39.9

D0817022

THE WORD IN THIS WORLD

THE NEW TESTAMENT LIBRARY

Editorial Board

C. CLIFTON BLACK
JOHN T. CARROLL
BEVERLY ROBERTS GAVENTA

Colorado Christian University
Library
180 S. Garrison
Lakewood, Colorado 80226

Paul W. Meyer

The Word in This World

Essays in New Testament Exegesis and Theology

Edited by John T. Carroll

Westminster John Knox Press

LOUISVILLE • LONDON

© 2004 Paul W. Meyer

Foreword and "A Personal Word" © 2004 Westminster John Knox Press

All rights reserved. No part of this book may be reproduced or transmitted in any form or by any means, electronic or mechanical, including photocopying, recording, or by any information storage or retrieval system, without permission in writing from the publisher. For information, address Westminster John Knox Press, 100 Witherspoon Street, Louisville, Kentucky 40202-1396.

Scripture quotations from the New Revised Standard Version of the Bible are copyright © 1989 by the Division of Christian Education of the National Council of the Churches of Christ in the U.S.A. and are used by permission. Scripture quotations from the Revised Standard Version of the Bible are copyright © 1946, 1952, 1971, and 1973 by the Division of Christian Education of the National Council of the Churches of Christ in the U.S.A. and are used by permission. Scripture quotations from *The Jerusalem Bible,* copyright © 1966, 1967, 1968 by Darton, Longman & Todd, Ltd., and Doubleday & Co., Inc. Used by permission of the publishers. Scripture quotations from *The New English Bible,* © The Delegates of the Oxford University Press and The Syndics of the Cambridge Press, 1961, 1970. Used by permission. Scripture quotations from the *Good News Bible*—Old Testament: Copyright © American Bible Society 1976; New Testament: Copyright © American Bible Society 1966, 1971, 1976.

Chapter 1, "The This-Worldliness of the New Testament," was first published in 1979 in the *Princeton Seminary Bulletin.* Used by permission. Chapter 2, "Faith and History Revisited," was first published in 1989 in the *Princeton Seminary Bulletin.* Used by permission. Chapter 3, "The Problem of the Messianic Self-Consciousness of Jesus," was first published in *Novum Testamentum* 4 (1960), 122–38. Used by permission of Brill Academic Publishers. Chapter 4, "'The Father': The Presentation of God in the Fourth Gospel" was first published in *Exploring the Gospel of John,* ed. R. A. Culpepper and C. C. Black (Louisville, Ky.: Westminster John Knox, 1996). Used by permission. Chapter 5, "The Worm at the Core of the Apple: Exegetical Reflections on Romans 7," was first published in *The Conversation Continues: Studies in Paul and John in Honor of J. Louis Martyn,* ed. Robert T. Fortna and Beverly Roberts Gaventa (Nashville: Abingdon, 1990). Used by permission. Chapter 6, "Romans 10:4 and the 'End' of the Law," is reprinted here by permission of James L. Crenshaw. Chapter 7, "Pauline Theology: A Proposal for a Pause in Its Pursuit," is used here by permission of the Society of Biblical Literature. Chapter 8, "The Holy Spirit in the Pauline Letters: A Contextual Exploration," was first published in *Interpretation* 33 (January, 1979), 3–18. Used by permission. Chapter 9, "Augustine's *The Spirit and the Letter* as a Reading of Paul's Romans," is reprinted by permission from *The Social World of the First Christians: Essays in Honor of Wayne A. Meeks,* edited by L. Michael White and O. Larry Yarbrough, © 1995 Augsburg Fortress (www.fortresspress.com). Chapter 12, "The Polarity of Faith: A Johannine Paradigm for Our Time," was first published in 1965 in the *Union Seminary Quarterly Review.* Used by permission. Chapter 13, "An Exegetical Note on John 2:10," is used here by permission of the Society of Biblical Literature. Chapter 14, "An Exegetical Note on John 10:1–18," is used here by permission of the Society of Biblical Literature. Chapter 15, "An Exegetical Reflection on Matthew 21:1–11," was originally published under the title "Matthew 21:1–11" in *Interpretation* 40 (April 1986), 180–185. Used by permission of Union Theological Seminary and Presbyterian School of Christian Education. Chapter 16, "Context as a Bearer of Meaning in Matthew," was first published in 1988 in the *Union Seminary Quarterly Review.* Used by permission. Part III, "Romans: A Commentary," was published under the title "Commentary on Romans" from *HarperCollins Bible Commentary, Revised Edition* by James L. Mays, General Editor. Copyright © 1988, 2000 by The Society of Biblical Literature. Reprinted by permission of HarperCollins Publishers Inc. Chapter 17, "The Parable of Responsibility: A Sermon," was first published in 1985 in the *Princeton Seminary Bulletin.* Used by permission. Chapter 18, "The Door That Closes: A Sermon," was first published in 1979 in the *Princeton Seminary Bulletin.* Used by permission.

Book design by Jennifer K. Cox

First edition
Published by Westminster John Knox Press
Louisville, Kentucky

This book is printed on acid-free paper that meets the American National Standards Institute Z39.48 standard. ∞

PRINTED IN THE UNITED STATES OF AMERICA

04 05 06 07 08 09 10 11 12 13 — 10 9 8 7 6 5 4 3 2 1

Library of Congress Cataloging-in-Publication Data is on file at the Library of Congress, Washington, D.C.

ISBN 0-664-22701-5

CONTENTS

PREFACE TO *THE WORD IN THIS WORLD: ESSAYS IN NEW TESTAMENT EXEGESIS AND THEOLOGY*

Sometimes a single moment tells the tale. At the annual meeting of the Society of Biblical Literature in 1991, a seminar convened to consider once again the much-disputed question whether the phrase *pistis Christou* refers primarily to Christ's own faithfulness or to faith in Christ. The room was full, and the temperature had risen as presenters and respondents alike vigorously pressed their views. In the middle of this intense discussion, the moderator recognized Professor Paul W. Meyer. Almost immediately, people ceased clamoring for time to assert their own views and began to listen. Many started to take notes as Meyer carefully laid out some fundamental exegetical points and their implications for the debate. That memorable scene—scholars crowded together in a conference room, straining to hear Paul Meyer's words—gives eloquent expression to the respect commanded by this scholar's scholar and teacher's teacher.

This volume demonstrates how it is that Professor Meyer gained such respect. It brings together for the first time numerous publications that range across the New Testament canon and encompass a variety of interpretive forms, from thematic essay to commentary, from close exegesis to homily. The volume also presents two major essays and two homilies that have not previously appeared in print. All these studies are distinguished by Meyer's characteristic attention to detail, precision in argument, and elegant prose. Readers will encounter on every page perceptive historical and literary analysis and deep theological wisdom from the pen of a master exegete.

Readers who possess long acquaintance with the work of Paul W. Meyer will understand the editors' delight and pride in making this collection available. Those for whom this book comes at the beginning of critical study of the New Testament can glimpse here what genuine exegesis involves and what theological fruit it has to offer.

THE EDITORS
THE NEW TESTAMENT LIBRARY

AUTHOR'S PREFACE

It is a pleasure to voice here some deeply felt thanks. My first and most obvious debt is to the Editorial Board of the New Testament Library for first suggesting, then encouraging, and above all facilitating this collection of shorter pieces into a full-length book. Of the members of that board, John Carroll, as editor of this volume, has been both a selfless contributor of his time and skill and a loyal and understanding friend.

The manifold other debts incurred over the years of the composition of these essays are far too numerous to list individually. It may be best simply to list the whole communities of theological discourse and worship in which I have been privileged to live and learn: Union Theological Seminary in New York, Yale Divinity School, Colgate Rochester Divinity School, Vanderbilt Divinity School, and Princeton Theological Seminary—places where along the way I have had colleagues, graduate assistants, students and friends who create the sort of theological setting to which I allude at the beginning of the opening essay.

In addition to the formal acknowledgments that appear elsewhere, I wish to record my special gratitude to the Society of Biblical Literature for allowing the reprinting of the brief commentary on Romans that occupies a central place in this collection and that first appeared in the Society's joint production, with the publishers, of the *Harper's Bible Commentary*.

One person who has been singularly involved in this project is J. Louis Martyn. As everyone knows, this generous teacher of teachers has profoundly affected the public course of the study of both the Fourth Gospel and the Pauline letters in our lifetime. "Much more surely," to use a phrase from the apostle, he has inspired, encouraged, and informed the work, both public and private, of a host of students of New Testament theology and exegesis. Over a period of almost fifty years, I have been a privileged beneficiary of his talents and have become a grateful member of that host.

P. W. M.

FOREWORD FROM THE EDITOR

This book is a gem. Editorial labors on this collection of essays and studies by Paul W. Meyer brought delight upon delight. There was, of course, the deep personal satisfaction of close collaboration with an esteemed teacher, collaboration that strengthened also the bonds of respect and friendship. Yet editorial effort on a project of this kind is demanding. The task of reading and rereading these studies became sheer grace for me, because every page offers elegant exegesis and theological interpretation of depth and power. The realization that I could play a small part in helping this master biblical interpreter convey his wisdom to a wider audience, and to a new generation of scholars, teachers, and students, afforded the greatest pleasure of all.

The volume opens with four essays (one previously unpublished) that probe difficult questions of perennial concern for exegetes, theologians, and ethicists. The complex interplay between matters of faith and history, and between close readings of texts and theological and ethical reflection, finds subtle and sophisticated treatment here. Readers meet in Part I a question that returns in various guises throughout the volume: What difference does the historical figure of Jesus, and especially his public death by crucifixion, make for Christian theological reflection and Christian life in the world?

Part II follows with five essays in which Paul Meyer shows himself to be a profound exegete and theological interpreter of Paul the apostle. (In an extended footnote, chapter 7 presents for the first time in print remarks given at a session of the Society of Biblical Literature's Pauline Theology seminar.) Part III then offers a sustained reading of Paul's letter to the Romans.

In the five essays of Part IV (including one previously unpublished), Meyer brings the same exegetical precision and theological insight to the interpretation of the Gospel of John. The book closes (Part V) with two brief essays on the Gospel of Matthew and four sermons (two published for the first time here) dealing with gospel texts. In the sermons no less than in the scholarly studies, readers find in Meyer both discerning exegete and creative theologian.

Appreciation is due the publishers of the seventeen previously published pieces for permission graciously extended to reproduce them, with some revision, in this volume. Specific acknowledgment of those debts is given at appropriate points throughout the book.

Special thanks are owed to J. Louis Martyn, longtime friend and conversation partner of Paul Meyer, for contributing a volume introduction that weaves together personal reminiscence and substantive exegetical engagement with Meyer's work. Much as twenty-first-century readers of Paul's letters or John's gospel overhear ancient conversations between those authors and their first-century audiences, readers of Martyn's "personal word" are privileged to listen in on a fascinating and rich conversation between these two scholars that has spanned more than four decades.

While these collected studies also span nearly four decades and address a range of biblical texts, authors, and themes, readers will discover a perhaps surprisingly coherent presentation of theological conviction and exegetical approach. Surprising, however, only for those who do not already know Paul Meyer. It is time that they become acquainted with this master exegete, and to such persons I simply say: Read on!

J. T. C.

ABBREVIATIONS

General Abbreviations and Latin Terms

B.C.E.	before the Common Era
bis	twice
ca.	circa
C.E.	Common Era
cf.	*confer* = compare
ch(s).	chapter(s)
col(s).	column(s)
ed(s).	edition(s); editor(s); edited by
e.g.	*exempli gratia* = for example
esp.	especially
ET	English translation
et al.	*et alia* = and others
f(f).	and the following page(s) or verse(s)
i.e.	*id est* = that is
idem	*idem* = the same (name previously mentioned)
lit.	literally
MS(S)	manuscript(s)
n(n).	note(s)
NS	New Series
NT	New Testament
OT	Old Testament
p(p).	page(s)
Q.E.D.	*quod erat demonstrandum* = which was (the matter) to be proved
sc.	*scilicet* = namely
s.v.	*sub verbo* = under the word
trans.	translated (by)
v(v).	verse(s)
viz.	*videlicet* = namely
v.l.	varia lectio = alternative reading recorded in MS(S)
vol(s).	volume(s)

Ancient Versions and Modern Translations of the Biblical Text

LXX	Septuagint
MT	Masoretic Text
JB	Jerusalem Bible
KJV	King James Version
NAB	New American Bible
NEB	New English Bible
NRSV	New Revised Standard Version
RSV	Revised Standard Version
TEV	Today's English Version

Biblical Books (including OT Apocrypha)

Gen	Genesis
Exod	Exodus
Lev	Leviticus
Num	Numbers
Deut	Deuteronomy
1–2 Sam	1–2 Samuel
1–2 Kgs	1–2 Kings
Ps(s)	Psalm(s)
Prov	Proverbs
Isa	Isaiah
Jer	Jeremiah
Ezek	Ezekiel
Dan	Daniel
Hos	Hosea
Joel	Joel
Amos	Amos
Hab	Habakkuk
Zech	Zechariah
Mal	Malachi
Wis	Wisdom of Solomon
Sir	Sirach (Ecclesiasticus)
1–4 Macc	1–4 Maccabees
1–2 Esd	1–2 Esdras
Matt	Matthew
Mark	Mark
Luke	Luke
John	John
Acts	Acts

Rom	Romans
1–2 Cor	1–2 Corinthians
Gal	Galatians
Eph	Ephesians
Phil	Philippians
Col	Colossians
1–2 Thess	1–2 Thessalonians
1–2 Tim	1–2 Timothy
Titus	Titus
Phlm	Philemon
Heb	Hebrews
Jas	James
1–2 Pet	1–2 Peter
Rev	Revelation

Old Testament Pseudepigrapha

Let. Aris.	*Letter of Aristeas*
2 Bar.	*2 Baruch (Syriac Apocalypse)*
1 En.	*1 Enoch (Ethiopic Apocalypse)*
4 Ezra	*4 Ezra*
Jub.	*Jubilees*
Sib. Or.	*Sibylline Oracles*
Pss. Sol.	*Psalms of Solomon*

Apostolic Fathers and New Testament Apocrypha

1–2 Clem.	*1–2 Clement*
Did.	*Didache*
Ign. *Eph.*	Ignatius, *To the Ephesians*
Ign. *Smyrn.*	Ignatius, *To the Smyrneans*
Gos. Thom.	*Gospel of Thomas*

Other Classical, Early Jewish, and Early Christian Authors

Augustine
Conf.	*Confessions*
Praed.	*The Predestination of the Saints*
Ep.	*Letters*
Retract.	*Retractions*
Epictetus
Disc.	*Discourses*

Euripides
  Hipp.   *Hippolytus*
  Med.   *Medea*
Hippolytus
  Haer.   *Refutation of All Heresies*
Ovid
  Metam. *Metamorphoses*
Philo
  Leg.   *Legum allegoriae I, II, III (Allegorical Interpretation I, II, III)*
  Opif.   *De opificio mundi (On the Creation of the World)*
Plato
  Prot.   *Protagoras*

Journals, Book Series, and Reference Works

AB	Anchor Bible
ABD	*Anchor Bible Dictionary.* Edited by D. N. Freedman. 6 vols.
BAGD	Bauer, W., W. F. Arndt, F. W. Gingrich, and F. W. Danker. *Greek-English Lexicon of the New Testament and Other Early Christian Literature.* 2d ed., 1979
BDAG	Bauer, W., F. W. Danker, W. F. Arndt, and F. W. Gingrich. *Greek-English Lexicon of the New Testament and Other Early Christian Literature.* 3d ed., 1999
BDF	Blass, F., A. Debrunner, and R. W. Funk. *A Greek Grammar of the New Testament and Other Early Christian Literature*
BEvT	Beiträge zur evangelischen Theologie
BJRL	*Bulletin of the John Rylands University Library of Manchester*
CSEL	Corpus scriptorum ecclesiasticorum latinorum
EKKNT	Evangelisch-katholischer Kommentar zum Neuen Testament
EvT	*Evangelische Theologie*
FRLANT	Forschungen zur Religion und Literatur des Alten und Neuen Testaments
GCS	Die griechischen christlichen Schriftsteller der ersten [drei] Jahrhunderte
GNS	*Good News Studies*
HBC	*Harper's Bible Commentary.* Rev. ed. Edited by J. L. Mays et al. 2000
HNT	Handbuch zum Neuen Testament
IB	*Interpreter's Bible*
IBC	Interpretation: A Bible Commentary for Teaching and Preaching

ICC	International Critical Commentary
IDB	*Interpreter's Dictionary of the Bible.* Edited by G. A. Buttrick. 4 vols.
IDBSup	Supplementary volume to *IDB*
Int	*Interpretation*
IRT	Issues in Religion and Theology
JBL	*Journal of Biblical Literature*
JSNT	*Journal for the Study of the New Testament*
JSNTSup	Journal for the Study of the New Testament: Supplement Series
KD	*Kerygma und Dogma*
LCC	Library of Christian Classics
LCL	Loeb Classical Library
LSJ	Liddell, H. G., R. Scott, and H. S. Jones. *A Greek-English Lexicon.* 9th ed.
MeyerK	Meyer, H. A. W. *Kritisch-exegetischer Kommentar über das Neue Testament*
NovT	*Novum Testamentum*
NovTSup	Novum Testamentum Supplements
NTD	Das Neue Testament Deutsch
NTL	New Testament Library
NTS	*New Testament Studies*
PL	Patrologia latina. Edited by J.-P. Migne. 217 vols.
PSB	*Princeton Seminary Bulletin*
PW	Pauly, A. F. *Paulys Realencyclopädie der classischen Altertumswissenschaft.* New edition G. Wissowa. 49 vols. Munich, 1980
RB	*Revue biblique*
SBB	Stuttgarter biblische Beiträge
SBLDS	Society of Biblical Literature Dissertation Series
SBS	Stuttgarter Bibelstudien
SBT	Studies in Biblical Theology
SHAW	Sitzungen der heidelberger Akademie der Wissenschaften
SNTSMS	Society for New Testament Studies Monograph Series
SP	Sacra pagina
TDNT	*Theological Dictionary of the New Testament.* Edited by G. Kittel and G. Friedrich. Trans. G. W. Bromiley. 10 vols.
TLZ	*Theologische Literaturzeitung*

TRE	*Theologische Realenzyklopädie.* Edited by G. Krause and G. Müller
TS	*Theological Studies*
TU	Texte und Untersuchungen
TWNT	*Theologisches Wörterbuch zum Neuen Testament.* Edited by G. Kittel and G. Friedrich
TZ	*Theologische Zeitschrift*
UBSGNT	United Bible Societies *Greek New Testament*
USQR	*Union Seminary Quarterly Review*
WBC	Word Biblical Commentary
WUNT	Wissenschaftliche Untersuchungen zum Neuen Testament
ZKG	*Zeitschrift für Kirchengeschichte*
ZNW	*Zeitschrift für die neutestamentliche Wissenschaft und die Kunde der älteren Kirche*
ZTK	*Zeitschrift für Theologie und Kirche*

A PERSONAL WORD
J. Louis Martyn

Yale University

One of Us, Yet Unique

I first met Paul Meyer in the fall of 1954, shortly after his appointment as Assistant Professor of New Testament at Yale. Barely thirty, he was in the general age group of those of us who were doctoral students in the biblical field, and even with his ever present, professorial bow tie, he looked it. To be sure, he had already served for three years as instructor in New Testament at Union Theological Seminary in New York, but we soon learned that like several of us he was still at work on his own dissertation, anticipating its defense at Union the following spring. We did not know, of course, that in a few years he would be a giant in biblical studies. Given his genuine modesty, we tended to see him, in some measure, as one of us.

At the time, Yale had two senior New Testament professors. Erich Dinkler, a German not yet fully at home in the English language, was a thoroughgoing Bultmann student in whose seminars we tasted not only his own gifts but also the genius of that master. Paul Schubert, another German, shared with us the importance for New Testament study of the Greek classics and of philosophical traditions of the Hellenistic period. Into this context came the young Paul Meyer, teaching undergraduates in Yale College, ministerial students in the divinity school, and New Testament doctoral candidates. It was quickly apparent that he had the respect of both senior colleagues, partly perhaps because he shared with Dinkler a palpable theological interest and with Schubert an insistence on meticulous scientific analysis of the text. There was also the simple fact that with Meyer's appointment the Teutonic cast of Yale's New Testament Department was both maintained and enriched.[1]

Reared in a Reformed missionary home in India in which Hindi was accompanied by German, and instructed at Elmhurst College by teachers marked by German scholarship, Meyer was permanently stamped by the year in Basel and

---

1. When wishing to speak privately to Meyer without taking him aside, Schubert occasionally addressed him in German.

xvii

Zurich that lay between his seminary degree and his doctoral studies (1949–50). In quite general terms I sensed in him something notably absent in Dinkler and Schubert, namely, the influence of Karl Barth. As I learned with time, however, "Barthian" would have been the wrong word. Indeed, there is in Meyer's writings an expression that is helpful in relating his work to that of the Swiss theologian. If Barth had an "uncanny sense for the theological jugular of the text" without always being able to say how he managed to find it, Meyer has that same invaluable sense for the text's foundational element.[2] In Meyer's case, however, there is always clarity about the route by which he has come upon it. Everything Meyer learned from his teachers—Americans such as Reinhold Niebuhr, F. C. Grant, and John Knox, and Swiss such as Karl Barth and Eduard Schweizer—was ground in his own mill, the Greek text in hand. There was never less a "school" man.

I remember the "early Meyer" particularly in the setting of the Biblical Colloquium, a monthly evening presided over by Dinkler that brought together Yale's Old Testament faculty, New Testament faculty, and doctoral students in both testaments. It was there that I first saw in Meyer elements of the staunchly Calvinist tradition, with its insistence that the New Testament is given its primary theological context when, joined with the Old Testament, it is read as *part* of the Christian Bible—a matter of great import with respect to nothing less than the identity of God.

In a somewhat different way that issue also takes center stage in one of Meyer's essays on the Gospel of John. Leaping chronologically ahead for a moment, we note that for the Festschrift of Moody Smith he advances Johannine research by speaking of John's presentation of God himself (ch. 10 in this volume). While Ernst Käsemann and others attributed to the Fourth Evangelist a massive and exclusivistic Christology similar to that of Zinzendorf ("I have but one passion. That is He and only He"),[3] Meyer offers a correction that is at once simple and profound. He first makes a modest but generally overlooked linguistic observation about the famous "sending formula" in John. Instead of employing the passive voice in order to refer to *Jesus* as the one who was sent, John consistently puts the formula in the active voice: "*the Father who has sent me*" or "*he who has sent me.*" From this modest linguistic observation Meyer notes that at its base the sending formula is virtually one of God's names, an epithet for God. In the Fourth Gospel "[t]he language of 'sending' is *theo*logical language that undergirds Christology but refuses to be absorbed into it."[4]

---

2. See ch. 4, p. 47.
3. E. Käsemann, *The Testament of Jesus* (Philadelphia: Fortress, 1966), 38.
4. Ch. 10, pp. 235–36.

Returning to the Yale scene of the 1950s, I recall noting that, young as he was, Meyer established himself alongside his older colleagues as a sage with extraordinary gifts as a doctor father. No dissertation writer was ever more self-lessly and creatively guided than were Meyer's advisees. In addition to invest-ing numerous hours in patient conversation over the text itself, he penned detailed marginal notes, supplementing them with comments that were in effect outlines for virtually publishable essays.

Here too one thinks in the first instance of Meyer's influence on the inter-pretation of the Gospel of John. Having written his Union Seminary dissertation on the eschatology of John, he began to publish his own Johannine contributions with an article on the shepherd discourse in John 10 (ch. 14). In this same period he also contributed to Johannine studies by directing the dis-sertations of Moody Smith and Wayne Meeks, both quickly published and both permanent items in New Testament research.[5] With some modification one might apply to the early Meyer a remark made of Robert Calhoun by Roland Bainton: "[He] teaches our generation [to a large extent] through those whom he has taught."[6]

Acquaintance, Friendship, Comradeship

My acquaintance with Paul Meyer became friendship in 1963. In the summer of that year a number of New Testament scholars participated in the Faith and Order conference in Montreal. To one of the planners, Paul Minear, it seemed a splendid opportunity to hold a postconference meeting of several days focused on theological issues in New Testament studies. As I recall, Britain was represented in the main by Hugh Montefiore and G. W. H. Lampe; Germany by three Bultmann students, Erich Dinkler (by then at Bonn), Günther Bornkamm, and Ernst Käsemann; Switzerland by Eduard Schweizer; the United States by Paul Minear and Albert Outler, accompanied by several younger scholars, James Robinson, William Farmer, Paul Meyer, Leander Keck, and myself.

I recall productively provocative discussions, enlivened notably by Käse-mann. I remember equally well and with gratitude leisurely conversations with Meyer on the lengthy trips north and south in his Volkswagen bus.[7] Here I began

5. D. Moody Smith, *The Composition and Order of the Fourth Gospel* (New Haven, Conn.: Yale University Press, 1965); Wayne A. Meeks, *The Prophet-King: Moses Traditions and the Johannine Christology*, NovTSup 14 (Leiden: E. J. Brill, 1967).

6. Roland Bainton, "Tribute to Robert Calhoun," *Yale University Divinity News* 62, no. 4 (1965): 4.

7. In these conversations I was being given a foretaste of the two-day exegetical discussions Meyer and I have had twice a year since 1978. The creative and energizing impact of those unhur-ried hours lies beyond measure.

to see a factor that cannot be taken for granted among theologians, one that became ever more clear as our acquaintance ripened into friendship, indeed into a genuine comradeship. Recalling that hobbies are often revealing, I noted that, having grown up in India and having had army service there during the Second World War, Meyer was a short-wave radio enthusiast with a keen interest in international politics. I was not conversing with a purely cerebral biblical scholar who lived in ethereal mists detached from the everyday world. This was a person with both feet on the ground, a fact made doubly clear when he addressed the American Society of Christian Ethics on the role of exegesis in ethical reflection (see ch. 4), and climactically when he gave his inaugural lecture at Princeton Seminary on "The This-Worldliness of the New Testament" (see ch. 1), a piece to which I will return.

Colgate Rochester Divinity School

Shortly after the Montreal meeting, the faculty at Colgate Rochester launched a courtship with Meyer, both vigorous and graceful. Seeking to woo this promising young biblical theologian away from the halls of ivy, every member of the Colgate Rochester faculty sent a personal telegram of warm invitation, a stratagem that eventually met with success. His appointment as Professor of New Testament Interpretation (1964–70) commenced appropriately with a public lecture focused on the dynamics of belief and unbelief in order to throw light on the issue of faith's origin (see ch. 12).

During Meyer's years at Colgate Rochester, I saw him from time to time at the monthly meetings of the Columbia University New Testament Seminar, a group including in that period such northeastern savants as Morton Smith, W. D. Davies, Cyril Richardson, Paul Schubert, Nils Dahl, Otto Piper, and Bruce Metzger. With some exceptions those discussions were quite different from the ones we had known in Montreal, being focused largely on scientific issues to the exclusion of theology per se.

I recall an evening in which Meyer and I walked back to Union Seminary with my colleague and friend Cyril Richardson, a humorist almost without peer. As we moved along, Richardson treated us to a devastating story. As a guest the previous year in the New Testament seminar at the University of Cambridge, he found that the paper one evening was read by a professor of chemistry and directed to the question of the chemical formula of salt that had lost its saltness. It was, of course, a story concocted in the moment with an eye to the meeting just concluded. Both Meyer and I knew it to be thoroughly apocryphal, but we also grasped its pertinence. I must add, however, that the Columbia seminar was often highly enlightening. I remember clearly, for example, a Johannine evening made rich by the prepared remarks of Raymond Brown, at the time a visiting professor at Union, and Meyer's former student Wayne Meeks, enticed to that meeting from Indiana.

Vanderbilt University

During his Vanderbilt period (1970–78), Meyer and I saw each other occasionally at national and international meetings, but for the most part we stayed in touch by mail. It was then that I began to learn what a letter from Paul Meyer can prove to be: a substantive work of art. In this period, and especially in his subsequent years at Princeton Seminary, I may have received an occasional note, but in general the body of a Meyer letter was a carefully crafted essay designed to be read by one who was altogether awake, Greek Testament in hand. It is no exaggeration to say that many of these letter-essays were meticulous, carefully wrought analyses of important interpretive issues, and thus forward steps in New Testament interpretation. Having missed the opportunity for formal study with Meyer at Yale, I pondered these modern Pauline missives at length, learning as I went.

At Vanderbilt, Meyer enjoyed and profited from team teaching with his Jewish colleague Lou Silberman. It seems clear that this teamwork deepened in Meyer the Calvinist tradition to which I have already referred, the one in which, joined with the Old Testament, the New Testament is consistently read as part of the Christian Bible. The values of this tradition are well reflected, I think, in all of Meyer's labors, especially in the article on Augustine written for the Meeks Festschrift (see ch. 9) and in his "Romans 10:4 and the 'End' of the Law," an essay honoring Silberman (see ch. 6).

It was also in the Vanderbilt years that Meyer was composing the Shaffer Lectures given at Yale in 1976 and titled "The Justification of Jesus." When he kindly sent the typescript to me, I read with keen interest to see how and why he had brought to the study of Jesus a term we generally associate with Paul. There were themes here that would thread their way through much of Meyer's later work, reflecting especially his concern with the issue of faith and history.

Princeton Theological Seminary

In Meyer's Princeton years (1978–89), I was delighted to see him again at meetings of the Columbia University New Testament Seminar, now often in the company of his new colleague Chris Beker. Equally important, I was glad to witness in his work a new burst of energy, indeed a level of boldness that can be identified, I think, as his own form of admirable radicality. Even more clearly than before, I saw that, while perceptively surveying the landscape, he also goes consistently to the root of an issue, thus painting with a broad brush that is itself equipped with fine bristles.

This-Worldly Faith and History

The breadth of Meyer's interpretive brush is altogether clear in his inaugural lecture at Princeton (see ch. 1) and in his presidential address to the American

Theological Society (see ch. 2). I have already noted his sustained concern with the matter of faith and history, an interest reflected in the title of his Festschrift.[8] Characteristic of his calling as a biblical theologian is the fact that, instead of following tradition by posing that issue yet again in a philosophically abstract fashion, he approaches it in a fresh and fundamentally exegetical way, relating history specifically to Jesus' public crucifixion and faith specifically to Jesus' resurrection.

Jesus' Death by Crucifixion

This event was without doubt a devastating defeat, a sure indication that Jesus was a loser:

> [O]n the level of sober historical reality Jesus' career had ended in failure, his teaching and above all the expectations he had generated in his followers were finally discredited by the deliberately demeaning way in which in the end his life was taken from him. For his crucifixion was, and remains, the one historically most certainly known detail of his life . . . and the one thing that seemed most clearly to destroy the credibility of Christian teaching.[9]

In light of the disorienting horror of Jesus' crucifixion, the Christian historian has to join the New Testament witnesses by asking what it means to be a follower of this crucified Messiah. That question brings us to Easter, and specifically to the relation of Easter to Good Friday.

Jesus' Resurrection at the Hands of God

When we turn from the cross to Jesus' resurrection, doing so by reading and rereading our sources themselves, we see—perhaps with a stabbing disappointment—that Easter is not the comforting "answer" to Good Friday. Nor, by extension, is faith the "solution" to history. Jesus' resurrection, that is to say, was not, is not, and cannot be an escape from the cross into a form of other-worldliness. God's resurrection of Jesus is the event that takes us back to the cross, making and keeping Christian faith and life inevasibly this-worldly. Facing the this-worldliness of the New Testament witness, Meyer states, "We need sometimes to think about the crucifixion of Jesus *as if* there had been no resurrection."[10] Here we encounter one of Meyer's radical theological challenges. Creatively linking Jesus' resurrection to the motif of justification/vindication,

---

8. *Faith and History: Essays in Honor of Paul W. Meyer*, ed. J. T. Carroll, C. H. Cosgrove, and E. E. Johnson (Atlanta: Scholars Press, 1990).

9. Ch. 2, p. 23.

10. Ch. 1, p. 12.

Meyer notes that that event is "God's elevation of [the] public and indisputable historical reality of the cross to the status of the critical norm by which the authenticity of the distinctive Christian message to the world is . . . established."[11]

We can and must note that in the life, death, and resurrection of Jesus there is an essential continuity with Jewish tradition. The earliest missionaries were proclaiming neither a new God nor an unknown Jesus. Their received traditions had passed, however, through a crucible fired by the public act of Jesus' humiliating crucifixion. They were declaring, therefore,

> that the God of their fathers had made of the discredited Jesus of Nazareth the right clue and the criterion for discerning God's true intentions; the measure of the right way to talk about salvation. . . . [A]ll has been stamped with the branding iron of the crucifixion. All has become irreversibly this-worldly. . . . [T]here is something on the stage of history [something in this unredeemed world] that was not there before: a community that calls itself by the name of the crucified Messiah.[12]

It is possible, of course, to imagine an otherworldly escape from the brutal event of Jesus' crucifixion, taking a romantic "walk in the garden alone, while the dew is still on the roses." A distinctively Christian theology, however, begins in this world, focused firmly on the cross.

Paul's Letter to the Roman Church

From the Princeton period we also have three seminal contributions to the interpretation of Romans, a full-dress commentary that is the mature fruit of numberless exegesis courses (Part III), and two exegetical essays that make indelible contributions to our understanding of the letter (see chs. 5 and 6).[13]

Romans 10:4 and the "End" of the Law

Those who teach courses of a basically exegetical sort are well advised to send their students to this piece and to the one on Romans 7, for, in attending carefully to these essays, the students will learn by observing a master artist at work.

Romans 10:4 is often interpreted in its immediate context, beginning with 10:1. When we read it in this way, we see that, having voiced his concern for

11. Ch. 2, p. 25. A major value of the sermons wisely included in the present volume (chs. 17–20) lies in their demonstration of what we might paradoxically call this crucified authenticity.

12. Ch. 1, p. 14.

13. Regarding Meyer's Romans commentary see esp. Charles Cousar's review of *Harper's Bible Commentary*, ed. J. L. Mays (San Francisco: Harper & Row, 1988), in *Int* 44 (1990): 291–92. Meyer's illuminating article on the Holy Spirit in the Pauline letters (see ch. 8) also comes from the Princeton years.

the salvation of his own people, having identified as unenlightened their zeal for God, and having credited them with an attempt to establish their own righteousness rather than submitting to that of God, Paul says pointedly that Christ is the *telos* of the law (10:1–4). He then contrasts the righteousness based on the law with the righteousness based on faith, adding that, whereas Moses "writes" about law-righteousness, faith-righteousness (being personified) "speaks" about Christ (vv. 5–6). Interpreted in this immediate context with its pattern of sharp polarity, does not Rom 10:4 refer to Christ as the salvific *termination* of the law, rather than as its *goal?* (The term *telos* itself can be taken either way.)

With many others I myself had long thought so, and the first reading of Meyer's essay did not change my mind. His concerted argument for finding a reference to Christ as "the intent and goal of the law" seemed to me to be purchased at a high price. Does not that reading inevitably ignore—at least partially—the specific and striking polarity between law-righteousness and faith-righteousness, the former being replaced by the latter?

A few years later, however, I returned, attending to this essay a second time as I read Meyer's theologically profound commentary on Romans. And now, to borrow an expression from the Gospel of Luke, my mind was opened to understand the radicality of the scripture that is here uncovered by Meyer's own radicality (Luke 24:45).[14] I saw more clearly that Meyer takes quite seriously the immediate context with its pattern of polarity, even adding similar notes struck in earlier parts of the letter:

> The two kinds of righteousness in vv. 5–6 are indeed opposites, as irreconcilable as obedience and disobedience, as "submitting to God's righteousness" and "seeking to establish one's own" in v. 3. They repeat the contrast between "from faith" and "from works" in 9:32. There is no compromise between an election "by grace" and one "by works" (11:6), between what depends "on the God who calls" and what "on works" (9:12), between what comes "as a gift" and what "as one's due" (4:4).[15]

He begins his analysis, however, at Rom 9:30, thus honoring the literary structure of Paul's argument (9:30–10:21 clearly forms a unit). And, beginning at this point, Meyer provides a stunning reading of 9:30–33.

Here Paul bears witness to the God who, prior to confounding his own people with a crucified Messiah, confounded them via the law. In Rom 9:30–33, we see, that is, Paul's most astonishing rhetorical use of the image of the racetrack. God's own people are on that track, pursuing the law of righteousness. In giving the law, however, God himself placed in the path of his people the "stone"

---

14. Reading an essay by Wayne A. Meeks also played a role at this point: "On Trusting an Unpredictable God: A Hermeneutical Meditation on Romans 9–11," first published in Meyer's Festschrift (see n. 8) and now included in Meeks, *In Search of the Early Christians* (New Haven, Conn.: Yale University Press, 2002), 210–29.

15. Ch. 6, p. 89.

that is at once the base for the runner's trust in God *and* an object that trips the runner up![16] And now God's people have tripped over God's law-stone itself.

But how? It is significant that in answering this question Meyer does not refer to Christ.[17] Racing in the nomistic way that is oriented to works rather than racing in the nomistic way that is focused on trust in this confounding God, Israel did indeed trip on the Torah stone itself. In giving this answer, has Meyer forgotten what he said in his Princeton inaugural about the discredited Jesus being the criterion for discerning God's true intentions? No. He is here simply and patiently listening to what Paul actually says in Rom 9:30–33, thus noting that it is the law itself to which this unbelieving Israel has not attained. This Israel has missed the good news of God that is spoken to it in the words of the law. And that is a major clue to Paul's understanding of the law, for, while Paul speaks forcefully of a pattern of polarity, he is certain that in itself

> the law does not belong on the side of this polarity that is alien to God or opposed to God. When it is found to function there, it does so as a consequence of a fundamental and tragic misunderstanding (9:32), or as an instrument of human disobedience and failure to recognize God and his righteousness (10:3), or as an opportunity seized by the demonic power of sin (7:11) for its own nourishment. But even when it is found to function in these ways, it has not been torn out of God's hand and it does not cease to be God's holy instrument, for ultimately it does not contradict even then but advances, however indirectly, the carrying out of God's purpose (Rom 5:20–21; 7:13; 11:32; Gal 3:21–22, 24).[18]

An important caveat is to be added:

> To make such a claim is not to deny the presence of evil, the power of sin, the tragedy of the distortion of the divine intent in the name of religion. It is rather . . . to claim in them and beyond them the ultimate manifestation of God's righteousness, impartial goodness, and sovereignty. Of course this is for Paul the Christian to read history in a pattern of meaning derived from the crucifixion of Jesus. But it is also for Paul the Jewish Christian to trace in the movements of history the sovereignty of the God of Abraham, Isaac, and Jacob, the God of Moses, the Judge and Comforter of the exile, who is also the Father of the Crucified.[19]

16. See Part III, pp. 198–99.

17. The pronoun in Rom 10:11—a quotation of Isa 28:16—has the same referent as do the instances of *kyrios* in 10:12 and 10:13, this last a quotation of Joel 2:32. Reading Rom 10:11 in its context, then, and bearing in mind with L. Cerfaux that in Paul's Old Testament citations *kyrios* is always a name for God, Meyer finds the pronoun in 10:11 to be a reference to God rather than to Christ (cf. L. Cerfaux, "Kyrios dans les citations pauliniennes de l'Ancien Testament," in *Recueil Lucien Cerfaux* [Gembloux: Duculot, 1954–62], 1.173–88). See p. 200.

18. Ch. 6, p. 89.

19. Ibid., 89–90. Meyer's reference to the distortion of the divine intent in the name of religion is his own exegetical finding. It can be compared, however, with a comment of Dietrich Bonhoeffer: "God has founded his church beyond religion" (*No Rusty Swords* [New York: Harper & Row, 1965], 118).

Following Meyer, then, as he patiently listens to Rom 10:4 in the context of 9:30–33, we see how that single verse is to be read. Failing to attain to the law—tripping over that Torah stone—unbelieving Israel has missed the good news of God spoken to it in the words of *the law*, the law that continues to stand firm (Rom 3:31), the law that finds its goal and intent in Christ.

Meyer's interpretation of Rom 9–10, then, was truly instructive to me. In two further regards, however, I had yet more to learn. First, I now paused over Meyer's charge that finding in Rom 10:4 a reference to the termination of the law "depends on decisions that one has made elsewhere."[20] Clearly that had been true of me. A sustained preoccupation with Galatians had caused me to interpret Rom 10:4 as though Paul had placed it in the argument of Gal 3, with the latter's picture of the law as a temporary parenthesis lasting "*until* the seed [Christ] should come to whom the [Abrahamic] promise had been made" (Gal 3:19; cf. 3:23, 25). Even today I remain convinced that in the third chapter of Galatians Paul does indeed portray the law as a parenthesis, but that portrait is not to be read into Rom 10:4. How then are we to understand this and other differences between Gal 3 and Rom 3; 9; 10? In recent conversations I have been privileged to have with Paul Meyer, that issue has occupied the two of us hour after hour. Here I will say only that one of Meyer's gifts to us all lies in his pedagogical ability to bring insights that lead to further interpretive questions. His work does not end!

The second instance of additional instruction came in Meyer's warning that an apocalyptic reading of Paul can be quite misleading.[21] That caveat caused me to pause for some time! Had I misinterpreted not only Rom 10:4 but also the pattern of polarity evident in Rom 10:2–3, 5–6? Specifically, had I read that pattern too narrowly in light of what I had come to think of as apocalyptic antinomies in Paul's theology generally, especially in Galatians and 2 Corinthians? Again, I am left with an open question. Meyer is surely right to draw from Romans the conclusion that in itself the law does not belong on the side of Paul's apocalyptic polarity that is alien to God. He is also right, however, to point out that it is sometimes found to *function* there. Can the law be, then, in two places at once? That question brings us to Meyer's essay on Rom 7, yet another example of exegesis at its best.

The Worm at the Core of the Apple: Exegetical Reflections on Romans 7

If I were to suggest reading this piece twice, that would not indicate a lack of clarity on Meyer's part but rather his faithfulness to the extraordinary complexity of Paul's text. The essay includes meticulous linguistic analysis, illu-

20. See p. 93.
21. Ibid.

minating rhetorical and *religionsgeschichtlich* comparisons, and finally an honest wrestling with profound theological issues, all of this serving Meyer's single-minded passion to discern "the design and argument" of the text itself.[22] I think one cannot carefully attend to this essay without its having a significant effect on one's reading of this famous passage.[23]

Here I must limit myself to a single issue, the full identity of the "I" who delights in God's holy law, yet finds that "the very commandment that promised life proved to be death to me" (Rom 7:10). Who is this "I" described by Paul in such an arresting fashion? Meyer's initial answer is similar to that of numerous other exegetes: "Paul is employing . . . a rhetorical style [well represented in the Qumran hymns] in which the self functions in a representative way as a type or paradigm for others. . . . [The pronoun 'I' is not used, however] in a purely fictive way, as though Paul were excluding himself from its pattern."[24] But this observation is no more than the beginning of an answer. The crucial issue lies deeper, its symptoms emerging when we pose a series of questions. How is the wretchedness with which Paul closes the chapter to be understood (v. 24)? Why exactly does this wretched "I" cry out for redemption? In what regard is the "I" deceived and indeed killed by sin (v. 11)? Of what, precisely, does that deception consist?

Most pressing are questions focused on the roles played in the story of this "I" by the law and sin. If the law is emphatically not sin (v. 7), then how are the law and sin and the "I" related to one another? Does sin deceive the "I" by causing him to think that he can truly observe the law—the God-given antidote to sin—whereas, being weak of will, he cannot actually do that? Or does he in fact observe the law, only to find that in the course of such observance he is deceived by sin?

In a tightly constructed analysis Meyer argues—successfully I think—for this last reading. As Rom 8 shows, the impotence darkening the story lies with the law itself, not merely with a weakness of will on the part of the "I." Sin deceives the willing "I" by causing him to think that law observance—the highest good—will assuredly lead to life. In truth, however, even the holy and just and good law of God is impotent in itself to play this role (Rom 8:3). An indelible mark of sin's deception emerges, then, when the observant "I" is astonished at the product of its own acts:

> What it means to this person to be "sold under sin" is manifested in the discovery that what one in fact "produces" by one's actions is not recognizable, because

---

22. The words quoted are drawn by Meyer from Moses Stuart (see ch. 5, p. 57), but I mean to suggest that they can serve as a signature of Meyer's own labors.

23. See, e.g., "Meyer" in the author index of E. P. Sanders, *Paul, the Law, and the Jewish People* (Philadelphia: Fortress, 1983).

24. Ch. 5, p. 60.

it is exactly the opposite of what was intended, just what one hoped to avoid in one's reliance on the law.[25]

The villain, then, is not *akrasia*, weakness of will, but rather sin, a power that is not only alien to the "I" but also capable of employing the law to slay precisely the observant "I."[26]

> The experience of the demonic power of sin to use the Mosaic law to effect just the opposite of what its devoted adherents expect, even and especially when it is obeyed, manifests not only the sinister nature of sin itself (v. 13) but also how profoundly the religious self is "sold" under it and indeed possessed by it (vv. 14–20).[27]

In a word, what the observant self does not recognize is the effect of its own action, not the effect of its failure to act. And, lest one think that this reading of Rom 7 proves to be anti-Judaic, it must be added that

> [t]wo thousand years of Christian history have shown that in the presence of [the power of sin] there is no distinction between the "godly" and the "ungodly." As the Latin maxim puts it, *corruptio optimi pessima*, "the worst evil consists in the corruption of the highest good." That is not depicted here simply as a private experience from Paul's Jewish past. It is all part of Paul's explanation of why God sent God's own Son, on behalf of *all*, to deal with sin as the law could not (8:3–4).[28]

Paul Meyer as Teacher and the Task of Biblical Interpretation

I have now offered an introduction to some of Paul Meyer's work, treating pieces collected in this volume in light of the growth of a comradeship for which I remain deeply thankful. I am far from being a disinterested observer.[29] Just

25. Ch. 5, p. 73. The clause *ho gar katergazomai ou ginōskō* in Rom 7:15 is to be rendered "I do not *recognize* the effect of my own action."

26. One notes especially the exegetical reasons Meyer gives for considering the often cited references to a divided self in Ovid, Euripides, et al., to be nothing more than "seemingly impressive parallels" (see ch. 5, p. 74). Contrast the readings of Rom 7 proposed by S. K. Stowers, *A Rereading of Romans* (New Haven, Conn.: Yale University Press, 1994), and T. Engberg-Pedersen, "The Reception of Greco-Roman Culture in the New Testament: The Case of Romans 7:7–25," in *The New Testament as Reception*, ed. M. Müller and H. Tronier (London: Continuum, 2002), 32–57. If we read Rom 7 in light of Rom 9:30–33, are we to conclude that the "I" in the former passage is observing the law in the nomistic way that is oriented to works rather than in the nomistic way that is focused on trust in God?

27. Ch. 5, p. 77. Cf. the comment of Bonhoeffer cited in n. 19 above.

28. Ibid.; emphasis added in final sentence.

29. See the reference to Meyer in the preface to J. Louis Martyn, *Galatians*, AB 33A (New York: Doubleday, 1997), xi.

so, I trust that my personal word will function as an enticement, leading one to climb the Meyer tree and taste its fruit for oneself. And that fruit can be truly nourishing. To read with care Meyer's Romans commentary and his essays is to be ushered metaphorically into the arresting scene well portrayed in the New Testament Library editorial board's preface, the hushed roomful of biblical scholars realistically expecting instruction from a colleague as learned as he is modest. Something similar is to be said of the sermons. We find ourselves imaginatively sitting in a chapel, listening attentively as scripture becomes gospel.

To attend carefully to these chapters is, however, to risk having one's mind changed without one's permission. As I have shown in my own case, the pieces in this volume come to us from the hand of a giant in biblical interpretation who is able to disturb us creatively. They also come from the last century. Is their collection an exercise, then, in retrospective hagiography?

Hardly! They had striking effects when they first appeared, but only today do they come fully into their own. The current scene in biblical studies, and in homiletics as well, is marked in part by a loss of nerve, by a retreat from the holistic task of interpretation, and thus by the substitution of ethics for theology, at least in effect. Meyer's work is a salutary antidote to that halting anxiety.

True enough, current labors in New Testament interpretation are carrying us forward in a number of subdisciplines, such as exercises in rhetorical analysis; sociological readings that put us in touch with real, ordinary flesh-and-blood Christians of the first century; and comparative studies that give us an effective entry into the various ways in which early Christians dealt with the need for character formation in their communities. Our debt to the pioneers in these areas is large indeed; their work opens our eyes to factors that are essential to the interpretive task.[30]

Alongside these welcome advances, however, we now find in some instances what is in effect a retreat from the grand task of holistic interpretation. Some followers of the pioneers, that is, seem inclined—however unconsciously—to take one or another of these subdisciplines as a definition of exegesis itself, leaving theological issues largely unattended. The result is a reductionistic view of New Testament research and of the preacher's task as well.

It is here that Paul Meyer's labors provide sorely needed guidance, for in them we see the justified boldness of a master artist at work in what we might

---

30. A sterling example of rhetorical analysis is M. M. Mitchell, *Paul and the Rhetoric of Reconciliation* (Louisville, Ky.: Westminster/John Knox, 1992). Wayne Meeks is one of our pioneering masters in the sociological reading of early Christian texts, and also one who makes those readings productive for comprehensive interpretation (for an example see his article on Rom 9–11, mentioned in n. 14 above). And the work of Abraham Malherbe continues to advance our knowledge of the traditions of ancient parenesis, especially as those traditions help us to understand Paul's letters; see his *The Letters to the Thessalonians*, AB 32B (New York: Doubleday, 2000).

call his holistic atelier. Gratefully drawing on the labors of fellow painters expert, for example, in the reds of rhetoric, the greens of historical sociology, and the indigos of moral exhortation, this is a painter who uses in his own work all the colors and shades in an effort fully to discern the theological "design and argument" of early Christian texts. And because these texts come to us from the hands of those who understood themselves to be witnesses to the God who calls into existence the things that do not exist (Rom 4:17), it is clear that with his holistic understanding of interpretation Meyer fixes his eyes on a remarkably elevated goal.[31]

Equally clear is Meyer's gift as a pedagogue who passes that holistic task along to us in the present, doing so with a contagious confidence that is drawn from the nature of the ancient texts themselves.

---

31. As Princeton Seminary was the scene of Paul Meyer's full flourishing, it may be more than interesting to note that that institution continues to echo his elevated interpretive goal. That is obvious in the work of the biblical field. Equally important, one notes in the teaching of homiletics a passion for holistic interpretation that reaches from meticulous exegesis through the disciplines of historical and systematic theology to theologically authorized rhetoric in the pulpit. See James F. Kay, "Reorientation: Homiletics as Theologically Authorized Rhetoric," *PSB* 24 NS (2003): 16–35; and idem, "The Word of the Cross at the Turn of the Ages," *Int* 53 (1999): 44–56.

THE WORD IN THIS WORLD

Part I

Essays in Theological and Historical Interpretation

CHAPTER 1

THE THIS-WORLDLINESS
OF THE NEW TESTAMENT*

Two years ago, in his own address, Professor Karlfried Froehlich referred to the venerable history from which the institution of the inaugural derives; it had its origin, he said, in the opening lecture on method with which the medieval master of theology began his teaching career. Personally I am happy to note that there have been some changes since then.

For one thing, I may have been very much the stranger and the newcomer at my installation at Opening Convocation in September. But as I stand before you now to try to make good on the unfulfilled obligation of that memorable evening, I have first to express my profound gratitude for the hospitality and reception already accorded to my family and to me by the Princeton Seminary community for more than a full semester. I am very much aware that I still have a long way to go to meet the expectations of the invitation that brought me here, but already I feel myself to be a part of this school, and I am relieved that this afternoon's lecture does not have to bear, as such lectures once did, the full burden of introducing myself to you or of establishing my credentials to be here.

The other most important change from those medieval antecedents is that inaugural lectures in modern academe come at a later time in a teacher's career. Of course the start of one's teaching is a very significant moment, both professionally and personally, and it remains so to this day. In this past semester I have had more than one occasion to be vividly reminded of my own. But those later times in which so-called inaugurals fall in the present scheme of things are significant for a teacher in other ways and for other reasons. One has had time and occasion to try out different methods; to learn at first hand some of the frustrations as well as the joys of teaching; to discover that one never works alone in such an enterprise but is always bound to colleagues in complex reciprocal relationships of debt and obligation that change, sometimes drastically, as the

*This essay re-presents in slightly revised form Paul W. Meyer's inaugural lecture as Helen H. P. Manson Professor of New Testament Literature and Exegesis at Princeton Theological Seminary (February 28, 1979), which was published in *PSB* 2, no. 3, NS (1979): 219–31.

colleagues themselves change; to ascertain that student generations change as one undergoes change himself or herself, and that the subtle chemistry of a course never repeats itself no matter how many times the catalog announcement is duplicated. Old answers don't work any longer to meet even the old questions, to say nothing of the new.

When the pace of change is rapid, profounder effects have begun to make themselves felt, whether recognized or not. New methods, new discoveries, new claims within one's discipline succeed each other with such rapidity as to threaten the continuity of one's work. Today's news wraps tomorrow's fish, even in scholarly circles. Significant change is at first indistinguishable from passing fad, and the old ways of keeping one's bearings and of maintaining one's integrity are put severely to the test. The methods we use in our work are important to all of us as furnishing clarity and precision to what we do. We cannot engage in common work, in teaching and learning from each other, if we cannot devise rules of procedure on which we agree and which make what we do compelling and persuasive for others. But it belongs to the nature of method that when it dilates at the expense of content and, by preoccupying us, usurps the place of those ends which it is devised to serve, it becomes an ideology. It is no longer possible to establish one's credentials simply with a discourse on method or a *specimen eruditionis*.

These factors are perhaps only the normal and ordinary concomitants of being a professor getting a little bit older. They are sharply reinforced by a major move from one institution to another, with which an inaugural occasion in mid-career may or may not nowadays coincide. But they are raised to the bracket of another order, it seems to me, when one is talking not simply about academe but about theological education. For now the mutual bonds of colleagues in a common enterprise, the interaction of students and teachers across the generation gap or across differences in social and regional background or race and sex or country and culture, and the efforts of the individual teacher to find professional integrity in the diversity of disciplines and in the unavoidable process of change—all these turn out to be our way of participating in the pain and the promise of the church in our day. The truth we are after is never perceived alone or in abstraction from obedience; method and integrity have become part of the quest for faithfulness to the gospel and its ministry in a changing world, and finding and keeping one's bearings as a student or as a teacher cannot be separated from working out one's identity as a Christian, that is, one's calling. Here to know is at once to be known; to find our way to faithful ministry is to learn to rely on God's faithfulness; and to act out our calling as individuals and as a school is, as the very word so clearly implies, to respond to a summons that has not originated with us or politely awaited our bidding.

If the burdens of proof attendant upon an inaugural are thus different but not really less than before, I should like to claim the opportunity that follows from its being now a later occasion in life to reflect briefly on some concerns that have been on my mind for some time and that appear to have some connection with these midstream ruminations about change, faithfulness, integrity, and identity in theological education.

I

I have given out as my topic "The This-Worldliness of the New Testament," and I should like to say first what I intend with this rather clumsy title and why I believe it to have some significance; to offer at the same time some indications of this characteristic as we encounter it in the New Testament itself; and finally to mention some implications it might have for the way in which we think of the unity of the New Testament, its functioning authority for the community of the church, and its connection to our sense of identity as Christians.

By the phrase "the this-worldliness of the New Testament" I am *not* in the first instance thinking of the historically conditioned character of the New Testament writings or their situation-bound particularity, even though the proper recognition of both these features is today utterly indispensable for the work of honest exegesis. And I certainly do not mean to convey the notion that the New Testament belongs without remainder to the everyday world of the secular and the profane. Part of our problem is that the *mundane* so often connotes the *profane,* the earthly has become the God-forsaken, and we can no longer tell the difference. And the last thing I mean to suggest is a hermeneutic of the New Testament that would deny the deliberate preoccupation of its writers with the actions and the presence of the living God and his transcendence. No, clumsy as it may be, the term "this-worldliness" has been chosen simply because it has no substitute as the opposite of "otherworldliness." Otherworldliness is our problem, a problem of our religion and our theology, a problem in our ways of reading the New Testament. What I aim to urge is simply that we seriously misunderstand the New Testament when we ignore what it supplies for the correction of this problem.

What then is the "this-worldliness of the New Testament"? In a letter written in 1926, Martin Buber put into the language of the twentieth century what has been called the perpetual and unchanging Jewish protest against the central claim of Christianity. Peter's confession at Caesarea Philippi, that Jesus was the Christ, he wrote, was a sincere confession but not a true one, and it has not become any less untrue for having been repeated down the centuries. Why? The Messiah cannot have come at a particular moment of history because his appearing can only mean the end of history. The world was not redeemed nineteen centuries ago because we still live in an unredeemed world.[1] How can the Christian community withstand, how has it withstood, the withering force of that elemental refutation? It does no good to refer to the putative fact that Jesus was certain in his own mind that he was the Messiah, or to prove that the conversation with Peter at Caesarea Philippi actually took place. Both the consciousness of the one and the confession of the other were thought by Buber to belong to the realm of the humanly possible, but to the merely human all the same. If they can be proved, they prove in turn only that Jesus was a messianic-minded sort of human being. Either one takes the condition of the world seriously or one does not. If one does, then its transformation has clearly not occurred and the Christian claim to have found in Jesus of Nazareth the Messiah of God cannot be honored.

The argument has particular force because it comes from a respected and honored religious leader who stands in the tradition from which the New Testament writers also drew, and which we cannot disown. Buber's God is the God of the Bible. Yet his challenge comes from outside the church and so effectively poses the question of our Christian identity. At the same time, it is not solely a Jewish demurral. It taps a problematic running deep within the Christian consciousness itself, so it poses a significant challenge to Christian integrity from within. As Sydney Cave wrote in 1949:

> There was a time when men rejected Christianity because they disbelieved in miracles or in the Divinity of Christ. In our age a commoner cause is this: what they understand by Christianity has been disproved by their experience of life.[2]

"What they understand by Christianity"—that is the issue, not only for Buber and anyone else who stands outside it, but more painfully and acutely for anyone who claims to belong within. Buber's challenge takes the world and its condition very seriously, and that is where its surface force is felt. But it does something else, and that is where I propose to locate both its inner force and its flaw. It links the Messiah with redemption, and both of these to the transformation of this world into another, or its supplanting by a new order. There does not seem at first to be anything odd in that; the New Testament appears to do the same, and for three quarters of a century we have been trained to honor the

---

1. The letter is preserved in Franz von Hammerstein, *Das Messiasproblem bei Martin Buber* (Stuttgart: Kohlhammer, 1958), and quoted by H. J. Schoeps in his review of the book, *TLZ* 84 (1959): 348–49. See also Reinhold Niebuhr's tribute, "Martin Buber: 1878–1965," *Christianity and Crisis* 25 (July 12, 1965): 146: "Speaking to an audience of Dutch Christian pastors, he [Buber] made this highly illuminating comment on Jewish and Christian attitudes toward Christ as the Messiah: 'To the Christian the Jew is the stubborn fellow who in a redeemed world is still waiting for the Messiah. For the Jew the Christian is a heedless fellow who in an unredeemed world affirms that somehow or other redemption has taken place.'"

2. Sydney Cave, *The Christian Way* (New York: Philosophical Library, 1949), 24.

continuities between the New Testament writers and the eschatological tradition that made up so large a part of their Jewish background. Nevertheless—and this seems to me the crucial point—the premise of the argument, from which it draws all its force, is that both the Messiah and his redemption are here construed in unambiguously otherworldly terms. In the New Testament, on the contrary, this otherworldliness has been changed in consequence of the claim that the Messiah *has* come in an *unredeemed* world. The eschatological tradition has not continued unbroken; it has passed through a crucible fired by a public act not only available but also inevasible to every onlooker and every inquirer—the crucifixion of Jesus of Nazareth. It has irreversibly become "this-worldly."

This still is not to suggest a simple and sharp discontinuity between the Christian faith and its Jewish antecedents. On the contrary, the resources for coming to terms with the crucifixion of Jesus were drawn by the early Christians from the very tradition that was being recast under its impact, from the Psalter, from the prophets of the exile, from the actual history of a beleaguered and delivered people and its memories of past deliverance. That tradition itself was not simply otherworldly but very much in touch with the realities of earthly human life, and that is still one of the things that binds Christian to Jew in our time. Nevertheless, the way in which this characteristic "this-worldliness" is riveted to the central religious categories, myths, images, symbols—whatever we call them—of the new faith under the impact of a distinct historical event lies close to the very heart of what gives Christianity an identity of its own. But what kind of an identity! Other religious communities celebrate their new years, commemorate the births of their founders or the founding of their institutions, recall to consciousness past alienation and its reconciling, present guilt and its atoning, and clothe with religious solemnities the high points and the low in the cycles of human life, individual and corporate. But only Christians have a Good Friday. Only they recall in text and liturgy a public historical event that once made, and still makes, a mockery of their most central claim, and yet return to it as their most central truth: the coming of the Messiah in an unredeemed world. That cross, which so vividly defies the natural and inevitable otherworldliness of human religious tradition, including that of the Christian first and most of all, has been a key mark of Christian identity from the beginning.

To understand more accurately what is involved in Christian recollection of this event, more precisely what accounts for the central place it occupies in the early stages of emerging Christian confession, we need to take cognizance of at least two important points.

a. One has to do with the sheer historical givenness of the crucifixion. Because of the use I have made of Buber's argument, it would be easy to misconstrue the point and conclude that Christian identity here boils down to a matter of a simple logical choice. After all, when it comes to ultimate truth, who is to decide whether redemption must first be conceived in otherworldly terms that forever preclude the notion of a Messiah's having come in an unredeemed world, or whether the Messiah's having come in an unredeemed world must forever alter the conventions by which we comprehend redemption? On the level of logic, the meaning that comes out at the end is but determined by the premise adopted at the start.

The fact is, of course, that the Christian movement did not have its origin in a logical or semantic premise arbitrarily arrived at. The whole point in the "this-worldliness of the New Testament" is that truth for its writers, "what they understood by Christianity," began in an important sense from "their experience of life." This does not simply mean that they stood in a Jewish tradition that had always taken seriously social injustice, the undeserved suffering of the righteous, the reality of pain and grief, or the stark threat and fact of death. Of course that is also true, and remains immensely significant. To this day it is the presence of those Hebrew scriptures in the Christian canon that often prevents this faith from falling back into a private and interior piety, from reverting to an existentialist reduction to the way in which Christians "receive" or construe the unredeemed world around them. Yet all the evidence is that the event of the crucifixion of Jesus was an unexpected and unbidden "experience of life" that forced itself upon the circle of his disciples and followers as a brutal intrusion. We may have some trouble locating the precise year in which it occurred, but nothing in the entire Bible is so historically certain or so secure from historical doubting. Jesus certainly did not die from so-called natural causes at the culmination of a successful career as a popular teacher. His life was taken from him. (Incidentally, we probably ought to contemplate occasionally what the devastatingly destructive consequences for our theology would be if this certainty could be overturned, especially since we sometimes talk and think as though Jesus had died in that other way; it would remind us of the theological importance of what we do know historically.) And whatever the complex causes behind the taking of his life may have been (unless we abandon all historical perspective, this fatal opposition had something to do with what he said and how he lived), the *way* in which it was taken mattered greatly.

Martin Hengel has recently documented in overwhelming detail the shocking, offensive, and degrading connotations that shaped the public quality of this form of execution in the Greco-Roman world.[3] Of course the evangelists do not dwell on gruesome detail for its own sake; the community recollections on which they draw already represent the event in terms of what was believed

---

3. Martin Hengel, "Mors turpissima crucis: Die Kreuzigung in der antiken Welt und die 'Torheit' des 'Wortes vom Kreuz,'" in *Rechtfertigung: Festschrift für Ernst Käsemann zum 70. Geburtstag,* ed. J. Friedrich, W. Pöhlmann, and P. Stuhlmacher (Tübingen: Mohr [Siebeck], 1976), 125–84.

about it. But we forget at our own peril that this belief had nothing to do with knowing about this event, but only with surviving its impact as an utterly discrediting outcome. To survive at all meant using the once-familiar religious terms and ideas in new and unfamiliar ways. That is what is meant by speaking of a crucible through which the eschatological tradition passed. But the important point here is to note the force with which the historically given event compelled such revision. I will suggest that it was here that a distinctively *Christian* theology began.

An incidental observation may not be out of place here. It is curious that in the long history of debate about Paul's relationship to Jesus,[4] no one seems to have noticed how far a simple point of chronology might go to explain many of the differences between the ways in which the synoptic tradition and Paul refer to Jesus. The disciples of Jesus, the bearers of the synoptic tradition in its early stages, were in a position to perceive, interpret, and understand Jesus, to respond to him and to set their hopes in him, with available Jewish categories, either before his death or out of their memories of him before his death—as a leader and teacher, as an authoritative interpreter of the law, as a prophet, perhaps even one designated to be God's anointed, and (some would say) even as the Messiah. The crucifixion would have forced a new meaning upon these only after such initial connection with Jesus. But for Paul, the persecutor of the Christians, such a beginning was precluded from the start by Jesus' ignominious death. There was for him no way to accept the claims made in undoubtedly Jewish terms on behalf of Jesus by those whom Paul persecuted. The merest term of respect, teacher or sage or prophet, to say nothing of a full titular designation such as the Christ, had for Paul first to be reconciled with Jesus' death before its application to him could even be contemplated; that is, it had from the very start to be redefined, or, one might say in hindsight, "Christianized." Is it really any wonder that Paul begins with Christ crucified and risen, and that, for example, whatever new perspectives upon the Old Testament scriptures were opened up to him, these were triggered first from that event rather than from any of the community's memories about Jesus' own teachings and debates concerning the Torah?

b. So the crucifixion must have had an impact in its sheer historical factuality, its givenness. But why was this earthly discrediting of Jesus of Nazareth, in all that he had taught and done, not the end of the movement, the final obliteration of whatever hopes and beliefs in the presence of God and his kingdom Jesus might have aroused or rekindled? Why did the early community *not* draw the conclusion voiced by Buber? Why did this ultimate demonstration that they lived in an unredeemed world not force them to revert to an otherworldly hope

---

4. See Victor P. Furnish, "The Jesus-Paul Debate: From Baur to Bultmann," *BJRL* 47 (1965): 342–81.

and retire to await the end of history? By itself the cross was a devastating defeat, a sure indication that Jesus was a loser. The very public quality that made it inevasible closed off any other religious alternatives.

In seeking some answer here, the *historical* problem of reaching some kind of plausible understanding of the emergence of Christian faith and the *theological* problem of discerning what is most central in that faith coalesce. A Christian faith that is satisfied to locate its authorizing warrants in what Jesus said or did is bankrupt before Buber's challenge. That includes not only the Christian apologetic of an earlier time which would have us believe that Jesus was the Christ because of his miracles, or because of the authority with which he surpassed the scribes and the Pharisees, or because of the putative originality or moral superiority of his teachings. It applies with equal force to those latter-day apologetic eulogies which would justify the place accorded to Jesus in Christian memory by extolling the existential profundity of his perception, or the disclosive nature of his language, or the power of his parables to evoke from the human religious imagination visions of realities yet to be, and so lay upon Jesus such modern and humanistic messianic titles as "the fabulator of fabulators." One mark of all such arguments is that they take Jesus out of his time and separate him from his Judaism. But they also separate him from his humanity; they seek to secure Christian faith by turning Jesus into a Superman. What are they but all-too-modern forms of otherworldliness?

It is at this point that recent studies of the earliest stages of Christian creedal formulation and of the resurrection traditions in the New Testament acquire a special kind of interest and theological and historical significance. These traditions are themselves complex and intricate, fascinating and rich in ways we cannot here pursue. For our purposes we may say that they are summed up in the two very early and very basic confessional formulas which Paul sets side by side in Rom 10:9. One is "Jesus is Lord"; the other is "God has raised him from the dead." The two serve to interpret and illumine each other.

Of course we all know that the resurrection of Jesus has as firm a place in Christian confession as his death, and that it has a great deal to do with the fact that the early community was able to "survive" the impact of that public crucifixion at all, that its hopes and beliefs in the presence of God's delivering power and his kingdom in the person of Jesus were not simply obliterated. But why should this not have been mentioned long ago? The fact is that our otherworldly ways of reading the New Testament often do their worst at just this point. We need sometimes to think about the crucifixion of Jesus *as if* there had been no resurrection just so that we might understand what the resurrection itself meant for those early Christians when they linked the latter so closely to the former. Theological reflection and personal piety tend to leap ahead to seize upon the resurrection as the Christian answer to the historical givenness of the crucifixion and to its massive and devastating impact. But the inevitable temptation is to rest the case for the Christian faith upon an interpretation of the resurrection that makes of it an even more massively demonstrative display of supernatural power. In that case one can only tremble at the thought that its historical certainty may not equal or may even be less secure than that of the crucifixion. Not only do both the frantic exaggeration of the first and the nagging uncertainty of the latter betray themselves all too readily in the schizophrenic joylessness of many Easter Sunday sermons, but those folk who come back from the margins of the church into its sanctuaries for that Sunday (as one of the two in the whole year that still hold them) return to their homes only confirmed in their suspicion that "what they understand by Christianity has been disproved by their experience of life."

In the New Testament, on the contrary, the resurrection is not the same kind of public event as the crucifixion; indeed, nowhere in the New Testament is the claim made that it was witnessed by anyone at all. It was instead the risen Lord who made himself known; and those to whom he did appear became without remainder his witnesses, which meant that being able to say "God has raised him from the dead" was the same thing as being able to say "Jesus is Lord." No wedge can be driven between knowledge of the resurrection and confession of Jesus as Lord. For the heart and nucleus of resurrection faith in the New Testament, the conviction "that forms the basis of the theology of the New Testament in all its varieties," as Professor Nils Dahl has said, is "that the crucified 'King of the Jews' was right and had been vindicated by God, who raised him from the dead."[5] In short, the crucial issue in our understanding of the resurrection is what it means in relation to the one whom all the world knows to have been crucified.

II

I have said that a Christian faith satisfied to locate its warrants in what Jesus said or did is bankrupt before Buber's challenge, and it is first of all the cross that makes it so. Jesus' teaching about the radical imperative of God's grace has no convincing claim—until God shows him to be right. His unorthodox moves to establish human community with the outcast are no different from the madness of any revolutionary—until God identifies himself with this madness. His challenges to religious tradition and convention are only as interesting or as tiresome as a thousand other religious radicals—until the early preachers talk of God's having confirmed this servant, this protégé of his. But conversely also, this crucified, this discredited Jesus, whom God is said in these creeds to have

5. Nils Alstrup Dahl, "The Neglected Factor in New Testament Theology," in *Jesus the Christ: The Historical Origins of Christological Doctrine*, ed. Donald H. Juel (Minneapolis: Augsburg Fortress, 1991), 157–58.

acknowledged as his own, is not an otherworldly Jesus. Resurrection, as an idea in the world of the New Testament, has no messianic content of its own. Judaism knew nothing of a messiah raised from the dead. And even a proposal that God had raised from the dead some faithful prophet or rabbi would probably have created no great stir; it surely would not have upset any conventions in the understanding of God. There is nothing distinctively Christian about the notion of a resurrection—until it is given content by the this-worldliness of Jesus and his cross. Those earliest missionaries were proclaiming neither a new God nor an unknown Jesus. Instead, they were declaring that the God of their fathers had made of the discredited Jesus of Nazareth the right clue and the criterion for discerning God's true intentions; the measure of the right way to talk about salvation and God's kingship and their obedience; the way to face what was for them a clear and self-evident part of their future, namely, the coming judgment of God. This Jesus, and no one else, had now become: as Son of Man, the answer to this problem of God's future judgment; as Son of David, the bearer of Judah's hopes for a king who would one day transcend the corruptions and infidelities of human dynasties; as Servant of God, the one who by his righteous suffering could atone for his people's sins; as Messiah, the one anointed by God to effect a new sort of deliverance; as Lord, the one to be served and obeyed in this earthly life.

The titles quickly multiply and develop, but all are used in new ways. The old scriptures are consulted, but always with new perspectives. The familiar language is employed, but with unfamiliar connotations: God himself, his presence and his freedom, his mercy and his judgment, his faithfulness and his salvation, or love, righteousness, sin, suffering, life, and death—all has been stamped with the branding iron of the crucifixion. All has become irreversibly this-worldly, because the transcendence and authority of God himself now underscore and authorize that this-worldliness. And there is something on the stage of history that was not there before: a community that calls itself by the name of the crucified Messiah. It is one that can say now with integrity that it has been brought into being not by a flight into another world or by visions of things yet to be, but by its experience of life and by God's confirmation of the same.

III

I have spoken of all this in terms of the sheer historical givenness of the crucifixion as a public event and its impact upon the community of Jesus' disciples and followers, and have suggested that this has some connection with establishing the distinct identity of the Christian movement. The work of New Testament studies in recent decades has helped us to appreciate as never before the diversity of the New Testament writers in their theological perceptions, their conceptual language, their concrete historical intentions. In my own teaching I am committed to honoring that diversity and indeed elaborating upon it with as much precision as possible. Exegetical honesty requires that of us. When we contemplate the early Christianity of the New Testament, however, we also ask whether there is anything that gives it a distinguishable identity of its own, and if so, what that is. That is a legitimate question for a deliberately disinterested historian, whose descriptive task requires him to ask it sooner or later; it is at the same time a necessary and deeply interested question for one who stands within the Christian tradition and who sooner or later inquires what that means. For the student of the New Testament it is also the question whether any unity is discernible behind or within its theological pluralism.

In general, the search for some kind of doctrinal common denominator on which we might find unanimity among the New Testament writers has been given up—and rightly so. That procedure is so reductionist that what it yields is too meager to deserve our giving it status as the nourishing heart and center of our faith. All the most interesting and valuable insights of Paul, of the Fourth Gospel, of Matthew, are sacrificed for the sake of such a bland uniformity. Although our religious vocabulary is profoundly shaped by the New Testament, we discover that the meaning of each term and each theme—whether it be faith itself, or God's love, or some title by which Jesus is known, such as the Son of God—is different according to the writer who uses it. Each interprets the sense of God's presence and action in Jesus differently as he understands the predicament of the world and the perplexities of human life within it differently.

Under such circumstances, one is tempted to single out some special facet of New Testament teaching—such as Paul's truth that God justifies not the righteous but the ungodly—and to make of it the "canon within the canon," a *discrimen* derived from the New Testament itself for distinguishing what is more central from what is peripheral within it. To some extent that is unavoidable. Each of us, in our reading of the New Testament, will always appropriate from its diversity what most meets a present need; and that has been the case throughout the history of exegesis, not only for individuals but for whole stages and periods, for every crisis, of the church at large. But we harden and systematize such choices at our peril, for then we truncate our scriptures, reduce them to the familiar and the already known, and deprive ourselves of those unexpected and unanticipated insights they supply for our nourishment on unexpected occasions. No curse lies more heavily upon our study of the Bible, especially in a theological seminary, than the confidence that we already know what is written on its pages. It is worse than ignorance or indifference, for like the unforgivable sin of blasphemy against the Holy Spirit, it is beyond being taken by surprise, even by God himself.

IV

One of the most tempting alternatives in this connection is to find the heart of the New Testament message in a *theology* of the cross, for one of the things that ties the New Testament most closely to our own condition is the fact that other-worldliness was a problem among Christian folk from the very start. The most startling and thoroughgoing illustration for this is provided by the Corinthian church, which had fallen prey to otherworldliness, to a Christian triumphalism, at almost every point: in their understanding of the office and credentials of an apostle, in their esoteric definition of his message, in their belief in the power of the sacrament to guarantee a future life, in their use of ecstatic speech to qual-ify a special elite, in their ascetic and libertinist disdain for human sexuality, in their claim to have taken part already in the resurrection.

Paul's response is a sustained exposition of the bearing of the cross upon their understanding of both Christian existence and the ways in which God is known: the apostles are a spectacle, like men condemned to the arena, marked as fools by the world; their message is one of God's sovereign use of what is despised by the world to confound the wise; eating the bread and drinking the cup remain a proclamation of the Lord's death until he comes; their vaunted gifts will pass away and only faith and hope and love will abide; the life of marriage relation-ships is one in which the husband does not rule over his own body but the wife does, and vice versa; freedom is a life that is bound to the other's conscience rather than one's own; and this earthly life is one in which Christ is known only as the firstfruits, one over which a lordship is exercised by a Christ who has not yet defeated death and not yet delivered up all things to the Father. Why *not* make such a theology of the cross the canon within the canon by which to know the identity of our Christian faith, especially its this-worldly application?

A theology of the cross in this Pauline sense is a critical and polemical instru-ment for correcting an otherworldliness that has perverted the gospel. As a knife it lends itself to the surgery needed to cut back religious pretension, the flight into idealism and supernaturalism, both in the New Testament and in the Chris-tian piety of our time. And Paul is not the only one in the New Testament to develop such a theology of the cross. His most notable partner is undoubtedly the Gospel of Mark, contending for a true versus a false understanding of the transcendent power and authority of Jesus as the Christ, and using the cross as the discriminating mark to tell the difference. Only recall Mark's account of that conversation at Caesarea Philippi with which we began (8:27–33). The wither-ing rebuke tendered to Peter by this Messiah is to the effect that his otherworldly notions of victory and discipleship are satanic until revised by the correction that the true disciple must take up his cross and follow the Crucified.

Such a surgical knife has a kind of immediate appeal for our preaching by virtue of its critical power. But we need to beware. This kind of theology of the

cross, used only in this way, cannot be itself the center of the New Testament
or of Christian faith. It is used, rather, to protect and to preserve that center. Yet,
of course, just in that protective function it directs our attention to what is central. I have tried to define that center not as one theology within the New Testament but as the historical event of the crucifixion, a public, certain, and
inevasible event that has left its distinguishing mark on every theology, every
narrative, every interpretation of Jesus and every memory of Jesus, every admonition to Christian living, every exhortation and every consolation within the
New Testament.

Some parts of the New Testament remain only indirectly related to that center, serving themselves to protect the center from serious misunderstanding and
distortion; one would have to say something of that sort about the Epistle of
James. Some appeal to the center, as I have just said, as the critical negative
instrument for warding off threats to Christian identity. But others use it more
positively, as Paul himself also does. It would take more than another lecture to
trace all the ways in which that is done, and in some ways that is the unending
task of appropriating for ourselves the message of the cross. But who will deny
that Matthew's portrait of the Messiah as a lowly king riding into Jerusalem, as
the scripture said, "mounted on an ass, and on a colt, the foal of an ass" (Matt
21:1–9), has likewise been shaped by the impact of the cross? Or who will claim
that the Gospel of John could have come to the notion that the one who genuinely claims to be a shepherd of God's people is the one who distinguishes
himself from every hireling and every fraudulent claimer of that title by laying
down his life for the sheep (John 10:1–18) if it had not been for that event? Or
that in a world full of otherworldly notions of the elixir of life, of heavenly food
and drink, the same evangelist should have identified the bread of the faithful,
their food which endures to eternal life, as the flesh which the Son of Man gave
for the life of the world (6:52–58) apart from the impact of that same event?
That event could not of course have served such a defining and sustaining role
without the authorizing confirmation of God in the resurrection, but that is only
to say that God has not disclosed himself in relation to the life of men and
women in this world otherwise than in that event and in the one whose life on
earth it ended.

V

The resurrection makes the crucifixion (or, more exactly, the One who was crucified) normative for Christian faith. It does not require us to make of the crucifixion a supernatural event or an event unique in kind, cutting faith off from
the realities of history. It does not make one language about the event normative, as was once maintained when people thought the Greek of the New Testament was unique. It does not require us to locate the warrants for our faith in

some intrinsic quality of the New Testament documents so that we have to fear
the very critical disciplines that can unlock for us their precise meanings. And
it does not require us to abandon the insight that scripture itself partakes of the
nature and fullness of religious tradition, flexible and changing as human situations and needs change. All of these are symptoms of our proclivity to otherworldliness and only block our vision. Rather, the resurrection makes the cross
the paradigm, the clue, the source of the disclosing impact that is sedimented
in various ways within our New Testament. Indeed, it is only an understanding
of the New Testament as tradition that enables us to trace the functioning presence of this paradigm and to appreciate the truly historic (in the sense of his-
tory-creating) character of this event and then of the scriptures in which it
comes to us. When it functions in that way in our time, the New Testament can
reshape our Christian consciousness and provide again the reliable index we so
urgently need to authentic Christian speaking about God and his presence and
care in an unredeemed world. Then it can again become for us the scripture
which it was my vow last September to accept and to teach.

CHAPTER 2

FAITH AND HISTORY REVISITED*

Presidential addresses, at least in academic fields, tend to have about them a touch of both the programmatic and the autobiographical—the first because one feels called upon to address a larger project than one's own specialty and to speak on such an occasion to issues that engage others on a broader front; the second because one cannot essay to do so apart from one's own experiences and experiments in that enterprise. "Faith and history" is, from one point of view, an insanely comprehensive topic. If I venture now as an exegete to wander into the garden of the theologians, it is not to lecture to you about the fate of this tortured topic from the days of Schleiermacher, Strauss, and Bauer, or to unravel its tangled intricacies. You know much more about these matters than I. But neither is it simply to smell or even pick the flowers. It is rather to reflect briefly, in your presence, on a very particular web of theological questions from which I have not been able to extricate myself in some thirty-five years of teaching in the field of New Testament. Whether this is because I am slow-witted and simply haven't been aware of what has been going on, or whether—and this is my claim—it is because there really is an issue here that has not been laid to rest or gone away, will be for you to decide.

I

My starting point is really very simple. It is a given of the study of the New Testament in our time that it is both a theological and a historical discipline. It cannot escape having to render some kind of account, in terms comprehensible beyond the faith community as well as within it, of the origins of the Christian movement in the eastern Mediterranean world of the first century and of the emergence in that context of the twenty-seven books that have been added to the Jewish scriptures, more or less, to form the canon of the Christian churches. New Testament study, as a discipline, cannot run away from that historical assignment.

*This essay, first published in *PSB* 10, no. 2, NS (1989): 75–83, was originally presented as Paul W. Meyer's presidential address to the American Theological Society meeting in Washington, D.C. (April 15, 1988).

In the course of carrying out that task, one of its basic discoveries has been this: the historical and literary evidence is overwhelming that the gospels cannot be taken at face value as disinterested reports of the life and teachings of Jesus of Nazareth; every student of the New Testament has to come to terms with the differences between the outward and publicly accessible course of events in that life and the representations and interpretations of those events that early Christian faith has produced in these confessional and kerygmatic documents. Failure to recognize the historical evidence that has compelled this conclusion and to come to terms with it can only produce misunderstanding—not only of the gospel materials themselves and their nature as sedimentations of the church's didactic and kerygmatic traditions, but also and consequently misunderstanding of both early Christian faith and history. Professionally I have to regard serious engagement with these matters as an essential ingredient of beginning theological education—exactly *not* because it is somehow destructive of Christian faith but because this is the only way in which Christian faith can be honest, informed, and disciplined in its understanding of itself.

The realization of this elemental distinction, even, if you will, this discrepancy, has its roots, of course, in the modern development of historical consciousness and method. It has resulted in a kind of loss of innocence that is as irreversible as it is far-reaching in its consequence. By it, in the first place, a multitude of new questions has been generated and an equal number of old ones of long standing exacerbated. What binds the early church to Jesus of Nazareth? What is the nature of the historical and theological continuity between them? Is it a continuity of form and substance between the preaching of Jesus and the kerygma of the early church, or something quite different, such as the prolongation of the cause of Jesus into the mission of the church, or yet something else? Indeed, deeper down, why is continuity, once so easily taken for granted, even important? In what way are the teaching and life of the church "grounded" in Jesus? And why in one way rather than another?

Another set of questions is this: once this fissure has opened up beneath our feet, it has become impossible to ignore the variety and diversity among the gospels and among the traditions utilized within each one of them—diversity of theological perception, of conceptual language and religious idiom, of historical occasion, and of strategic and pastoral intent, all the time a diversity in ways of claiming that Jesus to be the Christ. The duty of the discipline is not only to render a plausible historical account of the emergence of the Christian movement in its variations; like every historical description, it is bound to do so in such a way as to expose those characteristic features of this movement that distinguish it from its antecedents and its environment and so to display its identity and coherence—a goal demanded by disinterested historical integrity but at the same time freighted with immense consequence for those who stand within the tradition and want to know its value and meaning. The historical inquiry into the origins and essential characteristics of early Christianity cannot be divorced from the theological search for the criteria of its authenticity. This is also the question whether there is any unity behind the theological pluralism of the New Testament, any center at its core, and leads back again to that open issue of the relationship of those confessional claims made about Jesus to the historical reality of his life—in short, to that issue of faith and history.

So there has been a loss of innocence and a burgeoning of new questions. But there has been also, in the second place, irreversible gain. I can hardly emphasize this enough, for although the point is not a new one, as you will immediately recognize, it is troubling how widespread is the neglect of it today. To acknowledge this historical gap, this gulf between the life of Jesus, even his preaching, and the good news proclaimed by the evangelists, is to realize that in an important sense Jesus himself was not a "Christian." This does not mean that he was merely a presupposition of the early church's theology. But we cannot reverse the discovery that *Christian* faith only begins after Jesus' teachings and life form a completed whole and the early community can look back on it and say, as Peter is represented as doing in his Pentecost sermon, that this Jesus is the one whom God has made by his resurrection the authentic clue to God's own relationship to the world and the norm for Christian faith and life. To be a Christian can no longer be reduced to living a kind of life and speaking a kind of language about God for which Jesus of Nazareth provides the precedent and the model—for one thing, simply because the documents do not permit a sufficient reconstruction of that precedent. Such a definition leaves death and resurrection out of the identifying heart of Christian teaching. To be a Christian must now be much more like doing what the sources in fact do—looking back on Jesus' life and his death, and understanding, on the grounds of God's vindication of that whole, that the world is a different place because of it.

It is this basic historical recognition, arrived at by historical means, that opens up the possibility of understanding the gospels as a unique product of the fusion of historical memories and traditions with a post-Easter perspective, an ex post facto disclosure that related this human being's life to God's purpose and so to salvation. Such a shift renders viable again a genuine Christology—for Christology is not merely an answer to the question of who Jesus was and what he has done for others; it is born, instead, only when this Jesus of Nazareth is significantly related to the God of Abraham, Isaac, and Jacob—his purpose, and power, and judgment, and love. This historical recognition opens up the way to an interpretation of all the gospel materials as expositions of this central christological and messianic claim. It frees the interpreter from the impossible burdens of extracting from the gospels the historical "proof," however crude or subtle, that Jesus was the Christ because of his authoritative impact as a teacher upon his audiences, or because of the profundity of his existential insights, or because of the originality of his teaching (especially its purported superiority to the Judaism within which it is so deeply set), or because of his language about God (however intimate, or generative in its symbol-creating power). Jesus is not only the Christ because he aided human beings in distress—but he is represented here as healing with God's own power because he is already perceived as God's anointed. Jesus is not only the Christ because he taught about the kingdom of God and interpreted the Hebrew scriptures with authority—but he is pictured as interpreting Israel's Torah with authority because this is one way of representing him in Jewish idiom as one greater than Moses. Jesus is not only the Christ because he died willingly for his beliefs and in devotion to his God—but the story of his death is told in a certain way, under the impact of the Hebrew Psalter, because he is already viewed as the paradigmatic righteous sufferer who in solidarity with all humankind is dependent on God alone for his vindication and salvation.

Such a historical understanding of the gospels has had many other liberating consequences: a new freedom to understand Jesus as a Jew in his own time and context; a new freedom to see the continuities and similarities between the gospels and the other non-narrative, epistolary, catechetical, creedal, hymnic, and apocalyptic passages of the New Testament (a showing that in an earlier time of the "Lives of Jesus" was often exceedingly difficult to come by); and above all, a new freedom to explore, to penetrate, and to appropriate for our own age the surprisingly rich nuances of the theologies of the evangelists.

II

Perhaps I have begun to belabor what is for many of you the obvious, but I have two points to make. One is that, in a time when it has become a rather popular pastime to trash historical-critical methods, it is easy to forget how much of theological substance we owe to them. There are increasing signs, and not just in the Southern Baptist Convention, of a growing indifference to critical history in dealing with biblical texts, a contempt for the scholarly guild as beholden to an alien loyalty irreconcilable with that which the gospel invites, and thus of an increasing expectation in seminaries and beyond that one should choose *between* historical and theological integrity, between "faith" and "history." The second point, which I want to explore briefly in the remainder of these remarks, is that this is an unacceptable alternative, that the two kinds of integrity go together, and that one cannot have one at the price of the other.

I submit that the issues may be clarified if we focus on the question of the origins of Christology and on the question of the warrants that authorize and legitimate the Christian claim that Jesus is the Christ. These are but two sides of the same question, one side put historically, the other theologically. This way of putting the matter may help identify within the long and tortuous history of the issue—which in any case cannot be rehearsed here—a few clear patterns and alternatives. I ask your indulgence if under constraints of time these are sketched now in a somewhat crude and oversimplified way.

a. Almost from the time when it was first drawn, the distinction between the so-called historical Jesus and the "biblical" Christ or "Christ of faith" was connected with a realization that the warrants for christological doctrine were not to be sought in the historical figure of Jesus, but had to be located elsewhere. To say that Jesus was not himself a "Christian" was another way of taking seriously the historical finding that Jesus did not make on his own behalf, as the Fourth Gospel above all represents him doing, the claims that Christian teaching made about him. But it also meant, for one pattern of reflection, that the historical reality of Jesus took a decided second place. Understandably so, perhaps, as the historical Jesus, so confidently known in the nineteenth century, receded farther out of reach behind the preaching and teaching of the New Testament writers. But there was a deeper realization, powerfully supported within the New Testament itself by the Pauline letters, as well as by indirect evidence within the gospel tradition; namely, that on the level of sober historical reality Jesus' career had ended in failure, his teaching and above all the expectations he had generated in his followers were finally discredited by the deliberately demeaning way in which in the end his life was taken from him. For his crucifixion was, and remains, the one historically most certainly known detail of his life, the one best attested in non-Christian sources, the most public—the one thing that no Christian teaching could deny without paying the price of its own credibility, and the one thing that seemed most clearly to destroy the credibility of Christian teaching. So the claim that he was the Christ sprang from beyond that life, most notably in the preaching of the post-Easter church. These preachers may have derived their authorization for that preaching from their conviction that God had raised him from the dead, so in one sense it was God who provided the warrant, but the materials that supplied new meaning came from a vast treasury of first-century religious traditions, expectations, and theologoumena. Jesus' otherwise insignificant life took on meaning because of the context in which it was placed, or (to reverse the image) because of the patterns of meaning that were imposed upon it: the hypostatization of wisdom into a narrative account of God's search for a dwelling place among human beings; the Hellenistic redeemer figure; the *kyrios*-cult of the mysteries or of the Roman emperor; the Logos-figure of Alexandrian Judaism; the synagogue traditions about Moses or Elijah; the Davidic hopes of a politically subjugated Jewish nation; the "suffering righteous" one of apocalyptic longing; and so on in almost infinite variation. The important point is that the earliest Christian confession is interpreted as a kind of "synthetic judgment," a creative act that *bestows* meaning where it did not previously reside and confers religious significance on the otherwise insignificant. Christian faith here takes its place rather comfortably in the rich human history of religious ideas, almost as if it had been achieved in defiance of historical reality. On these terms, it has been hard to locate a center to early Christian confession; its content is as variegated as the syncretistic world from which it has drawn and on which in many ways it is primarily dependent. The form of Christian faith has appeared here to be the somewhat arbitrary result of a peculiar constellation of accidental cultural and religious circumstances which New Testament studies may describe but which they have trouble in the twenty-first century commending as normative.

b. Such an appeal to the creative power of the church's confession and preaching has, understandably, provoked reactions that may not easily be brought under a single head. One temptation has been to turn the clock back, to reverse the loss of innocence that came with critical history, to reunite the claims of history and of confession by restoring to the confessional language of the New Testament the standing and authority of historical accuracy and reliability. Such attempts have varied from the crude to the fairly sophisticated manipulation of historical evidence and method. But they have been accompanied by an important theological argument. This has also appealed to the resurrection as the point from which the New Testament writers themselves drew the authorization for their claim. Only now the resurrection is interpreted not as God's vindication of the Crucified, but rather as the supernatural disclosure of the divine nature of Jesus of Nazareth; not God's declaration that the crucified Jesus was right, but his empirical demonstration that the evangelists were right in their ways of describing the historical reality of Jesus. The resurrection is here the bestowal of an epistemic privilege that rehabilitates faith *as* history and permanently discredits human historical investigation as reductionist, as the suppression of God's truth. The important point is that Christology here is interpreted as a kind of "analytic judgment" that lays bare the truth and reality that Jesus' life has in and of itself as a supernatural intrusion into human history, before and independently of death and resurrection. Faith—that is, the confession that Jesus is the Christ—is the necessary and inescapable inference from the empirical datum of the resurrection. The responsibility for the apotheosis of Jesus' historical life has been shifted from the shoulders of the *Gemeindetheologie* to those of God himself. But the price is to wreak havoc with the humanity of Jesus, to isolate his history from that of the world, and to abandon the attempt to provide a plausible historical account of the Christian movement or explanation of how others might come to share in its privilege.

c. There seems to have emerged also a fairly clear third position. This is to accept the conclusions of critical history, to recognize that the gospels have resulted from the fusion of historical memory and post-Easter confession and are the literary end products of a historical process, but then to take them, like other such literary artifacts, exclusively on their own terms—to let the matter of their historical referents or the authorial intentions that produced them drop away altogether. Christian confession is neither a synthetic nor an analytical judgment; it is a "language game," the language of a community. It creates a luxurious narrative world in which the community can live and thrive. Such an interpretation of the New Testament, if it does not abdicate the historical task, at least prescinds from it. But the danger is a retreat into the ghetto of a world created rather than illuminated by the confessional texts of the early community. One senses almost a kind of despairing of the historical reality of Jesus of Nazareth; his place has been taken by another figure who is "rendered" by the narrative texts of the New Testament. Such a procedure, too, seems unable to give any meaningful historical account of the origin of Christian faith or of the dynamics that gave it this historical shape rather than another. It has a great deal to teach us about the role of faith and its artifacts in the life of a human community, but it has difficulty assigning to Jesus of Nazareth a reality that is independent of, much less prior to, that faith, and thus raises in new and only more insistent form the question of the warrants of Christian confession. "Faith" seems here to be bought at the price of relegating history in its harsher realities to a shadowy and marginal existence.

III

What is a New Testament exegete and historian to do? Am I wrong in suggesting that there is more than a whiff of docetic unreality about all these options? Are they more than defense mechanisms set into motion to avoid the consequences of that distinction between history and faith that I have called the irreversible inheritance of our historically conscious age?

Perhaps one should turn everything exactly around the other way and begin by giving priority to that one thing that is most certainly known about the historical Jesus—his crucifixion. Of course the resurrection is appealed to by all branches of New Testament theology as the authorizing warrant for Christian confession and preaching. But what if one were to understand that resurrection as God's elevation of that public and indisputable historical reality of the cross to the status of the critical norm by which the authenticity of the distinctive Christian message to the world is to be established? Not as the wiping out of the crucifixion but as its confirmation and finalization?

There is much in the New Testament to suggest following such a course. And it is not confined to Paul's theology of the cross or to the Johannine coalescence of the divine glorification of Jesus with his elevation on the cross before the world. To pursue that topic would involve an exposition of much of the best that is currently being produced in New Testament exegesis, and I cannot do that here. Let me only make a few suggestions in relation to the problematics of the discipline outlined at the start, particularly the double burden of the exegete to provide both an accounting of the origins of Christian faith and a clue to the distinctive identity of Christian faith—a burden that blends on both sides the historical and the theological.

The extreme pluralism of the New Testament is the pluralism of the ways of perceiving and talking about God that its writers bring with them from their immensely rich and complex religious world. The Christians did not invent language about God's presence and freedom, his mercy and his judgment, his faithfulness and salvation, or the religious categories of righteousness, sin, love, suffering, life, and death—nor did the reality of God's power and presence begin with them. One can make the case, I believe, that these all become distinctively *Christian* in a way that differs from what preceded or surrounded when they were *all* altered under the impact of the brutal historical reality of the crucifixion of Jesus of Nazareth and the reflections that reality set into motion. Take, for example, the kingdom of God. On the lips even of the historical Jesus, so far as we can see, it is nothing different from being another variation on the theme of the Jewish world in which Jesus lived, untouched by crucifixion. That is not to demean it or oversimplify it. But on the lips of the early Christians, and of Jesus in the Christian gospels, it is something that cannot long be separated from the crucifixion—and becomes one of the richest resources by which the early Christians came to terms with the crucifixion and were enabled to interpret it.

What results is no monolithic or closed system. New Testament theology becomes on these terms a movement of response and interpretation, better perhaps a form of religious *relexicalization,* that is open to its future, capable of great diversity and development, yet marked by a distinctive branding mark that has ever since identified it and provided at the same time a criterion for its faithfulness and authenticity. New Testament theology does not depend solely on the final form of the New Testament texts, as though their literary forms are forever frozen and absolute. Nor does it depend on absolutizing the individual parts that make up the whole, as though the historical moment that produced each fragment were forever final and as though each were not a product of a theological and historical process. The identity-sustaining center and norm do not lie in either a literary form or the content of a contingent theological affirmation—for both are aspects of an interpretive tradition that is set in motion by the same impulse, and that has always had both aspects: historical concreteness and continuing applicability to the ongoing life of the church.

There are analogies for such a creative impact upon human religious thought by a historical reality that is never exhausted in its subsequent appropriations; one may think in the biblical tradition of the deliverance from Egypt, or the exile. The repercussions set into motion by these events are not constrained by the rational schemata that they disturb. Rather, historical reality becomes here a vehicle for the intruding presence and prevenience of God, but does so in such a way as to avoid and prevent all flight from concrete reality and so to attest to God's own involvement in this world.

That is how I should like to continue to explore some of these issues: with a renewed sense of the historical reality of Jesus of Nazareth and its importance for understanding the bearing of the New Testament message on the historical reality of our own lives.

CHAPTER 3

THE PROBLEM OF THE MESSIANIC SELF-CONSCIOUSNESS OF JESUS*

It is impossible within the scope of a brief essay to say much that is very new or even to repeat in significant proportion what has already been said about this problem, which has exercised the minds of New Testament scholars from the very beginnings of historical criticism. I have chosen to approach this problem, however, for the very reason that it has *not* come to rest but has been appearing with renewed urgency and frequency in the most recent exegetical discussions. It has a kind of symptomatic value; it helps, I think, to lay bare some of the crises and challenges in the study of the Synoptic Gospels, and the first part of the essay will consider some of the varying fates encountered roughly since 1900 by the problem of the messianic self-consciousness of Jesus, loosely and rather widely defined as Jesus' own understanding and interpretation of his message and his mission. At the same time, the problem in one of its most specific and concrete forms, the question whether Jesus applied to himself the title "Son of Man," has recently come to lively and intense debate after a period of relative dormancy, and we shall turn at the very end of the essay to consider this renewed discussion and its bearing on our total understanding of the synoptic tradition.

The problem of the historical Jesus is usually said to have begun with Hermann Samuel Reimarus.[1] This teacher of Oriental languages in Hamburg composed a critique of Christianity from a radical deistic position, portions of which were posthumously and anonymously published by Lessing between 1774 and 1778. The last of these "Wolfenbüttel Fragments" bore the title "Concerning the

---

*First published in *NovT* 4 (1960): 122–38, this essay appears here with minor modifications, and is used by permission. Although these observations on the historical study of Jesus (and its theological significance) are now over forty years old, readers familiar with the current vigorous discussion of these matters will recognize the continuing relevance and the importance of Paul Meyer's insights in this study.

1. Cf. Joachim Jeremias, "The Present Position in the Controversy Concerning the Problem of the Historical Jesus," *EvT* 69 (1957–58): 333–39; Werner Georg Kümmel, *Das Neue Testament: Geschichte der Erforschung seiner Probleme* (Munich: Karl Alber, 1958), 105–6 (ET: *The New Testament: A History of the Investigation of Its Problems*, trans. S. McLean Gilmour [Nashville: Abingdon, 1972], 89–90); Albert Schweitzer, *The Quest of the Historical Jesus* (New York: Macmillan, 1968 [German orig., 1906]), 13–26.

Aims of Jesus and His Disciples"; in it a distinction was sharply drawn between the aims of Jesus and those of his followers. Jesus was a Jewish political aspirant intent on delivering his people from a foreign yoke, an aim in which he completely failed; his disciples, confronted by their leader's defeat but unwilling to accept this shattering of their dreams, stole the corpse of Jesus, invented the message of the resurrection and of a suffering Savior, and so produced the church. As a historical reconstruction, the thesis was full of fantasy, but it introduced in a clear and irrevocable way the fundamental distinction between the historical Jesus and the Christ proclaimed in the gospels and by the church.

Two things should be noted. The first is that the problem did not actually start here. The Reformation had worked out, in its own understanding of scripture over against the tradition and authority of the Roman Catholic Church, an answer to the question of the identity of the earthly man Jesus of Nazareth with the contemporary Lord of the church. This answer lay in its understanding of the preaching function, which it put at the center of the church's life. But the confidence of Protestantism on this matter had already begun to crack when, in reply to the counterproposals of the Council of Trent, Protestant orthodoxy was driven to elaborate a doctrine of the verbal inspiration of scripture that, by buttressing the authority of scripture, could validate and guarantee the continuity between the earthly Jesus and the Christ of faith. But with Reimarus, the dawning of historical inquiry has been so linked with the problem as to raise the question not simply of the earthly Jesus but now of the historical Jesus, that is, of a Jesus who is accessible and knowable to a strict historical method operating independently from and in conscious repudiation of the dogmatic tradition. In the case of someone like Francis of Assisi, it is not necessary to add this adjective "historical"; it can be assumed that the historical Francis is equivalent to the earthly Francis, Francis himself in contrast to the Francis of pious legend. But in the presence of the Christian claim, this assumption can no longer be taken for granted. To speak of the "historical" Jesus is precisely to raise the challenge whether the "true," the "real" Jesus, Jesus himself, is to be found in the historian's reconstruction or in the theological tradition.[2] Throughout the nineteenth-century quest for the historical Jesus, orthodox Christianity was consistently on the defensive because it was unable to meet this challenge convincingly.

The second point to note about Reimarus's attack can be put very briefly: he sets Jesus' own intentions and aims over against those of his disciples. This is to define the problem from the very start in terms of Jesus' understanding of his own mission. The issue must become, ultimately, the issue of the messianic self-consciousness of Jesus, broadly understood.

---

2. Cf. G. Ebeling, "Die Frage nach dem historischen Jesus und das Problem der Christologie," *ZTK* 56 (1959), Supplemental Volume 1: *Die Frage nach dem historischen Jesus*: 14–30, esp. 16ff.

We need not survey the history of the subsequent "quest." It is enough to note the appearance in 1901 of those two books which for Albert Schweitzer marked its end: Wrede's *The Messianic Secret*, and his own *The Mystery of the Kingdom of God*.[3] To these books Schweitzer attached the labels "thoroughgoing skepticism" and "thoroughgoing eschatology." They were at one in demonstrating that it was impossible to construct from the gospel narratives a Life of Jesus without an arbitrary reading between the lines, without a continuous compromise of the claims of either theology or history. The two books represent, then, the two remaining alternatives. To quote from Schweitzer (who puts his own position first):

> The inconsistency between the public life of Jesus and His Messianic claim lies either in the nature of the Jewish Messianic conception, or in the representation of the Evangelist. There is, on the one hand, the eschatological solution, which at one stroke raises the Marcan account as it stands, with all its disconnectedness and inconsistencies, into genuine history; and there is, on the other hand, the literary solution, which regards the incongruous dogmatic element as interpolated by the earliest Evangelist into the tradition and therefore strikes out the Messianic claim altogether from the historical Life of Jesus. *Tertium non datur.*[4]

Wrede's book stands for the second of these alternatives. Its thesis is that the Markan gospel is by nature, even in its structure, a dogmatic affirmation, the chief purpose of which was to cover over the vast discrepancy between the historical reality of a non-messianic Jesus and the messianic claims of the early Christian community. Here, in sum, is a drastic *denial* of the messianic self-consciousness. Schweitzer's book takes the first; it is a drastic historical *affirmation* of this consciousness on the part of Jesus, resulting in the well-known picture of Jesus as a hero who in the end is but a deluded fanatic.

Of course, Schweitzer did not ultimately subscribe to his own disjunctive proposition; he was himself still so contained by the historical positivism of the nineteenth century that for him only one of these two options was really live: to take the gospels as history in the most radical way. Since both he and Wrede appeared to pay their ultimate respects to the Jesus of history over against all the orthodoxies around them—the one to a Jesus devoid of messianic pretensions,

---

3. William Wrede, *Das Messiasgeheimnis in den Evangelien: Zugleich ein Beitrag zum Verständnis des Markusevangeliums* (Göttingen: Vandenhoeck & Ruprecht, 1901) (ET: *The Messianic Secret*, trans. J. C. G. Greig [Cambridge: James Clarke & Co., 1971]); and Albert Schweitzer, *Das Messianitäts- und Leidensgeheimnis: Eine Skizze des Lebens Jesu* (Tübingen: Mohr [Siebeck], 1956; orig., 1910) (ET: *The Mystery of the Kingdom of God: The Secret of Jesus' Messiahship and Passion*, trans. Walter Lowrie [London: A. & C. Black, 1925]).

4. Schweitzer, *Quest of the Historical Jesus,* 337. Cf. with the following the quite different treatment of the same passage in T. W. Manson, "The Life of Jesus: Some Tendencies in Present-Day Research," in *The Background of the New Testament and Its Eschatology* (in honor of C. H. Dodd), ed. W. D. Davies and D. Daube (Cambridge: Cambridge University Press, 1956), 211–21.

the other to a Jesus consumed by his messianic passion—the vast difference which separated them, and which had been correctly divined in Schweitzer's disjunctive proposition, was for the time being not apparent.

I should like to propose the thesis that it was form criticism that made this difference clear and confronted New Testament scholarship with the kind of critical choice that has divided the heirs of Wrede from the heirs of Schweitzer ever since. The cardinal tenet of the form critics (let me hasten to point out that this group was composed of a number of scholars and is not to be simply identified with the position of Rudolf Bultmann) was that the gospels are to be understood as the deposit of a religious tradition. The materials from this tradition which they contain have been retained and have been given their present form because of the needs and affirmations and activities of the early Christians (e.g., preaching, catechetical instruction, confession, and cultic observance) over a considerable period of time and in diverse geographical locations and cultural surroundings. Properly understood, of course, form criticism never claimed to account for the existence of this tradition; rather it presupposed this, and claimed to be a study of it as a living movement and of the gospels as its living written echoes. It declared that this tradition, in all its varieties, its messianic titles, its Old Testament citations, its portrayal of Jesus as an authentic expositor of the meaning of the Mosaic law, its representation of Jesus as one who restored the brokenness of human life and fed the hungry, its description of Jesus as a suffering Messiah, a king of Israel who wore a crown of thorns, as one who in the calling of a group of disciples had created a new people of God— that the tradition in all these aspects and many more is so thoroughly and profoundly an interpretative tradition that it will not yield to the kind of historical reconstruction represented by Reimarus, which operates independently from and in conscious repudiation of theological assertion. To peel off the layers of the tradition is like peeling off the layers of an onion; what one finds is not apple or orange or walnut, but still onion, still this variegated interpretation that starts not from historical interest but from religious commitment. Form criticism, in short, represents an evaluation of the nature of the synoptic materials that, insofar as the present problem is concerned, comes down unequivocally on the side of Wrede and against Schweitzer. It gives an answer to the question *why* a Life of Jesus could not be written—especially such a sketch as Schweitzer himself produced. As far as I can see, this answer has not been conditioned or refuted by subsequent development but only confirmed and extended.

I have been careful so to phrase this definition of the form-critical enterprise as not to imply that its acceptance necessarily involves one in a radical historical skepticism. The period of the form critics saw the *end* of modern attempts to deny the existence of Jesus of Nazareth, not a new beginning of them. If the movement stamped the synoptic traditions as "interpretative" in character, this designation does not in principle imply that early Christian faith has no relation to concrete historical events or that the tradition is in essence the production of early Christian fantasy and imaginative fervor. That form criticism could be understood as implying this, and was so understood, is, however, a matter of regrettable record.

Again, even if we may be confident that the fundamental conclusion of form criticism has not been refuted, we must observe that it has nevertheless been repudiated in a variety of ways. It is in effect repudiated when form criticism is understood in purely formal terms as a classification of literary types (a rather dubious and unworkable classification at that) which brings no significant historical or systematic consequences in its train. Or it is repudiated when it is conceived, not as a total method demanded by the nature of the materials but rather as a point of view which one can take or leave—preferably leave, since it represents a kind of typical German extravagance. So Conzelmann can complain that from abroad the form critics are looked upon as a small, rather ludicrous sect devoid of healthy common sense; his complaint will be found fully justified by any reader of the recent works of Vincent Taylor, the man usually regarded as a chief exponent of form criticism in the English-speaking world.[5]

My working thesis, again—although I don't want to claim too much for it—is that subsequent students of the gospels divide into two main groups that can be understood as the heirs of Wrede and the heirs of Schweitzer, and that can be distinguished by their adoption or their rejection, respectively, of the form-critical protest. Perhaps this is not true in all respects; it seems, however, to be quite clearly true in respect to the problem of the messianic self-consciousness of Jesus, which concerns us here.

It may be profitable simply to recall two major treatments of this problem that we find in Bultmann's *Theology of the New Testament* and Hoskyns and Davey's *The Riddle of the New Testament*.[6] Both treatments rest upon literary and form-critical studies. The documentary hypothesis plays an important role in the argument of each; the British scholars clearly show the influence of the form-critics' work on the Continent (in fact, Hoskyns had distinguished himself

5. Hans Conzelmann, "Zur Methode der Leben-Jesu-Forschung," *ZTK* 56 (1959), Supplemental Volume 1:7. Cf. Vincent Taylor, *The Life and Ministry of Jesus* (London: Macmillan, 1954), 26–27; idem, *The Gospel according to St. Mark* (London: Macmillan, 1952), passim, esp. 17–20. The attitude of most British scholars appears to be nicely summed up in the words of T. W. Manson: "After thirty years it is possible at least to attempt a rough appraisal of Form-Criticism; and it may perhaps be suggested that it has by now done about all that it could do, and more than it ought" ("Life of Jesus," 212).

6. Rudolf Bultmann, *Theologie des Neuen Testaments* (Tübingen: Mohr [Siebeck], 1953), 25–33 (ET: *Theology of the New Testament*, trans. Kendrick Grobel, 2 vols. [New York: Charles Scribner's Sons, 1951–55]), 1:26–32; Edwyn Hoskyns and Noel Davey, *The Riddle of the New Testament*, 3d ed. (London: Faber & Faber, 1947). I owe some of the following observations to a very illuminating comparison and critique of these two books submitted on assignment by one of my students at Yale University Divinity School, Wayne Sibley Towner.

in his other work by his sensitivity to Continental theological developments). Both treatments agree that the task of ascertaining Jesus' self-estimate belongs to the critical historian, and is independent of the question whether this estimate of Jesus' own is either true or realistic. Both are prepared in advance to recognize the possibility that the early church, through the tradition and in the persons of the evangelists, may have imposed upon the life of Jesus a messianic character he himself never claimed to possess.

But from this point on the two writers' presuppositions diverge sharply. Bultmann lays it down that the question whether Jesus considered himself the Messiah is a historical point irrelevant to faith's "acknowledgment of Jesus as the one in whom God's word decisively encounters man";[7] the locus of significant assertions regarding Jesus' messiahship is in the earliest church's kerygma, not in Jesus' own message. The historical question submits for him to a clear and definite answer. Jesus' life and work did not fit traditional messianic definitions; there is no clear indication in the tradition that Jesus reinterpreted the traditional concepts; nowhere are sayings preserved in which Jesus promises to return again or soon. The Son of Man sayings constitute the key category. These divide easily and naturally into three groups, which speak of the Son of Man (1) as coming, (2) as suffering death and rising again, and (3) as now at work. These three groups coincide with the three layers of the tradition. The first comes from old tradition, is alone found in Q, and alone has any claim to authenticity; here Jesus speaks of the coming Son of Man as of another person. The second comes from the church's tradition, and arises in conscious reflection upon the events of the passion narrative. The third comes from the editorial tradition and is to be credited to mistranslation in the transition from Aramaic to Greek. Jesus' life itself is wholly *unmessianic;* it has messianic character in the gospels—including the dimension of self-consciousness—simply because, from the church's perspective, it seemed entirely self-evident that Jesus Christ, the Son of God, should have authenticated himself as such during his lifetime.[8]

On the other hand, Hoskyns and Davey stipulate that if the great blocks of synoptic material (Mark, Q, Matthew, and Luke) and the various types of material (miracles, parables, and aphorisms) all show the same definite messianic understanding of Jesus, this understanding must go back to Jesus himself since such a daring conclusion could not be arrived at in four separate and independent traditions by coincidence. It is no surprise that they so find. Where the dominant motif in the materials, for Bultmann, is the impending reign of God, for Hoskyns and Davey it is Jesus' utter obedience to the Father's will. The christological consciousness that is found to be implicit in all the sources is one Jesus himself drew from the Old Testament; he is consciously and intentionally

---

7. Bultmann, *Theology of the New Testament,* 1:26.
8. Ibid., 32.

engaged in rendering that obedience to God which is demanded by the law and foretold by the prophets. The cart and the horse have now been turned around. What is for Bultmann the church's *later* interpretation of Jesus' role and mission is, for Hoskyns and Davey, Jesus' own *prior* image of that role, which inspires him and thus not only shapes and guides his personal history but creates it. Where for Bultmann the focus is on the early witnessing community, for Hoskyns and Davey it is on the mind and resolve of Jesus of Nazareth. Bultmann frankly accepts the discontinuity between the message of Jesus and the preaching and teaching of the early church; Hoskyns and Davey insist upon continuity, and define it as a direct reflection in the kerygma of Jesus' own conscious intent. The generating impulse for the Christian movement is located by Bultmann in the Easter faith of the witnessing church so that the life and death of Jesus of Nazareth fade into the background, taking the position finally of being presuppositions to the message. The generating impulse for Christianity is located by Hoskyns and Davey in the unique image and practice of obedience wrought by Jesus out of the Old Testament materials so that the resurrection fades into the background as the divine appendix to Jesus' life. For Bultmann, the fundamental problem of contemporary New Testament theology is to explain how Jesus, the preacher of a coming kingdom, became himself the one preached; for Hoskyns and Davey, the fundamental task is the discovery of the Jesus of history.[9]

The Riddle of the New Testament is a great classic; it is an instructive book and inspiring. But when one comes right down to it, it is perfectly apparent that Bultmann has the better of the argument. Hoskyns and Davey's supposition that they have before them four *independent* traditions whose agreement cannot be coincidental is sheer illusion. They are unable to make important distinctions between the church and Jesus or to explain why Jesus appears to refer to a coming Son of Man different from himself. They ignore the years of oral transmission and uneasily skirt the questions posed by the future reference that bulks so large in Jesus' message as the tradition depicts it. Their book is inspired by the passion to avoid a docetism that rests Christianity upon a myth, but what they produce in the end is a historically implausible Apollinarian Christ who lives a human life but has no human will, who is motivated rather by a divine purpose and consciousness. In sum, they have evaded the form-critical protest and aligned themselves with Albert Schweitzer, insisting on treating the gospels as history.

What is so fascinating about this British book is not this or that weakness or strength. It is rather that combination of symptoms which it displays, for which medical science has given us the very apt term *syndrome*. This constellation of symptoms tends to recur in the heirs of Schweitzer: a healthy concern to meet the problem of discontinuity bequeathed by Bultmann, but an inveterate desire

9. Hoskyns and Davey, *Riddle of the New Testament*, 172.

to trace the affirmations of the church right back to the *ipsissima verba* of Jesus; a preoccupation with his messianic consciousness; an evasive posture with regard to form criticism; and a curious indifference to the death and resurrection of Jesus as definitive factors in the emergence of Christian conviction. (This last explains the energy frequently devoted to demonstrating that Jesus interpreted his own death in terms of the Suffering Servant passages of Second Isaiah.) The syndrome appears very clearly in Vincent Taylor's *The Person of Christ in New Testament Teaching*, where the "divine" consciousness of Jesus is a historical phenomenon that can be plotted and ascertained by historical argument and in its demonstrability is made to authenticate the content of the church's dogma.[10] It also appears in Oscar Cullmann's *Christology of the New Testament*, which opens with the premise that early Christian faith could hold Jesus to be the Messiah only on the condition that it was sure he held himself to be such.[11] This is a curious argument. Of course the figure of Jesus had a kind of self-evident integrity for the early Christians, so that they could not separate their assertion that he was God's Son from assertions about his acting and speaking as one who was aware of his sonship. But this simply means that they could not and did not pose Reimarus's rationalistic challenge; their inability to do so cannot be used today to ward off that challenge, to buttress historical arguments about Jesus' self-consciousness. Again, in Cullmann's book, form criticism receives less rebuttal than silent disregard. And what he offers us, in the end, is a treatment of New Testament theology that comes very near to ignoring the resurrection as a definitive formative factor; a brief acquaintance with the letters of Paul reveals what an anomaly that is.

My intention here is not to paste labels, but it is deeply troubling to hear it claimed today that historical reconstruction can bring us into the presence of God himself,[12] or that Jesus' interpretation of his own death is a question so vital for faith that it takes precedence over all others,[13] or that the authority of the church's message rests upon our ability to reconstruct the very words of Jesus.[14] These are all ways of asserting that the historically reconstructed Jesus is the *real* Jesus on whom faith rests. Indeed, on these terms it is impossible to

10. Vincent Taylor, *The Person of Christ in New Testament Teaching* (New York: St. Martin's, 1958); cf. my detailed review in *Religion in Life* 29, no. 1 (1959–60): 135–38.

11. Oscar Cullmann, *The Christology of the New Testament*, trans. Shirley C. Guthrie and Charles A. M. Hall, NTL (Philadelphia: Westminster, 1963), 8.

12. "[I]f, with the utmost zeal and conscientiousness, using the critical resources at our disposal, we occupy ourselves with the historical Jesus, the result is always the same, we find ourselves in the presence of God Himself" (Jeremias, "Present Position," 338).

13. Ibid., 336. Cf. the conclusion drawn by W. Farmer and N. Perrin at the end of their article "The Kerygmatic Theology and the Question of the Historical Jesus," *Religion in Life* 29, no. 1 (1959–60): 97, or the conclusion to which T. W. Manson arrives in the above-mentioned article ("Life of Jesus," 221).

14. Joachim Jeremias, *The Parables of Jesus* (London: SCM Press, 1954), 7.

draw any meaningful distinction between faith's response to Christ (as the recognition of his reality and redemptive meaning), on the one hand, and intimate personal familiarity with his thoughts and intentions, on the other. Faith *is* knowledge of the historical Jesus and stands or falls as such, being wholly delivered to the uncertainties of historical reconstruction. Here, it seems to me, is the common error in both the liberal and the fundamentalist understandings of the gospels. In the nineteenth century, historical reconstruction was wielded as a sword by the opponents of orthodoxy, and in the end the result was healthy; today, orthodoxy enjoys more status and wields the historical reconstruction of Jesus' self-consciousness as a shield to defend the integrity of the New Testament portrait of Jesus. If this involves, as I think it does, a continual attempt to make of the gospels and of faith what form criticism taught us they are not, the effect cannot in the long run be healthy.

What then about the heirs of Wrede who *are* prepared to treat the gospels as kerygma? Everything depends now on what one understands by this term, and the curious phenomenon of our time is that the opposite syndrome has begun to fall apart. It is all very well to emphasize the resurrection in the genesis of Christian conviction, but neither faith nor historical honesty can remain satisfied with a radical discontinuity between the church's proclamation and the earthly career of Jesus. Bultmann has not been able to render intelligible the sudden appearance of the disciples' Easter faith or the one most indisputable fact in the entire tradition, namely, Jesus' having been put to death. Why was it "self-evident" to the later church that the Son of Man whom Jesus seems to have understood as another figure was really Jesus himself? Form criticism itself has shown us, in laying bare the diverse movements of earliest Christian theology, that it has a backward reference to certain events that have transpired independently of faith's evaluation of them, and that this happened-ness of the earthly Jesus is a constitutive element in his significance for faith. The New Testament kerygma does not float, devoid of mooring, in the realm of myth. And so the problem of continuity has forced itself afresh upon the pupils and successors of Bultmann. Their resolve is not to abandon what they have learned from him, so they have been exceedingly reluctant to give an affirmative answer to the problem of the messianic self-consciousness of Jesus; yet they have clearly moved in that direction.

One attempt at a solution has been offered by the more radically existentialist members of the group, represented in the English literature by James M. Robinson's book *A New Quest of the Historical Jesus*.[15] Robinson argues that our time is distinguished from the nineteenth century by a new understanding of history in which it is discerned to be nonexistent apart from the intention,

15. James M. Robinson, *A New Quest of the Historical Jesus*, SBT 25 (Naperville, Ill.: Alec R. Allenson, 1959).

commitment, and meaning of those who participate in it. The kerygma, for all
its mythological forms, does not have for its content a mythology but rather the
existential meaningfulness of a historical person. The kerygma invites us to
understand the cross not as a natural occurrence, a brute fact, but in its relation
to Jesus' own existential selfhood; it is Jesus' own act of accepting death and
"living out of transcendence." Since it is only as such a really historical event,
the kerygmatic and historical understandings of it coalesce.[16] Beneath the surface, and not very far down, lies the existentialist axiom that historical event is
constituted by the person, and the person in turn by his or her own appropriation of existence. Clearly Robinson wishes to affirm the continuity of the
kerygma with the historical Jesus; he wishes to insist that the kerygma has not
superimposed upon the life of Jesus a meaning foreign to it. But in the end he
prescribes that the meaning elaborated in the kerygma must coincide with
Jesus' own intention and commitment, his own existential appropriation of
death. The purpose of the new quest for the historical Jesus to which Robinson
summons his readers is to test and substantiate the fundamental agreement of
the kerygma with Jesus' own understanding of himself and his mission. This
kind of test is possible because Jesus is accessible to us not only in the kerygma
but also independently via the medium of historiography. And this test is necessary since faith now means one's repetition of Jesus' decision, one's appropriation of his understanding of existence. In form, this parallels perfectly the
older liberal understanding of faith as the reproduction, in one's religious experience, of Jesus' feeling of sonship in relation to God—and it is, like the other,
totally dependent on historical familiarity with Jesus' person.[17] We seem to
have here a complete capitulation to the heirs of Schweitzer.

Ernst Käsemann, another one of Bultmann's pupils, has been much more
cautious.[18] The form-critical enterprise for Käsemann has rendered the historical value of the whole synoptic tradition so dubious that we must assume the
burden of proving authenticity before we can draw historical deductions from
it. Yet we almost completely lack the precise criteria by which that proof might
be furnished—*almost* completely, that is, for we can tell we are in touch with
authentic material when we come across something in the tradition that can be
derived or explained neither from Judaism nor from early Christianity, especially something that early Jewish Christianity could not tolerate and so was

---

16. Ibid., 89.

17. Cf., as an extreme example, Walter Bell Denny, *The Career and Significance of Jesus* (New
York: Thomas Nelson & Sons, 1933), esp. 172–84. See also the article by Ernst Fuchs, "Die Frage
nach dem historischen Jesus," *ZTK* 53 (1956): 210–29, in which occurs the remarkable statement,
"An Jesus glauben heisst jetzt der Sache nach, Jesu Entscheidung wiederholen" (227).

18. Ernst Käsemann, "Das Problem des historischen Jesus," *ZTK* 51 (1954): 125–53 (ET: "The
Problem of the Historical Jesus," in *Essays on New Testament Themes*, trans. W. J. Montague [Lon-
don: SCM Press, 1964], 15–47).

compelled to water down or revise. Käsemann points to the antitheses of the Sermon on the Mount: "You have heard it said, . . . but I say unto you . . ." Any rabbi can redefine the Torah in the sense of disputing another rabbi's interpretation, but no rabbi can set himself over against Moses and the whole rabbinic tradition; this is to shatter the definition of a rabbi as one who derives his authority via the teaching tradition from Moses. To this there can be no parallel on Jewish soil; the Jew who does what Jesus does here has separated himself from Judaism—or else he is the Messiah of Judaism. The very radicalness of this utterance is to be taken, accordingly, as an index of its authenticity.

This is a very tempting argument; however, one should notice its double edge. On the one hand, authenticity is deduced from the non-Jewish dimension of the saying; no Jew, theologizing about Jesus, could have invented it. But on the other hand, the very sense of the antithesis rests upon a precise understanding of the nature of rabbinic tradition. To speak in this way, Jesus must know the Judaism of his time, and any really non-Jewish features in these sayings would immediately be credited to the later Hellenistic community. Can we operate with both criteria without their canceling each other in the sense of rendering dubious any clear distinction between authentic and unauthentic? What we have in these antitheses, in the end, is a claim to authority, a "messianic" claim if you will, couched in the terms of rabbinic authority, as something transcending rabbinic authority. But we are no closer at all to answering the question whether this claim is made by Jesus himself or by early Christian faith which has learned to view his total career in the light of his death and resurrection.

Take another illustration. On the face of the tradition, Jesus is portrayed as one so steeped in the Old Testament that he finds there delineated his own task. Part of the theological profile of Jesus as the Christ consists of this representation of *his* knowledge of the Old Testament texts with which earliest Christian theology operates. But historically speaking, it is perfectly plausible to suppose that Jesus did read and know the Old Testament, so that the historical and theological statements cannot be disentangled from each other—until, says Käsemann, we see such a thing as Jesus' break with his family, an action totally uncalled for in the Old Testament ethos. Thus we are brought to feel the inescapable presence of another factor in his life, a disturbance of the conventions of Jewish piety which the historian must recognize as authentic to remain a historian.[19] Perhaps so. But is not Jesus' break with his family simply a part of that total portrait of him which describes him as living out in his own life the allegiance to God that he demands? All we have *clearly* demonstrated is that a certain incongruity exists in the representation between the Jesus who obeys God by being steeped in the scriptures and the Jesus who obeys God by putting

19. Ibid., 147, 152 (ET: "Problem of the Historical Jesus," 40, 46).

God ahead of family. All we have clearly demonstrated is the rich variety of the interpreting tradition!

Shall we leave it there, abandoning resolutely all attempts to use the early church's tradition in order to wrest verification of Christian confession from the words and conceptions of a historically reconstructed Jesus? The teachings of Jesus, his activities (the miracles), his interpretation of the law, his call to discipleship, his death—all are qualitatively of a piece from the perspective of the kerygma. None can be used independently to verify the messiahship; instead, all are but the function of Jesus' messiahship, variously understood and interpreted from the vantage point of cross and resurrection. Jesus is not the Messiah *because* his teaching is authoritative, but he teaches with authority because he is the Messiah. So also with the "self-consciousness." This is not something to which we have access independently of the kerygmatic picture; instead, there must be a certain integrity to this picture which demands that the kerygma also portray him as conscious of messiahship, since his fate on the cross cannot be torn loose from his intention and resolve. But to speak of the inner integrity of this picture is to speak of something that is not susceptible to proof; it is to speak of its ultimate validity or truth. It is to speak not of the historical Jesus in the polemical sense of Reimarus, but of the earthly Jesus and the real Jesus who is not the creature of historical reconstruction but God's new gift to the world. On these terms, his messiahship is not a "consciousness" at all but his redemptive meaning.

But we cannot leave the matter there, for this would be to leave unanswered the problem of continuity that has been the concern of both groups outlined so far. Historical understanding cannot be summarily barred from theology. Even more important, precisely the form-critical legacy—which once taught us negatively the impossibility of reconstructing the life of Jesus from the synoptic materials and positively the interpretative richness of that tradition—now requires of us some answer to the question of the relation of that tradition to the one historical figure it interprets, some historically intelligible notion of how the variations in the traditions are related to each other. The very tradition that refuses to yield to the historicizing of Schweitzer, and so forbids us from securing the content of Christian confession by recourse to a construct of the mind of Jesus, compels us to enlist historical reconstruction in our attempts to comprehend its manifold variety and its relations to the other parts of the New Testament. The New Testament problem of our time is the question of "continuity"—of the correspondence between the worship, the creedal formulations (the "titles" for Jesus), and the documents of the early church, on the one hand, and the historical reality of revelation, on the other. But this is a problem in our *comprehension* of the tradition and must not be allowed to become a problem in the verification of revelation; the latter is, and must remain, outside of the historian's domain, Reimarus notwithstanding.

Many aspects of what we have called the problem of continuity, as well as of the historical tasks which it involves, have become clearer in the currently renewed discussion of the title "Son of Man" in the synoptic tradition, a matter long closely associated with the problem of the messianic self-consciousness of Jesus. The recent discussion has yielded two constructive attempts, by Eduard Schweizer and Heinz Eduard Tödt, to provide a plausible historical explanation for the puzzling complexities of this title's occurrence in the Synoptic Gospels.[20] These attempts differ sharply and cannot as they stand both be right: the greatest claims to authenticity are assigned by Schweizer to sayings that speak of the "earthly" Son of Man; for Tödt they belong to the references to a coming heavenly figure. But these attempts fruitfully reopen what had become very nearly a sterile debate, and this for a number of reasons. Both see the historical problem essentially as one of illuminating the details of the tradition we find before us, not one of estimating its "worth." Some explanation has to be given for the fact that this title invariably occurs in the tradition on the lips of Jesus and only there; some explanation has to be given for the way in which the tradition holds together three quite different kinds of sayings without resorting to such rationalizing devices as the modern notions of a "hidden" Son of Man or a "Son of Man designate." And above all, light needs to be shed on the ways in which each evangelist understood and shaped the tradition for the needs of the church; here must be included the Q traditions as a separate entity.

The special peculiarity of the "Son of Man" problem is that the carrying out of these tasks requires, sooner or later, some kind of historically educated guess concerning Jesus' own use of the term, not necessarily as a self-designation but in some relation to his own mission and message. Thus both writers come to some fairly clear conclusions about authenticity. Authenticity, however, is a question now wholly within and subservient to an understanding of the synoptic tradition and not a point outside it that can be appropriated for purposes of legislating its "truth." The problem has come to fruitful debate because the false apologetic burden of reconstructing the messianic self-consciousness of Jesus has been lifted from it. And yet at the same time the message and challenge of Jesus as the starting point (together with his death and resurrection) of the interpreting tradition have come back into focus here in a surprising degree of unanimity between the two authors. Schweizer finds the historically and theologically illuminating core of the Son of Man sayings in those passages that deliberately employ this ambiguous title to relate the humiliation of the eschatological Righteous One of Israel to the claims and authority implicit in his

---

20. Eduard Schweizer, "Der Menschensohn," *ZNW* 50 (1959): 185–209; and idem, "The Son of Man," *JBL* 79 (1960): 119–29; Heinz Eduard Tödt, *Der Menschensohn in der synoptischen Überlieferung* (Gütersloh: G. Mohn, 1959) (ET: *The Son of Man in the Synoptic Tradition*, trans. Dorothea M. Barton, NTL [Philadelphia: Westminster, 1965]).

whole earthly career. For Tödt, this illuminating center is to be found in those sayings in which reference to a heavenly Son of Man, as guarantor of the promises extended by Jesus in calling people from "this evil and adulterous generation," is made to enforce the authoritative claim with which Jesus confronted his hearers. Both writers agree that the apocalyptic imagery that goes at times with the term is wholly secondary and subservient to its central meaning in the tradition—as should have been surmised long ago from the stereotyped quality of these features. And the debate promises to be fruitful, finally, because we have here two significant attempts to solve the problem of continuity between the message of Jesus and the message of the early church without falling again into the fateful syndrome that repudiates the lessons of form criticism respecting the nature of the synoptic tradition. It is along these lines, it seems to me, that a proper historical concern with the real, earthly Jesus must proceed.

CHAPTER 4

SOME CONSIDERATIONS ON THE ROLE OF EXEGESIS IN ETHICAL REFLECTION*

This sounds like an enormously presumptuous title, and it doesn't seem to have helped much to have begun it as "*Some* Considerations." The subject is all the more difficult because I cannot come before you with a clear and sharply profiled definition, made to order, of just what is meant by *exegesis.* In one sense, of course, we all know what this means: the elucidation of the biblical text, particularly (for us) in its theological and ethical dimensions. But the problems only begin there; there does not exist, so far as I can see, a single exegetical method which the biblical scholar can fashion and then commend to his theological and ethical colleagues. Exegesis has its disciplines and tools, but their application and use is in many ways an art, which no one "has" but all strive to attain. Again, the very fact that I am here is an acknowledgment, from at least two sides, that the descriptive and the normative tasks in exegesis can never be cleanly separated from each other. The assumption already lies behind us, as taken for granted, that the ethical reflection we are talking about is Christian ethical reflection, that it is theological in its grounding if not in its nature, and that, in both theology and ethical reflection, scripture exercises some kind of authority. Yet I do not presume to speak here about the character of this authority, to defend it, to place it in the pluralism of authorities (or perhaps the pantheon of authorities) with which we live, or to offer some kind of measure by which we could test the theological-ness of ethical reflection—that is, by measuring the extent or nature of the authority which it allows to the Bible. Christian ethics *is* theological and it uses the Bible, but the problems only begin there.

James Gustafson, in his fine introduction to H. Richard Niebuhr's posthumously published volume *The Responsible Self,* identifies the two biblicisms against which Niebuhr used to react, implicitly or openly, whenever the place of scripture in Christian ethics came under consideration.[1] I suggest taking these as our starting point, because, whatever Niebuhr's own words to us on

---

*This essay presents in slightly revised form Paul W. Meyer's address to the American Society of Christian Ethics (Washington, D.C., January 1965). Unless otherwise indicated, biblical quotations come from the RSV.

1. H. Richard Niebuhr, *The Responsible Self* (New York: Harper & Row, 1963).

this matter might have been, these two points still shape our situation and define our problem.

The first of these two biblicisms characterized the Christian ethics of liberalism, which always made of the teachings of Jesus the foundation upon which to erect its edifice. Such a procedure could, of course, vary from a rigidly reductionist repetition and reaffirmation of what it took to be Jesus' teaching, to the looser form exemplified by T. W. Manson's *Ethics and the Gospel*, in which the building is spoken of as a "work of art," but in which the foundation is essentially the same.[2] The problematic of this procedure is that, from the side of critical exegesis, it oversimplifies the problem of reconstructing the material content of Jesus' teaching; from the side of ethics, it oversimplifies its applicability to life in the world of the twenty-first century; and from the side of theology it assumes too readily that the essence of Christianity (*das Wesen des Christentums*) is to be located in this teaching material. So far as the New Testament materials go, it puts the cart before the horse, making the messiahship of Jesus of Nazareth rest upon some quality of this teaching rather than finding in this teaching tradition the reflection, the exposition, and the proclamation of Jesus as the (teaching) Messiah. So it fails to raise adequately the crucial question about the fulcrum of Christian existence in the world, the point of authentication for the Christian message, and the distinctive mark of *Christian* ethics. This problematic continues to be very much with us in the field of New Testament studies; as the "post-Bultmannians" pursue the important and necessary question about what authenticates the early Christian kerygma, in all its variety, for the early writers, they are (as I see it) much too inclined to take recourse to the parabolic and teaching material in the synoptic tradition, and not enough to assess the importance of the one, universally attested datum that needs no new quest to establish it: the crucifixion as the one thing that most demonstrably transformed all thought about God, salvation, and human responsibility.

In the second biblicism, the Bible becomes too exclusively the source of knowledge about humanity's ethical responsibility, the source of moral wisdom. The problematic, from the side of critical exegesis, is that it wrongly makes moral wisdom the heart of the Bible's content; from the side of ethics, it unjustly repudiates the contributions and insights of all extrabiblical analysis and perception of the human condition and situation; and from the side of theology, whatever else it does, it denies the relativity and concreteness, as well as the vitality and dynamics, of that history in which the one who raises the ethical question in fact lives. One form of this biblicism is the ethics that uses scattered biblical quotations, without regard either to the original contexts of the passages cited or to the discussion of these texts among biblical scholars, as the pliable and sometimes slippery mortar to hold together the irregular and het-

2. T. W. Manson, *Ethics and the Gospel* (New York: Charles Scribner's Sons, 1960).

erogeneous stones that have been quarried from every available source. This kind of biblicism has probably done most to discredit the very use of the Bible in ethical discussion and reflection—not only before professors of ethics but also before students of the Bible!

The question now becomes this: given a necessary connection between ethics and theology, and between theology in turn and the Bible, is there some alternative to these biblicisms? Is there some way in which exegesis can play a significant role in ethical reflection? I believe there is, because this is a question about what *kind* of exegesis we pursue, and because contemporary work in New Testament is also involved in the search for an exegesis that will meet some of the problematics we have enumerated: an exegesis that has become sensitive to the question about the distinctive *proprium* of Christianity, the authentication for a Christian understanding of God, the world, and humanity (I intentionally avoid the term *self-understanding*)—and does so not by avoiding but by entering seriously into the pluralism of the New Testament and its strictly historical character, in the sense of its historical contingency and con- ditioned-ness. An exegesis that has become critical in this sense can play a nec- essary and convincing role in ethical reflection that will be more than simply haphazard and ludicrous. The rest of my remarks will be an attempt to pursue and support this argument.

This is not to deny that there is such a thing as moral wisdom in the pages of the New Testament. There is a lot of it, and sometimes a direct exposition of it can become surprisingly relevant to our time. An example is provided by this unlikely passage from the *Haustafel* material in Ephesians:

> Slaves, be obedient to those who are your earthly masters, with fear and trem- bling, in singleness of heart, as to Christ; not in the way of eye service, as men- pleasers, but as servants of Christ, doing the will of God from the heart, rendering service with a good will as to the Lord and not to men, knowing that whatever good anyone does, he will receive the same again from the Lord, whether he is a slave or free. Masters, do the same to them, and forbear threatening, knowing that he who is both their Master and yours is in heaven, and that there is no partiality with him. (Eph 6:5–9)

A truly historical exegesis will not allow its ears to be immediately stopped to this admonition simply because it is addressed to slaves. Rather, a careful reading of the text at its face value, and in full recognition of its time-bound connections with slavery, as one of those institutional structures in the Mediter- ranean world in which Christians came up most directly against human inequal- ity, will see at once that the task of Christian ethics is more complex than the inveighing against social usage or inequality as such. The subject of this text is not slavery but motivation and responsibility, and that from *both* sides, the side of the master as well as that of the slave. Its orientation is decidedly not pity for the "underdog," a sentiment unstable and one-sided, never able to offer correction or assistance to the person "on top." Again, its orientation is not provided by the secular principle of *noblesse oblige*, which, whatever its truth may be, will always remain in practice as ambiguous as privilege itself. Nor is it some abstract principle of equality; these have a way of breaking down before the actual inequalities of life, which always remain even where justice is found.

The strategy of the text is rather to speak of two orders or levels of life upon which one meets the contrast between master and servant: there is a lordship of earthly masters, and there is another lordship in heaven. As the latter is allowed to color and qualify the former, the earthly structure of authority and submission, a way is opened up to pose a more basic question about integrity and responsibility, and to do that in the context of *mutual* relationships. The temptation of the slave is to act by way of eye-service, to please the momentary mood and whim of the master, to "read off" from the mercurial shifts of his temperament the standard of his own life, what to do and what not to do. To succumb to this temptation is to lose integrity—not because of the master, not because of the institution of slavery, but because he himself has turned himself into a human weathervane. We may retort that it is just this kind of integrity and sincerity that the institution of slavery in the first century or segregation in the twentieth century made impossible, but then we admit that the text has actually provided a rationale for reform that cuts far deeper than pity and does not have to pay the price of becoming sentimental or unrealistic about human power structures. The text does not ask the master to renounce a position of power; it does, however, enjoin him to forbear threatening and put him on guard concerning that point in his relation to his subordinates where human relationships are broken, where trust is destroyed, and where power reaches for absoluteness. The corrective lies in the knowledge that there is a Lord over both slave and master—in heaven. This theological corrective is as much embedded in a first-century three-storied worldview as the human problem to which it is addressed is embedded in first-century social structures. But are we to say that it is not a real and substantial corrective, or that it is irrelevant to the problems of motivation and integrity in the twenty-first century, from the slave of the giant corporation to the civil rights worker dedicated to overcoming the American inheritance from slavery?

Finally, reciprocity is the key to this piece of New Testament admonition—the very feature of it that was mutilated in every attempt to use this text in support of slavery! Reciprocity, as a mutual readiness to consider this heavenly lordship, became here a clue to a realistic working out of Christian equality in a world where all things are not simply equal, whether because of human creatureliness (parent and child), or because of human activity (master and slave), or because of a mystifying combination of both (husband and wife).

But this is too easy an example. The text itself holds the contrary injunctions addressed to slave and master together, so that there is a built-in safeguard against a biblicism that absolutizes a single one of them. It is quite another matter when these occur in widely different contexts that have little to do with each other; historical considerations become then proportionately more crucial. The writer of 1 Peter, addressing Christians under the heavy shadow of impending persecution, tells them not to be surprised by any fiery ordeal, to find rather in eventual unjust suffering evidence of their true community with a Christ who has already suffered in the pattern of Isa 53—a confirmation, therefore, of their true calling, and the grounds for rejoicing.

The author of James, in quite another situation, knows perfectly well how easily such an admonition can be perverted into the inhumanity that, in the name of faith, condescends in cruel benevolence to the brother or sister who is ill-clad and lacks daily food, with the words "Go in peace, be warmed and filled" (Jas 2:15–16). The writer presses home his point that faith without works is dead: "You believe that God is one? Well, bully for you! Even the demons can do that, but at least they shudder in the presence of God." In the situation of ethical indifference, which remains one of the identifying hallmarks of the gnostic religious mentality, James was not really an epistle of straw; the Suffering Servant profile of the Christ of 1 Peter could only have aggravated the inhumanity that this epistle lashes with its aphoristic Greek. Here, in short, is situational ethics with a vengeance, but even more: situational theology!

Does historical exegesis, then, yield us only an antiquarian relativism? Ethical reflection might well in that case abandon the New Testament entirely for a more up-to-date version of the same thing. But what led Luther, after all, to speak so disparagingly of James? We may at once concede that Luther was too quick to single out one canon within the canon by which to set up his hierarchy within scripture, and that some of his theological heirs have inherited this weakness. Yet it is hard to avoid the recognition that the passages just used in 1 Peter and James do not really stand on the same level. When the writer of 1 Peter penetrates to the paradox of joy *in* and *because* of suffering (something that cannot really be paralleled from the Greek and Roman moralists), even the descriptive exegete must recognize a profound kinship with the apostle Paul and with the Farewell Discourses of the Fourth Gospel (John 15:18: "If the world hates you, know that it has hated me before it hated you"). This notion that suffering is not accidental to the Christian life but essentially bound up with it, so susceptible to abuse as it was to be in the period of martyrdom, is nonetheless closer to the *proprium* of Christianity than the delicious irony of James. And note well: this is *not* because some majority vote can be mustered for this notion in the parliament of New Testament witnesses, but because behind it lies the recognition that God's way of dealing with the human condition lies itself along the way of suffering, namely, the historically given *proprium* of the faith in the crucifixion of Jesus. This is what counts, even for—nay, especially for— the historian. An exegesis that has become historically sensitive and critical cannot be satisfied to catalog the theological, conceptual, and ethical pluralisms of the New Testament (to name only three), along with their diverse historical settings, for history and life itself are not atomistic. It must seek also to discern the continuities and the relationships among these pluralisms, even sometimes their internal, intensely polemical relationships.

No one will claim that this is an easy undertaking, but it is here that the excit- ing work of New Testament study is now going on. We are beginning here to see Christian life and reflection emerging from its environment before the period of conformity, before there is such a thing as "normative Christianity." In this period of diversity and ferment, the question about what is really dis- tinctive in, and proper to, Christianity, and whether what we observe is more than Christianity's being simply a norm unto itself from one occasion to the next, is an acute one—for the first-century writers as well as for their twenty- first-century interpreters. Clearly, every step that is made here has theological significance, ethical bearing, and import for the question whether ethical reflec- tion can become in some sense biblical without becoming biblicistic. All of which is to say that the most serious use of historical considerations, especially the attempt to put a text firmly into its historical setting and to understand it there, is at once the most successful and the most reliable way of penetrating its theological meaning and releasing it for ourselves. (I might comment par- enthetically that exactly the same thing is true, for instance, in the study of Augustine or Luther.)

The remainder of this essay attempts to illustrate some of these points from Paul's First Letter to the Corinthians, that open strip mine so denuded by the passing shovels of writers on New Testament ethics (myself included). This fre- quent use of 1 Corinthians has been both child and parent of an exegetical understanding of the letter as a collection of disparate loci of Pauline instruc- tion, yielding conveniently to the familiar headings: partisanship and schism, church and world, law courts and fornication, marriage and divorce, meats and idol worship, veiling of women and abusing of the sacrament, glossolalia and love. The fifteenth chapter, to be sure, deals with resurrection, but despite a gen- eral admission that eschatology and ethics have something to do with each other in the New Testament, the specific connection of *this* eschatology with *this* ethics has not been at all plain. This last of the Corinthian "problems" has seemed to belong in an area of right thinking or right hoping quite isolated from right acting, and many an exegete has in fact so treated it.

Exegetical, theological, and historical considerations come together in the question: Just who were the opponents in chapter 15? To what kind of a posi- tion is this strangely composite block of material directed?

Albert Schweitzer identified the target as a Jewish ultraconservatism that was engaged in a kind of Sadducean denial of the resurrection; the issue then is a more or less inner-Jewish debate in eschatological dogmatics.

For Johannes Weiss as well, the issue was a doctrinal dispute, but of a different sort. For him, Paul's teaching about an afterlife is produced by the friction between the discredit, on the one hand, into which the peculiarly Jewish doctrine of a return of the dead from their graves (with the same bodies with which they had been buried) had fallen among the cultured of the Hellenistic world and, on the other, Paul's inability to imagine the "naked" existence of a disembodied soul after death. The flour produced by this grinding is a new doctrine that occupies a middle position between popular and crude physical conceptions of resurrection and Hellenistic notions about the immortality of the soul. Such a reading of Paul still enjoys considerable vogue.

Karl Barth's famous treatment of 1 Corinthians represented a radical change from this perspective, for his first question was whether a single theological theme cannot be discerned beneath all the disparate subjects discussed in the letter. His answer was an emphatic *Ja;* all the way through, Paul defines the life of Christian believers as shaped by faith in the resurrection of Christ and by the hope of their own resurrection. The theme of *all* of 1 Corinthians is the "last things," not as an object of speculation but as the prime reality in the Christian life. For Barth, this hidden theme becomes explicit in the discussion of "last things" in the concluding chapter. In this, as in his treatment of the Christ hymn in Phil 2 and comparably great passages, Barth displayed his uncanny sense for the theological jugular of the text, without being able to provide either the literary analysis or the historical setting that could refine and clinch his argument.

On these two points—violence to the text and to the historical setting—Rudolf Bultmann was quick to raise his protest, even though in general he was compelled to agree with and to praise Barth's understanding of Paul. Bultmann's contention was that the literary unity of 1 Corinthians is a result not of a thematic coherence in Paul's exposition but of the unity or totality of the Corinthian crisis; the subjects discussed by Paul are in themselves not simply disparate but all arise out of one and the same situation. This situational unity was at first bought by Bultmann at the price of the theological one. He considered the appeal to tradition in the opening verses of 1 Cor 15 to be a fateful relapse on Paul's part into an attempt to buttress the resurrection of Christ as an objective historical *factum*; the theological unity of the chapter in itself, not to mention that of the letter as a whole, thus rests at best on blunder. Bultmann's instinct was for the right historical clue: the opponents in Corinth are neither Sadducean conservatives nor idealists who believe in the immortality of the soul, but early gnostics like those mentioned in 2 Tim 2:18 who understand the resurrection as having already taken place. They claim full present possession of eschatological life in the Spirit; they strike out the future dimension of

Christianity not because they deny life after death but because they believe themselves to possess it already.

A great deal of what has happened since Bultmann's essay in 1926 confirms this insight of his and does in fact link chapter 15 with the rest of the epistle. These fanatical spiritualists, or spiritualist fanatics, are the ones who in chapter 1 understand baptism in terms of initiation into the mysteries and so "empty" the cross of Christ; they do this not by a denial of Jesus' humanity or death but by a denial that the death of Jesus should decisively color and shape the present life of the Christian, a denial of the permanent bearing of the crucifixion upon human life. To these who are already filled, who have already become kings, Paul sets up the spectacle of the apostles as men condemned in the arena, fools, weak, reviled, the refuse of the world (1 Cor 4:8–13), those who in a way prototypical for every believer are "united with Christ in a death like his" (Rom 6:5).

The same Corinthians consider themselves above what even pagans regard as the elementary requirements of morality, and sexual license belongs for them on one level with the passing hungers of the belly. Their disdain for the body, with its resulting and characteristic oscillation between asceticism and promiscuity, raises a whole nest of questions concerning marriage—about which Paul too has his reservations, albeit for eschatological reasons of an entirely opposite sort, creating not a little difficulty for his argument. Their fanaticism is characteristically impatient with the particularities of life in the world in which one hears God's call, whether circumcised or not, whether slave or free (the famous "calling passage" in 1 Cor 7:17–24). Against their sovereign indifference to the needs and conscience of the brother or sister for whom Christ died, Paul has to set up the apostolic prototype of freedom as a freedom to become all things to all people in order to be a slave to all for the sake of the gospel.

It is exactly these same early gnostics who elicit from Paul that troublesome chapter 11; here the newer manuscript discoveries really help, for example, logion 114 of the *Gospel of Thomas*: "Jesus said: See, I shall lead her [i.e., Mary], so that I will make her male, that she too may become a living spirit [*pneuma*], resembling you males. For every woman who makes herself male will enter the Kingdom of Heaven."[3] If Gnosticism equates bisexuality with sinfulness, the reverse side of the coin is the almost exhibitionist repudiation of every token of distinction between the sexes in the gathered community, as proof to itself that it participates already in the spirit and the age to come, where they neither marry nor are given in marriage but are equal to angels and sons of God, being sons of the resurrection (I am using the language of Luke 20:34). *Formally* Paul agrees that in Christ there is neither male nor female, but their presuppositions and the material of their contention are entirely contrary to his.

---

3. The translation is that of *The Gospel according to Thomas*, Coptic text established and trans. A. Guillaumont et al. (New York: Harper & Brothers, 1959), 57.

His appeals to nature and to general custom—these reasons are so awkward because the situation is even more so—amount in the end to a reminder that neither men nor women live in the church without the other, and so to a defense of the freedom of Christians to be men *and* women (the central assertion here, vv. 11 12, ending with "all things are from God," is put by a horrible mistake into parentheses in the RSV). (It is one of the cruelest ironies of Christian history that for almost two millennia this argument, intended for freedom, has been understood to abrogate that freedom.)

Finally, the matter of glossolalia: this is not a parlor debate on the relative merits of different gifts of the Spirit; rather, the same virulent religious understanding that assigns bisexuality to the realm of sin and flesh and locates the true self in *pneuma* produces in Corinth an ecstatic elite that identifies the presence of God with the contemptuous cancellation of every "merely human" gift. But for Paul the pouring out of God's Spirit is the same as the pouring out of divine love into human hearts (Rom 5:5); this spirit is not the prerogative of an elite, but all who have been baptized into one body have been made to drink of the one spirit, and all human functions in the body, especially those rational ones that seem to fade out in ecstasy, are the gift and fruits of this one spirit. No room is left for the feeling of inferiority that can cause the ear to say, "Because I am not an eye, I do not belong any more to the body," or for the feeling of superiority which can cause the eye to say to the hand, "I have no need of you." In sum, Bultmann was right: correct historical identification of the Corinthian opponents does in fact give to the letter an amazing unity and coherence. All the details in the text, for many of which Paul has been so cavalierly treated, now return to drive home exegetical recognition.

Is this unity only situational or accidental? Is it only a unity of the Corinthian situation and crisis? What about Barth's question concerning the theological pulse that beats beneath the manifold replies and admonitions of the apostle? Can the historian discover here some clue to the fundamental authentication behind Paul's injunctions? Barth was quite right in looking to chapter 15 for the answer, but I venture to propose that he found the wrong one, or at least looked there for the wrong reason.

Verse 19 begins to pose the issue. The RSV offers two translations. The one in the margin represents the interpretation of the KJV, the Phillips translation, and Barth's exposition, and reads: "If in this life only we have hoped in Christ, we are of all men most to be pitied." The implication is that the Corinthians deny any bearing of the Christian hope upon the future. But this translation cannot be sustained from the Greek, in which (a) "only" clearly belongs with "hope" and not with the phrase "in this life," and (b) the prepositional phrase "in Christ" does not go naturally with the noun "hope" but stands more independently in the meaning that it normally has in Paul. All this supports the translation in the RSV text: "If in this life *we who are in Christ* have *only hope*, we are of all men most to be pitied." For purposes of argument, Paul adopts hypothetically for the moment the Corinthian premise, which for him clearly carries with it a denial of Christ's resurrection. The shame and misery of this premise then is that they have only a hope. If this is what they have in this life, they have no *present* release from their sins, and those who have fallen asleep in Christ are lost. Then there is no substance to their faith; it is in vain and the apostle's preaching is in vain. But of course this is not really the Corinthian position. They do have a substance to their *pistis* that is more than a pious hope; look at their glossolalia! Moreover, they do not directly deny the resurrection of Christ (there is no hint in the text that they do). Christ has now in fact been raised from the dead, and Paul counts on their agreeing (this is not yet the turning point in the argument). This is the content of their *pistis* because in this the testimony of the apostles agreed: "Whether then it was I or they, so we preach and so you believe" (v. 11). The appeal to the kerygma in vv. 1–11 is not to prove the resurrection as a *factum* but to confirm the agreed-upon premise that those who are in Christ have more than a mere hope; they know already his death for their sins and his resurrection, both according to the scriptures.

So far in his argument, Paul is propounding a "realized eschatology" of his own, a fact that has made it appear to many a commentator that he has misunderstood the Corinthian gnostics. They too affirm the conquest of sin as a reality in their lives; they too affirm the resurrection of Christ and subscribe to the position that "as by a man came death, by a man has come also the resurrection of the dead" (v. 21). Is not Paul playing right into their hands?

The decisive turning point in the passage seems to me to come with verse 23: "But each in his own *order:* Christ the first fruits, then at his coming those who belong to Christ." What the Corinthians deny, in every aspect of their conduct, is not the resurrection of Christ but the limiting, reserving, qualifying affirmation that is involved in taking him seriously as a "first fruits." Where this is gone, they can both claim to be Christians (i.e., assent to the proclamation that Christ has been raised) and at the same deny the future resurrection—just that combination which Paul repudiates. Twice in this long chapter, Paul puts unmistakable emphasis upon order and sequence (*tagma*), first here in vv. 23–28, then again in vv. 46–49: "[I]t is not the spiritual that is first, but the physical, and then the spiritual" (v. 46 NRSV). This latter reference to the first and last Adams is an explicit repudiation of the inverse order of gnostic anthropology, but it is at the same time a repudiation of the enthusiastic fanaticism for which no eschatological reservation remains. The destruction of the last enemy and God's being all in all belong to the end (*telos*), which can come *only* by a transformation of both the living and the dead (vv. 50–57). It is above all this order that divides Paul from the gnostics, for it alone means that there is a "not yet" to the Christian life; it divides Paul from the gnostics because it unmistakably divides the life of imperishability and immortality from this present life in which the Christian must live and act. What the Corinthians in fact deny is the bearing of the Christian faith on *this* life. In this life, Paul protests emphatically and with an oath, "I die daily." The arguments from seeds, from different kinds of flesh (of people and animals and birds and fish), from different kinds of glory (of sun and moon and stars), and from different kinds of body (physical and spiritual) are all arguments for *dis*continuity. The central *mystērion* of the chapter is the change that must take place for all flesh and blood before it can inherit the kingdom of God. What the chapter proves is not the certainty of resurrection so much as its *futurity* and the affirmation this involves for the present life that is so discontinuous with it and from which the Corinthians are trying to flee. *This* life is the life of human bisexuality, the life of marriage relationship in which the husband does not rule over his own body but the wife does, the life of not many wise and not many powerful and not many of noble birth, the life in which one is called to glorify God *in* the body, the life that is bound to the other's conscience rather than one's own, the life in which those who think that they stand need to take heed lest they fall, the life in which eating the bread and drinking the cup remain a proclamation of the Lord's death until he comes, the life in which we see in a mirror dimly and in which we know in part. This is not a life of mere hope only, but it is a life in which Christ is known as a "first fruits." Every description by Paul of his apostleship is a confirmation of this "I die daily," a confirmation of the claim upon him in the present of a Christ who has not yet delivered up all things to the Father.

That brings us to Paul's final discontinuity, which is such a unique feature of this chapter and yet so much an unrecognized part of it: the distinction he draws here, and here alone, between the kingdom of Christ and the kingdom of God the Father. In the *telos*, God will be all in all, but until every rule and authority and power is destroyed, it is "necessary" (Paul's language means: within the divine strategy and purpose, not as a limitation imposed upon it from without) that Christ rule. And what does Christ's rule mean for Paul? (That is the question about the real *proprium* of Christianity for him.) It is not an imperfect or a partial rule. It certainly does not mean that the prince of this world still rules! Rather, it is that rule of God which has the shape and structure manifest in Paul's own life—"always carrying in the body the death of Jesus, so that the life of Jesus may also be manifested in our bodies" (2 Cor 4:10). It is that rule of God which follows the death and resurrection of Christ as the place where God has reasserted himself to be the one who is himself righteous and who justifies (i.e., manifested his righteousness apart from the law). It is that rule of God which is given shape in the cross, in a crucified Messiah who is a scandal to the Jews and foolishness to the Greeks, but to those who are called, both Jews and Greeks, God's power and God's wisdom. It is the rule of God as known now under the impact of the historically given Golgotha. In short, it is that rule of God which gives human life and action and responsibility the shape and profile of every plea and every admonition throughout 1 Corinthians.

The resurrection of Christ cannot be separated in Paul from that rule. It is not some massive metaphysical catastrophe but the designation of the crucified—"as Son of God in power by the spirit of holiness" (Rom 1:4). It is God's own affirmation of this crucified, whom alone Paul resolved to know among the Corinthians, as the arbiter of human life and conduct, of human right and wrong. It is the point at which this crucified is known as *kyrios* and where the question of authority receives its answer and at the same time its redefinition. That curiously inverted argument of 1 Cor 15 seems only on these terms to make some clear sense: a denial of the futurity of the resurrection, in and by the kind of fanaticism which the Corinthians exhibit all along the line, is a denial that Christ has been raised from the dead because it is a denial that this crucified Christ is *Lord*.

"But in fact, Christ has been raised from the dead, the first fruits of those who have fallen asleep" (1 Cor 15:20). Of course the first fruits is also the guarantee of that which lies yet hidden in the power of God. "Just as we have borne the image of the man of dust [not Adam in his sin but Christ in his death!], we shall also bear the image of the man of heaven" (v. 49). As Christ the first fruits provides the shape of this life we now live by faith, in the flesh (Gal 2:20), and the motivation for the ethical injunction, so he provides also the undergirding and the surety of the hope. Both of these, ethics and eschatology, coalesce perfectly in the final verse of the chapter: "Therefore, my beloved brethren, be steadfast, immovable, always abounding in the work of the Lord, knowing that in the Lord your labor is not in vain" (1 Cor 15:58).

Can we, by way of a provisional conclusion, draw some consequences from this review of 1 Cor 15? Paul's citation of tradition is an important part of his argument for a number of reasons. It provides him with a vehicle for his affirmation of the resurrection of Christ, and enables him to align himself with a commonly acknowledged consensus and to include himself (by his additions to the list) within a closed circle of authentic witnesses—thus implicitly closing off any independent claims to access to the risen Lord that the Corinthian ecstatics might be inclined to put forward. Moreover, it allows Paul to emphasize the unanimity of apostolic proclamation and provides a common base for discussion between himself and the Corinthians.

But if our reading of the chapter is correct, while it contains the seeds of Paul's own resolution of the problem at hand, this tradition does not itself offer the criterion or norm by which Paul's argument gains its telling thrust. The assertion of Christ's lordship does not in itself settle the issue, and neither does the affirmation by itself that Christ has been raised from the dead. The effective fulcrum is provided to Paul's argument by the way in which he takes seriously the epithet "first fruits"—by his refusal to let the resurrection tradition be pushed in the direction of a *theologia gloriae* by the Corinthians. He presses to the thought of a lordship of Christ that is qualitatively different from the *telos* in which God will be all in all; this compels him to an understanding of deliverance and freedom, along with its responsibility, which is present in full and compelling force but which is *not* equivalent to the transformation of the world in which human beings live into the transcendent pneumatic realm anticipated in fanatic spiritualism. This lordship ties one to others and to one's world, enabling life in an "unredeemed world" (in Martin Buber's phrase), and confirming such life as not being "in vain."

The authentic content of resurrection faith is the identity of the Risen One with the Crucified, *that* identification which forbids the transformation of the earthly Jesus into a cult god known independently in the church as *pneuma*. It is not a formula or a doctrine, but God's own identification and confirmation of Jesus as his Son. This is what provides Paul with the measure for proper talk about the living God who is wiser and stronger than human beings. We would not be wrong, surely, in identifying the resurrection faith, so understood, as the *proprium* of Christianity at this particular historical juncture, the crucial matter by which what Paul elsewhere refers to as the "truth of the gospel" was to stand or fall.

Was such resurrection faith not already present in the tradition and known in Corinth? All we can say is that if it had been, Paul would not have had to reaffirm and reinforce his gospel *against* the Corinthians as he in fact does. What he does is to bring both the tradition and the Corinthians back under the normative impact of the historically given *proprium* of Christianity, the death of Jesus of Nazareth—under the same impact that had started this movement in the first place—and to do that just at the point of their ethical responsibilities.

Part II

EXEGETICAL AND THEOLOGICAL ESSAYS ON PAUL

CHAPTER 5

THE WORM AT THE CORE OF THE APPLE: EXEGETICAL REFLECTIONS ON ROMANS 7[*]

First, it is [a] just principle of interpretation, that we should understand every writer, when this can be done in consonance with the laws of language, as speaking to the purpose which he has immediately before him. There are very many truths of the gospel, and many plain and important truths, which are not taught in this or that passage of Scripture. The question concerning [Romans] chap. vii. 5–25 is not, whether it be true that there is a contest in the breast of Christians, which might, at least for the most part, be well described by the words there found; but, whether such a view of the subject is congruous with the present design and argument of the apostle.[1]

These words were written over a century and a half ago by Moses Stuart, one of America's pioneers in biblical exegesis. If the words bear the unmistakable marks of his time, their point is so contemporary and possesses such undiminished pertinence to theological discourse today that they may still serve as a kind of motto for exegesis. One of the major tasks of exegesis, in our day no less than in earlier ones, is to check the arbitrary exploitation of passages from scripture to score points in theological controversy, to inhibit their use for purposes alien to their original form and function, to prevent their being made simply subservient to the interests of those who use them. One might, of course, ask why such tendencies need to be restrained. Why should anyone not be free to make whatever one wishes of these familiar and fondly held texts? People will be found, after all, to do just that. But if these texts were composed initially to guide, correct, and reform the community's perceptions and understanding, to clarify and restore its identity and direction, and if this role was recognized and conceded to them in the process of canonization by the community that still uses them as scripture, then their own power to shape rather than to be shaped by contemporary interests must be respected. Whatever one may have to say

---

[*]This essay presents with minor revisions the study first published in *The Conversation Continues: Studies in Paul and John in Honor of J. Louis Martyn*, ed. Robert T. Fortna and Beverly Roberts Gaventa (Nashville: Abingdon, 1990), 62–84.

1. M. Stuart, *A Commentary on the Epistle to the Romans*, ed. R. D. C. Robbins (4th ed.; Andover: Draper, 1868), 463.

about the failings and inadequacies of actual biblical exegesis in its practice, this continual search to recover and reinstate in the first instance the texts' own integrity must remain its ideal.[2]

In that search, the tools and methods of historical study—defined in the broadest sense as the attempt to understand these texts in their original historical, literary, and cultural contexts—take on growing rather than diminishing significance and urgency. Indeed, one may even redefine the major task of exegesis under discussion here as the purification of all anachronistic understandings from our reading of biblical passages. These anachronisms comprise more than the deliberate uses of texts for purposes that have nothing to do with their original composition. They are even more likely to be the unintended or even well-meaning interpretations that read back into the texts the lexical usages, the debates, the anxieties and designs, and the theological claims of later times in the church's life. It is ironic, but true, and amply documented in the history of biblical interpretation, that one of the major barriers to the recovery of the texts' integrity is often the accumulated freight of the church's own long history of the use of scripture, the sedimentation left behind by its own previous attempts to honor and appeal to these very texts! This surely does not mean that the texts have no integrity of their own. It is the situation and needs of those who take recourse to them that never remain the same. But the task becomes more pressing than ever of distinguishing carefully, in Stuart's words, between what "might, at least for the most part, be well described by the words there found" and what is "congruous with the present design and argument" of the writer. The power of a biblical text to transcend the subsequent tradition in such a way as to perform a regulative function upon it depends on this preservation of its historical distance and priority as much as it does on the continuities that bind the biblical materials to the church's life and thought, by virtue of which they remain "the church's book." This in turn requires giving heed in every particular instance to "the purpose which [the writer] has immediately before him."

Recovering that purpose, of course, is just the problem. To re-create the situation that called forth a New Testament text and shaped it requires all the resources and skills the exegete can muster: detailed familiarity with available

---

2. Bultmann's classic essay on the problem touched on here, "Is Exegesis without Presuppositions Possible?" in *Existence and Faith: Shorter Writings of Rudolf Bultmann* (New York: Meridian Books, 1960), 289–96, starts from this need to respect "what the text actually says"; "exegesis must be without prejudice" (289). In her presidential address to the Society of Biblical Literature ("The Ethics of Biblical Interpretation: Decentering Biblical Scholarship," *JBL* 107 [1988]: 3–17), E. Schüssler Fiorenza probes the issue raised here and advocates the adoption of a "critical theory of rhetoric" for which "context is as important as text" (5). Unfortunately, despite a wealth of insight on the responsibilities of biblical interpreters, she does not give any guidance on the most pressing hermeneutical issue of our day: By what criteria can one determine where responsible attention to context ends and ideological manipulation of a text begins?

sources, balanced judgment in their evaluation and use, knowledge of the complex processes by which tradition grows, but above all a sympathetic historical imagination that can use such information in a disciplined projection of the interpreter into another place and time. It requires the ability to sit loose to previous interpretations of a text rather than to let false modesty absolutize these; a willingness to let issues of sometimes immense theological import take on unsuspected and unforeseen contours under the promptings of the text itself and its oft-unnoticed details, sometimes in defiance of what the interpreter or the community has previously held most dear; and a readiness to seek out the critical and reforming intent of the text without the defensive or manipulative reactions that so often distort both historical reconstruction and exegesis.

Simply to list these requisite qualities for recovering the setting of a biblical text is already, for those who know him and his work, to describe the gifts that Lou Martyn has brought in special measure to the interpretation, first, of the Fourth Gospel and, more recently, of the Pauline letters. Some of the most rewarding hours I have been privileged to enjoy have been those spent in unhurried conversations with him, exploring "the design and argument" of this or that Pauline text, especially from Galatians or Romans. What I offer here as a token of gratitude and respect is but an attempt to continue such conversation, now in a fashion more one-sided than usual, but more open to public perusal and discussion.

I

Romans 7 is a showcase of the issues in exegesis that have just been outlined for at least two major reasons. The first is clearly suggested in the passage quoted from Moses Stuart. It is a quality of the text itself: its location at a critical turning point in the general argument of Romans, its susceptibility to a variety of interpretations, and its seeming propensity to evoke from the reader analogy and comparison with one's own apparently similar experiences.[3] These characteristics of this particular text are well known, and every commentary lays out to some extent the choices with which it confronts the thoughtful reader. Paul's extended use of the first person singular pronoun "I" is one of the features of the text that most notably imparts to it this ostensible multivalence. We need not review here the various proposals that have been made to identify more precisely the antecedent of this pronoun.[4] A fairly strong consensus seems

3. Of the seven reasons for the attention devoted to Rom 7 listed by W. G. Kümmel in his influential monograph *Römer 7 und die Bekehrung des Paulus* (Leipzig: Hinrichs, 1929; reproduced with unchanged pagination in *Römer 7 und das Bild des Menschen im Neuen Testament* [Munich: Kaiser, 1974], 1), this is the first.

4. The various suggestions are surveyed in Kümmel, *Römer 7*, 74–132; and C. E. B. Cranfield, *A Critical and Exegetical Commentary on the Epistle to the Romans*, ICC, 2 vols. (Edinburgh: T. & T. Clark, 1975–79), 1:342–46.

to have emerged that the passage is not autobiographical in any sense that allows it to yield details about Paul's personal life, either before his conversion or after. Paul is employing rather a rhetorical style in which the self functions in a representative way as a type or paradigm for others.[5] At the same time, the pronoun is not used in a purely fictive way, as though Paul were excluding himself from its pattern. The closest parallels in his own letters to this intense and vivid device of casting fundamental religious affirmations involving the self into first person singular language are provided by Gal 2:18–21 and Phil 3:7–14. Both passages follow so closely upon obviously autobiographical references that it is impossible to dismiss all personal nuances from his use of "I."[6] Moreover, the closest formal literary analogies to this style are found in the individual laments and thanksgivings of the Hebrew Psalter and the Qumran hymns. These reinforce the view that Rom 7:7–25 is a theological description, cast in a retrospective and reflective mode, of the destructive power of sin—by one who has himself known it and been delivered from it—and that its antithesis, announced already in the contrasting phrases of v. 6b, is provided by Paul in 8:1–11.[7] Yet the question remains: Whom is Paul describing? Who is embraced by this paradigmatic rhetorical style? The answer is not a function of the style itself, but must depend on "the present design and argument of the apostle." In other words, a correct answer cannot simply precede exegesis, but follows it and depends on it.

If one major reason why a consensus in the reading of Rom 7 has been so elusive lies in a certain quality of the text itself, the second lies in the accumulated freight brought to it by its interpreters. The literature on this text seems to offer some particularly striking examples of the anachronistic reading referred to earlier, and it is on these that I should like to focus. The barriers to understanding thrown up by the legacy of past interpretations are the hardest ones to identify because they are so intricately interwoven with the positive debts every exegete owes to those who have gone before. Indeed, it is sometimes precisely some insight that once opened up with fresh vitality the force of Paul's gospel that now, taken as self-evident in another situation and frozen into convention, impedes the interpreter's ability to cross the differences of historical space and

5. BDF § 281. Kümmel adds many examples (*Römer 7,* 126–32), but his list was drawn up before the discovery of the manuscripts at Qumran (see also n. 7).

6. When E. Käsemann (*Commentary on Romans* [Grand Rapids: Eerdmans, 1980], 192) pronounces that an autobiographical reminiscence in the "I" "is refuted by Phil 3:6," he must not have the first-person language as such in mind, which is patently autobiographical and supports such a self-reference in vv. 8–14, but the putative contradiction in the content of what is said about this "I" in Rom 7 and Phil 3:6. This is another issue to which we must return.

7. See the more recent discussion in U. Wilckens, *Der Brief an die Römer,* EKKNT, 3 vols. (Neukirchen-Vluyn: Neukirchener Verlag, 1978–82), 2:76–78; and G. Theissen, *Psychological Aspects of Pauline Theology* (Philadelphia: Fortress, 1987), 190–201. Theissen has a particularly instructive treatment of the "I" in Rom 7.

time in order to approach again that elusive intent of the author. To remove these barriers requires something akin to the paradigm shifts of other disciplines. It can come about only when proposals that may initially seem outlandish can win their way to new acceptance.

II

What would be an example of such an apparent "dogma" that has once appeared in the course of the interpretation of Rom 7:7–25 but now has become an impediment to our understanding of Paul's words?

In one of the most well-known and fateful shifts in the history of exegesis, Augustine changed his mind about Rom 7:7–25. In his own words, he at first understood Paul in these verses to be "describing the man who is still under the law and not yet under grace. Long afterwards I learned that these words could also describe the spiritual man and indeed in all probability do so."[8] There had been differences of opinion on these verses before Augustine,[9] but like so much else he wrote and thought, his later view is particularly significant for the influence it has exercised, first, on the Protestant Reformers and then, through them, on subsequent interpretation right up to some of the most recent commentaries. The reasons why the Reformers were so attracted to Augustine's interpretation are complex, and they are not by any means identical with the ones that moved Augustine to alter his view.[10] Nevertheless, on an attentive reading of a few of the key paragraphs, an important element in this line of exegesis emerges quite clearly. A few sentences will suffice.

First, from Martin Luther:

> First, this whole passage clearly reveals disapproval and hatred of the flesh and love for the good and the law. Now such an attitude is not characteristic of a carnal man [*carnalis homo*], for he hates and laughs at the law and follows the inclinations of his flesh.

8. Augustine, *Retract.* 2.1.1, in *Augustine: Earlier Writings,* LCC (Philadelphia: Westminster, 1953), 370. Fuller documentation of Augustine's different views is given by Kümmel, *Römer 7,* 90–94.

9. For the patristic exegesis, see the bibliography in Kümmel, *Römer 7,* 75 n. 1, and more recently K. H. Schelkle, *Paulus: Lehrer der Väter* (Düsseldorf: Patmos, 1956), 242–58. The best recent review of the whole history of the exegesis of Rom 7:7–25, with bibliographical notes, is to be found in Wilckens, *Römer,* 2:101–17.

10. The reasons behind Augustine's change are discussed by Kümmel, *Römer 7,* 93–94; and especially Wilckens, *Römer,* 2:105–7. The shift is usually connected with Augustine's conflict with Pelagius and dated in 418–419 C.E. (Kümmel, 91; Wilckens, 102). Nobody, in this literature at least, seems to have noticed that the later position is already emerging in Augustine's *The Spirit and the Letter,* 26—that is, in 412 C.E.; this would seem to reinforce the view that the factors behind the shift are more complicated. This subject, and in particular the nature and quality of Augustine's exegesis of Romans in his *The Spirit and the Letter,* requires further discussion elsewhere. See pp. 133–48 in this volume.

Yet a spiritual man [*spiritualis*] fights with his flesh and bemoans the fact that he cannot do as he wills. But a carnal man does not fight with it but yields and consents to it. Hence, this well-known judgment of Blessed Augustine: "The will to be righteous is a large part of righteousness."[11]

The first word, then, which proves that a spiritual man is speaking here is this: *But I am carnal* (Rom. 7:14). Because it is characteristic of a spiritual and wise man [*spiritualis et sapiens homo*] that he knows that he is carnal . . . and that he praises the law of God because it is spiritual.[12]

Certainly no one will declare himself wretched except one who is a spiritual man. For perfect self-knowledge is perfect humility, and perfect humility is perfect wisdom, and perfect wisdom is perfect spiritualness [*perfecta spiritualitas*]. Hence, only a perfectly spiritual man can say: "Wretched man that I am!"[13]

And then a comment by Philipp Melanchthon: "For Paul is speaking here of the sort of person he was after his conversion. For before his conversion that conflict did not exist since an ungodly person [*impius*] does not will from the heart what the law admonishes."[14]

One is naturally drawn to concur with what Luther is doing here. A few sentences after the last words quoted from him, he moves directly into a reassertion of his characteristic claim, made familiar in the formula *simul iustus ac peccator:* "The saints in being righteous are at the same time sinners."[15] Faced with a "Christianized" society in which every citizen was also a baptized Christian, Luther was insisting with that formula that Christian perfection was not to be claimed as a quality of the self in this life, but belongs to it only by imputation in the gospel's promise of God's forgiveness. As Wilckens has pointed out, Luther was taking the experience of confession, the starting point of Christian conversion, out of daily monastic practice and making it the permanent center of personal piety.[16] The religious application of Luther's exegesis is explicit and unmistakable: "Indeed, it is a great consolation to us to learn that such a great

11. Martin Luther, *Luther: Lectures on Romans*, trans. W. Pauck, LCC (Philadelphia: Westminster, 1961), 201. Luther's Latin words are taken from Martin Luther, *Vorlesung über den Römerbrief 1515/1516*, 2 vols., Latin-German ed. (Darmstadt: Wissenschaftliche Buchgesellschaft, 1960), 2:24, which reproduces the Ficker Latin text. The reference is to Augustine, *Ep.* 127, 5.

12. Luther, *Lectures on Romans*, 201–2; *Vorlesung über den Römerbrief,* 2:24.

13. Luther, *Lectures on Romans*, 208; *Vorlesung über den Römerbrief,* 2:42.

14. Philipp Melanchthon, *Römerbrief-Kommentar 1532,* Latin text ed. Rolf Schäfer; vol. 5 of *Melanchthons Werke in Auswahl* (Gütersloh: Mohn, 1965), 224; my translation. In this context the terms used by Melanchthon to contrast with *impius* are *renati* ("reborn persons") and *sancti* ("saints").

15. Luther, *Lectures on Romans*, 208; *Vorlesung über den Römerbrief,* 2:44 (*simul sancti, dum sunt iusti, sunt peccatores*).

16. Wilckens, *Römer,* 2:109.

apostle was involved in the same grievings and afflictions in which we find ourselves when we wish to be obedient to God!"[17] Nevertheless, from these last words one may begin to suspect that the pastoral end has captured and distorted the exegetical means. The suspicion hardens into certainty when one notes how Paul's anguished cry in v. 24a is turned into an expression of "perfect spiritualness." If Augustine's exegesis here constitutes a celebrated volte-face, Luther's is a no less notable tour de force. It does not just water down Paul's language (as do all attempts to make the words of v. 14b, "I am sold under sin," apply to life in Christ). It turns Paul's text on its head and makes it mean its own opposite. The disparity between text and interpretation is painfully manifest as well in the "judgment" or axiom (*sententia*) of Augustine to which Luther appeals: "The will to be righteous is a large part of righteousness." Not only is there no basis for such a claim in Rom 7, but also it is altogether un-Pauline and irreconcilable with Paul's argument in chapter 2 (especially vv. 3, 6, 13, 22, 25–27).

What shall one make of this disparity? Is this a case in which, to paraphrase what Wilckens says about Augustine, Luther has the substance (*Sache*) of Paul's theology in his favor, even though he has Paul's text against him?[18] Is the meaning of Paul's passage to be accessible only at the price of doing such violence to the integrity of the text?

When one looks more closely at these sentences from Luther and Melanchthon, one discovers something else. In v. 14, Paul uses the contrasting terms πνευματικός ("spiritual") and σάρκινος ("fleshly, consisting of flesh" or "belonging to the realm of the flesh") to mark the gulf between *God's* law and the *human* self confronted by it. These adjectives are not used again in this section, although σάρξ ("flesh") reappears by itself in v. 18 and in contrast to νοῦς ("mind") in v. 25b. But under the influence of Augustine's language, these adjectives have been deflected from Paul's usage and their new meanings have come to dominate the exegesis. They are now made to differentiate two classes of *humans:* the religious person who is righteous, wise, understanding, reborn, perfect in self-knowledge and humility, on the one hand, and the irreligious, the ungodly, and the sinner, on the other, who is utterly devoid of genuine religious impulse. This is the language of binary opposites, used by triumphalist religion to separate humankind into two groups of people, the saved and the damned. This language has been perpetuated in Protestant commentaries with such generic terms as *regenerate* and *unregenerate.* Such language must have had a certain appeal in the sixteenth century to distinguish the "godly" denizens of Europe from the non-Christian infidels pounding on the eastern gates of Constantinople. So it is not at all surprising that the Reformers, wishing to deflate such natural religious pretension in the apostle's name, should jump to

17. Luther, *Lectures on Romans,* 208.
18. Wilckens, *Römer,* 2:107.

the conclusion that Paul must be describing the tension proper to Christian existence in 7:7–25. He does speak of continuing conflict between flesh and Spirit "in the breast of Christians," to use Moses Stuart's words, most explicitly in the next chapter, in 8:5–8 (cf. Gal 5:16–18). So well-intentioned commentators have continued, with the Reformers, to think that it is the part of true Christian humility and self-knowledge to find that conflict to be "the present design and argument of the apostle,"[19] even though there is not a syllable in Rom 7:7–25 about life in Christ, and even though Paul himself has signaled to his reader in both 7:6b and 8:1–2 that the rest of chapter 7 is to be understood as the antithesis to chapter 8 and not in simple continuity with it.[20]

The flaw lies in the binary language that has been imposed on Paul's text: the "I" of Rom 7 must be either a "godly" or an "ungodly" person; there is no third possibility. That this reading coerces a false alternative on the text is betrayed by the harsh anachronism that results. It leaves no room for the historical Paul or his kind, the deeply religious Jew devoted to the God of Abraham and Moses. There are complex historical reasons, no doubt, why no living Jew sat in that empty chair at the Reformers' exegetical table. But whatever the reason, this absence permitted the deeper misunderstanding. Like the perfectionist piety that produced it, this binary mode of thinking dismisses with scarcely disguised contempt the religious seriousness of any person outside its own group. Melanchthon's comment is particularly revealing: "An ungodly person [anyone prior to Christian conversion] does not will from the heart what the law admonishes." Its modern counterpart is Cranfield's comment: "A struggle as serious as that which is here described can only take place where the Spirit of God is present and active."[21] The clear assumption here is that the Spirit of God is not at work anywhere outside of the Christian church—even though Paul himself has just stated in unequivocal terms that the (Mosaic!) law is "spiritual"—and so the inference is drawn with Luther and Melanchthon that the "I" of Rom 7 can only refer to the Christian.

19. See, e.g., Cranfield, *Epistle to the Romans,* 1:246–47, who uses the flagrantly ad hominem argument that one should question the moral seriousness of anyone who finds it hard to believe that Paul was describing life in Christ with his words "sold under sin" (v. 14b).

20. "Not until we come to ver. 25 is there a single expression used which belongs to Christianity" (W. Sanday and A. C. Headlam, A *Critical and Exegetical Commentary on the Epistle to the Romans,* ICC [New York: Charles Scribner's Sons, 1906], 186). Dissenting interpretations rely heavily on equating what is taken to be Paul's use of fairly conventional Hellenistic distinctions within the human self (between ὁ ἔσω ἄνθρωπος, "inmost self," and μέλη, "members," in vv. 22–23, and between νοῦς, "mind," and σάρξ, "flesh," in v. 25b) with his distinction between "spiritual" and "fleshly" in v. 14. Such an interpretation of "inmost self" cannot be supported from 2 Cor 4:16, where the context is entirely different; see Wilckens, *Römer,* 2:93–94; and Kümmel, *Römer* 7, 14–15.

21. Cranfield, *Epistle to the Romans,* 1:346.

But this refusal to take seriously any religious vitality other than Christian, even the apostle's Jewish past, this inability to concede any consequence or substance to a religious existence other than one's own, which breeds that pernicious binary language and feeds on it, has bedeviled the discussion of Rom 7 even among those commentators who have concluded that this section of the letter is to be sharply distinguished from chapter 8 and is Paul's negative description of life under the Mosaic law. They, too, perceive that Paul is saying some positive things about the "inmost self" and the "mind." If Paul is referring here to the unredeemed, one is confronted with what Käsemann identifies as the central hermeneutical quandary of Rom 7: "How can the predicates and capacities of the *redeemed* person be ascribed to the *unredeemed?*"[22] What follows is one of the more opaque sections of Käsemann's magisterial commentary. He simply puts the problem in different words when he asks how it happens that "in some sense the Christian situation of Gal 5:16ff. is here transferred to pre-Christian existence."[23] No reason is given; instead Käsemann insists that the force of Paul's words "sold under sin" must not be compromised by finding something good said about the human will in these verses.[24] Only Wilckens, who singles out Käsemann's formulation of the quandary for quotation and comment, seems to have broken through the tyranny of that false dichotomy. All those positive things said about the "I" in Rom 7 can be taken at face value because they actually redound to the glory of the *law* and not to the praise of the human self.[25] With that we reach a new stage in our reflections on Rom 7, to which we must return in a moment.

But before we take up the implications of this last move, another observation is needed to conclude the present line of thought. These binary categorizations of religious human beings existed, of course, in Paul's day as well; they were not invented by Luther or by Augustine or by other Christians. Indeed, the depth to which any reading of Paul that clings to such a division between the "godly" and the "ungodly" has misunderstood the apostle is sounded accurately only when one realizes that the whole of Paul's epistle is but a single massive argument against the conventional uses of this distinction. In his own religious tradition the division was between Jew and

---

22. Käsemann, *Commentary on Romans,* 207, italics added. See also n. 20. The quandary produces elaborate—one may even say tortured—discussions of Paul's use of these predicates. Does the "inmost self" refer to the spirit-endowed persons ("pneumatic"), and if so, what kind of relapse into the idealistic motifs of Greek religion does this signal (Käsemann, *Commentary on Romans,* 206–8)? What sorts of contradictions and inconsistencies is Paul generating with these concessions to the general moral capacities of human nature in view of his more pessimistic assessments elsewhere (Kümmel, *Römer 7,* 134–38)?

23. Käsemann, *Commentary on Romans,* 208.

24. Ibid.

25. Wilckens, *Römer,* 2:94.

non-Jew.[26] Paul never erases this historical or cultural distinction completely, but the whole first part of Romans is aimed at showing it to be a distinction without a difference and without consequence. When it comes to accountability before God, possession of the law, around which all the prerogatives of the Jew in 2:17–20 revolve, or nonpossession, which defines the Gentile as Gentile (so twice in one verse, 2:14), makes no difference, as circumcision or its absence do not (2:25–29), for there is no favoritism with God (2:11).[27] All have fallen short of God's glory (3:23). Since a right relationship to God cannot be brought about by the fulfilling of any conditions from the side of human beings, or by anything men or women have done or not done (4:4–5; 9:11, 16), but only by God's free and undeserved gift (3:24), the new terms on which God's power to save operates are that both Jew and non-Jew, "the Jew first but also the Greek," relate to God in trust, for only these terms put Jew and Greek on the same footing before God (1:16, the statement of the theme of Romans). The central creed of Judaism, the acknowledgment that God is one, requires that one abandon the notion that God is the patron of one constituency against another (3:27–30). The definition of God's election as the calling of those who were not God's people to be "my people" applies equally to both Jew and non-Jew (9:24–26); the cultivated branch and the wild branch belong to God's olive tree on the same terms (11:20–24).

Abraham provides the inclusive patriarchal precedent for the way in which God deals with all human beings and the model for the way in which all human beings rightly relate to God—by trusting in what God has promised. God has not changed. In Christ, God has done what Abraham trusted God to do: to give life where from a human point of view the only prospect is death (4:11b–12, 19–22). Nowhere in this argument does Paul draw a distinction between Jew and non-Jew that is not aimed at showing that there is no privilege before God on the one side or the other. Nowhere in Romans does Paul draw a distinction between an authentic Jew (2:28–29) and an authentic Christian (4:18–25; 9:24; 15:7–13). "The same God is Lord of all, rich and generous to all who call upon him" (10:12). Nowhere does Paul draw a line through himself, to distinguish the authentic Jew from the non-Jewish Christian in his own person, or through God, to distinguish a God of the one from a God of the other (11:1–5). What Paul has found in Christ is not an alternative God to the God of Abraham and

26. For non-Jews, Paul uses the terms *Gentiles* (τὰ ἔθνη, "the [non-Jewish] nations") and *Greeks.* Sometimes they are simply interchangeable, as in 1 Cor 1:22–24. In his letters the former is always a collective designation (the singular ἔθνος ["nation"] occurs only in an Old Testament quotation in Rom 10:19). The latter is always used for the singular individual, and even in the plural the emphasis seems to be on the members of the group (Rom 3:9; 1 Cor 10:32; 12:13).

27. For further treatment, see J. M. Bassler, *Divine Impartiality: Paul and a Theological Axiom,* SBLDS 59 (Chico, Calif.: Scholars Press, 1982).

Moses, but God's own gift to restore integrity to obedience to the God of Abraham and Moses.

The problem with human religion rests not with the "ungodly" but with those who separate themselves as the "godly" and in that way seek to establish "a righteousness of their own" (10:3). These "do not submit to God's righteousness," which, since its terms are trust in God, puts all on the same footing. Not a failure to keep and obey the law, but the attempt by those who do keep it—and think they have every right to condemn others as "ungodly"—to escape their own accountability to God, is what "stores up wrath on the day of wrath when God's righteous judgment will be revealed" (2:3–5). The conclusive demonstration of the power of sin over all, not just the "ungodly" but most especially the "godly" as well, is its power to destroy that inner integrity of trust, to make every genuinely religious person deny that all stand on the same footing before the same God and in that way to blaspheme God's good name. To the extent that Christians for 1,900 years have continued to divide up the world into the "godly" (themselves) and the "ungodly," they have merely remained caught within the very problem that Paul diagnoses in his own religious tradition. Its only remedy is a fresh disclosure of God's righteousness as the undeserved vindication of the unrighteous. Only this eliminates the self-defensiveness Paul calls "enmity" toward God, and by the power of the life-giving Spirit sets men and women on the way to an obedience that the law itself has remained powerless to produce (8:1–11).[28]

III

We come back to that difficult question of "the present design and argument of the apostle" in Rom 7. If the history of exegesis has imposed on Paul's argument the not uncommon pattern of conventional human religion to separate the "godly" from the "ungodly," what would an interpretation look like that takes its cue from Paul himself and eschews this elitism? Would it provide some relief from the quandaries and anachronisms sketched above? It will be the aim of this final section to explore this possibility.

Due to limitations of space, certain preliminary observations can be noted only briefly. First, the subtleties and complexities of Paul's argument in chapters 5–8 have rightly led most commentators to abandon as overly simple the thematic proposal that Paul describes the Christian life as freedom from a series of powers: in sequence, freedom from wrath (ch. 5), from sin (ch. 6), from the

---

28. For a more sequential and comprehensive treatment of the argument of Romans, see my commentary "Romans," in *HarperCollins Bible Commentary*, ed. J. L. Mays (2d ed.; San Francisco: HarperSanFrancisco, 2000), 1038–73; reprinted with minor revisions in this volume, pp. 149–218.

law (ch. 7), and from death (ch. 8).[29] Instead, the argument advances by cues that it has itself generated, as points require clarification, as potential misunderstandings need to be deflected, and as objections are anticipated. While these movements and turns sometimes have the form of "digressions," they are indispensable stages in the argument, for which rhetorical questions are often the major literary markers.[30]

Second, I take Rom 6:1–7:6 to be one of these larger units, so that 7:1–6 belongs with the preceding more closely than with 7:7–25. The question of 6:1 ("Are we to continue in sin in order that grace might increase?") arose inevitably out of Paul's previous description of the lavish generosity of God's gift in Christ, which the "intruding" law showed to be as undeserved and gracious as it showed the death that otherwise has come upon all since Adam to be deserved and due. Whereas in chapter 5 justification as God's restoration of integrity and righteousness to human life is presented as "a matter of grace" (cf. 4:16), 6:1–7:6 reverses the argument to show that God's grace involves a new righteousness and integrity that alter life's previous patterns. Employing the polarities of sin and grace, death and life, and disobedience and obedience that were set up by contrasting Adam and Christ in chapter 5, three separate trains of thought turn aside that essentially libertinistic deduction to answer the question "Why not sin?" First, an irrevocable death (Christ's) has taken place, in which the destiny of all for whom he died is reshaped. It follows that justification involves a new life of righteousness because it is a death to sin (6:1–14). Second, justification is a change of controlling allegiance; it sets one free from sin only insofar as it makes one an obedient "slave" to God (6:15–23). Third, both these aspects of justification are illustrated by an example from the general area of human social law: While living with another man before her husband's death brings upon a married woman the damning epithet of an adulteress, exactly the same action after her husband's death has no such result, and she is free to enter the new relationship. The marriage legislation is not abrogated, but a death has broken its power to condemn (the point resumed in 8:1). Just so, by the death of Christ all those for whom he died have been "vacated" from that power of the law, and a new allegiance and a new productive life have been legitimated for them (7:1–6).

---

29. A clear example of an exegesis of this type is A. Nygren, *Commentary on Romans* (Philadelphia: Muhlenberg, 1949), 191–349, summarized on 265–67. This summary shows the extent to which this reading of these chapters is shaped by appeal to statements made by Paul in Galatians rather than by attention to the internal movement of the argument in Romans itself.

30. For fuller discussion, see N. A. Dahl, "The Missionary Theology in the Epistle to the Romans," in *Studies in Paul* (Minneapolis: Augsburg, 1977), 70–94, esp. 82–83; and the work there referred to by Stanley Stowers, since published as *The Diatribe and Paul's Letter to the Romans*, SBLDS 57 (Chico, Calif.: Scholars Press, 1981).

This illustration from everyday legal experience provides one of Paul's most striking definitions of justification, explaining both how a person is put into a completely new situation by the death of another party (Christ) and how that change carries with it new social and moral obligations. It is the quintessential Pauline refutation of all the antinomian constructions that have been laid upon him from his own lifetime (3:8) until now.

Yet the choice of this very example creates a grave difficulty. While it does not start out as a specific allusion to Mosaic law, its application pertains unmistakably to release from the condemning power that Paul's previous argument has consistently assigned to the Mosaic law, which impartially silences every human attempt to evade God's indictment, imparts to human conduct the dimension of transgression against God, and so discloses the presence and power of sin (3:19–20; 4:15; 5:13, 20). The flow of the argument has progressively confused the roles of the law and the sin it condemns and discloses, so that "dying to sin" in 6:10 has become "being put to death to the law" in Paul's little tableau (7:4), and "being set free from sin" in 6:18 has become a "being vacated from the law" (7:6). The confusion is complete in 7:6a. The grammatical antecedent of the relative clause ἐν ᾧ κατειχόμεθα ("what bound us," NAB) is the law. Ironically, an illustration initially intended to rebut an antinomian argument has suddenly become itself susceptible to an antinomian interpretation, as if God's law and the demonic power of sin are to be identified.[31]

From that result, Paul "draws back with a kind of horror,"[32] and it is to ward off such a misunderstanding that Rom 7:7–12 is written. Verse 12 is Paul's Q.E.D.: the Mosaic law is not demonic and not to be confused with sin, nor is it responsible for producing sin.[33] This demonstration, however, is not carried out by directly defending the goodness of the law but by giving an account of how it has been used by sin. The focus is on the other side of the mistaken confusion:

---

31. Many of the difficulties attendant upon the interpretation of Rom 7 arise from a failure to respect the differences between Romans and Galatians and from importing elements from Paul's argument in Galatians into Romans—another form of anachronistic fallacy. The Galatians background makes the developing antinomian entanglement of Paul's exposition here in Rom 7:1–6 plausible and understandable, but his clear and emphatic repudiation of this logical consequence shows how he has changed since Galatians. There the law still seems to play an adversarial, not to say quasi-demonic, role (Gal 3:19, 23; 4:4–5; 5:18). Here that has been more clearly transferred to the personified power of sin that uses God's good law (Rom 7:12–14). That the condemning power of the law is now more firmly subsumed under a consistent theocentrism is apparent from the subtle but clear differences between Gal 3:22 and Rom 11:32.

32. J. Knox, "The Epistle to the Romans: Introduction and Exegesis," in *IB* 9 (New York: Abingdon, 1954), 491.

33. See the excursus in Wilckens, *Römer,* 2:80–81, for a decisive refutation of the notion that in Paul's view the law produces sin because the very desire it awakens, to commit one's efforts to the fulfillment of its precepts, is itself sinful, whether these efforts actually succeed or not. This notion is a particularly harsh anachronism.

the central protagonist in the whole of 7:7–25—not just in vv. 7–12—the adversary of that "I," is not the law at all but sin as a personified power.[34] Once this is seen, it becomes clear that 7:7–25 advances the main argument of Romans in a variety of ways. In addition to the manifest intention of answering the question in v. 7 and warding off a misunderstanding of the law, this unit forms the first part of an exposition of the contrasts between past and present with which Paul in vv. 5–6 has brought the whole preceding section (6:1–7:6) to its climax. The obsolete quality of life in "what bound us" is depicted and analyzed in 7:7–25 in preparation for the discussion of the eschatological quality of life in 8:1–11.[35] Paul calls the one "letter" and the other "Spirit." This contrasting word pair has been used earlier in 2:29 to distinguish spurious religious identity from authentic (beginning with the Jew), and its introduction here signals another level of Paul's argument. Chapter 8 forms the second part of the exposition and returns to the theme of what God has done for the restoration of human life by means of the life-giving Spirit; 7:7–25 prepares for that by showing what the law, despite its being God's own holy and good commandment, has not been able to do (8:3), because sin's use of it has produced death instead of life.

Clearly 7:7–25 proceeds in two movements, the first being vv. 7–12. Here the greatest difficulty has been caused by Paul's use of the first-person verbs in past tenses, particularly in vv. 8b–9. When was Paul, or anyone else, "once alive apart from law," and when did the commandment "come"? It is useless to look for some point in Paul's own lifetime, so increasingly commentators find in these verses allusion to the story of the fall in Genesis 3, even though the "commandment" Paul has in mind here is patently the Decalogue (v. 7d).[36] Most of the difficulties disappear if one notices that Paul is resuming with dramatic juxtaposition and reversal the motifs of death and life in their association with sin already used in 5:12–14. That explains the "epic" use of past tenses here. "In the absence of law" (χωρὶς νόμου, vv. 8b, 9) picks up 5:13; the "entry" (ἐλθεῖν,

---

34. Two stereotypes about Rom 7 that are particularly hard to uproot are the conventional views that vv. 7–12 constitute an "apology for the law" (questioned by Käsemann, *Commentary on Romans,* 192) and that in vv. 13–25 "everything focuses on anthropology" (ibid.) and the divided self. O. Michel, *Der Brief an die Römer,* MeyerK (5th ed.; Göttingen: Vandenhoeck & Ruprecht, 1978), 225 n. 7: "What is distinctive about our section [Rom 7:7–25] is its description of the cleavage of the human self" (my translation).

35. Many commentators have noticed that the statements of 7:5–6 are resumed and elaborated in what follows (e.g., Dahl, *Studies in Paul,* 85). The problem lies in identifying just how that is done. Nygren (*Commentary on Romans,* 275–76) finds the two complementary "panels" of the Pauline exposition in vv. 7–13 and vv. 14–25, respectively, which lands one right back in the problem presented earlier.

36. For the general trend to appeal to Genesis 3, one may note Käsemann, *Commentary on Romans,* 196; Wilckens, *Römer,* 2:79; Cranfield, *Epistle to the Romans,* 1:351–52; Theissen, *Psychological Aspects,* 202–11. There is strong evidence in Jewish tradition for taking the commandment of v. 7d, "Thou shalt not covet," as representative of the whole Decalogue or the law as such (Käsemann, *Commentary on Romans,* 196; Wilckens, *Römer,* 2:78–79; Michel, *Römer,* 226–27).

v. 9) of the commandment repeats 5:20, presupposed already by the mention of Moses in 5:14, and thus fits naturally with Paul's quotation from the Decalogue. At the same time, one need not deny the presence of such an echo of the fall narrative as the "deceived" of v. 11. But clearly the allusion is to the Mosaic Torah, which, as the example of the prohibition of covetousness shows, is not only powerless to prevent what it prohibits but in fact produces the very thing it is supposed to prevent. The climax and center of the whole paragraph is provided in vv. 10b–11: "The very commandment that was supposed to lead to life turned out for me to lead to death; for sin, by taking advantage of me through that commandment, tricked me and by using it killed me" (my paraphrase).

The point of these verses and this section is entirely lost if one understands Paul to be talking only about the "ungodly" Jew who "does not will from the heart what the law admonishes" (Melanchthon), or if one takes the point to be the effect of the *law*.[37] The clear meaning of these sentences is that the effect of *sin* on the genuinely religious person who looks to God's Torah for life has been to produce exactly its opposite, death. This is not because the law has not been obeyed or because there is something demonic about the law. It is not because looking to God's Torah for life is somehow a lower order of human religion. The transcendentally (καθ᾽ ὑπερβολήν, v. 13) demonic nature of sin is its power to pervert the highest and best in *all* human piety, typified by the best in Paul's world, his own commitment to God's holy commandment, in such a way as to produce death in place of the promised life.

What these much disputed verses bring to expression is not despair over one's inability to live up to a demanding requirement—such as Luther's experience in the monastery at Erfurt—nor is it the pain of discovering that one has oriented one's life around a lesser surrogate in place of God as one's highest good, which Augustine repeatedly describes in his *Confessions*. It is the realization that one has been deceived by a much more sinister power, capable of making the best and the most genuine devotion to the one true God produce, as in the case of God's own commandment in the Decalogue, the very thing it is supposed to vanquish. There is no contradiction between these verses and Paul's claim in Phil 3:6 that the life he came to count as "loss" was "as to righteousness under the law blameless."[38]

---

37. "[Verses] 7–13 have in view primarily people under the Torah. . . . [T]he apostle wants to illustrate the effect of the law concretely by using the example of the recipient of the law and of Jewish piety" (Käsemann, *An die Römer* [Tübingen: Mohr (Siebeck), 1973], 187, my translation; cf. ET: *Commentary on Romans,* 197).

38. See n. 6. The immense pressure exerted upon the exegesis of Rom 7 by the perception that what Paul writes here cannot be reconciled with Phil 3 is plain from Kümmel's discussion (*Römer 7,* 111–19; see also Wilckens, *Römer,* 2:76–77 and n. 292; Cranfield, *Epistle to the Romans,* 1:344). The degree to which this perception, in turn, has been kept alive by the influence of the Reformers' exegesis should now be clear. Theissen (*Psychological Aspects,* 234–50) seeks to resolve the putative contradiction by using the distinctions of depth psychology between the conscious and the unconscious, a recourse fraught with difficulties that is simply unnecessary if the conflict does not exist!

Such a reading of 7:7–12 puts us in a position to take a fresh look at the second movement in the rest of the chapter. The transitional v. 13 does two things. In emphatically repeating first the question of v. 7 and then the substance of the answer in v. 11, but adding two purpose clauses, it makes clear that even when it has been used by sin, the law has remained God's and has continued to serve the divine purpose of disclosing and intensifying sin, attributed to it earlier in the letter. In this way v. 13 rounds out what precedes. At the same time, it begins to shift categories in such a manner as to open up a new level of discussion in the next section. In very much the same way, a change of terms from "life" and "death" to "freedom" and "slavery" marked the break in chapter 6 from vv. 1–11 to vv. 15–23, while vv. 12–14 modulated the transition with language about obedience. This time there is a change from the words for "life" and "death" (both nouns and verbs) that have colored the imagery in 7:8–11 to the vocabulary of "good" and "evil," signaled by the fact that in v. 13 "the good" replaces the law. Of course, this is because Paul has just called the law itself "good." But there is more involved. In a brilliant exegetical observation, Bultmann noticed that "the good" in this new section is equivalent to "life" in the preceding verses.[39] "The object of 'willing' is not the fulfilling of the 'commandments,' but 'life' (ζωή). What is really willed in all our doing is 'life,' but what comes out of all our doing is 'death' (θάνατος)."[40] "Good" and "evil," then, are not labels for conventional moral values that Paul simply takes for granted. They are "the two eschatological possibilities" of "life" and "death."[41] As a result, "that which is good" (v. 13) is not simply the law itself, but *the good* that the law holds out "to me" (twice in v. 13) in its promise of life, exactly as in v. 10.

This is confirmed by the contrasting verbs that increasingly carry the argument in this next section. They are still in the first person singular of Paul's paradigmatic style, but they shift to the present tense as he describes the self's encounter with the power of sin, the perennial human quandary that is the consequence of that "epic" event of sin's "entry." Since the opposite of "to will" is now "to hate," it is clear that the verbs, too, are not to be understood in any narrowly volitional sense. The "common Greek meaning"[42] of θέλειν is "to prefer, to want, to desire," and this is retained in the LXX where it often translates *ḥāpēṣ*, "to delight in" (echoed in Paul's συνήδομαι in v. 22). In v. 15 "the good"

---

39. R. Bultmann, "Romans 7 and the Anthropology of Paul," in *Existence and Faith,* 147–57, esp. 154–55. See also his *Theology of the New Testament,* 2 vols. (New York: Charles Scribner's Sons, 1951–55), 1:248. Bultmann's exegetical insights here have been neglected because they are buried beneath a debatable argument about theological anthropology. They are nevertheless recognized by Käsemann, *Commentary on Romans,* 202–3; and Wilckens, *Römer,* 2:88 n. 358 (see also 114–15 for a comprehensive assessment of Bultmann's exegesis of Rom 7 in general).

40. Bultmann, "Romans 7," 152.

41. Ibid., 154.

42. *TDNT* 3:44; cf. LSJ s.v. ἐθέλω.

becomes "what I want" and in v. 19 "the good that I desire." Its opposite in v. 15 is "what I hate" and in v. 19 "the evil that I do not want." In short, the verbs help to circumscribe "the good" as that which every genuinely religious person longs for. The appeal and attraction and promise of the law, especially since it is God's own instruction, is that it will lead to the life that human beings want and desire more than anything else. When Paul says that he "delights" in God's law (v. 22), he is giving clear expression to the devotion to this law that echoes throughout the Hebrew Psalter (see Pss 1:2; 119:16). In it the desire to find life and the desire to live by the good that God commands are fully merged, and that desire is the greater the more any religious person realizes that "the good" that amounts to life in this ultimate sense is not available in one's human resources taken by themselves (which is the meaning of "my flesh" in v. 18). There is nothing at all in this paragraph to suggest that this longing and desire, exemplified at its highest in the Jewish allegiance to Torah in which Paul was raised from infancy, is either illegitimate or misplaced.[43]

But now something has happened to contradict this expectation. "What a person wants is salvation. What he creates is disaster."[44] What it means to this person to be "sold under sin" is manifested in the discovery that what one in fact "produces" by one's actions is not recognizable, because it is exactly the opposite of what was intended, just what one hoped to avoid in one's reliance on the law (v. 15); κατεργάζεσθαι ("to bring about or achieve") has the same meaning throughout vv. 15–20 that it has in v. 13. It is clear that the fault does not lie in the law. Instead, the self, no longer the agent of its own actions, is con-

---

43. It is at this point that Bultmann's exegesis seems to remain under the spell of that aspect of the Reformation tradition from which we have been proposing we need to free our reading of Romans. Paul's "fundamental reproach," Bultmann writes, is "that the *direction* of this way [of the law] is perverse, and this for the reason that it intends to lead to 'one's own righteousness' (Rom 10:8; Phil 3:9). It is not evil works or transgressions of the law that first make the Jews objectionable to God. Rather the intention to become righteous before him by fulfilling the law is their real sin, which is merely manifested by transgressions" ("Romans 7," 149; translation slightly corrected from the German, "Römer 7 und die Anthropologie des Paulus" [1932], in R. Bultmann, *Exegetica: Aufsätze zur Erforschung des Neuen Testaments,* ed. E. Dinkler [Tübingen: Mohr (Siebeck), 1967], 200). By thus leaving no room for an authentic religious motivation from the law for obedient action, Bultmann seems to eliminate the very distinction Paul is making between sin and the law. This is exactly the issue at stake in interpreting Romans 7. Another symptom of the continuing force of this Reformation legacy may be seen in Theissen's elaborate attempt not only to make ἁμαρτία ("sin") the replacement for ἐπιθυμία ("covetousness") in vv. 7–8, but also to treat θέλειν ("to want") in vv. 15–21 as a functional equivalent to ἐπιθυμεῖν ("to covet") in the commandment of v. 7 (*Psychological Aspects,* 210–11). He can mount such an argument only by importing elements from Galatians and 2 Corinthians (209). But it is already circular. The equivalence is assumed, and when there is no evidence to support it ("Zeal for the law, *which is the nomistic sin,* is *never* interpreted as a manifestation of covetousness," 208, italics added), the very lack of correlation with Gen 3 is taken to show that Paul is reading his own experience into the role of Adam when he does not find it there.

44. Käsemann, *Commentary on Romans,* 203.

trolled by the alien power of sin (vv. 16–17). The thought in these verses is exactly the same as in vv. 10b–11, only now it is not the Mosaic Torah but the religious self devoted to it that is powerless to achieve what it longs for, that in fact produces the very thing that it is supposed to avoid. The early chapters of Romans have already unfolded this unexpected power of sin to reverse and subvert the integrity of the relationship all religious persons have to God, both Jews and Greeks (3:9), especially those who know God's commands and judgments (1:31; 2:2) but use that knowledge to exempt themselves from accountability and to deny that all stand on the same footing before God, and so abuse God's goodness and blaspheme God's name (2:4–5, 17–24).

Commentators have made many quite different proposals for understanding the structure of vv. 13–25 in detail. Most suggestions fail in plausibility because they are wedded to prior decisions regarding the subject matter of this section, especially to the effect that Paul is primarily concerned with the malevolent power of the law rather than that of sin, or that he is describing a divided self. Again it was Bultmann who clearly saw that the seemingly impressive parallels to Paul's language that can be found in Greek and Latin literature really have little to do with the purpose his words serve in the present argument.[45] Paul is not talking about the conflict between the rational and the irrational in the human self, nor about two selves at different levels, as though one were under the power of sin and the other not. Both "inmost self" (v. 22) and "members" (v. 23) are but two aspects of the same self that is "sold under sin." The symptom of this enslavement is not simple frustration of good intent, but good intention carried out and then surprised and dumbfounded by the evil it has produced, not despair but the same disillusionment so clearly described in v. 10. What should have effected life has produced death!

Close scrutiny of Paul's verses shows a striking progression that confirms this interpretation.[46] The leading clue is provided by the quite complete and precise parallelism between vv. 15–17 and vv. 18–20, running twice through the same sequence of ideas.[47] Each series begins with an essentially negative proposition

45. Bultmann, "Romans 7," 148; *Theology of the New Testament,* 1:248. Careful attention to the contexts of these "parallels" confirms his judgment. In Ovid, *Metam.* 7.18–21, one of the most frequently cited passages, the conflict is between reason (*mens*) and desire (*cupido*); in Euripides, *Med.* 1076–80, it is between resolution (*bouleumata*) and passion (*thymos*). See also Plato, *Prot.* 352D; Euripides, *Hipp.* 375–85; Epictetus, *Disc.* 2.26.1–2, 4–5. A recent discussion that collects and presents these texts and some secondary literature on them, even though it comes to entirely different conclusions, is found in Theissen, *Psychological Aspects,* 211–21.

46. Despite strong disagreement with his interpretation, my own observations have been whetted and refined by the "text analysis" in Theissen, *Psychological Aspects,* 186–90; see also 187 n. 11, for reference to other constructions.

47. The phenomenon is not an isolated one in Paul's letters. A close analogue in Romans is the parallelism in ch. 6 between vv. 5–7 and 8–10, pointed out by G. Bornkamm, "Baptism and New Life in Paul," in *Early Christian Experience* (New York: Harper & Row, 1969), 71–86, esp. 74–75.

introduced with the phrase "We/I know": vv. 14–15a ("I don't recognize what I am bringing about, the results of my own actions") and v. 18 ("To desire the good is within my capacity but I cannot bring it about"). In the second place, this is followed each time by a short description of the experience behind this proposition, in almost identical language ("For I do not do what I intend, desire or prefer, but do the very thing I do not want or wish to avoid," vv. 15b, 19).[48] In the third place, now in even more striking repetition of linguistic detail, each sequence draws the same conclusion: "If this is my experience, it follows that I am no longer the one producing this result but rather the sin that dwells in me" (vv. 16–17, 20). By their repetition these conclusions forcefully declare what it means to be "fleshly, sold under sin." The opening proposition for the second sequence (v. 18) rephrases that of the first (vv. 14–15a) in language colored by the intervening verses, and the detail that distinguishes the second sequence and marks its advance over the first is the addition of those eschatological categories "good" and "evil" in vv. 18 and 19, expanding the incidental remark in v. 16b about the law's being itself "good." This new ingredient continues into v. 21 and provides a bridge to the concluding verses of the chapter.

This conclusion comes in vv. 21–23. The last time the law seriously entered Paul's argument was v. 12, his emphatic repudiation of the suggested identification of the law with sin in v. 7b. The place of the law was taken in v. 13 by "the good" (which, incidentally, Paul equates with God's will in 12:2). A brief reminder of 7:12 reappears in v. 14, but it functions only as the foil for its opposite, "I am fleshly, sold under sin," which it has been the main burden of vv. 15–20 to elaborate. There is also a parenthetical remark about the law's goodness in v. 16b, but the parallel in v. 20 shows that it can be dropped without loss to the argument—it only anticipates v. 22—and that the real purpose of the conditional clause in v. 16a is to serve as a protasis to v. 17. But now that thematic undercurrent of the law bursts to the surface and dominates the discussion in the form of *two* diametrically opposed laws: (1) ὁ νόμος τοῦ θεοῦ ("the law of God"), vv. 22 and 25b, which is also "the law of the mind"—that is, the law I intend to serve—in v. 23; and (2) ἕτερος νόμος ("a different law," not just another law), which is also ὁ νόμος τῆς ἁμαρτίας ("the law of sin") "which is in my members," vv. 23 and 25b. Verse 22 confesses allegiance and delight in the first. Verse 23 reports the discovery of the second. The contrast could scarcely be sharper. In sum, 7:13–25 culminates with a cleavage, but it is in the law and not in the self.

48. If there is any point in these verses where Paul is appropriating conventional or stereotyped phrasing, it is here in the *first* sequence (i.e., in v. 15b), and it is confined to the ordinary observation of a discrepancy between intention and action, without any moral complications. Of the "parallels" cited above (n. 45), only the wording that Epictetus repeats as a sort of refrain in *Disc.* 2.26.1–2, 4–5 ("he does not do what he wishes"; "he does what he does not wish") is really similar. The paraphrases of Rom 7:15–20 in this section are mine.

Attention to this movement toward an antithetical climax helps to solve two perennial difficulties in the exegesis of these verses. One is v. 21, in which commentators struggle both with the meaning of ὁ νόμος ("the law") and with the syntax. It strains credulity to read Paul's definite noun in this context as "a law" (RSV) in the sense of a perceived regularity of experience. Serious lexicographical difficulties stand in the way of this translation as well, despite its natural sound in English. It must, instead, refer to the same law that is called a "different" law, or "the law of sin" in v. 23.[49] But what law is that? The polarized duality of "laws" at the end of chapter 7 provides the bridge to chapter 8, and this "different law" must be the same as "the law of sin and death" in 8:2. But the transitional verses in 8:1–2 also serve as a parenthesis with 7:6b to enclose the whole of our passage. The phrase "the law of sin and death" in 8:2 can only be intended as a shorthand summary of the whole point of 7:7–25: It is the *law* that has been used by *sin* to produce *death*. But that means that not only the "law of God" (v. 22) but also this "different law" (v. 23) is the Mosaic law! We will return to this in a moment.

In the meantime, the problem of the syntax of v. 21 is now also eased. The dative participle and its infinitive have been advanced for emphasis, but they belong syntactically to the ὅτι-clause that is the direct object of εὑρίσκω.[50] To take τὸν νόμον as an adverbial accusative of respect is not nearly as harsh as is commonly argued if one realizes that the present active εὑρίσκω has simply taken the place of the deponential aorist εὑρέθη of v. 10,[51] to fit the altered context and its present tenses, but without significant change of meaning. Just as Paul said there, "the law that was supposed to lead to life has turned out for me to lead to death," so also he now opens this final section of chapter 7 by writing, "So then, as far as the [Mosaic] law is concerned, the outcome [of the above experience] is that for me, the very one who wishes to do the good, evil is what I find at hand" (v. 21, my paraphrase). He goes on:

> I delight in the law of God . . . but what I see is a quite different law, operative in my members [that aspect of my self that ought to be at God's disposal, 6:13]; it is in conflict with that law of God that I adhere to in my intentions, and keeps me imprisoned to the law that controls me and that is used by sin. (vv. 22–23, my paraphrase)

The other celebrated crux of chapter 7 is v. 25b, which has created difficulty both by its position, which has seemed to interrupt or even reverse the natural

---

49. The decisive lexicographical arguments are noted by Wilckens, *Römer,* 2:89 and n. 371. Even Cranfield (*Epistle to the Romans,* 1:361–62), while he finds all explanations of the term as a reference to the Mosaic law so forced as to be "incredible," recognizes the continuity with the "different law" in v. 23.

50. BDF § 475 (1). See the examples listed by Cranfield in his discussion of 11:31 (*Epistle to the Romans,* 2:583–84).

51. BDF § 313.

and logical movement of thought from v. 25a to chapter 8, and by its content, which has seemed to betray an anthropological dualism uncharacteristic of Paul and out of place in this chapter.[52] Here too the difficulty disappears once one observes that the load-bearing words in v. 25b are not "mind" and "flesh," even though these have the article, but rather the contrasting datives at the end of each clause, "*God's* law" and "*sin's* law."[53] The verse not only fits the context but also confirms our reading of it. As a summary, it tightens the link with 8:1–4. The same contrast between God and sin reappears in the subject and direct object of 8:3.

The translation of vv. 21–23 we thus arrive at makes "the present design and argument of the apostle" plain. The experience of the demonic power of sin to use the Mosaic law to effect just the opposite of what its devoted adherents expect, even and especially when it is obeyed, manifests not only the sinister nature of sin itself (v. 13) but also how profoundly the religious self is "sold" under it and indeed possessed by it (vv. 14–20). God's own good law takes on a quality and character opposite to that which a person knows to be true, so that the religious self is put in the wretched position of serving sin in its very service of God. Two thousand years of Christian history have shown that in the presence of this power there is no distinction between the "godly" and the "ungodly." As the Latin maxim puts it, *corruptio optimi pessima,* "the worst evil consists in the corruption of the highest good." That is not depicted here simply as a private experience from Paul's Jewish past. It is all part of Paul's explanation of why God sent God's own Son, on behalf of all, to deal with sin as the law could not (8:3–4). In the end, as Lou Martyn has also argued, the guiding theme of Paul's theology is not the law but Christ.[54] A more adequate penetration of Paul's diagnosis of the condition under which all human religion suffers may lead to a more profound understanding of his gospel.

---

52. Almost every commentator discusses these problems. The two major solutions are transposition (see James Moffatt, *The Bible: A New Translation* [New York: Harper & Brothers, 1935]) and excision (see Bultmann, "Glossen im Römerbrief," in *Exegetica,* 278–79).

53. The articles with νοῦς and σάρξ simply function in place of the possessive pronouns, "with *my* mind." See R. Kühner and B. Gerth, *Ausführliche Grammatik der griechischen Sprache: Satzlehre,* 2 vols. (4th ed.; Leverkusen: Gottschalksche Verlagsbuchhandlung, 1955), 1:555–56, 581. There is no discussion of this common phenomenon in BDF, but see H. W. Smyth, *Greek Grammar* (Cambridge, Mass.: Harvard University Press, 1956), § 1121. On the other hand, the omission of the article with the datives underlines the qualitative nuance provided by the modifying genitives; see BDF § 252.

54. J. L. Martyn, "Paul and His Jewish-Christian Interpreters," *USQR* 42 (1988): 3: "Paul was firmly of the opinion that the nub of the matter was not the issue of the law, but rather christology." Contrast Michel, *Römer,* 239: "An der Gesetzesfrage hängt das Verständnis des ganzen Urchristentums" ("The understanding of the whole of early Christianity hinges on the question of the law").

CHAPTER 6

ROMANS 10:4 AND THE "END" OF THE LAW*

> Paul defined the relationship of Christianity with Judaism and in this way gave it
> a structure which was never subsequently modified in spite of Marcion's attempts
> to do so, and so far as can be seen could never be called in question without shak-
> ing the very foundations of Christianity.[1]

Maurice Goguel used these words a half century ago to comment on the historical significance of the apostle Paul for Christian origins. One will of course not
hear them today quite as Goguel wrote them. He described the cause for which
Paul struggled as "Christian universalism freed from all ritualism." When he
varied this terminology to say that Paul "cut the gospel free from the chains with
which Judaism was in danger of strangling it,"[2] he was skirting close to that
equation of Judaism with "ritualism" which has become unacceptable today on
grounds both historical and theological. And what he meant by "universalism"
seems to have been a capacity on the part of the early Christian movement to
adapt to its future in Greek culture rather than any fruition of its legacy from its
Jewish past. Today one will be more inclined to argue that it was Paul's view of
the relation of Israel to the Gentiles that gave to his doctrine of justification its
characteristic structure and shape.[3] Or, as I would prefer, one might argue a similar case with respect to Paul's Christology: that he so defined the meaning of
Jesus as the Christ for the new movement as to clarify for it at the same time its
relation to the Judaism from which it emerged and so contributed to its identity;
or that it was Paul's definition of the relation of Christianity to Judaism that gave
his peculiar signature to his exposition of the meaning of Christ for the church.
Yet all these are but variations that confirm the truth of Goguel's remark, not as

---

*This essay is a slightly revised version of Paul W. Meyer's contribution to a volume honoring
Lou H. Silberman: *The Divine Helmsman: Studies on God's Control of Human Events, Presented
to Lou H. Silberman*, ed. James L. Crenshaw and Samuel Sandmel (New York: KTAV, 1980),
59–78. It is used by permission.

1. Maurice Goguel, *The Birth of Christianity* (London: Allen & Unwin, 1953), 195 (French
orig., 1946).

2. Ibid., 195 and 194.

3. N. A. Dahl, *Studies in Paul* (Minneapolis: Augsburg, 1977), 156; cf. 148.

an axiom settled for all time but as a heuristic proposition to be tested as one continues to explore the absolutely fundamental place occupied in Paul's letters by the matter of Christianity's relation to Judaism. Goguel rightly saw that in one way or another this theme, and the problem of the right interpretation of it, lies at "the very foundations of Christianity."

Nowhere are these themes more incontestably intertwined than in Rom 9–11, which is at the same time the one place in Paul's letters where the historical horizons of his theology become most apparent, where he grapples most directly with the question whether God's purposes and judgments are sustained in the history of his people or whether that history shows God's word instead to have failed (9:6). Here we come, in other words, as close as Paul himself will allow us, to the question of God's control over the course of human events or lack thereof, in appearance and in reality. Yet just because of the presence of those other themes that run through the rest of Romans—justification and the righteousness of God, the meaning of Christ, and the relation of Jew and Greek, of Israel and the church—these chapters do not yield to being isolated from their epistolary and historical context and treated as if they constituted an independent treatise upon "salvation history" or were the composition of a "theology of history."[4] Their most adequate interpretation is likely to continue to be located in full-length interpretations of the letter, that is, in commentaries on Romans.[5] For in these the interpreter will remain to some extent accountable, if not in practice then at least in principle, to the combinations and conjunctions, the ordering and disposition, the arrangements and sequences of thought that were Paul's own at the time of his writing. This will not preclude the selection of some discrete aspect, even some minute detail, for separate discussion. But it will serve as a reminder of that constant reciprocal bearing of the whole upon

---

4. For the necessity and at the same time the problematic of using such modern terms in connection with Paul, the essential discussion for the present is E. Käsemann's essay "Justification and Salvation History in the Epistle to the Romans," in *Perspectives on Paul* (Philadelphia: Fortress, 1971), 60–78.

5. To the full commentary treatment by Käsemann, *An die Römer* (Tübingen: Mohr [Siebeck], 1973), 241–308 (ET: E. Käsemann, *Commentary on Romans*, trans. and ed. G. W. Bromiley [Grand Rapids: Eerdmans, 1980], 253–321), there must now be added the even longer discussion by O. Kuss, *Der Römerbrief*, vol. 3 (Regensburg: Verlag Friedrich Pustet, 1978), 662–935; see pp. 667–68 for a select bibliography of earlier special treatments of Rom 9–11. This literature has witnessed explosive growth; other major commentaries on Rom 9–11 in the context of the whole letter have appeared in recent years. See, e.g., U. Wilckens, *Der Brief an die Römer*, EKKNT, 3 vols. (Neukirchen-Vluyn: Neukirchener Verlag, 1978–1982); J. A. Fitzmyer, *Romans: A New Translation with Introduction and Commentary*, AB 33 (New York: Doubleday, 1993); B. Byrne, *Romans*, SP 6 (Collegeville, Minn.: Liturgical Press, 1996); J. D. G. Dunn, *Romans*, WBC 38A–B, 2 vols. (Dallas: Word, 1988). Cf. also the discussion (with reference to other literature) in E. E. Johnson, "Romans 9–11: The Faithfulness and Impartiality of God," in *Pauline Theology, Volume III: Romans,* ed. D. M. Hay and E. E. Johnson (Minneapolis: Fortress, 1995), 211–39.

the part and of the minute part upon the understanding of the whole which it has seemed always in my association with Lou Silberman to be his special genius to keep before the human interpreter.

I

One verse in which these problems of interpretation come to a head is Rom 10:4: *telos gar nomou Christos eis dikaiosynēn panti tō pisteuonti.* This is variously translated as "For Christ is the end of the law, that every one who has faith may be justified" (RSV); "For Christ ends the law and brings righteousness for everyone who has faith" (NEB); "But now the Law has come to an end with Christ, and everyone who has faith may be justified" (JB); "For Christ, by realizing righteousness for every believer, proves to be the end of the law" (C. K. Barrett).[6]

The passage is a well-known, not to say notorious, crux primarily because of the lexical possibilities available for *telos* ("end"). Here they are mainly two: "termination" (as in Luke 1:33), or final state or "outcome." In this latter sense the word may, depending on context, refer to a goal intended in advance (1 Tim 1:5) or to a consequence or outcome reached quite apart from any deliberate intent on the part of the one who reaches it (Rom 6:21–22).[7] In the alternative translations just quoted *telos* is uniformly rendered by "end" not simply because the translators have chosen the first of these options but also because it preserves some of the ambivalence of the Greek term. It will be noted that no such uniformity marks the very diverse treatments given the prepositional phrase at the end of the verse.[8] The RSV rewords it with a purpose clause. The NEB and JB appear to think rather of result, though for the JB this result is clearly potential,

---

6. C. K. Barrett, *A Commentary on the Epistle to the Romans* (New York: Harper & Row, 1957), 195.

7. Cf. BDAG, 998–99. It should be noted that if one sets aside the more specialized meanings *telos* may have as "tax, duty" (Rom 13:7) or in stereotyped adverbial prepositional phrases such as *heōs telous* (2 Cor 1:13) or *eis telos* (1 Thess 2:16), all occurrences in the undisputed Pauline letters apart from Rom 10:4 fall into the second group ("outcome," "conclusion"). This preponderance of meaning is especially clear in 1 Cor 15:24; 2 Cor 3:13; 11:15; Phil 3:19. In these letters the word never means simply "cessation"; such a meaning is to be found in the whole of the traditional Pauline corpus only in Heb 7:3. These proportions clearly conform to the general picture of Greek usage provided by LSJ, 1772–74.

8. All do connect the dative participle with the prepositional phrase rather than with the main clause. To construe it in the latter way ("in the judgment of every believer Christ has become the end of the law [as a way] to righteousness") might appear plausible in terms of classical usage (R. Kühner and B. Gerth, *Ausführliche Grammatik der griechischen Sprache,* Satzlehre, 2 vols. [4th ed.; Leverkusen: Gottschalksche Verlagsbuchhandlung, 1955], 1:421), but three internal reasons are strongly against it. First, Paul's use of the dative alone is never so purely "subjective"; cf. 1 Cor 1:18, the nearest parallel I can find. Second, the frequent close association of *pisteuein / pistis* with *dikaioun / dikaiosynē* throughout Paul's letters and in this context (9:30; 10:6) speaks against separating them here. Third, the need to supply the words in brackets in order to yield some sense shows how awkward such a construal is.

a resulting possibility. Barrett treats the phrase as an expression of purpose or goal in his discussion, but he translates it as a modal parallel to the main clause as though it were a participial construction in Greek.[9]

Given these difficulties in the verse as it stands, it is no surprise that the major grounds for preferring one interpretation over another are taken from the context or related considerations. The crucial decisions are made elsewhere, and this part of Paul's text is in fact and in practice understood within and from a wider whole. We need briefly to examine this context before we consider just how some of these decisions are made.

There is first of all the context preceding 10:4 and the issue where the present unit of Paul's argument may properly be said to begin. Romans 10:1, inasmuch as it makes a personal affirmation of Paul's concern for Israel and his identification with her, seems at first sight to be quite parallel to 9:1–5 and so also to be making a fresh start. If that is the case, 9:30–33, beginning as it does with the rhetorical question "What shall we say, then?" is a brief aside or interlude. But Paul does not this time follow the question by formulating a conclusion that might have been drawn from his own preceding argument only then to repudiate such a conclusion as wrong ("God forbid") and to go on to correct it, as he does in 9:14 and often. The "conclusion" here is supplied by Paul as a legitimate one that needs only further explanation and elaboration, which the next question and its reply in v. 32 proceed to furnish. Moreover, this "conclusion" does not clearly and easily follow from the preceding argument at all, and Paul's explanation of it is clearly continued in 10:2–3. It turns out that the personal asseveration does not then open a new argument but is evoked by Paul's own statement about Israel in 9:32: "They have stumbled over the stumbling stone." Thus many commentators take 9:30 to be the beginning of a major section that runs through 10:21.[10]

9. Barrett, *Epistle to the Romans,* 197. See p. 198: "He puts an end to the law, not by destroying all that the law stood for but by realizing it." Such a strained modal translation is the price Barrett seems to believe himself compelled to pay for the choice of a final meaning for *telos.* It is, however, not a necessary price. Leenhardt (*L'Epitre de Saint Paul aux Romains* [Neuchâtel: Delachaux & Niestlé, 1957], 151) translates easily with a purpose clause: "Christ est cependant but et terme de la loi, pour mettre quiconque croit au bénéfice de ce jugement de grâce." This shows too that in the other direction a natural final translation of the prepositional phrase (as purpose or result) does not require in its wake interpreting *telos* as "termination," as in RSV, NEB, and JB.

10. So Käsemann, *Römer,* 264–65 (ET: *Commentary on Romans,* 276); Kuss, *Römerbrief,* 740–48. Dahl (*Studies in Paul,* 147) calls 9:30–33 a "provisional summary" that "functions as a transition to the following section," but significantly he goes on to say that what it summarizes is not the preceding argument of ch. 9 but "Paul's view of the contemporary situation." Romans 10:1–3 seems to him to make a new start because "only at this point does Paul explain what prompts the sorrow and anguish about which he spoke in 9:1–3," and Dahl finds that explanation in v. 3. But v. 3 is nothing else than Paul's interpretation of 9:32. For Dahl both verses have to do with the Jews' rejection of Jesus as Messiah, so even on his terms 9:30–33 functions as a "transition" mainly by introducing new elements for the next stage of Paul's argument (cf. *Studies in Paul,* 143 n. 24).

The opening sentences of this section in 9:30–31 are on any reading of Paul's argument a remarkable statement. By skillful rhetorical use of "antithetical parallelism"[11] they underscore the presence of a historical paradox crying out to be made in some measure intelligible. It is important for just that reason not "to rewrite Paul's sentence for him according to our own notions of what he ought to have said."[12] What Paul writes is: "Gentiles, who did not pursue righteousness, (nonetheless) achieved righteousness, to be sure one that comes from faith; but Israel on the other hand, while (or though) pursuing a law of righteousness, did not attain to law" (my translation). By very wide agreement among commentators, the language is unmistakably that of the racecourse: achievement and attainment here are matters of catching up with the pursued quarry or rival or arriving at the aimed-for goal. The tripping of the next verse merely sustains the figure. "A law of righteousness"[13] must in this context have reference to a law that holds out the promise of righteousness in return for the effort given in its observance and pursuit. The paradox is not devoid of irony, but the irony lies in the unforeseen, in the reversal of normal expectations, and these in turn are formulated from what would have to be characterized as a Jewish rather than a Gentile perspective. The foil is provided by Gentiles who are not only indefinite (the article is absent) but also unidentified except by the trait of their non-pursuit of righteousness, just as in 2:14 they are identified simply (but twice in one verse) by their nonpossession of the Torah. Of these it is said that they have achieved the un-sought-for goal, just as in 2:14 it was said of them that they do occasionally on their own (*physei*) and without the promptings of the Torah what it requires. To be sure, Paul adds, the righteousness these Gentiles have achieved is the sort that comes from faith. It could hardly be otherwise; their achievement of this un-sought-for goal is "apart from law," to echo 3:21. Against such a background it is then said of Israel (with what is now a modal rather than an adjectival participle) that either in spite of or alongside that very pursuit that distinguishes Jew from Gentile, of a divine instruction that Israel alone is distinguished for having and that holds out the promise of righteousness, her goal remains unattained—not the goal of the promised righteousness, it should be noted, but even more drastically the goal of the prior divine instruction. It is Torah itself that has inexplicably become the unattained goal, the destination not reached. One is compelled by such assertions to resort to the term

11. Käsemann, *Römer,* 265 (ET: *Commentary on Romans,* 277).

12. C. E. B. Cranfield, "Some Notes on Romans 9:30–33," in *Jesus und Paulus: Festschrift für Werner Georg Kümmel,* ed. E. E. Ellis and E. Grässer (Göttingen: Vandenhoeck & Ruprecht, 1975), 36. A good example of such rewriting is found in H. Lietzmann, *An die Römer* (Tübingen: Mohr [Siebeck], 1971), 94, but others abound in the commentary literature on these verses as already in the manuscript variants and conjectural emendations to the text.

13. The phrase *nomos dikaiosynēs* is a *hapax legomenon* in the New Testament; in the LXX it occurs only once (Wis 2:11) and then clearly *in malam partem*.

dialectic in order to designate adequately not only the rhetoric operative here but the very notion of Torah that it conveys as well. Israel does not "have" this Torah so much as she pursues it. Israel is distinguished from the Gentiles by the pursuit of it—and distinguished from the Gentiles at the same time by the odd fact that her pursuit, unlike theirs, remains without consummation.

Normal expectations straightforwardly fulfilled are like the proverbial dead men: they ask no questions and demand no replies. But this unforeseen reversal is of another order. No sooner has Paul formulated it than he proceeds to try to make it intelligible with a new question and answer in v. 32. But the most remarkable feature of the new verse is the simple fact that it is there at all. For by being there it shows that while vv. 30–31 document the ironical reversal, in themselves they offer no word of resolution or explanation. The modal participle in v. 31 cannot be translated "because of pursuing a law of righteousness"; like the adjectival participle in v. 30, to which it corresponds, it is part of the puzzle and not its solution. The historical paradox is not caused by Israel's pursuit of the law.[14] Rather, Paul goes on, it is due in the first instance to a misunderstanding,[15] a false assumption with which the pursuit was undertaken. "Why? Because not deriving from faith, but as if derived from works" (*hoti ouk ek pisteōs all' hōs ex ergōn*). The severe elliptical brevity of the explanation strips it down to its one basic essential, misunderstanding, but there is little doubt about Paul's meaning.[16]

Returning to the imagery of running pursuit in v. 32b, Paul supplements this first accounting with the flat assertion, in language taken from Isaiah, "They have stumbled against the stone of stumbling." By at once expressly identifying the scriptural source of this language with his usual formula "just as it is written" and offering the well-known and oft-discussed composite quotation from Isa 8:14 and 28:16 ("Behold I am laying a stone in Zion . . .") Paul takes the significant further step of implying that this unexpected outcome was no merely subjective vagary but was rooted in God's deliberate intent. If this seems

14. On this detail Cranfield is quite correct ("Some Notes," 39). But to go on, as he does, triumphantly to declare "fundamental agreement" between Paul and Jesus on the law is a sharp abridgment of Paul's complex reflections on the law and can only result in caricature. There is nothing in the tradition of Jesus' teaching to compare with Rom 5:20; 7:13; or Gal 3:21–22.

15. H. J. Schoeps, who in his very instructive book on Paul's theology climaxes his discussion of Paul's treatment of the law with a whole section on the fundamental Pauline misunderstanding of the Torah, never once mentions this verse of Romans (*Paul: The Theology of the Apostle in the Light of Jewish Religious History* [London: Lutterworth, 1961]).

16. Both Käsemann (*Römer,* 265 [ET: *Commentary on Romans,* 278]) and Kuss (*Römerbrief,* 745) refer to L. Radermacher's discussion of the expressly Greek nuancing of the verse (*Neutestamentliche Grammatik* [Tübingen: Mohr (Siebeck), 1925], 26) in the absence of any mention of it in BDF. There can be little doubt, in view of Paul's common use of these contrasting prepositional phrases, that the governing word intended but only implied is either the substantive "righteousness" or a cognate verbal form such as "being justified."

to complicate Paul's explanation by reintroducing from chapter 9 the tension between divine purpose and instigation on the one hand and human response and accountability on the other, that is no more and no less than what is involved anyway in the mere appropriation of LXX terminology for "a stone of stumbling" and "a rock of offense."[17] The traditional language about such a stone combines the elements of an unavoidable obstruction and an avoidable encounter with it. Indeed the double form of the citation confirms this tension by setting alongside the offense the alternative possibility of believing trust, and assigning this equal sanction in the divine utterance. In the end, Paul's "explanation" is hardly less complex than the baffling and unexpected double reversal it was called forth to illuminate, and it is neither jarring nor surprising that the first verse of chapter 10 should consist, as we have seen, of a renewed asseveration by the apostle of his deep concern for his people and their salvation in the presence of this confounding God, both his and theirs.

It will be noted that we have left unspecified the matter of the application of the composite quotation from Isaiah. What did Paul have in mind as the stone that has been placed by God in Zion and that has confronted Israel with the alternatives of believing or stumbling? The line of thought Paul has been pursuing and the racecourse imagery with which he has been working—in short, the context read on its own terms—suggests that the Torah is the rock placed by God in Zion. There is nothing in the antecedent context, in the whole of chapter 9 or all of Romans before it, to suggest anything else. Yet all seem to have missed Paul's intent; no commentary on Romans known to me departs from the unanimous opinion that for Paul this stone is Christ. There is no more striking example in the Pauline letters of a crucial exegetical decision made on grounds extrinsic to the text itself. The reason usually given for the latter interpretation is that Paul is drawing upon a tradition of early Christian use of these texts from Isa 8:14 and 28:16 which had already sufficiently established the identification of Christ as the stone so that Paul could take it for granted. Yet this argument has come under increasing attack and has, I think, been decisively undermined.[18] Otherwise, one must in order to sustain this interpretation simply read Paul as anticipating here his mention of Christ in 10:4. But this remains mere

17. Cf. G. Stählin, *"skandalon, ktl," TDNT* 7:341–42. The parallel *proskomma* adds the further nuance of "being taken unawares."

18. John E. Toews, *The Law in Paul's Letter to the Romans: A Study of Romans 9:30–10:13* (Ph.D. diss.; Northwestern University, 1977). One central argument of this dissertation, that Rom 9:33 is not a messianic stone testimonium, was presented by Toews in a paper on "Romans 9:33 and the Testimonia Hypothesis" to the Pauline Epistles Section of the Society of Biblical Literature, meeting in New Orleans on November 20, 1978. In this paper he showed that the Christian christological use of Isa 8:14 everywhere else presupposes the use of Ps 118:22, just what is absent in Rom 9:33. For a general view of the state of the discussion on the so-called testimonia, see J. A. Fitzmyer, " '4Q Testimonia' and the New Testament," in his *Essays on the Semitic Background of the New Testament* (Missoula, Mont.: Scholars Press, 1974), 59–89. Klyne R. Snodgrass ("I Peter

conjecture unless one makes additional assumptions: that Paul's view of Jewish reaction to the preaching of the cross (1 Cor 1:23) was already so generalized, so polarized, and so fixed, and his own thinking so exclusively christological, that it was impossible for him to think that God would cause his people a theological and religious difficulty in any other way; or that *telos* in 10:4 means "abolishment," so that the cause of offense to the Jew is not the messianic claim of the Christians as such or the preaching of the cross but the fact that the Jew cannot accept God's abolishment of the Torah. The first assumption is refuted by chapter 9; the second falls by its own circularity. Except in the total absence of any alternatives, that is, unless one is reduced to looking ahead because one cannot make sense of an unintelligible passage, Rom 10:4 has little evidential value for the meaning of 9:33.

If Paul makes a "new start" in 10:2–3,[19] it is a renewed attempt to shed light on just the state of affairs with which he began in 9:30–31, another try at reducing what obstinately remains a very intricate explanation to a more manageable dimension. He has no new subject in mind. This is clear from the fact that in v. 3 he returns to the same verbal form (aorist third person plural) he used in 9:32; the same event or sequence of events is in view. Righteousness and justification—that is, the question who may stand in God's presence and on what grounds—is still at stake as it was in 9:30–31. And though Paul has shifted the categories from pursuit and the failure of attainment to obedience and disobedience, the same reversal is being described. Now the foil is a deposition by Paul on behalf of his people: what distinguishes them is "zeal for God," nothing else than that eager and devoted commitment to the service of God and to living in accordance with his will and claim which elsewhere Paul alleged without apology or dissimulation to be his own proud legacy from his Jewish past (Phil 3:6). But now against that background there is the same baffling and unexpected outcome: "[T]hey did not submit to God's righteousness" (v. 3 RSV). There is even something of the same dialectic as in 9:30–31, only without the complicating presence of the Gentiles it comes out much more straightforwardly: Obedience, real and genuine in both its intention and its fervor, has turned out as disobedience. Why? Again the explanatory middle link in vv. 2b and 3a has two sides: a passive one in a failure of recognition (*epignōsis*),[20] a

---

II.1–10: Its Formation and Literary Affinities," *NTS* 24 [1977–78]: 97–106) shows that the connection of Isa 8:14 and 28:16 was made already in Jewish tradition, and that the *ep' autō* of Rom 9:33 is not the result of Christian interpolation; this means that this phrase cannot be taken as evidence for a christological application by Paul.

19. Dahl, *Studies in Paul,* 147.

20. The word *epignōsis* occurs in the undisputed Pauline letters here and in Rom 1:28; 3:20; Phil 1:9; and Phlm 6. The contexts always show the presence of the connotation "recognition" or "acknowledgment" (e.g., in Phil 1:9 the parallel term is *aisthēsis*).

knowledge of God's righteousness that has aborted (*agnoein*);[21] and a more active side in a contrary search to establish "one's own" righteousness.

Kuss points out an important detail in the grammar of the verses we have been following, one to which we have tried to hold.[22] Verses 2, 3, 4 (and 5 as well) all begin with the conjunction *gar* ("for"). Verse 2 gives the grounds for (i.e., explains) Paul's statement of involved concern by characterizing his people both positively and negatively; v. 3 in turn explains v. 2 by elaborating on both aspects of the analysis. Verse 4 next explains v. 3—but how? If v. 4 makes Christ God's termination of the Torah, it can "explain" as disobedience only continued adherence to law, the "zeal" of v. 2 and the pursuit of 9:32; but these are not in themselves perverse for Paul. If v. 4 makes Christ the termination of Torah, it can "explain" then not the main clause of v. 3 but only its subordinate participle ("seeking to establish their own"), and then only on the secondary premise that there is no way for the Jews to live by Torah without seeking to establish their own righteousness. But then Paul could have spared himself all the dialectic of 9:30–10:3, just as he could have spared himself the defense of the law's holiness in 7:7–12. To read 10:4 in this way is to compel Paul into a simplistic antinomian position and to make unintelligible his present intricate argument. It also requires one arbitrarily to fill in an ellipsis in the verse (cf. n. 8): "Christ is the end of the law *as a means to* righteousness." In fact, however, Paul nowhere suggests that the way to obedience to God for the Israelite lies in abandoning the Torah. If, on the other hand, v. 4 makes the crediting of righteousness to everyone who believes and trusts God the goal and intent of Torah, it explains directly and straightforwardly, without any need for supplementation by the reader, why the failure to acknowledge God's righteousness and the attempt to establish one's own is an act of disobedience and defiance.

Paul's new explanation is no more simple than his earlier one. But readers, no longer merely baffled, find themselves instead coming out into the clear on familiar Pauline terrain. In the first place, the language has become reminiscent of Phil 3:9 and the paradigmatic way Paul writes of himself there, contrasting two kinds of righteousness: one which belongs to God or comes as a gift from God and can only be recognized and acknowledged in faith, and the other which human beings strive to establish out of their own resources. But more significant than this echo of Phil 3:9 are those other passages from earlier parts of Paul's argument in Romans that now enter into and shape the recognition process. For to understand God's righteousness, to "attain to" it in faith (9:30), means also to submit to it, to acknowledge God as the one who defines righteousness as well as good and evil, truth and falsehood (3:4); it is to recognize

---

21. Cf. R. Bultmann, *"agnoeō, ktl,"* *TDNT* 1:116.
22. Kuss, *Römerbrief,* 748.

his prerogative as well as his claim (3:6); it is to add to the knowledge of him the recognition of him as God with praise and thanksgiving (1:21); it is to believe after the manner of Abraham, trusting him to carry through what he has promised (4:21).

Indeed, the coalescing of Paul's experience with his perception of his people and of his analysis of his people's experience with his own penetrates to a still deeper level. He gives here no hint whatsoever that in Israel's past the Torah was identified mistakenly, or was of demonic origin, or was corrupted in its transmission. There is no suggestion that Israel's knowledge of God was unreal or ever diverted into idolatry and the worship of false gods. There is no indication that Israel's zeal was halfhearted or cold, that it did not spring from genuine commitment. Yet, in spite of all that, there is a Torah given and "pursued" but not reached, a knowledge of God aborted in nonrecognition, a zeal for God that has turned into disobedience. Where do we find ourselves if not back in Rom 7, at the heart of Paul's own experience with God's holy Torah and with the transcendent (*kath' hyperbolēn,* 7:13) capacity of sin to pervert his deepest commitment to it? "[T]he very commandment that promised life proved to be death to me" (7:10 NRSV). "I do not understand what I bring about; for it is not what I intend or desire that I put into practice, but the very thing I want to avoid" (7:15, my translation).

It was after all not only Paul's discovery of the *iustificatio impii,* of God's vindication of the sinner, in the death of Jesus (and hence of the irreconcilable contradiction between that death and justification through the law, Gal 2:21), but also, and perhaps for himself personally more importantly, this experience, interpreted in the light of the cross, of the power of sin to convert even his delight in the Torah into captivity (7:22–23) that raised to the level of an axiom in Paul's mind the conviction that no person's standing before God could be secured by observance of the law (Gal 2:16; 3:11; Rom 3:20, 28; 4:5; 11:16). Even more: in Rom 7 the holiness of God's Torah was so far beyond dispute for him that even this perverse use made of it by the power of sin to trick and to kill had to be seen as serving the divine purpose, namely, to manifest the incalculable dimensions of that power. This point is made twice in 7:13, with two independent purpose clauses. (Unfortunately, the RSV here reduces the impact of these clauses by bringing them together and fusing them into one; worse, the NEB turns them into matter-of-fact result clauses, eliminating the divine purpose entirely; worst of all, the JB makes one a result clause but in keeping the other a purpose construction turns it into a reflexive and assigns the intent to sin itself.) Of course this simply develops a move already made in 5:21, where another purpose clause assigned a deliberate and ultimately redemptive design to the "increase" of sin by the law. The result is the most idiosyncratic feature of Paul's view of the law, the claim that, far from preserving its adherent from sin, it compounds sin.[23] Curiously, this feature has not infrequently been taken to show how far removed Paul had become from his Jewish roots; on the contrary, it shows how unshakable his attachment to Torah as God's and as gift really was.[24] And now—something completely missed in the conventional equation of the "stone" with Christ—just this peculiar but unmistakable signature of Pauline reflection and experience reappears in his backward look over Israel's corporate history when the law is identified as the "stone of stumbling" (9:32).

There is, to be sure, a difference. In Rom 7, speaking personally and for himself, Paul can thank God for a deliverance he has found in Jesus Christ. In Rom 10 and 11, speaking in solidarity with Israel, his thought can only come to rest in the future of God's irrevocable calling (11:26, 29). But the difference in no way impugns the impartiality of God, who has treated all on the same terms and can be counted on to do so in the future (10:12–13; cf. 2:6–11; 4:11–12; 9:11, 16; and 11:28–32). The end result in the case of those who are "in Christ Jesus" (8:1, 2) has been that God has done what the law could not do to bring about the fulfillment of the law's just requirement (8:4), a new obedience to God and a submission to God's will free of that hostility of the flesh that perverts obedience into the securing of a person's own righteousness (8:7–9). Paul does not yet say what the end result will be for Israel, but one can see that it too will be by faith (10:11; 11:23), and by calling upon the Lord, as scripture says (10:13). In any case, that kind of righteousness which belongs to faith and to trust in the God of Abraham, and which Paul now sees from his Christian perspective to have been God's intent all along (4:11–12, 23–24; 9:33b; Gal 3:8) will be for Israel as it is for himself the Torah arrived at, the knowledge of God made authentic in recognition and thanksgiving, the performance and zeal that deserves the name of obedience, the not-so-obvious Jewish identity and circumcision that receives its

---

23. There is a remarkable biblical precedent for Paul's view in Ezek 20:25, where concern with the holiness of God yields a unique reflection on the statutes and ordinances that, though intended for life (vv. 11, 13, 21), lead to death. The concrete allusion is to Exod 22:28 and the enigma of a divine judgment operating in the command itself (W. Zimmerli, *Ezechiel* [Neukirchen-Vluyn: Neukirchener Verlag, 1969], 1:449: "Die paulinische Erkenntnis vom Wesen des Gesetzes [Rö 5,20; 7,13; Gal 3,19] ist hier in einer eigentümlich begrenzten Formulierung von ferne zu ahnen").

24. Schoeps (*Paul,* 182), after remarking on the precedents in Jewish tradition for the claim that the law brings knowledge of sin, goes on to say that no Jew can follow Paul when he concludes from this that the law is a law unto death, and then refers to Rom 8:2–3 and Gal 3:21. But even Paul the Jew does not draw such a conclusion in the verses referred to. In Rom 8:2 the phrase "the law of sin and death" is a shorthand summation of Paul's account in 7:7–12 of (God's) law used by sin to produce death; v. 4 goes on to refer to what God has done to turn this state of affairs around in order that "the just requirement of the law might be fulfilled." Galatians 3:21 voices Paul's conviction that the law is powerless to make alive, but that is not yet to say that the *law* (in distinction from the *letter,* 2 Cor 3:6) kills; the very next verse explicitly makes the function of "scripture" to "consign all things to sin" subservient to the execution of the promise. The negative effects of the law are for Paul always penultimate.

praise and recognition from God and not from human beings (2:28–29). "For the intent and goal of the law, to lead to righteousness for everyone who believes, is (nothing different from) Christ" (my paraphrase).

With that we are back where we started. Before we leave Rom 10:4 we should note that in the next verse Paul goes on, with a new causal sentence, to demonstrate that the grounds for such an affirmation as he has just made are in turn to be found by turning to scripture (10:5–13). With that a new stage is reached which we cannot follow here, although it is of great significance for understanding the methods, intentions, and assumptions of Paul's exegesis.[25]

One point, however, needs to be recognized and accounted for: 10:5–6 is widely used as evidence to show that in v. 4 Paul uses *telos* in the sense of "abolition." The argument is essentially that the contrast these verses draw between "the righteousness which is based on the law" and "the righteousness based on faith" is so sharp and the resulting confrontation between the Moses who "writes" in v. 5 and a personified faith-righteousness that "speaks" in v. 6 so uncompromising that "law" and "Christ" in v. 4 can only be mutually exclusive and Christ can in Paul's mind only mean the termination of Torah.[26] We have examined enough of the context of 10:4 to see that such an argument seriously dislocates the polarity from the place where Paul places it, and does this in such a way as to alter crucially Paul's view of the law. The two kinds of righteousness in vv. 5–6 are indeed opposites, as irreconcilable as obedience and disobedience, as "submitting to God's righteousness" and "seeking to establish one's own" in v. 3. They repeat the contrast between "from faith" and "from works" in 9:32. There is no compromise between an election "by grace" and one "by works" (11:6), between what depends "on the God who calls" and what "on works" (9:12), between what comes "as a gift" and what "as one's due" (4:4). But the law does not belong on the side of this polarity that is alien to God or opposed to God. When it is found to function there, it does so as a consequence of a fundamental and tragic misunderstanding (9:32), or as an instrument of human disobedience and failure to recognize God and his righteousness (10:3), or as an opportunity seized by the demonic power of sin (7:11) for its own nourishment. But even when it is found to function in these ways, it has not been torn out of God's hand and it does not cease to be God's holy instrument, for ultimately it does not contradict even then but advances, however indirectly, the carrying out of God's purpose (Rom 5:20–21; 7:13; 11:32; Gal 3:21–22, 24). To make such a claim is not to deny the presence of evil, the power of sin, the tragedy of the distortion of the divine intent in the name of religion. It is rather

25. Cf. M. J. Suggs, "'The Word Is Near You': Romans 10:6–10 within the Purpose of the Letter," in *Christian History and Interpretation: Studies Presented to John Knox*, ed. W. R. Farmer et al. (Cambridge: Cambridge University Press, 1967), 289–312.

26. E.g., Käsemann, *Römer*, 272 (ET: *Commentary on Romans*, 282–83); on the other side, see F. Flückiger, "Christus, des Gesetzes *telos*," *TZ* 11 (1955): 155–56.

precisely to take all these with utmost seriousness, yet not absolutely, to claim in them and beyond them the ultimate manifestation of God's righteousness, impartial goodness, and sovereignty. Of course this is for Paul the Christian to read history in a pattern of meaning derived from the crucifixion of Jesus. But it is also for Paul the Jewish Christian to trace in the movements of history the sovereignty of the God of Abraham, Isaac, and Jacob, the God of Moses, the Judge and Comforter of the exile, who is also the Father of the Crucified.

II

If such reflections and conclusions as these can claim significant warrant in Paul's own text, it is very difficult to avoid reflecting on the reasons why they are not only not very widely held but also in some quarters, and in the commentary literature generally, firmly opposed, sometimes vehemently. The issue is significant enough to merit a brief postscript.

One matter that we have not mentioned but that has special bearing upon the interpretation of 9:30–10:4 is its relation to 9:1–29. What is the nature of the transition between the body of chapter 9 and 9:30–33? On its face this is a very simple question: How is chapter 10 related to chapter 9? But answering it is one of the major decisions facing the interpreter of Rom 9–11. For, as Dahl has pointed out,[27] through most of its history the interpretation of these chapters has been dominated by the problem of theodicy. More specifically, in the wake of Augustine's preoccupation with the issue of the freedom of the will, Rom 9–11 has been read as a discussion of divine predestination and human responsibility. On the assumption that what primarily troubles Paul in these chapters is his own Jewish people's rejection of the proclamation of Jesus as the Messiah, the three chapters are read as three different and rather unrelated, not to say logically incompatible, attempts to explain and understand this *contemporary* turn of events, this "disobedience of Israel":[28] in chapter 9, by attributing it to God's absolute sovereignty and freedom to elect and to reject (divine determinism); in chapter 10, by attributing it to the Jews' own responsible refusal of the Christ (human freedom); and in chapter 11, by describing it as a temporary expedient that makes possible the inclusion of the Gentiles in God's redemptive purpose and that therefore, frustrating God's sovereignty in appearance only, actually contributes to the salvation of "all Israel" (11:26) and the ultimate victory of God's purpose (not so much in spite of human resistance as in and through it, not wiping it out so much as using it). On such a reading, of course, the transi-

---

27. Dahl, *Studies in Paul,* 142–43.

28. The phrase occurs, for instance, in the opening sentence of Cranfield, "Some Notes," 34. Its use here, where Cranfield is summarizing 9:6–29, illustrates the problem we are addressing. How does one come, on careful reading of Rom 9, to speak at all about "Israel's disobedience," especially in the light of v. 11? What must such an interpreter be bringing to the text, and whence?

tion from chapter 9 to chapter 10 (at 9:30) is abrupt.[29] The discontinuity is as sharp as the contradiction between determinism and freedom. If there is logical coherence here, it would have to be something like the coherence of "thesis" and "antithesis" on the way to "synthesis." But it is questionable whether Paul's argument moves through the stages of this popular but simple and vulgarized schema somehow left to religious language by Hegel. In any case, such a reading of these chapters has had the effect, through a large part of the history of the exegesis of Romans, of isolating these chapters from the rest of the epistle and of creating unnecessary obstacles in the understanding of particular sections.

It is, to be sure, beyond doubt that the negative reaction of Jews to the Christian kerygma, especially in its contrast to the reception accorded by Gentiles, is one of the things on Paul's mind. It is no accident that Paul's use in 11:8 of language from Deut 29:3 and Isa 29:10 is very close in meaning ("eine Sinnparallele")[30] to the text from Isa 6:9–11 embedded in the evangelists' reflections on Jewish response to the gospel (Matt 13:14–15; Mark 4:12; Luke 8:10; John 12:40; Acts 28:26–27). But the issue in chapter 9 does not begin there, as a matter of "the disobedience of Israel." For Paul—the Jew—this discussion begins in 9:6 with the matter of the consistency and reliability of God's word. This is not a new issue in the text of Romans. It is rather a piece of unfinished business left over from a previous stage in the argument, specifically from 3:1–4, just as 6:1–7:6 deals with an issue abruptly turned aside by the apostle and left unresolved in 3:5–8.[31] There, after bluntly pressing the point of God's impartiality, before which Jew and Greek stand on an equal footing, Paul had himself given expression to the question he most naturally expected from a Jew: "What then is the point of being a Jew?" (3:1, my translation). His answer, too brief to be anything but a pointer, had been to say that that issue and the matter of God's faithfulness and truth stand or fall together, and to suggest with a quotation from Ps 51:4 that the real issue in justification is *God's* being "justified," that is, acknowledged as true, even if every human being turns out to be a liar. Clearly Rom 9 pursues that matter first. But that means—and this is the point that bears on our discussion—that what occupies Paul is God's faithfulness over the long past and the consistency of his dealings with his people over past and present. As 9:11 and 9:16 clearly show, Paul is aware of the extent to which his own descriptions of justification "apart from law" depend for their credibility on the case that he can make for this faithfulness and consistency on God's part. It is not at all merely a matter of a contemporary turn of events. It is a matter of

---

29. Dahl himself (*Studies in Paul,* 148) sees 10:4–21 to be an important digression, in some ways logically prior to ch. 9.

30. Kuss, *Römerbrief,* 791.

31. Cf. Dahl, *Studies in Paul,* 139. I owe my initial recognition of this feature of Romans and its significance to the valuable little commentary by E. Gaugler, *Der Brief an die Römer,* 2 vols. (Zurich: Zwingli-Verlag, 1945–52), 1:71.

surveying and reviewing (without a chronological retelling) essential features of Israel's past from his Christian perspective, just as he had been driven earlier to review (without autobiographical sequence) certain aspects of his individual past as a paradigm of human existence under the Torah (ch. 7).

Thus what we meet in Rom 9:30–10:4 is not an apostate Jew accusing his kinsmen of disobeying God because they have not been won over to his new interpretation of God's righteousness, or of persisting in an anachronism because they cannot accept God's putative termination of his Torah, or of being so attached to Moses that they have been unable to follow the living God in his new revelations of himself in unexpected ways.[32] Rather, we encounter a Jewish Christian whose new religious identity depends on continuity with his old; who must, for his own sake and the sake of those who have made the move with him, as well as for the sake of the right understanding of his gospel on the part of Gentile Christians (11:13), undertake such a review. Just as he had pressed the matter of God's consistency in the problematic of descent from Abraham in chapter 9, so now in chapter 10 he had to pursue God's faithfulness in the dialectic of obedience and disobedience (including Gentile obedience and Jewish disobedience), of Jewish devotion to Torah and Jewish failure to attain to Torah, of the problem of a defiance of God in the midst of the greatest possible human zeal for God, in order to be able to discover in his own kerygma the presence of his Jewish God and an answer to the question about that God's intentions in the giving of Torah.

But these are not the only reasons why an interpretation of Rom 10:4 such as we have suggested here has not commended itself. At once the most vehement attack against all translations of *telos* in 10:4 as "goal" and the most eloquent defense of its rendering as "termination" has been made by Käsemann in his superb commentary.[33] There is much in his argument with which one must agree. This applies especially to his polemic against a Christian moralizing, "pedagogical" interpretation of the law in its relation to Christ that derives from a false translation of *paidagōgos* in Gal 3:24 as "tutor" rather than "custodian." Such an interpretation makes of both the Jewish Torah and Israel's history a preparatory schooling for Christian truth, a halfway step on the liberal road of progressive religious development climaxing in Christian piety. Such triumphalism among Christians is not only the soil on which a patronizing view of Judaism grows (and worse, where Christendom dominates, a questioning of the Jew's right to existence); it is irreconcilable with Paul's understanding of justification. For Paul the problem with *homo religiosus,* the religious human being, is not that he has been on the right track, only has not exerted himself sufficiently (Paul could then never

---

32. The language used here echoes that used by Kuss, *Römerbrief,* 741. It is very doubtful that we should read Romans 10 as an attack ("Generalangriff") on Judaism at all, as Kuss does (753).

33. Käsemann, *Römer,* 269–71 (ET: *Commentary on Romans,* 281–83); cf. also idem, "The Spirit and the Letter," in *Perspectives on Paul,* 138–66.

have formulated the paradox of 9:30–31). Rather, human religious striving and "progress" has made more acute a fundamental problematic in humanity's relation to God, and God's gift of the Torah has deepened that crisis just where it has been obeyed (Gal 3:19–24). Here one can only agree with Käsemann.

The problem appears to me to lie elsewhere. Käsemann is quite ready to characterize Paul's understanding of the Jewish Torah in 9:30–31 as "dialectical,"[34] and reminds his readers that "Paul was a Jew, and remained one even as a Christian, in that he still allowed the Torah to be the kernel of the Old Testament."[35] Yet when he comes to 10:4 he insists upon a unilateral and undialectical view of Torah that prohibits *telos* from meaning anything other than "termination." The reason is that "law and gospel mutually exclude one another in an entirely undialectical way";[36] Christ and the Torah of Moses stand in the same kind of contrary relationship as Christ and Adam in 5:12–21, the one belonging to the new aeon and the other to the old.[37] In short, Käsemann's interpretation of Rom 10:4 rests on the premise that the Jewish Torah, the Mosaic law, belongs for Paul to the old aeon that must come, that has come, to an end in Christ. This is a kind of ultimate example of the way in which the understanding of 10:4 depends on decisions that one has made elsewhere.

What is it that casts this dark Manichean shadow across the pages of Paul and of his commentators? Is this the flaw in an apocalyptic reading of Paul, that it proves impotent to deliver us wholly from our Protestant habit of reading Paul through the eyes of Luther? In any case, this premise does not stand up under scrutiny in the light of such passages as are usually adduced in its support, especially 5:20; 7:1–6; and 8:2–4.

We have already alluded to the problem produced by the mislocation of the genuine Pauline polarity in relation to the Jewish Torah.[38] And we have also pointed out that the phrasing of Rom 8:2 ("the law of sin and death") is not to be understood apart from the dialectic of Rom 7 which it summarizes in shorthand form, in which God's holy law is described as having been used by sin in order to produce death.[39] Romans 8:3–4 shows that the counterpart in v. 2 ("the law of the Spirit of life in Christ Jesus") is the same divine Torah brought to fulfillment through the life-giving power which it was itself unable to provide but which belongs to the Spirit. The contraries are sin and righteousness, death and life. Law and Spirit, however, are not related as such opposites but as powerlessness and life-giving power.

---

34. Käsemann, *Römer,* 265 (cf. ET: *Commentary on Romans,* 277); idem, "Spirit and the Letter," 159.

35. Käsemann, "Spirit and the Letter," 154.

36. Käsemann, *Römer,* 269 (my translation); cf. ET: *Commentary on Romans,* 282.

37. Ibid., 270 (ET: *Commentary on Romans,* 282).

38. See p. 89.

39. See n. 24.

The case is similar in Rom 7:1–6. The first three verses are not unclear. In Paul's illustration, living with another man before her husband's death brings upon the woman the label and mark of an adulteress, the "scarlet letter." The very same action after the husband's death brings no such consequence. The law is not annulled by the husband's death, but the power of the law to *condemn* is broken—just the point that is resumed in 8:1 ("There is therefore now no condemnation for those who are in Christ Jesus"). That Paul wishes precisely to avoid suggesting that the law is no longer in effect is shown when he writes (literally translated): "she is annulled [*katērgētai*] from the law of the husband"; the Greek language is being strained to the breaking point to avoid the natural use of this verb, to avoid saying "the law of the husband has been cancelled." The whole purpose of 7:7–12 is to make clear that Paul wants no one to conclude that the Mosaic law is to be equated with the power of sin, and to insist instead that as God's holy, righteous, and good commandment it is not evil or demonic.

Finally, there is the much more complex matter of the law in Rom 5:12–21. One thing is clear: in vv. 20–21 the law intrudes itself as "the factor which disturbs the analogy in [the] contrast between Adam and Christ."[40] It functions for Paul on *both* sides of the divide between Adam and Christ, to make of death, on the one hand, not merely an inexorable fate inherited by all as a result of Adam's trespass alone but a condemnation deserved by the trespasses of all (v. 13), and to make life, on the other hand, not merely a neutral consequence inherited by all as a result of Christ's obedience but a gift that has its character most of all in being undeserved and gracious. That is why it deepens the trespass in order to deepen all the more the ensuing grace, to show that death is the symptom and result of sin's rule and power, but just as surely to show that life in Christ is the symptom and sign of the rule of God's undeserved grace. The law defines for both the old and the new their character; it does not stand unambiguously on the side of the old.

One might very well ask what the consequences would be of a consistent Christian interpretation that insists on identifying the Mosaic Torah with the old aeon. What would that mean for the Christian's relationship to Judaism, to the Hebrew scriptures, to the God of Moses? That consequence might not be as reprehensible as that other paternalizing view of Judaism as a lower order of religious commitment and behavior on its way to Christianity, but it surely would miss by an even wider mark Paul's deep engagement with the Judaism from which he came and to which he remained profoundly tied. To miss that engagement and so to abandon the structure which Paul gave to Christianity because of it would be, as Goguel observed in the passage referred to at the beginning of this essay, "to shake the very foundations of Christianity."

---

40. Dahl, *Studies in Paul*, 91.

CHAPTER 7

PAULINE THEOLOGY: A PROPOSAL FOR A PAUSE IN ITS PURSUIT*

The material produced by the Society of Biblical Literature's Pauline Theology Group between 1985 and 1995 attests to an immense amount of diligent analysis of Pauline texts, careful methodological reflection, and lively and earnest debate.[1] Nonetheless, in the prefaces to each of the earlier volumes of *Pauline Theology,* the editors call attention to the great diversity that has resulted both in the approaches taken by the essays that follow and in the interpretations of Paul's theology at which they arrive. A retrospective survey of what is here presented is thus an enlightening experience, but also a chastening one. On the one hand, the diversity of material shows that the task of understanding the apostle's theology remains unfinished, so that the termination of the group's existence can provide at best only a pause in its pursuit. On the other hand, that same wealth of material calls for taking such a pause as a fresh opportunity for reflection and appraisal. Not the least of the questions still open for discussion is the very central one: Just what do we mean by "Pauline theology"?

---

*This essay originated in a paper prepared for the Society of Biblical Literature Pauline Theology Group, meeting in Philadelphia, Pennsylvania (November 21, 1995), and later published in the final volume disseminating the group's work: *Pauline Theology, Volume IV*, ed. E. Elizabeth Johnson and David M. Hay (Atlanta: Scholars Press, 1997), 140–60. Footnote 82 of the present essay contains Paul Meyer's response to papers delivered by J. D. G. Dunn, R. B. Hays, and P. J. Achtemeier at the same group's meeting in Kansas City, Missouri, on November 26, 1991 (later published in *Pauline Theology IV*). This response, adapted and somewhat abbreviated here, did not appear in the original form of this study and is published here for the first time.

1. Most of this material is preserved and accessible in the *SBL Seminar Papers* of these years, but especially in selected and revised form in the three volumes: Jouette M. Bassler, ed., *Pauline Theology, Volume I: Thessalonians, Philippians, Galatians, Philemon* (Minneapolis: Fortress, 1991), hereafter simply *Pauline Theology I;* David M. Hay, ed., *Pauline Theology, Volume II: 1 and 2 Corinthians* (Minneapolis: Fortress, 1993), hereafter *Pauline Theology II;* and David M. Hay and E. Elizabeth Johnson, eds., *Pauline Theology, Volume III: Romans* (Minneapolis: Fortress, 1995), hereafter *Pauline Theology III.* In addition, at least three important articles, written independently by members of the group but with explicit reference to its work, should be mentioned: Victor P. Furnish, "Paul the Theologian," in *The Conversation Continues: Studies in Paul and John in Honor of J. Louis Martyn*, ed. Robert T. Fortna and Beverly R. Gaventa (Nashville: Abingdon, 1990), 19–34; idem, "On Putting Paul in His Place" (the 1993 SBL Presidential Address), *JBL* 113 (1994): 3–17; and Leander E. Keck, "Paul as Thinker," *Int 47* (1993): 27–38.

If there is no consensus at the end of this stage of the inquiry, there is one conspicuous thread that has run through the discussion; namely, the repeated use, in one way or another, of the uncommonly suggestive pair of terms, *coherence* and *contingency,* that J. Christiaan Beker brought into play early on.[2] Beker's own first definition, before the work of this group began, was:

> Paul's hermeneutic cannot be divorced from the content of his thought, because he relates the universal truth claim of the gospel directly to the particular situation to which it is addressed. His hermeneutic consists in the constant interaction between the *coherent center* of the gospel and its *contingent interpretation.*[3]

For some, the polarity of this language will recall issues that exercised New Testament interpretation at an earlier time under such rubrics as the universality and particularity of the gospel, revelation and history, and even, from longer ago, "the necessary truths of reason" and "the accidental truths of history."[4] Others may balk at even suggesting such a connection. Our subject, after all, is Pauline *theology.* What can the rational opposites of coherence and incoherence, of consistency and confusion in theology, have to do with the metaphysical difference between the transcendent and history? Furthermore, times have changed. One goal in the use of this "coherence-contingency scheme" is to try to get beyond some of those older antitheses and polarities. But that is just the point; it may be worth asking whether we have succeeded.

One may perhaps begin with *contingency* and with a brief historical reminder. Robert Morgan has written about a major turn in New Testament theology that took place about the time of the First World War.[5] The historical criticism of the closing nineteenth century had so driven home the contingency of early Christian history and its documents that all previous sense of divine transcendence had been rather thoroughly wrung out of it. The New Testament had become the merely human sediment left by a multiplicity of first-century developments in religion. The result was the loss not only of a sense of the unity of the New Testament but also of the very category of revelation. It was only the neo-Reformation "theology of the word" after the war that was able to recover

2. J. Christiaan Beker, "Recasting Pauline Theology: The Coherence-Contingency Scheme as Interpretive Model," in *Pauline Theology I,* 15–24.

3. J. Christiaan Beker, *Paul the Apostle: The Triumph of God in Life and Thought* (Philadelphia: Fortress, 1980), 11; emphasis added. The book's discussion after this opening definition should not be read without consulting Beker's own corrective and refining reflections in "Recasting Pauline Theology."

4. Gotthold Lessing, "On the Proof of the Spirit and of Power," in *Lessing's Theological Writings*, trans. and ed. Henry Chadwick (Stanford, Calif.: Stanford University Press, 1957), 53.

5. Robert Morgan, "Introduction: The Nature of New Testament Theology," in *The Nature of New Testament Theology: The Contribution of William Wrede and Adolf Schlatter,* ed. Robert Morgan, SBT 2/25 (Naperville, Ill.: Alec R. Allenson, 1973), 33–35.

the latter, and then only by relocating revelation in proclamation, as Morgan explains:

> Revelation occurs in the act of proclamation when the message is "got across" and a hearer "gets the message" and acknowledges Jesus as his Lord in faith. It is therefore no longer located in the documents (or tradition), nor in the history, but in the event in which, on the basis of the tradition, the Christ (who touches history only as a tangent touches a circle) is represented. This event is not within human control, but the human activity of proclamation sets the stage for it. God will enter the stage or speak to the hearer, evoking faith or rejection, where and when he wills.[6]

Such a relocation opened up some distinct advantages, the foremost one being the complete freedom with which the true historical contingency of all New Testament documents could now be acknowledged. One did not have to compromise historical evidence and findings about their provenance, date, authorship, and literary character or integrity, or suppress the discovery of real historical diversity or variation (including outright contradictions) for the sake of preserving the gospel "message." Of that freedom we have all been beneficiaries.

Other effects were less benign. The relocation itself can be regarded as an attempt to rescue Christian faith and the idea of revelation from the tyranny of the contingent. Separated from the particular historical occurrence of the life of Jesus of Nazareth and (to focus now more closely on the Pauline letters) his crucifixion, the revelatory event of proclamation was movable, and its relationship to the theology contained in the New Testament writings could vary. That act of proclamation, as the point at which human activity could become transparent to, and transmissive of, God's challenging presence and life-giving power, that founding *kerygma* that elicits and validates human believing, could be understood as coming *before* the written gospels and Pauline letters. This was the case in the generally more historical perspective of a Rudolf Bultmann, for whom "the kerygma of Jesus as Messiah is the basic and primary thing which gives everything else—the ancient tradition and Jesus' message—its special character."[7] What one finds in Paul's letters, then, are "theological thoughts" that "are the unfolding of faith itself growing out of that new understanding of God, the world, and man which is conferred in and by faith" (understood as "faith in the kerygma").[8] Here the revelatory event calls forth and shapes theology. Still, kerygma, as the event of the gospel's encounter, and theology, as its subsequent and derivative elaboration and elucidation, however important the living connection between them, are kept distinct in both function and

6. Ibid., 34–35.

7. Rudolf Bultmann, *Theology of the New Testament*, trans. Kendrick Grobel, 2 vols. (New York: Charles Scribner's Sons, 1951–55), 1:42.

8. Ibid., 2:239.

form.[9] This does justice to the event-character of the gospel—"For Paul, the gospel is first and fundamentally *an event,* not a message"[10]—but it draws a fairly sharp line between preaching and theology, a line that may be self-evident in later church life but is much harder to locate exegetically in Paul's letters.[11]

That founding act of proclamation could also be understood as coming *after* the written gospels and Pauline letters. This was the case in the generally more systematic and ecclesiological perspective of a Karl Barth and rather specifically in the words of Robert Morgan cited earlier; this is proclamation in the ongoing life of the church throughout its history. What one sees in Paul's letters from this point of view is the historically contingent "raw material" of early Christian tradition that is interpreted in the direct address of the sermon and only there becomes "gospel." Here the relationship between Paul's theology and preaching is reversed. Paul's letters are more like proclamation in form, which, even though now relegated to a past that has become distant and exotic, still provides both standard and example to the present; and their theological content, as tradition, shapes and provides norms for contemporary proclamation. Still, the distance between the "event" of the preached gospel and the historical event of the cross has become even greater.

In either case, no matter where the founding act of proclamation is understood to be located, the relationship of that proclamatory event to the preceding history that calls it forth and validates it remains in some doubt, and so too does the theological importance of that history. The historical contingency of the cross has been escaped or overcome or transcended. In the first instance this has been done by resort to an indefinable kerygma in which the historical Jesus of Nazareth *becomes* the Christ. This kerygma presupposes faith, so that the truly founding event is the rise of Easter faith. In the second instance, it has been done by shifting the crucial occurrence to the epistemological event, the "aural event,"[12] in which the hearer "gets the message." Either way, to the historical contingency of the cross there has now been added the existential or epistemological contingency of human believing. The attempt to rescue the Christian

9. So Furnish, "Paul the Theologian," 27.

10. Ibid., 26; emphasis original.

11. Furnish ("Paul the Theologian," 33 n. 70) tries to preserve this line when he questions Lou Martyn's language about a "theological event" Paul was confident God intended to occur at the reading of his letter in the Galatian congregation (see J. Louis Martyn, "Events in Galatia: Modified Covenantal Nomism versus God's Invasion of the Cosmos in the Singular Gospel: A Response to J. D. G. Dunn and B. R. Gaventa," in *Pauline Theology I,* 161, the revised version of the paper to which Furnish refers). But he implicitly concedes how hard this is when he remarks, "Paul's apostolic service, which includes but is by no means restricted to his preaching . . . , bears witness to this event [of the gospel] and is thus in its own way *eventful*" (ibid., 26; emphasis added).

12. The term is used by Martyn, "Events in Galatia," 161.

faith and revelation from the supposed and feared tyranny of the contingent has ended in the doubling of that tyranny.

Let us leave *contingency* and turn to *coherence*. In our discussions there have been many attempts to define and locate it, starting with Beker himself, the person responsible for putting it in the forefront of our vocabulary.[13] There has been widespread agreement with Beker concerning the occasional and situationally diverse character of Paul's letters, coming to a head in the discussion of Romans and the rejection of Melanchthon's now notorious assessment of it as a compendium of Christian doctrine. But, beginning with Beker's own initial juxtaposition of these two key terms, there has persisted a powerful tendency to use coherence as the *opposite* of contingency, to direct the search for it toward various strategies for transcending or even suppressing the historical and the contingent, and so to escape the supposed tyranny of the latter in still another way.

This search can take various forms. One is to look for coherence in a belief system that is assumed to be the single source behind all the variety of what Paul writes. N. T. Wright's very definition of Pauline theology has it "refer to that *integrated* set of beliefs which may be supposed to inform and undergird Paul's life, mission, and writing, coming to expression in varied ways throughout all three."[14]

> It is not enough, however, merely to consider the specific topics treated by Paul at this or that point in his letters. It is also important to ask questions about the underlying structure of his belief system. . . . Here we have to do with issues too large to be seen frequently on the surface: questions of monism and dualism; of paganism, pantheism, and polytheism; of monotheism, its alternatives and its implications. It is my conviction that if we are really studying Pauline theology these issues must at least be on the table, if we are not to condemn ourselves ultimately to shallowness. Ultimately, *theology is all about the great wholes,* the single worldviews that determine and dominate the day-to-day handling of varied issues. Most, perhaps all, great thinkers and writers can in the last resort be studied at this level.[15]

It is no surprise that immediately following these words, Wright devotes a rather full (and not uninstructive) discussion to such "worrying things" as "contradictions, tensions, inconsistencies, and antinomies." There is more than a hint here that greatness and substance and profundity in theology, as well as coherence, are to be found only beyond and behind the contingencies of history. Yet in the same context, Wright says of Paul's theology that it "consists precisely

---

13. See esp. Beker's "Recasting Pauline Theology," 15–18.
14. N. T. Wright, "Putting Paul Together Again: Toward a Synthesis of Pauline Theology (1 and 2 Thessalonians, Philippians, and Philemon)," in *Pauline Theology I,* 184; emphasis added.
15. Ibid., 186; emphasis added.

in the redefinition, by means of christology and pneumatology, of those two key Jewish doctrines [sc. monotheism and election],"[16] suggesting on the contrary that Paul's theology is after all deeply embedded in significant historical change. Part of what Wright is after is to counter "aggressively deconstructive analyses such as Heikki Räisänen's,"[17] and to make sure that we do not reduce Pauline theology "on the one hand to a mere function of social forces or rhetorical conventions nor subsume it on the other hand under the traditional loci of a different age."[18] So the search for coherence is motivated at least in part by the desire to respect Paul's integrity as a thinker. But that is not all.

Richard Hays looks for coherence in the symbolic world shared by Paul and other early Christians, including his readers, and shaped by tradition. He finds Noam Chomsky's model useful:

> Paul's particular statements, which are contingent pastoral responses to specific historical situations, are to be read as performances of a competence supplied by this larger communal symbol system; the symbol system is a language, and Paul's letters are utterances within the language.[19]

Pauline theology does not reside in this symbolic world, but consists of the "characteristic patterns of critical reflection" that recur as Paul "attempts to persuade his readers to interpret the practical consequences of *foundational assumptions (axioms)* that they putatively share with him in the light of his convictions."[20] Though such foundational assumptions still seem to be the origin of coherence, Hays is more ready to concede that "ideational coherence" is the product of *our* own constructive efforts "to make sense of Paul's writings by rearticulating their message in a form different from the form that Paul himself employed."[21] Why are such synthetic reconstructions important? They "hope to generate imaginative accounts of Pauline theology that have the power to *elicit consent* from the community of putatively competent readers"; they are our attempts by trial and error to reach a level of understanding that will strike informed readers as a satisfying account of the texts.[22] Coherence is here much more closely linked to the hermeneutic process of interpreting Paul's letters in the modern world, and Hays's essay in synthesis ends with a very useful summary of the unresolved issues with which anyone is left who attempts to interpret the five Pauline letters covered in *Pauline Theology I*. In the end, however,

---

16. Ibid., 184.
17. The words are those of Richard Hays, "Crucified with Christ: A Synthesis of the Theology of 1 and 2 Thessalonians, Philemon, Philippians, and Galatians," in *Pauline Theology I*, 229.
18. Wright, "Putting Paul Together Again," 196–97.
19. Hays, "Crucified with Christ," 228.
20. Ibid., 228–29; emphasis added.
21. Ibid., 230.
22. Ibid., 230–31; emphasis added.

Hays returns to Paul's own thinking rather than that of his interpreters; he finds "the ground of coherence in Paul's thought" to lie in "the narrative framework of the symbolic world presupposed by that theology," which has its heart in "the kerygmatic story of God's action through Jesus Christ."[23]

This turn to narrative has two consequences. One is that it encourages the idea of "the history of salvation" as the place to look for coherence in Paul's theology, thus renewing a debate that remains unresolved in our discussions. The suggestion is adopted and developed by David Lull and Robin Scroggs.[24] Hays himself, after making the suggestion that it is the narrative dimension of Paul's theology that supplies its coherence, raises the most serious problem with it:

> In other words, Paul does not interpret the foundational story as a simple linear *Heilsgeschichte* from Abraham to the present moment. Rather, for Paul, Christ's death has introduced a surprising discontinuity in Israel's story, simultaneously necessitating and enabling a new reading of scripture that discloses its witness to the gospel.[25]

The second consequence of Hays's move, and the net result, is this pointer to God's action through Jesus Christ as the root and fount of theological coherence in Paul. This is fruitful and promising, for it moves the discussion of coherence to another level since Jesus Christ (or Christology) is also for Paul the point at which ultimate theological meaning is most intimately linked to the contingency of a very particular historical event. We shall return to this point. For the moment, one further observation on the search for coherence may still be in order.

The question persists: What accounts for the urgency and drive behind this search? There can be little doubt that human understanding, by its very nature, reaches for inclusiveness and universality. There is always a touch of human hubris in that, but also of the human freedom that includes the impulse toward systematization. The inductive reasoning that shapes our work as historians aims at comprehensive conclusions, for what cannot be accounted for lives on to threaten the plausibility of every explanation. So, for example, as Victor Furnish reports, Joseph Fitzmyer does not hesitate to provide "a systematization of the Apostle's thought in a form in which he himself did not present it" since it is the task of the biblical theologian "to express the *total* Pauline message,

---

23. Ibid., 231–32.

24. David J. Lull, "Salvation History: Theology in 1 Thessalonians, Philemon, Philippians, and Galatians: A Response to N. T. Wright, R. B. Hays, and R. Scroggs," in *Pauline Theology I*, 247–65; Robin Scroggs, "Salvation History: The Theological Structure of Paul's Thought (1 Thessalonians, Philippians, and Galatians)," in *Pauline Theology I*, 212–26. For two vigorous rejections of "salvation history" as the solution to the problem of coherence in Paul's theology, see Martyn, "Events in Galatia," 172–74; and Keck, "Paul as Thinker," 33–34.

25. Hays, "Crucified with Christ," 237.

which *transcends the contextual situation* and embraces also the relational meaning of the Pauline utterances."[26] We may protest that the total Pauline message is beyond our reach, if for no other reason than the limitations of our sources. But even if we should narrow the theological interpreter's task within these limits to its more descriptive dimensions and eschew such systematization, and even when we have become less sanguine about the search for a "center" to Paul's thinking, there still remains that strong desire to find what it takes to integrate the apostle's thinking into a coherent whole, or to find, in the very expressive words of Jouette Bassler,

> a pattern, a center, a commitment, a conviction, a vision, an underlying structure, a core communication, a set of beliefs, a narrative, a coherence—*something*—in Paul's thoughts or behind them that dispels any abiding sense of mere opportunism or intellectual chaos on the part of the apostle. Yet nowhere, it seems, does this core, center, vision, etc. come to expression in a noncontingent way.[27]

Another clue to the pathos behind this search for an inclusive coherence appears in an observation made early in the Pauline Theology Group's discussions by Paul Achtemeier, who formulated the search for the coherence of Paul's gospel as a question, namely, "how to isolate from the welter of situation-conditioned material present in Paul's letter[s] that material which represents positions or expressions which themselves do not depend on a given contingent situation for their validity."[28] This suggests that what is at stake is to identify not only what controls or shapes the apostle's argument at any given moment but also what can so transcend the limitations of historical contingency as to supply warrant for its truth and reliability. That adds another dimension to the search. But it also raises a new set of questions. If we are dependent for that kind of warrant on a "coherence" that exacts from us the price of suppressing the historical and contingent, does that not disclose a new tyranny, this time of "coherence"? Can coherence supply what is here being asked of it? Is that the source, the originating fountain, the authenticating signature of the truth of the gospel for Paul?

Are we then torn between a tyranny of contingency and one of coherence? The material produced by the Pauline Theology Group is permeated with intimations that this polarity, useful as it has proven to be as a heuristic device, cannot provide the key to understanding Paul's theology. One may begin with Achtemeier again, who stresses the dynamic quality not only of Paul's thought

---

26. Joseph Fitzmyer, *Paul and His Theology: A Brief Sketch* (2d ed.; Englewood Cliffs, N.J.: Prentice-Hall, 1989), 38, as quoted by Furnish, "Paul the Theologian," 22; emphasis added.

27. Jouette M. Bassler, "Paul's Theology: Whence and Whither?" in *Pauline Theology II*, 6; emphasis added.

28. Paul J. Achtemeier, "Finding the Way to Paul's Theology: A Response to J. Christiaan Beker and J. Paul Sampley," in *Pauline Theology I*, 25–26.

but also of Paul's particular and occasional reactions to the various situations he addresses.[29] Of special importance are the many scattered observations that recognize the contingent character of Paul's *theology* and his core convictions. "We do not have a non-contingent expression of what Paul felt represented the coherent center of the faith."[30] We have seen that Bultmann already spoke of Paul's theology as an "unfolding" process. In offering retrospective modifications of his book *Paul the Apostle,* Beker speaks more and more of a hermeneutical process characterized by "the reciprocal and circular interaction of coherence and contingency."[31] Bassler prefers to speak of Paul's theology as an "activity"[32] and she is vigorously seconded in this by Steven Kraftchick, who develops the thought in his own way.[33] Furnish portrays the apostle's theology as a continuous working out of an understanding of the gospel, not merely the application to a "target" situation of a gospel already formulated.[34] In his earlier article, both the title and the concluding sentence imply that the search is not so much for Paul's theology as it is for "Paul the theologian."[35]

These intimations have deeply colored our discussions of Paul with the twofold benefit that his theology is conceived in a much more flexible and dynamic way, and the rigid polarization of coherence and contingency has broken down to the point where it no longer confronts us as an inescapable alternative. Nevertheless, these advances notwithstanding, something of the inherited model of theology still clings to many of our formulations. This is the assumption that Paul's relatively coherent thought world (rightly recognized to be highly complex and syncretistic) is always the starting point, the storehouse, the repertoire, the competence *out of which* Paul addresses each of the particular crises he confronts. This can be illustrated from Beker's own uncommonly suggestive, and for our discussions seminal, essay. A major step forward is taken when Beker identifies Paul's theology with his "interpretive activity." But in the next breath he locates coherence in the "convictional basis" from which Paul's activity moves, "the truth of the gospel" (Gal 2:5, 14).[36] Even if *coherence* refers to something "fluid and flexible," it "nourishes" Paul's thought.[37] It is "the abiding solution to Paul's private contingency (in answering the crisis of his personal life) but also the abiding solution to the various problems of his

29. Ibid., 33–34.

30. Ibid., 32.

31. Beker, "Recasting Pauline Theology," 24.

32. Bassler, "Paul's Theology," 10–12.

33. Steven Kraftchick, "Seeking a More Fluid Model: A Response to Jouette M. Bassler," in *Pauline Theology II,* 30–33.

34. Furnish, "On Putting Paul in His Place," 12–17.

35. Furnish, "Paul the Theologian," 30.

36. Beker, "Recasting Pauline Theology," 15.

37. Ibid., 16–17.

churches (answering their several crises)."[38] It does not matter how flexibly coherence is defined; if "the truth of the gospel" is understood as the "answer" to various problems, we are still stuck in the image of Paul as a problem-solver in the churches that came to him for "answers" and of the gospel as a resource in the tool-bag of this "fixer." The English word *answer* does not function here as *Antwort* (a response in a process of dialogue) but as *Lösung* (a solution to a puzzle). But the underlying conception of theology, not to mention this image of Paul, ill fits either the apostle's argument or Beker's. In both verses in Gal 2, "the truth of the gospel" is used teleologically; it is not something ready-made and given but is at risk and has to survive (διαμεῖναι, v. 5, a punctiliar aorist) or be attained (πρός and accusative case, v. 14). In the very same sentence, Beker himself also identifies "the truth of the gospel" as "the apocalyptic interpretation of the cross and resurrection of Christ." That is a powerful move in a different direction in which cross and resurrection are the "given," the precipitating occasion is the crisis confronting Paul, but the theology is the *Antwort,* the response, the resulting outcome of the process of interpretation. (If theological content is to be located anywhere, it is here; *content* and *process* may be a useful distinction, but in the end it is a false alternative for defining Paul's theology.)

It is the conception of theology operative here that is the issue. Once again, there have appeared, scattered throughout the Pauline Theology Group's materials, many pointers in this alternative direction. Andrew Lincoln's very careful and instructive analysis of the interplay among tradition, gospel, and audience in Rom 1:18–4:25 offers repeatedly a close-up look at Paul's argument as a theology in the making, though he stops short of calling it that.[39] "These insights [in Rom 2:17–27] produce finally a whole new perspective on who is a Jew."[40] "The early chapters of Romans show Paul forging a theology based on his gospel through creative interpretation of Jewish and Jewish Christian tradition."[41] Beker suggests that "a disclosure theory of truth" might prove to be more compatible with Paul's hermeneutic than "a coherence theory of truth," though he does not pursue the question of what the former might look like.[42] Troels Engberg-Pedersen writes: "All this tends to emphasize the dynamic and open-ended character of Paul's theologizing. What we see in the letters is a symbolic universe *in the making,* not a fully worked out, static, and final one."[43] This series of quotations may be ended with the arresting, and I

38. Ibid., 17.
39. Andrew T. Lincoln, "From Wrath to Justification: Tradition, Gospel, and Audience in the Theology of Romans 1:18–4:25," in *Pauline Theology III,* 130–59.
40. Ibid., 144.
41. Ibid., 157.
42. Beker, "Recasting Pauline Theology," 20.
43. Troels Engberg-Pedersen, "Proclaiming the Lord's Death: 1 Corinthians 11:17–34 and the Forms of Paul's Theological Argument," in *Pauline Theology II,* 106; emphasis original.

believe correct, observation of Steven Kraftchick: "Sometimes Paul discovered where he wanted to go during the act of composition rather than prior to it."[44]

In view of such suggestions, the proposal being made here is simply this: Instead of assuming most of the time that Paul's theology or convictions are the *resource* or starting point from which he addresses the issues placed before him, may one rather, as a kind of "experiment in thought," think of them more consistently as the end product and result, the outcome to which he arrives in the process of his argument, his "hermeneutic," or his "theologizing"? Many features of Paul's letters that have come under scrutiny in the course of these discussions recommend such a shift.

1. The later letters, most conspicuously of course Romans, incorporate the experiences and the theological formulations of earlier crises. It is not just the case that we find blocks of text in Romans that look like sermonic materials or arguments used on previous occasions. New contingencies produce new coherences in formulation; the process of reflection yields new theological affirmation, less inchoate, more pregnant. Can anyone deny the sense of progression in the work of the Pauline Theology Group as it has moved from 1 Thessalonians to Romans? Has this been only a progression in the scope and range of Pauline texts under review, or has it not also been a progression in the *emergence* of the Pauline theology/theologies we have been seeking, at a new level of coherence just because of the new diversity? If so, then the coherence of Pauline theology is itself the product of historical process; that is, it is itself contingent—as is demonstrated in the sometimes painful awareness that the end result of one line of theologizing on one occasion is not in all respects logically compatible with that of another and cannot be made to be so. Then one would no longer be able to speak of "the non-contingent bedrock of Pauline theological convictions."[45]

2. Romans 9–11 may well serve as exhibit no. 1. This is a matter of much dispute and hangs on the detailed exegesis of these chapters, about which there is important debate within the Pauline Theology Group.[46] But a not unpersuasive case has been made out by Nikolaus Walter for the view that Paul himself did not clearly see, when he wrote Rom 9:1, where chapter 11 would end, and "that we actually share in a mental struggle here, the outcome of which was not

---

44. Steven Kraftchick, "Seeking a More Fluid Model," 24. This observation recalls the striking declaration attributed to Daniel J. Boorstin, one-time Distinguished Service Professor of American History at the University of Chicago, Librarian of Congress, Pulitzer Prize recipient, and author, among many other books, of *The Discoverers* (New York: Random House, 1983): "I write to discover what I think."

45. Achtemeier, "Finding the Way to Paul's Theology," 31.

46. E. Elizabeth Johnson, "Romans 9–11: The Faithfulness and Impartiality of God," in *Pauline Theology III*, 211–39; and Douglas Moo, "The Theology of Romans 9–11: A Response to E. Elizabeth Johnson," in *Pauline Theology III*, 240–58.

already settled with the first sentences of chap. 9."[47] Despite wildly differing conclusions about where Paul comes out, many interpreters seem willing to agree on the highly contingent nature of Paul's theologizing here. The main disagreements over the coherence that does or does not emerge from Paul's mental struggle in these chapters boil down, it seems to me, to what Hays has called "vicarious inclusion in corporate salvation," the second of the three unmet "hermeneutical challenges" with which he ends his partial synthesis of the shorter letters.[48] But that is another matter that cannot be pursued here.

3. Galatians may provide an example on which we agree more quickly. Lou Martyn has observed, "Had the Teachers not had such extraordinary success with their Abraham sermons, we would probably know nothing of Paul's interpretation of the patriarch, for Romans 4 is clearly a reworking of Galatians 3."[49] Perhaps even more significant is the lesson he credits to E. Grässer and approvingly passes on:

> [T]he term "covenant" does not itself point to a fundamental element of Paul's theology. With few exceptions, Paul employs the term only when one of his churches has become enamored of the use being made of it by traveling evangelists who stand in opposition to his mission (Galatians 3–4; 2 Corinthians 3).[50]

It is actually a confirmation of this point when Richard Hays points out that "righteousness/justification language . . . appears only in the letters where the question of covenant membership for Gentile Christians is a disputed matter" (for the debated "covenant membership" one may substitute the more Pauline "standing in God's grace" [e.g., Rom 5:21] and the point still stands).[51] Despite the argument between Martyn and Dunn over whether "covenantal nomism" best characterizes Paul's theology or that of the Teachers he is opposing, they seem to agree "that the Antioch incident was a decisive factor in the development of Paul's understanding of the gospel."[52] The question whether the situational demands in Galatians *suppress* the coherent "core" of Paul's theology or rather *elicit* it and bring it into full view[53] has proven to be a fruitful test case

47. Nikolaus Walter, "Zur Interpretation von Römer 9–11," *ZTK* 81 (1984): 176; my translation.

48. Hays, "Crucified with Christ," 246.

49. Martyn, "Events in Galatia," 166–67 n. 15.

50. Ibid., 171 n. 26.

51. Hays, "Crucified with Christ," 237.

52. James D. G. Dunn, "The Theology of Galatians: The Issue of Covenantal Nomism," in *Pauline Theology I*, 144. Cf. Martyn, "Events in Galatia," 164–65 and passim.

53. In the context of Beker's claim that apocalyptic is the heart of Paul's gospel, this question has taken the specific form of a debate over whether Galatians is devoid of apocalyptic or "is fully as apocalyptic as are the other Paulines" (Martyn); see Beker, *Paul the Apostle,* 58; and Martyn, "Apocalyptic Antinomies in Paul's Letter to the Galatians," *NTS* 31 (1985): 410–24, esp. 410–12, 420–21.

for examining the validity of any definition of coherence, but either outcome to that debate will serve as a powerful support for the contention that coherence (and in its wake Pauline theology) is the result of Paul's theologizing and not its presupposition.

4. Paul's use of scripture seems also to justify this proposal. It turns out on closer observation that scriptural citations are in most cases not a starting point of Paul's theologizing but are drawn into the argument as a kind of ladder by which to reach a new level of meaning and coherence—a ladder on which Paul knows he can rely but one that he redesigns as he uses it. He has a certain confidence that scripture can help him reach a goal that is not yet in his grasp. The resulting pattern comes close to showing that theology is something one does or produces rather than has, and that Paul's theology in particular is not the father of his theologizing but its child. Much remains yet to be done in any analysis of Paul's use of scripture from this perspective; "interpretation of Israel's scripture" is another of Hays's unmet "hermeneutical challenges."[54]

5. In the early discussions of method in the Pauline Theology Group, Paul Sampley formulated a series of specific procedures for moving upstream, so to speak, "from text to thought world" in Paul's letters.[55] Although Sampley stresses "pervasive flexibility" and adaptability as characteristic of Paul's letters and the degree to which their agendas are "fundamentally set by his perception of the needs and struggles of a given community,"[56] these procedures were nevertheless formulated with an eye to moving backward "to the thought world from which his thoughts gain expression," in order from there to facilitate a "reconstruction of what we might call a theology of Paul"; this "will always be a modern abstraction, a distillation that we gain from his thought world."[57] What is being proposed here on the contrary is in many ways a reversal of direction in this procedure, in which "Pauline theology" would be less an abstraction or distillation on our part and more closely identified with the actual conclusions reached in Paul's arguments. But the point to be made now is that many of the procedures Sampley recommends turn out to be just as serviceable if one is asking where Paul's theology comes out. They include, for example, the questions "Where does Paul self-correct?"; "What matters are treated as indifferent?"; and especially "What shall we make of the frequency with which Paul mentions goals in his letters?"[58] Again, we cannot pursue that matter further here.

---

54. Hays, "Crucified with Christ," 246.
55. J. Paul Sampley, "From Text to Thought World: The Route to Paul's Ways," in *Pauline Theology I*, 3–14; see esp. 9–14.
56. Ibid., 5.
57. Ibid., 3.
58. Ibid., 10, 13.

These may be some of the reasons encouraging one to experiment with a different way of conceiving "Pauline theology." But the proposal implies some correlates and raises some questions to which we need to turn.

In the first place, a word about *argument*. Lou Martyn is not happy with a "definition of the theology of Galatians as a responsive argument" and proposes that the theology of the letter is much more closely connected with "the letter's work" and that Paul "does theology [here] by writing in such a way as to anticipate a theological event," an "aural event" in which "God will re-preach his gospel to the Galatians."[59] But as Martyn's own case unfolds, it becomes clear that the real issue at stake is not whether Paul's letter contains an argument that "responds" to the situation in that congregation or intends a certain result, but rather what the strategy of Paul's argumentation is and on whose terms and within whose frame of reference it is carried through.[60] Martyn's answers to those critical questions and the suggestion that they display Paul's way of doing theology seem to demonstrate that no clear line can be drawn in Paul's letters between argument, rhetoric (the art of persuasion, the producing of an effect) and theology, and even to raise doubts about how far we can go with the relatively useful but ultimately only heuristic distinction between proclamation and theology in Paul's letters.[61]

A more important point is that since Paul's theology has been so frequently spoken of in our discussions in terms of his foundational convictions, the present proposal might be construed to imply that Paul had no convictions before engaging in this activity and brought none to the writing of his letters. The absurdity of that implication might then count as a decisive reason for rejecting the proposal. This requires some discussion. Much depends, of course, on the definitions with which one starts. Bassler finds Daniel Patte's definition helpful: "A conviction is a self-evident truth." The way to locate convictions in theological argument is then to identify what in it is "established as self-evidently good and desirable."[62] Convictions remain here clearly within the

59. Martyn, "Events in Galatia," 160–61.

60. Ibid., 162–63.

61. The distinction is energetically defended by Furnish ("Paul the Theologian," 27). One may readily grant that the distinction is clear and even essential in the contemporary ecclesiastical and academic context. A flaw in Furnish's exceptionally clear and instructive article is that he first establishes a useful but modern definition of "Christian theology" independently of Paul and then asks whether Paul may be regarded as a theologian who fits it (ibid., 25–26). An alternative is to begin with an analysis of what the apostle does and then ask whether the umbrella of "theology" can be extended to cover that. Thus William S. Campbell: "It is a body of tradition rather than a system of theology with which Paul interacts. But if the creative reformulating and transforming of inherited images and metaphors are what constitutes doing theology, then Paul is certainly a theologian par excellence" ("The Contribution of Traditions to Paul's Theology: A Response to C. J. Roetzel," in *Pauline Theology II*, 254).

62. Bassler, "Paul's Theology," 12, citing Daniel Patte, *Paul's Faith and the Power of the Gospel: A Structural Introduction to the Pauline Letters* (Philadelphia: Fortress, 1983), 11, 17.

realm of that *from* which Paul argues. Yet Kraftchick points out that conviction statements function in different ways in Paul's letters and for that reason should not be identified as the foundation of Paul's theologizing but as its "presuppositions or products," part of Paul's "raw data."[63] Sometimes Paul's argument is directed at *changing* his readers' presuppositions about what is good and desirable, real or illusory, so that the conviction is something arrived at in a particular setting and occasion, not only by his readers but also, as we have suggested, even by Paul himself.

To propose that one should at least experiment with an understanding of Pauline theology as the product and outcome of Paul's various concrete and contingent acts of doing theology does not in any way call into question the importance of convictions that Paul brings to these enterprises. But "convictions" will now carry a somewhat different meaning. If anything comes close to being self-evident, it is that not only Paul but also his readers carry to the writing and the reading respectively of those letters a large freight of pre-understandings, assumptions, opinions, beliefs, and even convictions. Some are held in common; some are not. Some are silently taken for granted; some are named and drawn upon in argument. Some have been previously planted by Paul, wittingly or unwittingly; some have been planted by his opponents. Some Paul attempts to encourage and reinforce; some he aims to question and to change. This freight includes what some writers of our papers have referred to as "world view" and others as "symbolic world"; certainly we should think as well of scripture and even of pre-Pauline Christian traditions. For purposes of reflecting on Pauline theology, we may embrace most of this under the heading of (religious) tradition. Paul, after all, was not the first to read his Hebrew scriptures or to speak of God, of God's presence and action (even in Jesus of Nazareth), God's freedom and faithfulness, God's mercy and judgment, or of love, righteousness, sin, suffering, or of life and death. At this point Andrew Lincoln's careful analysis of Rom 1:18–4:25 is helpful. He has traced

> three main coordinates in the theology of Rom 1:18–4:25—*tradition,* which provides most of the symbol system within which the argument takes place; *gospel,* which supplies the convictions by which the symbols are realigned and reshaped; and *audience,* whose needs influence the argument but are interpreted in the light of the gospel.[64]

He has then summed it all up in one of the best one-liners of our material: "tradition, gospel and audience abide, these three; and the greatest of these is gospel."[65]

---

63. Kraftchick, "Seeking a More Fluid Model," 28–29.
64. Lincoln, "From Wrath to Justification," 159; emphasis added.
65. Ibid.

Clearly it is the gospel that ultimately controls the process of Paul's theologizing; on that there seems to be wide agreement. Leander Keck ended his major essay on Romans for the Pauline Theology Group, "What Makes Romans Tick?" with the statement: "Romans ticks because Paul did not allow his immediate situation to govern completely what he had to say, but allowed the inner logic of his gospel to assert itself even if that meant subjecting his first readers to a certain amount of theological overkill."[66]

But now, just what is that "gospel" and what is its "inner logic" that not only gives coherence to this multifaceted body of Pauline literature but also transcends the contextual situation of that literature so that it still calls for a hearing today? What is it that realigns and reshapes the symbols of Paul's tradition so that a distinctive Pauline theology that is also a Christian theology emerges? Lincoln still refers to "convictions" that the gospel supplies, but he has made the important step of making "convictions" depend upon and derive from this "gospel" instead of standing for its substance. Picking up Sampley's point that one clue to coherence in Paul is provided by basic points from which he argues,[67] Achtemeier focuses on "those generative statements or beliefs that seem to underlie larger developments in Paul's letters," and lists as one of these the resurrection. It is "a non-contingent component of valid Christian faith," which is affirmed as an act of God in the confessional formula of Rom 10:9b and which, as Achtemeier goes on to elaborate, can be shown to be not only central for Paul but also "generative of other beliefs and to that extent foundational for Paul's gospel."[68]

Here we have come, I believe, very close to our answer. But we have not quite reached it yet. In a crucial observation, Calvin Roetzel has remarked that "it is simply inadequate to say the cross is foundational without noting the way the interpretation of the cross is changed by its context and then bends back onto the context to shape that as well."[69] That is to say, every reference to the cross and resurrection in Paul's letters, every affirmation, conviction, or belief, even every pre-Pauline confessional formula, every human statement of it as "gospel" is shaped by historical, cultural, and personal circumstances and context, and so is embedded in historical contingency. There *is* no "non-contingent bedrock of Pauline theological convictions."[70]

Here, as often in the past, Leander Keck has come to our aid, in an article written to honor Achtemeier.[71] "Paul," he writes,

66. Leander E. Keck, "What Makes Romans Tick?" in *Pauline Theology III*, 29.
67. Sampley, "From Text to Thought World," 11.
68. Achtemeier, "Finding the Way to Paul's Theology," 35.
69. Calvin J. Roetzel, "The Grammar of Election in Four Pauline Letters," in *Pauline Theology II*, 228.
70. Achtemeier, "Finding the Way to Paul's Theology," 31.
71. Keck, "Paul as Thinker," 27–38.

was an ex post facto thinker. Ex post facto thinking occurs not only after an event but because of it, and with continual reference, explicit or implicit, to it. The event's very "happenedness" requires thinking. . . . For Paul, this given, this event, this compelling datum that evoked his ex post facto thinking, was the resurrection of the crucified Jesus.[72]

This is helpful for three reasons, which we may discuss briefly in turn in conclusion.

In the first place, these words help locate more precisely that bedrock of Pauline theological convictions. They remind us of the crucial distinction that must be drawn between human believing, confession, affirmation, and conviction on the one hand and the "event" on the other, the "compelling datum" that calls forth these human responses. In words now widely familiar, Nils Dahl has identified what can be called the "foundational conviction," from both a material and a historical perspective, of all New Testament theology:

> The central task of early Christian theology was to come to terms with the crucifixion of Jesus. The conviction that the crucified "King of the Jews" was right and had been vindicated by God, who raised him from the dead, forms the basis of the theology of the New Testament in all its varieties.[73]

Obviously, this conviction as such is part of early Christian theology. But just as clearly, the essential ingredient in this conviction is the certainty that it is not self-generating, that it has been called into being and derives its warrant and authorization from something God has done. As God's act, this is the bedrock that elicits and shapes convictions but is not itself a conviction—not the Easter faith of the early church or its proclamation, not some indefinable cipher labeled "kerygma" behind all the contingent theological formulations of the New Testament, not the apostolic act of preaching Jesus as the Christ, but God's act of confirming and vindicating the crucified Jesus.[74] To locate the

---

72. Ibid., 29–30.

73. Nils Alstrup Dahl, "The Neglected Factor in New Testament Theology," in *Jesus the Christ: The Historical Origins of Christological Doctrine*, ed. Donald H. Juel (Minneapolis: Fortress, 1991), 157–58. It should not be forgotten that Dahl played a significant role in the early formation of the Pauline Theology Group.

74. Cf. Hans Küng, *On Being a Christian* (Garden City, N.Y.: Doubleday, 1976), 352: "The Easter faith is not a function of the disciples' faith. . . . Even according to Bultmann, the formula 'Jesus is risen into the kerygma (proclamation)' is liable to be misunderstood. Even according to Bultmann, it does not mean that Jesus lives because he is proclaimed: he is proclaimed because he lives." See R. Bultmann, *Das Verhältnis der urchristlichen Christusbotschaft zum historischen Jesus*, SHAW 60/3 (2d ed.; Heidelberg: Carl Winter Universitätsverlag, 1961), 27; ET (from the 3d German edition): "The Primitive Christian Kerygma and the Historical Jesus," in *The Historical Jesus and the Kerygmatic Christ: Essays on the New Quest of the Historical Jesus*, trans. and ed. Carl E. Braaten and Roy A. Harrisville (New York: Abingdon, 1964), 42.

bedrock in this way does more than define the basic content of the conviction. It points the way to a solution to that other dimension as well of the search for what controls and shapes the apostle's argument, namely, the quest for what can so transcend the contingencies of human believing as to supply warrant for its truth and reliability. It is God's raising of the crucified Jesus that provides for Paul the authenticating signature for the truth of the gospel and for his own apostleship in its service as well.

In the second place, Keck's words open the way to a more satisfying formulation of the relationship between contingency and coherence. The crucifixion of Jesus is a contingent historical event in the full sense of the word. It is a public event, fully open to historical explanation and description (knowledge of which is subject to the same limitations of accessibility, information, and evidence as any other event of the past), but also fully susceptible to contradictory human responses and evaluations. In itself, its meaning remains open and uncertain. Yet its concrete givenness is remarkably fixed, even inescapable. Nothing in the entire Bible is so certain historically or so secure from historical doubting as that Jesus did not die from so-called natural causes at the end of a successful career as a popular teacher but that his life was taken from him. Moreover, the *way* it was taken from him constituted from the start a devastating threat to the meaning of his life and teaching, and especially to the coherence of all early Christian claims connecting him with God's purposes.[75] That is why Dahl has identified that "central task of early Christian theology" to be "to come to terms with the crucifixion of Jesus." Because of this threat, the necessary condition for receiving and understanding his death as a benevolent and salutary "divine act" was that certainty that God had identified himself with this crucified One and so confirmed and vindicated him. Apart from God's act, Jesus' death would remain devoid of special meaning, another merely historical and starkly contingent human defeat. The resurrection does not wipe out the death of Jesus or undo its contingent historical reality. Rather, as divine vindication, it makes the death of Jesus an apocalyptic event, and Paul uses apocalyptic categories and traditions to make clear what God's raising of this Jesus makes this death mean. "The very structure of reality is transformed."[76] So much is this the case that the death of Jesus plays a surprisingly more conspicuous role in Paul's letters than even the resurrection as such.

Of course the resurrection, too, is received and pictured and transmitted, in narratives of appearances, in empty tomb stories, in hymnic and creedal formulas—all historically contingent ways that can be traced by the historian as

---

75. For the factors that shaped the public meaning of this form of execution in the Greco-Roman world, see Martin Hengel, *Crucifixion* (Philadelphia: Fortress, 1977).

76. Hays, "Crucified with Christ," 239.

diverse and developing traditions.[77] The earliest affirmations of its reality are confessional in nature. Yet just because such confession included the realization that faith is not self-generating but has been called into being ex post facto, and because the reality being confessed cannot be reduced to or exhausted in the confessing and believing it elicits, these confessional utterances take the form of historical statements about a particular event of the past that parallel references to the contingent event of Jesus' crucifixion: "God has raised him from the dead" (Rom 10:9). But this does not mean that the resurrection itself is a contingent historical event of the same order as the crucifixion.[78] It cannot be. It has *God* as its actor. It has no eyewitness. It is not subject to historical verification or falsification. It has no content for unbelief; for belief, its content is the freshly disclosed status and identity of the previously known particular historical figure of the Crucified. Those twin confessional statements of Rom 10:9—"Jesus is Lord" and "God has raised him from the dead"—are equivalent and interpret each other: to say the second is to confess the first. Yet it is this resurrection that makes all the difference in authorizing an understanding of Jesus' death as itself a divine act, more than a merely contingent historical event.

To return to our pair of troublesome and yet illuminating terms, we may thus suggest that Paul sees this contingently historical event of the crucifixion not only to have been made normative by God's action but to have been made the point where human believing and knowing may genuinely transcend the contingent and find an authentic coherence to life and thought. It has become the eternally reliable clue and criterion for discerning God's true nature, presence, and intention, and thus the historical locus of revelation. This accidental truth of history has been made the disclosure point for the eternally valid and necessary inner logic of the gospel.

How does this work itself out in Paul's theology? This brings us to our third point, and to what is in the end the final and most telling argument for the proposal to conceive of Paul's theology as the resulting outcome rather than as the starting point of his theological activity. In the article referred to earlier, Keck also writes,

---

77. For the complexities of "resurrection symbolism" at the primary exegetical level and beyond, one may consult Pheme Perkins, *Resurrection: New Testament Witness and Contemporary Reflection* (Garden City, N.Y.: Doubleday, 1984). For the historical development of the diverse resurrection traditions as well as for the understanding of resurrection in Paul in particular, and as representative of a much larger literature, see Ulrich Wilckens, *Resurrection. Biblical Testimony to the Resurrection: An Historical Examination and Explanation* (Atlanta: John Knox, 1978).

78. For further discussion of the question whether the resurrection may be spoken of as an "event," historical or eschatological or otherwise, see Küng, On *Being a Christian*, 348–56; and Perkins, *Resurrection*, 28–30.

Paul had no Christian teacher. He was nobody's pupil, but was an *autodidact,* that is, a self-taught thinker who, while indebted to traditions, *never appealed to an authoritative teacher.* Nor did Paul's thinking develop in a collegial context as Johannine theology did, assuming that this tradition was formed in a school.[79]

This emphasis on the creative singularity of Paul and his position at the fountainhead of Christian theology (though he is not alone there) is, I think, extremely important—something lost in the "history of religions school" with its overemphasis on pre-Pauline Hellenistic Christianity. It is important because in Paul's theology (in his letters) we have ringside seats to watch what happens when the fully historical impact of the crucifixion, made the defining event by God's raising Jesus from the dead, forces the revision and recasting of all the traditional language, concepts, convictions, and categories, including the reading of scripture (God,[80] God's "anointed" [Christ], God's righteousness, mercy, calling, and so forth) not to mention the coloring and reconstruction of all the memories of the Jewish teacher of Nazareth. This may not be God's "invasion of the cosmos," but it is an invasion of the world of human religious thinking, speaking, and believing. It is a thoroughly historical process. This is how a revelation that is not only existential but also historical takes place. God is not understood to act here for the first time or for the last; God does not stop acting. But his acting can never again be perceived or understood in the same way as before. This process of revision, this "creative reformulating of inherited images and metaphors,"[81] this ferment that has been set in motion by this compelling datum and produces what can first be called by the historian distinctively *Christian* ways of speaking about God, about righteousness, sin, mercy, God's people, and so forth, does not all take place at one point in Paul. It keeps happening, in historically contingent ways: one way here in Galatians where the Teachers introduce Abraham into the discourse, another way in 1 and 2 Corinthians, another way in Romans. Thus Paul himself says that *God* is at work in the process ("event") of human persuasion and confessing. In an important sense, Paul is not an "autodidact"; he is a θεοδίδακτος ("God-taught") and he calls his converts θεοδίδακτοι because God has been present and active in their learning what it really means to love one another (1 Thess 4:9). How has God been present? Through the preaching of Christ crucified/risen, which is not unrelated to "the spirit of Christ" (= "the Spirit of him who raised Jesus from the dead" = "Christ in you" [Rom 8:11]).

Pauline theology, I have tried to suggest, is what emerged in these successive contingent "persuasion-events," not above or behind historical contin-

79. Keck, "Paul as Thinker," 28; emphasis added.
80. Küng, *On Being a Christian,* 361: "'He who raised Jesus from the dead' becomes practically the designation of the Christian God."
81. Campbell, "Contribution of Traditions to Paul's Theology," 254.

gency but in each act of αἰχμαλωτίζειν πᾶν νόημα εἰς τὴν ὑπακοὴν τοῦ Χριστοῦ (2 Cor 10:5). This phrase is not unlike that other one that has caused so much discussion: ἡ πίστις τοῦ Χριστοῦ ("the faith of Christ"),[82] and may

82. Translations vary as one takes the genitive τοῦ Χριστοῦ ("of Christ") as a subjective genitive, an objective genitive, or an adjectival genitive (or genitive of quality), respectively. A similar ambivalence or ambiguity of a genitive after ὑπακοή may be seen in Rom 1:5. For the so-called objective genitive after nouns whose cognate verbs are not transitive, i.e., which do not take a direct object in the accusative, see BDF § 168. The word πίστις is one of these nouns because the verb πιστεύειν is transitive only in the meaning "to entrust" (followed by two accusatives), but not when it means "to trust, believe" (followed by a dative or a prepositional phrase). The "objective genitive" after such nouns, strictly speaking a misnomer, is best translated by using the same prepositional construction as is used with the cognate verb form—e.g., "faith *in*," "trust *in*," and "reliance *upon*."

The debate over the construal of the genitive τοῦ Χριστοῦ in the Pauline expression πίστις τοῦ Χριστοῦ has been extensive and vigorous. See, e.g., Richard B. Hays, "ΠΙΣΤΙΣ and Pauline Christology: What Is at Stake?" in *Pauline Theology IV*, 35–60; James D. G. Dunn, "Once More, ΠΙΣΤΙΣ ΧΡΙΣΤΟΥ," in *Pauline Theology IV*, 61–81; and Paul J. Achtemeier, "Apropos the Faith of/in Christ: A Response to Hays and Dunn," in *Pauline Theology IV*, 82–92.

It seems to me that this whole discussion has been muddied by our social setting, more specifically by the freight we carry from church history and its confessional wars, from the Crusades to the Reformation, during and as a result of which faithfulness and trust have become *Glaubensbekenntnis*, a confessional *act*, and (even worse) "faith" has become "saving faith," "justifying faith."

Thus Dunn ("Once More," 69), for example, counters Hays's argument for the subjective genitive: "It now appears that a text (Galatians), which has provided such a powerful charter of 'justifying faith' for Christian self-understanding, *nowhere* clearly speaks of that 'faith'" (emphasis original). Such an argument has more apparent force than real because Paul nowhere speaks of *faith* as justifying. It is *God* who justifies, even in the case of Abraham.

When referring to Gal 2:20, Dunn rightly points to the clause "who loved me and gave himself for me" as reproducing or echoing the πίστις formulas (i.e., the ὅτι formulas we find with the verb πιστεύειν), and he then infers that the governing πίστις τοῦ υἱοῦ τοῦ θεοῦ describes "confessional faith, rather than the act of Christ's faithfulness" (ibid., 73). There would be no argument for me if Dunn had written that πίστις here denotes (human) reliance on the Son of God "who loved me and gave himself for me." The issue has not yet been exactly defined when identified as an issue of subjective versus objective genitive; the issue (to use another set of categories from the history of theology) concerns what really "saves" in Paul's theology: *that on which* I rely, or *my reliance* on it (*fides quae* or *fides qua*).

That is why I am troubled by what seems to me too easy an equation of "faith(fulness)" and "obedience"—that is, of "faith" and "faithfulness"—in Achtemeier's argument (e.g., "Apropos the Faith," 85, 88). This pushes Paul's use of πίστις consistently in the direction of Hebrews ("faithfulness"), where there are "heroes" of faith, and away from the center of Paul's own usage ("trust"). There is a significant difference here between *faithfulness*, as a reflection and imitation of God's faithfulness (Hebrews), and *trust*, as that human reliance that is the fitting counterpart to God's reliability and trustworthiness (Paul).

If we could see this more clearly—that for Paul it is not human relying and trusting that saves, but the God on whose faithfulness we can rely or set our trust (Paul's punctiliar aorist ἐπιστεύσαμεν in Gal 2:16)—we might be able to allay somewhat Dunn's fears that we leave Paul no word for human trust, Hays's fears that we are removing the theocentric dimension of the

be rendered "taking captive every thought, concept, category and conviction to the obedience of Christ/to obedience to Christ/to Christian obedience." It is the resulting outcome, which can only set the pattern for subsequent generations but remains before us for our continuing profit and reflection, that is "Pauline theology."

---

revelation of God's righteousness from these key references to trust in God's Messiah, and Achtemeier's worries that we might be divorcing obedience and faith for Paul.

Jesus' "obedience" is not the key christological category in Paul that it is in the Synoptics, John, and Hebrews. It appears only in Rom 5 and Phil 2. In the former, it is the contrast between Adam and Christ as apocalyptic *Schicksalträger* that governs the argument. In the latter, it is not at all certain that ὑπήκοος (with no modifier and no "objective genitive") means obedience to God. If anything, it means something more like submission (i.e., to the human condition) than faithfulness. Paul's Jesus is much less a Promethean believer than he is the vulnerable but vindicated sufferer who looks to God alone for vindication. It is not he but Abraham who provides for Paul the defining model of human trust.

CHAPTER 8

THE HOLY SPIRIT
IN THE PAULINE LETTERS:
A CONTEXTUAL EXPLORATION*

Anyone who is interested in determining what may be found in the New Testament to guide contemporary reflection about the Holy Spirit and who consults
a reasonably detailed lexicon or encyclopedia article under the heading "Spirit"
is immediately confronted by at least two circumstances.

The first is the great variety of meanings with which the Greek term *pneuma*
was used in the ancient world. These include breath or wind as an invisible yet
sensible phenomenon; the animating principle known by the life it imparts to
living creatures; an aspect of the human self, especially its inner side unavail-
able to sense perception and yet central to its identity as a self and to its knowing, feeling, and willing; a state of mind or disposition; an independent reality,
transcending the human and benevolent or malevolent in its working; and that
divine element or power which is reserved to God and distinguishes God from
all that is not God. Such range of meaning is the most striking feature of the terminological occurrences of both the Greek and Hebrew words we translate into
English as "spirit," and it is not confined to any single linguistic, cultural, or
religious tradition. Across the board, the most exalted use of these terms to refer
to transcendent divine reality seems scarcely ever to lose touch entirely with
the etymological origins that tie them to "wind, breath, air" or to lose that peculiar attachment to the world of experience or sense that comes from their application to perceived or felt phenomena of power—whether the experience of
having power or that of being touched or controlled or possessed by power. The
New Testament does not seem to differ at this point significantly from the
Judaism, Gnosticism, or Stoicism of its time. The problem in defining or clarifying the notion of spirit is a problem that is given for any religious movement
as soon as it uses this term for something more than air or the animating breath
of created life as such, that is, when it uses the term theologically.[1] The issues
then become a matter of reflection upon the ways in which God and his transcendence are related to human existence and experience in the world. As

---

*This essay was first published in *Int* 33 (1979): 3–18. It is reproduced here with revisions, and
by permission.
1. Cf. Eduard Schweizer, *"Pneuma, Pneumatikos, ktl," TDNT* 6:389.

Rudolf Bultmann has written, "This, then, constitutes the concept of *pneuma:* it is the miraculous—insofar *as that takes place in the sphere of human* life— either in what men do or in what is done to them."[2] If one leaves to one side the unquestionably anthropological and demonological uses of *pneuma,* the theological context for a discussion of God's Spirit or the Holy Spirit is thus unavoidably set within reflection upon the relation of the divine to the human, of God's transcendence to his presence and power in the world, of the eschatological to the historical.

The second observation compelled upon the reader of the usual encyclopedic discussion of "Spirit" in the Bible is that the New Testament draws heavily for its terminology and conceptualizations upon its background and shares the latter's diversity. There is little, if anything, distinctively Christian about either the language used of the Holy Spirit or the notions of Spirit found in the New Testament. One may catalog the continuities and discontinuities varyingly displayed by its writers at this level with the different traditions and currents present in their religious world, so far as we know them; the result is the same baffling lexicographical variety and the same confusion concerning the category or concept of the Spirit with which one began. But in view of what has already been said, this should occasion no surprise. The problem of understanding the Holy Spirit in the New Testament is a matter of exploring how these writers use the language of their world in relating God, his transcendence, his presence, and his power to their existence and experience. Such exploration can be carried out only in the context of interpreting the thought and argument in which each one of them seeks to elaborate his own distinctive understanding and application of the Christian gospel. It is not the words or the concepts but the problems of Christian understanding at issue for each writer in his time that must come first if we are to discover those distinctive assertions of the New Testament that can affect reflection fruitfully in our time.

On such terms we can hope to accomplish no more than an initial investigation of the undisputed letters of Paul. Of course we may choose to begin with him simply because of his commanding place in the development of the doctrine of the Holy Spirit in the history of Christian theology. But there is another reason for beginning here, and it constitutes the thesis of this essay: While there is little, if anything, distinctively Christian about either the language about the Holy Spirit or the notions of Spirit found even in Paul, *these become distinctively Christian precisely when they are related, and by virtue of being related, to the figure of Jesus Christ*—in Paul's terms, to the pattern of death and resurrection that is central to his credo. This is how Paul relates the powerful presence of God in and to the experience and existence of Christians in their

---

2. Rudolf Bultmann, *Theology of the New Testament*, 2 vols. (New York: Charles Scribner's Sons, 1951–55), 1:153–54; italics altered.

everyday life in the world. If this can be shown to be the case in Paul's letters, it will affect our discussion of the Holy Spirit in all its ramifications, as we reflect further upon the relation of the Spirit to God and his power, to salvation, to the individual, to the worshiping community, to the sacraments, and so on.

Such an approach requires above all close attention to the contexts in which Paul refers to the Spirit. Each letter, and often each of several parts of what has come to us as a single letter, has its own historical context; and ideally each one should be taken in detail and in turn. The space available here compels a more modest aim: Respecting the integrity of each larger theological context, what connections may we find Paul himself establishing as he refers to the Spirit of God, and what may emerge from these for our appreciation of its reality and significance in his theology? Where these show recurring patterns, we need not hesitate to group passages from different contexts together, for these will suggest characteristic features of Paul's understanding that remain his own as he moves from one context to another and that transcend each immediate occasion for writing.

We may begin with Romans. This letter presents Paul's most reflective and synthetic argument, least controlled by a specific crisis in the congregation addressed and most directly motivated by his own expository intent to make himself and his gospel understood. While we should not expect everything in the other letters to be entirely consistent with what we find here, there are good reasons for believing that this letter incorporates insights and conclusions that emerged for Paul from the separate polemical encounters that preceded its writing in his career.[3] It can therefore most quickly put us in touch with what we have referred to as his characteristic understanding.

1. Romans 5:5 is notable for its relative neglect in exegetical discussions of our topic. This section of Romans (vv. 1–11) interprets justification as access to grace opened up through Jesus Christ and as enabling "confidence" about future salvation (vv. 2 and 11; beginning and end). Such confidence has the form of hope of sharing in the glory of God, a hope that will not "put to shame" (i.e., turn out to be false and so expose to ultimate embarrassment those who have followed it) because God has already demonstrated his unparalleled love for humanity in Christ's death for the ungodly, a death interpreted in terms of reconciliation. Such confidence produces staying power in an as yet unredeemed life of affliction and testing (vv. 3–4). The translators' use of such English expressions as "to rejoice" (RSV), "to be filled with joyful trust" (JB), "to exult" (NEB), for all their appropriateness, hides the remarkable fact that Paul uses

---

3. The arguments underlying such an assessment of Romans are briefly set forth in Günther Bornkamm, *Paul* (New York: Harper & Row, 1971), 88–96. A more detailed presentation is given in his "Der Römerbrief als Testament des Paulus," in *Geschichte und Glaube,* vol. 2 (Munich: Kaiser, 1971), 120–39.

throughout the same Greek verb translated elsewhere "to boast," the very stance said in 3:27–31 to have been excluded through and for faith. What is there an illegitimate confidence, a claim on God for special treatment and a denial that God is the God of all people, is here in chapter 5 the legitimate refuge of the reconciled enemy of God when he or she takes recourse to what the God of all human beings, especially of sinners, has done on their behalf.

In this generally clear passage Paul makes in v. 5 both the first mention of the Holy Spirit in his positive argument (only 1:4 and 2:29 precede) and also the first mention of *agapē,* love. Nowhere else in the Greek Bible is God's *love* said to be "poured out" (once, in Sir 18:11, his mercy, *eleos,* is so spoken of; frequently it is his wrath). This language, however, is simply conventional for God's *Spirit.* It does not seem unreasonable to conclude that Paul, *speaking* about God's love, is *thinking* about God's Spirit; that is the clue to the importance of this passage for our topic. For this easy interchange of language means that the Christian's experience of the Spirit, and of the demonstration of God's love in the death of his Son as a sustaining power that comes to the Christian from outside himself, are here scarcely distinguishable sides of one and the same reality. In the language of a modern theologian, "Faith perceives God in Christ and this perception is itself the power of the Spirit."[4]

One may note in passing the fateful implications (whatever the causes) of Luther's firm attachment to the interpretation of "the love of God" in this verse as an objective genitive, referring to human love for God (*purissima affectio in Deum*), contrary to the clear evidence provided by verse 8.[5] On such a reading, the relationship between the Holy Spirit and love becomes entirely different: The power of the Spirit is a healing power that enables men and women to love God and so to fulfill the law. The consequences may be illustrated by the difference this shift makes for identifying the gift received in the sacrament of the Lord's Table. In the one case it is the sustaining power in this life of God's demonstration of his love; in the other it is a supernatural, transforming power that enables the recipient to lead a transcendent life.

2. It is an accepted fact that Rom 8 resumes themes struck in chapter 5, and it is here that the next references to both love and Spirit occur. The one intervening reference to "Spirit" in 7:6 belongs with 2:29 but serves also to define the context of 8:1–11. The contrast it draws between serving "in the oldness of the letter" and "in the newness of the Spirit" sums up the contrasts of 7:1–6 (the illustration of the married woman) and anticipates those of 8:2. The inclu-

4. Jürgen Moltmann, *The Church in the Power of the Spirit* (New York: Harper & Row, 1977), 33.

5. Martin Luther, *Lectures on Romans,* trans. and ed. Wilhelm Pauck (Philadelphia: Westminster, 1961), 162. Luther is here following the interpretation given this verse by Augustine, *The Spirit and the Letter,* 5, 42, and 56 (*Augustine: Later Works,* trans. and ed. John Burnaby [Philadelphia: Westminster, 1955], 198, 226, and 241).

sio thus created by 7:6 and 8:2 serves at the same time to set Rom 8 over against 7:7–25.

The last phrase of 8:2 ("the law of sin and death") can be interpreted as a shorthand summary of Paul's description in 7:7–25 of life under law from a Christian perspective, for that description consists of an account of the way in which the Mosaic law (holy and "spiritual") is used by sin as a power to effect death. The other phrase of 8:2 ("the law of the Spirit of life in Christ Jesus") appears to be formulated as an ad hoc parallel to this; so interpreted, as shorthand for the way in which the law, on the contrary, functions under the Spirit as power in order to produce life, it serves admirably to introduce 8:1–11. After 8:3, 4, 7, the law drops from view until the quite different discussion of 9:30–10:13. But before it disappears, it is clear that law and Spirit are linked; in the face of the incapacity and weakness of the law, one purpose served by the sending of God's Son is "that the just requirement of the law might be fulfilled in us, who walk not according to the flesh but according to the Spirit" (RSV). The law stands for the holy, just will of God (as in 7:12, 14); the life made possible by the Spirit is neither simply one of ecstatic freedom nor one transformed into a transcendent mode but is a fruitful commitment (7:4) in which the whole fabric of human allegiance is set right but not disintegrated. Only on such terms as these can an argument be concluded that began (Rom 1–2) with an impartial God whose righteousness and sovereignty are to be acknowledged by human beings if their relationship to him as the Creator is to have integrity. Verses 5–8 digress somewhat to elaborate on the continuing opposition of "Spirit" and "flesh." The Spirit, however, is here no merely mechanical force operating upon human beings; its reality creates for those who "are according to the flesh" a new "mind-set" which is not inimical to God and so prevented from submitting to God's will. We are thus not far removed from the starting point in Rom 5:5 where the effect on human life of the experience of the Spirit as the sustaining power of God's demonstration of his love in the Son is interpreted as the reconciliation of hostility. But there is now more emphasis on power; the present argument implies that this Spirit is a power operating in defiance of the power of sin and in place of the powerlessness of the law to produce liberation, life, and peace (vv. 2, 6).

This indirect implication comes to direct expression in vv. 9–11, which are truly central to our topic. Verse 10 is often mistranslated. I read it as follows: "But if Christ is in you, the body [i.e., your bodily existence] is, to be sure [concessive clause], dead [i.e., subject to the power of death] because of sin, but the Spirit is life for the sake of righteousness" (not: "your spirits are alive because of righteousness," RSV). The apparent parallel to the anthropological term "body" is not sufficient ground for interpreting *pneuma* here as also anthropological rather than as God's Spirit, in violation of the train of thought; when that shift is made in v. 16, it is clearly marked by the possessive "our." The sustaining parallels of the verse are rather death and life, sin and righteousness. The Spirit *is* life because it produces life (v. 11; this the law cannot do) just as sin produces death; and this the Spirit does for the sake of producing righteousness (telic *dia* with the accusative, as in 1 Cor 11:9), which is the fulfillment of the "just requirement" mentioned in v. 4.

The most remarkable feature of these verses is the apparently promiscuous interchanging of "God's Spirit," "Christ's Spirit," "the Spirit of him who raised Jesus from the dead," and "Christ in you" (this last is related to "belonging to him" just before). But v. 11 clarifies the possible confusion: the Spirit is a third power, the life-giving power of God by which he raised Jesus from the dead, operating already in the Christian toward the future ultimate defeat of present mortality in such a way as to liberate the Christian life now from its past patterns of obligation (vv. 12–13). The "logic" of these interrelationships of death and life, present and future, bondage and freedom parallels precisely that presented in Rom 6:6–11, especially in the persistence of the eschatological reservation which locates the resurrection life in the temporal future. What is new is that here the Spirit (not mentioned in ch. 6) as the creator of the new life dominates (the categories are more dynamic), whereas there it was the death of Jesus as the annihilation of the old that was primary (the categories were more juridical). The pattern of Jesus Christ's death and life is present, however, in both passages and binds them together.

Thus an understanding of Spirit that began in chapter 5 as indistinguishable from the sustaining power of the demonstration of God's love in the midst of affliction has been clearly identified with God's power by which he raised Jesus from the dead, and so shielded from too *subjective* an interpretation. At the same time, this Spirit emerges as the power of a new obedience to God and submission to his law free of the hostility that corrupts obedience into the securing of a person's own righteousness. It is a delivering power because where it operates in this way God's law is no longer the instrument by which sin holds human beings in its power (ch. 7). In the running course of the argument the term "Spirit" almost visibly fills with meaning: not only the power of God who shows his love in Christ's death and his power to give life in Christ's resurrection, but also the powerful presence of this Jesus who embraces us in his death and life and so takes us into the power by which he has been made alive ("Christ in you," "the Spirit of Christ"). This is another way of saying that in Jesus God has done what the law was powerless to do: to meet sin as power. But it says it in a new way that makes it clear that the felt effects, in human liberation and changed allegiance, of what God has done are just how God's power to give life, his Spirit, works in us.

But how this power of God is understood is crucial. If the identification of this power as God's prevents a too subjective interpretation of it, the close connection of this power with Christ and the pattern of Jesus' death and resurrection prevents a too triumphalist and otherworldly reading of it. For there is no suggestion that this power "makes Christians new creatures."[6] Its transforming force is promissory, operating not by transforming the Christian life into a supernatural one but by identifying the Christian with Christ ("Christ in you"). The resulting identity of destiny, already established and attested to as an identity in his death by baptism, *will become* (an eschatological future [Rom 5:10; 6:8]) and *ought to become* (an imperatival "future" pressing itself upon the present [Rom 6:4, 11]) an identity also in his life. The power of him who raised Jesus from the dead is the power that has made him Lord of human life (i.e., the one qualified to shape and direct it) in *this* world. That is why Paul does *not* say in 8:10b "your spirits are alive because of righteousness," as though a kind of "partial" resurrection were already realized.

From the slight rise in terrain we have thus gained, we can observe a number of further points that will now look familiar, that can now be seen in their relationships to each other, and that can now be noted more briefly even though they are no less important.

3. If God's power is not simply identified with human subjectivity, its experience and operation nevertheless are located in concrete human existence (Rom 8:12–27). To be "sons of God" (a claim made by Christian fanatics in all ages in the name of religious experience) is to be controlled by this power (8:14); the *habitus* ("mind-set," vv. 5–8) it produces is that of sonship in contrast to slavery and fear. But in describing the way in which it produces this, Paul shifts from the dynamic category of "being led" back to the juridical category (as opposed to a substantial one) of attestation or witness and returns once again in v. 17 to the root christological pattern that reserves transformation to the eschatological future. The Spirit is the spirit of sonship not because it transforms human beings into divine ones but because it enables persons to call God "Father" (v. 15, instrumental *en*). Galatians 4:4 and 6, where the terms "Spirit," "Son," "sonship," "slavery," "Father," and "heir" reappear in such similar association as to suggest a recurring pattern of exposition, sets up an express parallelism between God's "sending" of his Son and his "sending" of the Spirit that makes this sonship present and real to those who are sons. The two are correlative but cannot be collapsed into each other. It is important to note that this enabling result of the Spirit's presence is frequently communal as well as individual; it is not private. The inspired utterance that acclaims God as Father may be the liturgical response of the assembly; the movement of the "Spirit itself" (Rom 8:16, 26) in the congregation may thus be a transpersonal confirmation

---

6. The phrase comes from Bultmann, *Theology of the New Testament,* 1:159. The context is Bultmann's discussion of the theology not of Paul but of Hellenistic and "gnosticizing" Christians; the extent to which the Pauline passages here cited by Bultmann show that Paul shared such views is just what is uncertain.

of the gift of this presence of God's power to each individual. The Spirit's work in prophecy has a similar cultic context in 1 Cor 14:14–25. The Spirit's "intercession" assists in prayer, enabling it in spite of human weakness and ignorance to be "in accord with God" (Rom 8:27). This whole context is particularly important for showing that the Spirit-endowed community ("not only the creation but we too who have the firstfruits of the Spirit," v. 23) is not exempted from the world's "sighing" but only the more closely identified with it, for the Spirit itself participates in this sighing in its intercession. The distance between the world and God is not collapsed but heightened in this intensified dependence upon God's power in prayer. Therein is reaffirmed the supporting presence of God himself, the searcher of human hearts, but it is a presence with vulnerable human beings.

4. Such language about the Spirit as a forensic divine defender and supporter for a beleaguered community draws on a tradition that surfaces also in the Paraclete sayings of the Fourth Gospel and in the Synoptic Gospels (Mark 13:11; Matt 10:17–22, where it is taken out of Mark's apocalyptic context and made part of the discourse on discipleship; and Luke 12:12; cf. 21:15). It reappears in a striking way in Phil 1:19, where Paul, anticipating legal proceedings in which his life is at stake, counts on the prayers of the Philippians and on the "supporting provision" or "subvention"[7] of the Spirit of Jesus Christ to ensure that he will not be "put to shame." The unusual precision of language here seems to mean that the Spirit is quite specifically "the Spirit which will enable Paul to testify to Christ"[8] (cf. Matt 10:19) in this public forum, not only orally but in his person (*sōma*), no matter whether the outcome for him is life or death. The same language, in verbal form, is used in Gal 3:5 in the attribution of God as "the one who provides the support of the Spirit to you and works miracles among you" (my translation).

5. There is nothing surprising now about the way in which the "Holy Spirit" appears in perfect parallelism with "power" and "full assurance, conviction" to describe the way in which the gospel is present to its hearers (1 Thess 1:5–6). Specifically the effect of the Spirit's operation here is that the acceptance of the preached word is accompanied with "much joy." Similarly in Gal 5:5, the Spirit is the instrumentality or supporting power by which Christians are said to await in faith the hope of (hoped-for) righteousness.

6. If the experience of God's life-giving power is thus located in concrete human experience, it does not destroy or displace the ordinary processes of human decision-making and existence but operates to enable their proper functioning. If this Spirit is the instrumentality of right conduct and so of life (Rom

7. The latter translation for *epichoregia* is drawn from J.-F. Collange, *L'épître de Saint Paul aux Philippiens* (Neuchâtel: Delachaux & Niestlé, 1973), 58.
8. Ibid.

8:13), as the instrumentality of life it is also that of right conduct (Gal 5:25). No sharp line can be drawn between instrumentality and norm, between "to walk by the Spirit" (Gal 5:16), to be "led by [or in] the Spirit" (v. 18), and to be "according to the Spirit" (Rom 8:5). The line that counts is the one that contrasts all these to being (Rom 8:5), living (v. 12), and walking (Rom 8:4; 2 Cor 10:2) "according to the flesh." What this contrast means can be spelled out only by Paul's own linguistic substitutions, of which we may cite a few examples. The first is equivalent to "serving one another in love" and so fulfilling the law (Gal 5:13); it is "not to gratify the desire of the flesh" (singular, Gal 5:16; probably not the desires awakened by the flesh but the "intentionality" of which the flesh is the producer and the source; cf. v. 17 and Rom 8:6); it is "to serve God and rest one's confidence in Jesus Christ and not in the flesh" (Phil 3:3). "Flesh" on the contrary, in this last passage, is very specifically physical circumcision and the whole complex of illusory and destructive religious confidence that rests upon it. Orientation to it is that orientation to the law as the source of life which submitting to circumcision signifies for the Galatians (5:3); it is to "be under law" (5:18), to derive from the law a false understanding of justification as "a righteousness of my own" (Phil 3:9).

Are flesh and Spirit contrasting powers, demonic and divine respectively? The issue is important because if they are, the effect of the Spirit might seem to be the suppression or crippling of true human response. Galatians 5:17 and Rom 8:5–8 seem to suggest such a conclusion by their personifying language, to reduce the human self to the neutral booty in dispute between these powers, helplessly passive to their conflict, the more so as each is identified in Galatians by a catalog of the results that follow from it. Against such a conclusion, however, we may note that the context for these catalogs is set by the imperatives of Gal 5:16, which reaffirm by implication human responsibility in the setting and determination of allegiance (such close but paradoxical joining of human choice and fateful consequence reappears in Rom 6:12–13, 16, 19). Moreover, the catalogs list the "manifest works" (Gal 6:8) of the flesh but the "fruit" (singular) of the Spirit, suggesting that the first results arise from the intention of human beings to justify themselves and that the second series is in the nature of a gift not available to human control.[9] And, most importantly, Paul never speaks of flesh as power in the way in which he speaks of Spirit. Flesh is associated rather with weakness and insufficiency. Despite the personifying language of Gal 5:17 and Rom 8:5–8, "flesh" is human nature in its own desires and intentions and "hostility," as it is in itself apart from God's power, in the orientations and values that come naturally to it. The undeniable tension between fateful passivity and responsive activity in these passages does justice to the paradoxes of freedom and fatefulness in human existence, to the persisting and

9. Cf. Schweizer, *"Pneuma,"* 431.

self-perpetuating inevitabilities that follow from human choices of commitment and allegiance. Such a view draws deeply from a Jewish tradition in the understanding of sin. But in that tradition it is sin, not flesh, that is assigned demonic initiative and power.[10] Just for that reason the catechetical imperatives invite Paul's readers to open themselves to that profound change which consists in reorientation toward Jesus Christ and is possible only by virtue of the Spirit as the presence of *God's* liberating power vis-à-vis the power of sin. But just because this Spirit is God's, these imperatives operate also as divine sanctions. The one who refuses these imperatives, aimed toward sanctification in contrast to impurity, "refuses not man but the God who gives his *holy* Spirit into you" (1 Thess 4:7–8 [my translation], echoing Ezek 36:27; cf. also 1 Cor 3:16).

7. On three occasions Paul refers to the "firstfruits" (Rom 8:23, a harvest metaphor applied elsewhere to Christ, to first converts, and to Israel) or "promissory down payment" (2 Cor 1:22; 5:5; cf. Eph 1:14) of the Spirit. These metaphors do not mean that the Spirit is given partially now in anticipation or place of a full endowment of the same later on. The Spirit is itself the "firstfruits," anticipatory of redemption ("of our bodies," Rom 8:23, quite in line with what we have seen in Rom 8:11). In the second metaphor (the contexts of both occurrences allude to baptism) the sense is that the Spirit provides confirming surety, to God's "Yes" in Jesus Christ (2 Cor 1:22) or to God's provision of a future life free from death (2 Cor 5:5). Even this last difficult passage on the future life is not to be read in abstraction from Paul's Christology. J.-F. Collange argues persuasively that its point lies in the hope of the overgarment of the "man from heaven" which shall cover the present garment of the crucified Jesus that the Christian has already "put on" in baptism, "so that what is mortal may be swallowed up by life" (v. 4).[11] Its underlying theological structure relating present and future, the historical and the eschatological, is thus strikingly similar to Rom 6:1–11 and 8:11.

Caution is thus at least advisable against defining the Spirit as "the eschatological gift" or "the power of futurity."[12] To do so may result in reading Acts 2, with its use of the Joel prophecy, into Paul or hearing Paul in a manner (the Corinthians') he explicitly repudiates. The gift of the Spirit is not for Paul a partial resurrection, as baptism is not. It does not heal a "defect" in human nature

---

10. For a fuller discussion of the joining of fatefulness and freedom (guilt) in the Jewish understanding of sin, see Ernst Käsemann's discussion of Rom 5:12, *An die Römer* (Tübingen: Mohr [Siebeck], 1973), 138–39 (ET: *Commentary on Romans*, trans. and ed. Geoffrey W. Bromiley [Grand Rapids: Eerdmans, 1980], 147–49). For the difference in Paul between Spirit as power and flesh as power or weakness, see Eduard Schweizer, *"Sarx," TDNT* 7:131–34.

11. J.-F. Collange, *Enigmes de la deuxième épître de Paul aux Corinthiens* (Cambridge: Cambridge University Press, 1972), 199–225.

12. See, e.g., Bultmann, *Theology of the New Testament,* 1:335.

(as in Augustine's interpretation of Rom 5:5, referred to earlier). Of course we have seen in Rom 8:11 that this presence of "the power of him who raised Jesus from the dead" operates toward the future ultimate defeat of present mortality. But this transforming force is rooted in the promissory pattern of Jesus' crucifixion and resurrection, which clamps life to death; and it consists in making this Jesus present as the Lord of human existence in *this* world, both to liberate and to elicit allegiance, the two complementary aspects of the same lordship. Paul's Christology everywhere provides the context for his *pneumatology.*

One might wonder whether this reading of Paul is contradicted by 2 Cor 5:17, but it is not. Whether here v. 17 follows directly upon 15 or upon 16 (if there is a parenthesis in v. 16, it consists only of v. 16b, and v. 17 then follows from v. 16a), the conjunctions of sequential reasoning show that the newness of the "new creation" is a transformation not of substance but of perception and relationship; the next verses speak of "reconciliation." The change is grounded in the way in which, since "one has died for all," "all have died." That is how "what is old has passed away; behold, it has become new and fresh."

8. Another quite distinct set of assertions, of immense significance in the history of the doctrine of the Spirit, is found in 1 Cor 2:10–16. The Spirit appears here as the revelatory agent of God, the imparter of wisdom and insight into the mysteries ("depths") of God. The language employed here, unquestionably evoked by the Corinthian situation, reverberates to a wide spectrum of Hellenistic religion, including wisdom tradition, apocalyptic, Qumran, Stoicism, and Gnosticism, especially where and as it speaks of revelation. There is no critique of this language; it is used to refute the pretensions of the Corinthians. There is nothing here fundamentally inconsistent with what we have seen so far, or to justify the assertion that Paul joins the Hellenists so far as to "regard the Spirit as the power which takes man out of this aeon and sets him in that aeon."[13] Spirit is the divinely given efficacy that *enables* Christian insight, but what counts is the content thus revealed, "the gifts bestowed on us by God" (v. 12). If this content is interpreted with the help of the notion of a preexistent wisdom, that only radicalizes the gift character of this revelation. The same effect is produced by the use of the ancient principle "like by means of like"

---

13. The words are those of Eduard Schweizer, who refers to 1 Cor 2:6 in their support (*"Pneuma,"* 425). He immediately qualifies them by pointing to Paul's "decisive correction" to this notion, but the correction is so decisive as to throw the main assertion into serious doubt. The issue appears to me to be whether it is really possible to hold to the long-established and conventional dictum that for Paul the Christian has been transported into "the age to come." Paul nowhere makes such a claim, and his attachment to the so-called doctrine of the two ages is too loose to allow us to infer the claim from what he does say. This is an instance of the problem underlying the whole of the present argument: To what extent are we compelled on the basis of certain formal features of his language, by lexicography, to attribute to Paul views that the inner movements of his arguments repudiate?

and of the dualism of "natural" and "spiritual" (*psychikos* and *pneumatikos*). This latter dualism functions in the same way as the opposition of flesh and Spirit in Rom 8:5–8, to set the results of the Spirit's working sharply apart from all immanent capacities available to human insight from its own resources and by the world's standards. But the content of the divine mystery and wisdom, far from being some secret celestial knowledge, is the "folly" of the cross, so that the "mind of the Lord" in the concluding citation from Isa 40:13 is displaced by the "mind of Christ."[14]

The context of 1 Corinthians makes it clear that the effect of this Spirit-endowed insight is not to remove Christians from the world but to engage them more fully and realistically within it. Even the Hellenistic distinctions between *psychikos* and *pneumatikos*, between babes and mature ("perfect"), give way to Paul's more habitual contrasts between flesh and Spirit, between the conduct natural to ordinary human beings and the conduct that accords with his gospel and that all those to whom the Spirit has been given in baptism (6:11) ought to display in their daily relationships (3:1–4).

9. The "Spirit of holiness" (Rom 1:4b) belongs in a category by itself. Not a Pauline phrase, this occurrence of "Spirit" stems from a hymnic and creedal tradition and is paralleled by 1 Tim 3:16 and 1 Pet 3:18. "Spirit" and "flesh" appear here to contrast a heavenly, divine "sphere" of reality to an earthly, human one (cf. Isa 31:3); in christological terms they distinguish two aspects of Jesus' sonship, his earthly lineage and his resurrection status, which in this formula also represent successive stages in the Son's movement. The closest Pauline linguistic parallels are the qualifications of the sons of Hagar and Sarah in Gal 4 as "born according to the flesh" and "born through the promise, . . . according to the Spirit" (vv. 23 and 29). The literature on Rom 1:4 is extensive and the debate over how Paul has edited his tradition protracted, but in one way or another his editing has produced the kind of correlation of Spirit, resurrection, and power that confirms our previous emphasis on Rom 8:11. If Spirit and flesh are in this creedal language to be read more precisely as "spheres" of reality, we have here a link between Paul and the usage of the Fourth Gospel (John 3:6; 6:63).

10. First Corinthians 6:12–20 is a passage notable for some surprising turns of phrase. In contending that the body (*sōma*) is the locus of the Lord's claim for allegiance (v. 20) and is not to be relegated to the inconsequentiality of the transitory stomach and its foods, Paul appeals first to the parallelism of God's resurrection of the Lord (past) and of "us" (future) by his "power" (cf. "Spirit" in Rom 8:11), in order to ground the assertion that Christians' bodies are "mem-

---

14. Would Paul have thought of the "mind of the Lord" *here* if he had not been aware that the Hebrew in Isaiah is "the *rûaḥ* of *yhwh*"? Is then "the mind of Christ" a functional equivalent for "the Spirit of Christ"?

bers of Christ" and belong to him. This conclusion precludes "taking" one's self as body and making it a prostitute's, since to cleave to a prostitute is to become "one body [with her]" on the premises of Gen 2:24 ("the two shall become one *flesh*"). In contrast, "he who cleaves to the Lord is [becomes?] one *spirit* [with him?]." Some interpreters have thought Paul might have made his point just as well if he had used the term "body" again this last time, but his shift to "spirit" appears to be both deliberate and significant. (a) Unity with the Lord is never the consummation of a bodily encounter or described in sexual terms. (b) If such union is somatic, it is pneumatic first of all since it begins, as here, with the *power* of the resurrection. (c) The shift reintroduces the typical Pauline contrast between flesh and Spirit: union with the prostitute is "fleshly" and not merely "bodily" (i.e., human, cf. 3:3)—a distinction of some consolation to married folk who have trouble seeing how the logic of Paul's argument can avoid an ascetic condemnation of all sexual intercourse. And (d) *sōma* is at a person's disposal, but *pneuma* is at God's. This last comes out into the open in Paul's concluding move, which is quite similar to Rom 8:11–12: The gift of the *holy* Spirit claims the realm of bodily existence as its "temple" just as the "price" of Jesus' death claims the Christian person as God's. The implication is that what *is* at a person's disposal is to be placed at God's.

11. We must now briefly touch on a few points in Paul's debates with the Corinthians over their understanding of Spirit. The issues are posed by the phenomenon of ecstasy.

a. *1 Corinthians 12 and 14*. Paul's basic assumption throughout is that the Spirit as gift is given to all Christians. The classic reaffirmation of this appears in 12:12–13: that the unity of the corporate body of Christ results from common participation ("drinking" in baptism) in the one Spirit is structurally parallel to the unity that derives from common participation ("eating of one loaf" in the Lord's Supper [10:17]) in the benefits of Jesus' death. On premises drawn from a whole range of Hellenistic religion, however, the Corinthians (i) locate essential human nature, the true and eternal self, in *pneuma* (the corollary is to assign sexuality to an evil world, resulting in both ascetic and libertinist behavior in Corinth); and (ii) identify ecstatic phenomena as unambiguous manifestations of the direct presence of divine power to and in a select few. Here the precedents of some Old Testament and non-Pauline Christian usages of *pneuma* for miraculous and sporadic divine power certainly work in their favor. But the Corinthians understand this power also in triumphalist and substantialist terms, either as transforming human nature and transporting it in advance to its divine destination or as confirming its primordial kinship with the divine. Such understandings are utterly destructive of Paul's gospel. His concluding and climactic move against them, in 1 Cor 15, is radically to reserve the transformation of human existence by God's life-giving Spirit to the future resurrection (just as in Rom 8 and 1 Cor 6). His first move (in 1 Cor 12:3) is to make the Christian credo the test of the content of any ecstatic utterance claiming divine inspiration. In both moves, the bond between pneumatology and Christology that is broken on the Corinthians' terms is reestablished. This both qualifies the direct supernaturalism of their interpretation of *pneuma* and recalls them to a realistic acknowledgment of the finitude and mortality of human existence. Between these two moves, unable and unwilling flatly to deny the reality of divine inspiration as such, Paul develops his own understanding of "spiritual gifts."[15]

In this process Paul reaffirms the gift character of these *charismata* and the divine initiative that produces them, producing along the way a triadic formulation that anticipates the doctrine of the Trinity (12:4–11, esp. vv. 4–6). He disallows the Corinthians' restriction of inspiration to the ecstatic, a restriction that makes of it the prerogative of an elite within the community and so undermines the community-creating power of the Spirit; and he claims divine authentication instead for all the functions of the members of the body (vv. 14–31). He ties the gifts to the daily existence of the community in and for which they are given and to love as the greatest of the three things that transcend the ephemeralities of human life. Thus he derives another criterion, the "building up" of the community, to be used in adjudicating the claims that inspiration produces. In all these ways, he renews the call for responsible human behavior in this life, in place of the flight into chaos which the experience of God's power understood on their terms produces.

b. *2 Corinthians 3.* Here the situation in Corinth has worsened to the point of desperate conflict. The phenomenon of ecstasy, as the presence of "transcendent power" (2 Cor 4:7), has become both the ground and the instrument of rival claims to apostleship, even the proclamation of a rival Spirit, a rival gospel, and a rival Jesus (11:3–4). In the first of several letters that respond to this new situation, and prompted by the fact that his opponents use letters of recommendation where Paul has nothing but his churches to commend him, he contrasts letters written in ink with those written "by the Spirit of the living God," "tablets of stone" with "tablets of hearts of flesh." This leads into the contrast between a "covenant of death, carved in letters on stone," and a new "covenant of the Spirit." It produces the antithesis between "the *letter* which kills" and "the *Spirit* which makes alive" that surfaces again in Rom 2:29 and 7:6 to denote the lifeless and fruitless consequences that follow when sin's power corrupts religious tradition and the understanding of both circumcision and the law.

Given the polemical crisis that produced it and that can only be reconstructed with its aid, it is no wonder that this passage has proved immensely difficult.

---

15. Apart from a final echo in Rom 12:6, the term in this technical sense appears only in 1 and 2 Corinthians. The other occurrences, all in Romans, *could* have appeared if there had been no crisis whatever in Corinth (Rom 1:11; 5:15, 16; 6:23; 11:29), though it may be wondered whether they *would* have.

The tendency has been to read out of it or into it a fundamental polarization of the Mosaic covenant to the new and to see in the unique label Paul drops only once for the synagogue scriptures ("the old covenant," v. 14) an anticipation not only of the language that first appears in Melito of Sardis but also of the negative view of Judaism as such that has been associated with it and become conventional for Christians ever since. Worse, the language about the "veil" that lies over "their" heart and mind whenever Moses is read but is removed "when one turns to the Lord" has been universalized to refer to *all* descendants of the Israelites, to the Jew as such. Then, as though Paul were Justin Martyr or Irenaeus, this veil is taken in this universality to be both objectively the result of God's will and subjectively the responsibility of those who ignore its removal in Christ. The passage is made the warrant for the assertion that Jews read their scriptures in terms of "this age" and the "flesh," justly earning condemnation, and for an *interpretatio Christiana* that alone rightly understands the Hebrew scriptures.

Is not *our* tradition here too much with us, the tradition especially of the second-century apologists and the tradition of Luther? The issue is not whether Paul exercises freedom in his hermeneutics (often peculiarly Jewish!) or has such a thing as an *interpretatio Christiana*. The issue is not whether Paul can assign guilt for misunderstanding God's gift to his own people (Rom 9:30–32) or even find that misunderstanding to be mysteriously symptomatic of the working of God, his "gift" of a "spirit of stupor" (Rom 11:8). At issue is the fundamental credibility of Paul's appeals to his own Hebrew scripture, of his use of the exemplary faith of Abraham, of his reliance upon the "irrevocable gifts and calling of God"—in short, of his Jewish roots. And at issue is everything we have maintained and argued for so far, including by implication the value for Christian faith of careful exegesis and the historical study of both "testaments."

My space has been exhausted. Fortunately, the work of historical exegesis goes on. J.-F. Collange has written an impressive book which seems to solve this last enigma of 2 Cor 3 as follows: "their" minds refers to Paul's "Christian" opponents when they use his scriptures in a certain way; "letter" is their death-producing use of Moses' law; "Spirit" is the renewing power of God which creates a new covenant in human hearts and by which Paul exercises his ministry.[16] Neither Hellenistic nor rabbinic Judaism makes this kind of use of the radiant splendor of Moses' countenance in Exod 34:29–35; it is Paul's Christian opponents who use this text in support of a convention widespread in the history of religions, to connect divine possession and "transfiguration" with the radiant face of the ecstatic. The references to the "veil" originate in the opponents' mocking use of their proof text to deride Paul's apostleship and his gospel "veiled" under the indignities accepted by its messengers in the name of Jesus

16. Collange, *Enigmes,* 199–225, esp. 224–25.

Christ. The true intent of their text, Paul counters, is not to promote ecstasy but to bring people to turn away from seeking their own glory and to God (*kyrios* in 3:16 refers to YHWH, as in most Pauline citations of the LXX). Thus v. 17 begins Paul's exegesis of it (in form it is like 1 Cor 10:4 and 15:56), v. 18 completes it, and 4:1–6 expounds it. The Lord of their text is his God and theirs. His Spirit is the transformer of human hearts. The change it produces is a transformation not of the faces of some but of the hearts of all. Its model ("image," 4:4) is Christ, not Moses. It is progressive, not instantaneous. And its locus is the cult in which the glory of God is perceived immediately ("with unveiled face," without all the mysteries of the opponents) in the crucified and risen Lord. It is by this glory that the Christian is transformed toward glory, as by the Spirit and power of God himself. To this transformation Moses himself, rightly understood, invites the Corinthians to turn. In short, Paul is urging that it will be by turning to Jesus that his fellow Christians in Corinth will properly understand the transforming power and presence of Moses' God for this present human life.

CHAPTER 9

AUGUSTINE'S *THE SPIRIT AND THE LETTER* AS A READING OF PAUL'S ROMANS[*]

In the recent past, reflection on the importance of the *Wirkungsgeschichte* of religious texts (or the history of their influence) has given fresh impetus to the examination of the history of exegesis. Consideration of a text's posthistory, not only the more formal course of its interpretation as deposited in the commentaries but the much more variegated history of its effects, consequences, and repercussions in the continuing life of the community that uses it, can enrich the modern interpreter's encounter with the text in a variety of ways and so help breach that insulation from the contemporary world that seems inevitably to follow upon the necessary historical-critical discipline of locating a text in its original setting. Such consideration of the effect of a text, especially upon its interpreters, is not merely ancillary to understanding but a very part of it.[1]

Although it owes its title directly to the apostle's language (Rom 2:29; 7:6; 2 Cor 3:6), Augustine's treatise *The Spirit and the Letter* (*De spiritu et littera*) would not seem at first sight to provide a "reading" of Paul's letter to the Romans. What we have from Augustine as explicit commentary on Romans is highly fragmentary and, like so much else of his biblical interpretation, deeply imbedded in doctrinal, apologetic, and polemical argumentation.[2] This treatise,

---

[*]This essay was originally published in *The Social World of the First Christians: Essays in Honor of Wayne A. Meeks*, ed. L. Michael White and O. Larry Yarbrough (Minneapolis: Fortress, 1995), 366–81. It is reproduced here with minor modifications, by permission.

1. So concludes Ulrich Luz in the final section of the introduction to his *Matthew 1–7: A Commentary* (Minneapolis: Augsburg, 1989), 95–99. His methodological observations have been prompted in part by H. G. Gadamer's emphasis on "effective history" as an essential aspect of the historicality of human understanding (Gadamer, *Truth and Method* [New York: Seabury, 1975], 267–74). In "The Christian Proteus" (in his *The Writings of St. Paul: A Norton Critical Edition* [New York: Norton, 1972], 435–44), Wayne Meeks has summarized in an unforgettable way the results of his own vivid exhibition of the *Nachgeschichte*, or posthistory, of the letters of Paul in an anthology of responses and reactions to the apostle. Paul's texts not only provide access to the apostle, complex and elusive figure as he may be; they also shed light on and challenge his interpreters in every age.

2. See the introduction in Paula Fredriksen Landes, *Augustine on Romans: Propositions from the Epistle to the Romans; Unfinished Commentary on the Epistle to the Romans* (Chico, Calif.: Scholars Press, 1982), ix–xvi. For a brief survey of Augustine's biblical expositions, see B. Altaner, *Patrologie* (3d ed.; Freiburg: Herder, 1951), 380–82.

in one sense, is no exception; it belongs firmly, both by date and in Augustine's own retrospective view of it, to his anti-Pelagian writings.[3] It ought, therefore, to offer evidence primarily for the effects not of Paul on Augustine so much as of Augustine's theological preoccupations upon his reading of Paul. Furthermore, the treatise is strikingly absent from a number of major modern discussions of Augustine's exegesis of Paul, partly because the latter concentrate on specific theological issues or on particular passages in Romans (notably chs. 7 and 9) or on major turning points in the development of Augustine's thought, of which the writing of *The Spirit and the Letter* does not seem to have been one.[4] As a matter of fact, it is surprising, when one consults the catalogs and bibliographies, that books or articles devoted to a study of this treatise for its own sake are nearly nonexistent.

This first impression, however, needs correction. Peter Brown calls *The Spirit and the Letter* "the book which Augustine himself regarded as his most fundamental demolition of Pelagianism."[5] Yet the three richly documented and informative chapters Brown devotes to the Pelagian controversy contain only two other relatively peripheral references to this treatise. The reason is clear from Brown's own portrayal. Augustine "knew Pelagius only as an author, and he combatted him by books."[6] But *The Spirit and the Letter* is a sequel to Augustine's very first anti-Pelagian writing, On *the Consequences and Forgiveness of Sins and Baptism of Little Children,* and this in turn was Augustine's response to Marcellinus's account of the disturbance created in Carthage by Pelagius's zealous disciple, Caelestius, a response composed *before* the flood of materials to which Augustine was later to give detailed attention.[7] The point is that at this inchoative stage (411 C.E.) Augustine was confronted with questions for the answering of which he turned afresh to Paul—of course in the context of the

---

3. *Retract.* 63 (=2.37).

4. See, e.g., Paula Fredriksen, "Beyond the Body/Soul Dichotomy: Augustine on Paul against the Manichees and the Pelagians," *Recherches augustiniennes* 23 (1988): 87–114; W. S. Babcock, "Augustine's Interpretation of Romans (A.D. 394–396)," *Augustinian Studies* 10 (1979): 54–74; idem, "Augustine and Paul: The Case of Romans IX," *Studia Patristica* 16, no. 2 (1985): 473–79; Marie-François Berrouard, "L'exégèse augustinienne de Rom. 7,7–25 entre 396 et 418, avec des remarques sur les deux premières périodes de la crise 'pélagienne,'" *Recherches augustiniennes* 16 (1981): 101–96.

5. Peter Brown, *Augustine of Hippo: A Biography* (Berkeley, Calif.: University of California Press, 1967), 372. I do not know where Augustine makes this evaluation; the passage in *Retract.* 2.37, to which Brown refers, does not contain it.

6. Brown, *Augustine of Hippo*, 355.

7. Ibid., 345: "It is extremely difficult to identify the opinions and pamphlets that provided Augustine with the material for his first coherent picture of the ideas he would later ascribe directly to Pelagius." For Brown this makes all the more astonishing Augustine's quick grasp of the issues at stake: "Indeed, Pelagia*nism* as we know it, that consistent body of ideas of momentous consequences, had come into existence; but in the mind of Augustine, not of Pelagius" (ibid.). What role may Romans have played in shaping that "grasp"?

prior development of his own thought and understanding of the apostle. That the treatise has not served as a major resource for the reconstruction of Pelagius's teaching or of the main points of Augustine's response is the very reason why it invites fresh examination as a genuine act of "reading" Romans. That it belongs in the *Wirkungsgeschichte* of Romans is confirmed by the way it has served as a major vehicle for Augustine's influence upon the subsequent interpretation of Paul, most notably upon Luther and, through him, the whole of the modern history of the exegesis of Romans, but this lies outside our present concern.[8]

That *The Spirit and the Letter* deserves consideration in its own right as a reading of Romans is confirmed above all by closer analysis of the text itself. Of course, like so many writings of the church fathers, this treatise is liberally sprinkled with quotations and allusions from across the breadth of the Bible.[9] But the focus is clearly on Romans; of 171 New Testament citations and allusions, 124 are from the Pauline corpus, and over half of these (72) are from Romans. Such statistics tell only part of the story; it is the long quotations (of Romans, but also of 2 Cor 3–5, Jer 31, and Ps 103), from which verses and phrases not included in the counting are repeated in the ensuing discussion, and the *seriatim* quotation of verses, not always adjoining but nevertheless in their sequence in Paul's letter, that sustain Augustine's argument and capture him in the act of listening to his texts. With good reason, as he nears the end of the book, Augustine lays down the challenge that those who occasioned its writing will have to defend themselves "not against me, but . . . certainly against no less an apostle than Paul, speaking not in a single text but in a long argument of such power, intensity and vigilance" (61).

Since I have written a short commentary on Romans myself,[10] it is this aspect of *The Spirit and the Letter* that I have found most intriguing and that I propose to examine in what follows, by a cursory review of the structure and

8. For the indebtedness of Luther's lectures on Romans to *The Spirit and the Letter,* see Wilhelm Pauck, *Luther: Lectures on Romans,* LCC 15 (Philadelphia: Westminster, 1961), xxxiv–lxi. It is striking to what extent preoccupation with Augustine's influence on the Protestant Reformation has diverted attention in much scholarship from Augustine's own exegesis in this treatise. See, e.g., W. Anz, "Zur Exegese von Römer 7 bei Bultmann, Luther, Augustin," in *Theologia Crucis–Signum Crucis: Festschrift für Erich Dinkler zum 70. Geburtstag,* ed. Carl Andresen and Günter Klein (Tübingen: Mohr [Siebeck], 1979), 1–15; Reinhart Staats, "Augustins 'De spiritu et littera' in Luthers reformatorischer Erkenntnis," *ZKG* 98 (1987): 28–47; Hjalmar Sundén, "Der psychologische Aspekt in der Rechtfertigung durch den Glauben [Augustins *De spiritu et litera* und Luthers 'Turmerlebnis']," *KD* 32 (1986): 120–31.

9. Burnaby's footnotes (see n. 11) identify 55 quotations from 15 books of the Old Testament, including 2 books of the Apocrypha (of these, 28 are from the Psalms) and 99 quotations from 16 books of the New Testament apart from Romans (of these, 52 are from the larger Pauline corpus, not including Hebrews). The count for Romans is 72, but this is a misleadingly low figure.

10. P. W. Meyer, "Romans," in *Harper's Bible Commentary,* ed. James L. Mays (San Francisco: Harper & Row, 1988), 1130–67. This commentary could never have been completed without the editorial guidance and encouragement of Wayne Meeks. See now pp. 149–218 in this volume.

movement of Augustine's treatise, especially as he quotes and uses Paul, and by some summary characterizations of Augustine's interpretation in relation to modern understandings in order to identify some significant similarities and differences. The focus, it should be emphasized, is on this treatise alone; I make no claim to sufficient grasp of Augustine's other writings or of his thought in general to reach beyond this modest goal.

The Structure and Basic Argument

As one tries to see through and behind the conventional section divisions of this patristic work, certain structural features emerge rather quickly and clearly.[11] After an introduction in sections 1–7, the main body of the argument ends with a Q.E.D. in 42. It is followed by two appendixes dealing with difficulties raised in the course of the argument, one more exegetical in nature (43–51), the other more theological (52–60). A conclusion to the whole work follows in sections 61–66.

The introduction (1–7) defines the issue. In his first anti-Pelagian writing, *On the Consequences and Forgiveness of Sins,* Augustine had argued that, although God has without doubt the power to make a person entirely free from sin, no one in scripture or experience, apart from Christ, has reached this state. The reason is that

> men *will* not do what is right, either because the right is hidden from them, or because they find no delight in it. For the strength of our will to anything is proportionate to the assurance of our knowledge of its goodness, and to the warmth of our delight in it. . . . But that what was hidden may become clear, what delighted not may become sweet—this belongs to the grace of God which aids the wills of men.[12]

Marcellinus had asked Augustine to explain the apparent contradiction in claiming both that a sinless human life is possible with God's help and that it has never in fact been realized. Augustine dispenses with this question in sections 1–3 by showing that the two claims are not mutually exclusive and challenging anyone to provide the example of a sinless life that could falsify the latter.

Augustine then redefines the issue, stating the main thesis to be opposed (4) and formulating his own counterthesis (5). The issue is not whether the self

---

11. The text used here is the English translation and edition of John Burnaby, *Augustine: Later Works,* LCC 8 (Philadelphia: Westminster, 1955), 193–250. The Latin text is available in CSEL 60 (Vienna and Leipzig, 1913), 153–229. References in the body of this essay are to the shorter section divisions of Augustine's text (Arabic numerals in both versions above); references in the notes to "Burnaby" are to the page numbers of his edition.

12. *On the Consequences and Forgiveness of Sins (de pecc. mer.)* 2.26 (as quoted by Burnaby, *Augustine,* 186–87).

needs God's help to achieve righteousness but why and by what means. That divine help is required, that "God has both created man in possession of a will that chooses freely and teaches him by the gift of his commandments the right way of life," is not in dispute. What is to be vigorously resisted is "that God's help consists in the removal by instruction of man's ignorance," so that a person "by means of the power of free choice belonging to him by nature" may proceed along the path thus opened (4). In Augustine's contrary view (5), that is too narrow a perception of God's assistance, which consists not only in the endowment of freedom to choose, and not only in the instruction how one ought to live, but also in the gift of the Holy Spirit, "whereby there arises in [the] soul the delight in and love of God, the supreme and changeless Good."

> Free choice alone, if the way of truth is hidden, avails for nothing but sin; and when the right action and the true aim has begun to appear clearly, there is still no doing, no devotion, no good life, unless it be also delighted in and loved. And that it may be loved, the love of God is shed abroad in our hearts, not by the free choice whose spring is in ourselves, but through the Holy Spirit which is given us. (5)

Free choice, "whose spring is in ourselves [*quod surgit ex nobis*]," fails to provide the transcendent resource that is needed to motivate true devotion and bring about change.

Such formulation of the issue does not fit the popular definitions of Pelagianism on which many theological students have been brought up, as "the heresy that man can take the initial steps toward salvation by his own efforts, apart from Divine Grace."[13] But it fits much better what we know of the ascetic stringency of Pelagius, his sense for the incorruptible majesty of the God of the commandments, and his perfectionism.[14] In 418 the Synod of Carthage, which condemned Pelagius, "expressly emphasized that this grace of God does not consist only in instruction concerning the content of God's commandments, but that, above all, it imparts power for their fulfillment."[15]

It is noteworthy that this opening distinction between knowing the good and doing it parallels precisely Paul's distinction at the start of Romans (2:13) between hearing the law and doing it. By charging his Pelagian opponent with narrowing God's grace to divine instruction in right action, Augustine is positioning him where Paul positions the Jew in Rom 2, a strategy that becomes explicit later (13–14).

13. *The Concise Oxford Dictionary of the Christian Church*, ed. E. A. Livingstone (Oxford: Oxford University Press, 1977), 390.

14. Brown, *Augustine of Hippo*, 340–52 and passim.

15. B. Lohse, *A Short History of Christian Doctrine* (Philadelphia: Fortress, 1966), 121, paraphrasing Canon 4 of the Council of Carthage; the text is in H. Denzinger, *Enchiridion Symbolorum* (24th ed.; Barcelona: Herder, 1946), 104.

Section 6 takes another arrow from Paul's quiver. So far Augustine has not indicated why, apart from God's gift of the Holy Spirit, the good is not delighted in and loved by human beings. Several explanations are given during the subsequent argument, but for now Augustine simply turns rather suddenly to 2 Cor 3:6 in order to undermine from another side his adversary's "opinion": "The letter killeth, but the Spirit giveth life."[16] That instruction in "the way of truth" with which the Pelagian wants to identify God's gracious aid is not merely a benign gift. The Spirit has an active role in "shedding charity abroad in our hearts" (*caritatem diffudens,* echoing the Latin version of Rom 5:5: *caritas Dei diffusa est in cordibus nostris per Spiritum Sanctum*), thus inspiring good desire (*concupiscentia bona*). Where the Spirit is not present, there the law "increases by its prohibition the evil desire [*concupiscentia mala*]." The "Thou shalt not covet" of Rom 7:7 represents "the voice of the law forbidding all sin," and Rom 7:11 shows that it is this law that "killeth" (6). The very law that promises life cannot produce it; quite the contrary, the law generates the opposite. Once again, it follows that human righteousness is to be credited only to the operation of God's life-giving power, which is the Spirit (7).

Romans 2:29 is one of the three verses in which Paul (via the Latin rendering of *in spiritu non littera* for the Greek ἐν πνεύματι οὐ γράμματι) bequeathed to Christian theological vocabulary the pair of terms "letter" and "spirit." It is possible that it served as the springboard for the main argument through its proximity and parallelism with Rom 2:13, by thus sharply distinguishing the doing of the good from the knowing of it. While there is no clear evidence that Augustine had this verse in mind when he opened his argument, it is striking that he next turns to the second of those eponymous verses (2 Cor 3:6, rendering οὐ γράμματος ἀλλὰ πνεύματος) against the Pelagian. That the "letter" kills but the "Spirit" gives life provides the fundamental opposition. Then he at once appeals to Paul's own elaboration of the third (Rom 7:6 and the following verses, 7–12, *in novitate Spiritus et non in vetustate litterae*) to interpret and drive home the second. In the Latin text *littera* ("letter") renders both the sense of "written" and that of "literal." Paul's argument visibly affects Augustine's in other ways as well. Like Paul, Augustine takes the commandment "Thou shalt not covet" to be "the voice of the law" and to stand for the whole of the Decalogue, "for there is no sin whose commission does not begin with coveting" (6).[17] Again, the "letter" now clearly means the command of the Decalogue; Augustine expressly appeals to

16. The biblical quotations here follow Burnaby's translations from Augustine's Latin, since Augustine's biblical text often differs from modern versions; cf. Burnaby, *Augustine,* 14.

17. For Jewish traditions taking the command against coveting as representative of the Decalogue as a whole, see E. Käsemann, *Commentary on Romans* (Grand Rapids: Eerdmans, 1980), 196; U. Wilckens, *Der Brief an die Römer,* EKKNT, 3 vols. (Neukirchen-Vluyn: Neukirchener Verlag, 1978–82), 2:78–79. For Hellenistic-Jewish identification of coveting as the cause of all sinning, see Wilckens, *Römer,* 2:78.

Paul's language in order to reject the "figurative" and Origenistic uses of "letter" and "spirit" to distinguish the literal and the allegorical senses of scripture.[18] Finally, though Augustine began (4 and 5) with law as neutral instruction (Torah!) in "the right way of life" (both "what is to be avoided" and "what is to be sought"), under the influence of Paul's argument it has become negative and prohibitory in sections 6 and 7—with immense consequences later in the treatise.[19]

The Body of the Argument

The main body of *The Spirit and the Letter* consists of sections 8–42 and falls into two major divisions. The first (8–15) continues to draw upon diverse passages in Romans to interpret the topic verse from 2 Cor 3:6. That "the letter killeth" is given another dimension (8 and 9) by turning to Rom 5:20–21: coveting is evil in itself, but when "transgression of law is added to [that] evil," sin is "increased rather than diminished." But the contrast between Adam and Christ in Rom 5 shows that God's real goal is the giving of life: "The apostle's aim is to commend the grace which came through Jesus Christ to all peoples." Something of the universalism of Rom 5:12–21 comes through here. (When Augustine adds, without provocation from the immediate context, "lest the Jews exalt themselves above the rest on account of their possession of the law," his sense for the law as an identity marker reinforcing the Jews' self-consciousness may sound very modern,[20] but the remark may more likely be a passing rebuke to the claims of Pelagian perfectionism.) The reason for the law's "entry" and the consequent "abounding of the offense"[21] is

> so that thus convicted and confounded [man] might see his need for God, not only as teacher but as helper . . . : that he should flee to the help of mercy for his healing, and so . . . grace should yet more abound, not by the desert of the sinner but through the aid of the succourer. (9)[22]

---

18. According to *Conf.* 6.4, Ambrose's use of this distinction in interpreting the same text (2 Cor 3:6) played a part in his conversion.

19. Augustine has *not* gotten from Paul, though it has often been repeated in the interpretation of Romans, his "psychological" explanation of how sin "deceives" and "kills," viz., by making "the coveted object [grow] somehow more attractive through being forbidden" (6). For Paul, the deceit or trick lies in the fact that the commandment is unable to deliver what it promises (life) and in truth delivers the opposite, thus defrauding the desire for the good; for Augustine, it lies in the way it leads the self to desire the evil in place of the good.

20. Cf. James D. G. Dunn, "The New Perspective on Paul," in *Romans 1–8*, WBC 38A (Dallas: Word, 1988), lxiii–lxxii, esp. lxix.

21. In Augustine's Latin New Testament, what "abounds" is not sin but the *delictum,* the offense or transgression against express prohibition.

22. The assignment of this role to the law, here and elsewhere in *The Spirit and the Letter,* clearly anticipates (and prepares for) Luther, who called this the *usus proprius* (the special and characteristic function) of the law—a role it never plays in Paul.

On the heels of this use of Rom 5:20–21, still following Paul's text, Augustine introduces a long quotation of Rom 6:1–11 to explain and describe the "abounding of grace." This benefit, which cannot come "by the letter of the law but only by faith in Jesus Christ," is depicted with two images. One is supplied by the text and its references to Christ's death and resurrection. The other, without basis in Paul, introduced here for the first time in this treatise but loaded with associations that will emerge as Augustine proceeds, is the figure of grace as "healing medicine." Their combination means that death and resurrection are not the apocalyptic turning points by which God reverses the direction of human destiny and behavior, but become metaphors for a moral and spiritual process:

> It is plain enough that by the mystery of the Lord's death and resurrection is signified the setting of our old life and the rising of the new: there is shown forth the destruction of sin and the renewal of righteousness. (10)

By the very same token, however, Augustine is able to appropriate from Paul the indivisible unity of indicative and imperative, justification and sanctification. Illumined by the parallelisms of the psalmist's language (Ps 36:10), God's mercy and his righteousness are one, and the justification of the ungodly is God's free creation of righteousness where it did not exist before. After quoting a catena of phrases from this psalm (36:7–10 [35:8–11 LXX]), Augustine continues:

> He extends his mercy, not because they know him but in order that they may know him: he extends his righteousness whereby he justifies the ungodly, not because they are upright in heart, but that they may become upright in heart. (11)

Backing off for a moment from the details of his text, Augustine declares the preaching of this grace to be almost the apostle's sole concern in the manifold, persistent, and even wearying arguments of this epistle (12).

A significant new start is taken with section 13, which opens with a long quotation of Paul's apostrophe to the Jew and its sequel in Rom 2:17–29. Paul's original rhetorical aim seems to have involved three steps: first, to single out the Jew as representative of the best in his religious world, one whose religious identity and distinctiveness revolved around possession of the law; second, to deny that the law provides to those who possess it any exemption from accountability to its demands; third, thus to include the Jew in his argument that all human beings stand on the same footing before an impartial God and are all under the power of sin. The final words of the section (2:29) remind such a religious person that the ultimate evaluation of human life depends on the "praise" or commendation and vindication that only God can give. Like most Christian interpreters since, however, Augustine takes the passage as Paul's

Christian indictment of the discrepancy in the Jew between profession and performance.[23]

The Jews were indeed favored by God's gift of the law, "yet this law of God they supposed themselves to fulfil by their own righteousness, though they were rather its transgressors." Noticing, nonetheless, that Paul's apostrophe does not directly accuse the Jew of breaking the law, Augustine immediately adds, "even those who did as the law commanded." If performance is not wanting, their failure must be found at a deeper level; they

> did it through fear of punishment and not from love of righteousness. Thus in God's sight there was not in their will that obedience which to the sight of men appeared in their work; they were rather held guilty for that which God knew they would have chosen to commit, if it could have been without penalty. (13)

The charge is ruinous. A genuinely Pauline recognition that observance of Torah is not necessarily identical with obedience to God is combined with a wholly non-Pauline preoccupation with the motivation or "will" *behind* human action, to the point where, even when the outward action is right, the guilt that belongs to the action not done is attached to the fear that is presumed and attributed to the doer. The resulting polarizing of "the love of righteousness" (*amor iustitiae*) with the "fear of punishment" (*timor poenae*) becomes an increasingly important ingredient in Augustine's interpretation.

In section 14 Augustine gives "their answer," the wording of which shows that he now has his own Pelagian opponent in mind under the cover of Paul's Jew: "We do give praise to God as author of our justification, inasmuch as he gave the law, by the study of which we know how we ought to live." For his rebuttal Augustine draws on the continuity of Paul's text: "from the law shall no flesh be justified before God," and "through the law is the knowledge of sin" (Rom 3:20a, b). With the exegetically correct insistence that by "law" here Paul means the Decalogue, and not any "law of ancient rites" such as circumcision, Augustine goes out of his way to foreclose any move by the Pelagian to deflect Paul's text away from himself and upon the ancient ethnic Jew.

As Paul's text reaches a turning point in Rom 3:21 and its following verses, Augustine's reaches a preliminary climax in section 15. Insisting on human free will, the Pelagian will not dispute Paul's assertion that "from the law shall no flesh be justified" (3:20a), "since the law does but point out what is to be done or not done, in order that the will may carry out its promptings, and so man be justified not by the law's command but by his own free choice" (15). But for Augustine this is not enough:

---

23. The pejorative interpretation is aggravated by a forced syntactical substitution of a subjective genitive for an objective, so that "praise" (Greek ἔπαινος; Latin *laus)* is no longer the approbation conferred *by* God on the authentic religious person but the praise rendered *to* God by "the true Jew" in contrast to the self-praise implicitly attributed to the empirical Jew.

Nay but, O man, consider what follows!—"But now without law the righteousness of God hath been manifested, witnessed to by law and prophets." Can even the deaf fail to hear? . . . "The righteousness *of God*"—not the righteousness of man or the righteousness of our own will—the righteousness of God, not that by which God is righteous, but that wherewith he clothes man, when he justifies the ungodly. (15)

As Paul moves in these verses (Rom 3:21, 31) to more positive remarks about the Mosaic law, Augustine too leaves behind the language about its "killing." Now it is Paul's "without the law" (*sine lege* for χωρὶς νόμου) in 3:21 that serves as his weapon against the Pelagian: "The law . . . contributes nothing to God's saving act." Where for the Pelagian and for Paul's Jew God's gracious gift is the law, for Augustine that gift is "the righteousness of God without law": "It is indeed a righteousness of God without law, because God confers it upon the believer through the Spirit of grace, without the help of the law" (15).

We have already noted the Pelagian emphasis on free will. In this section (15), just where he is following each verse of Rom 3:21–24, Augustine makes clear how much he shares this preoccupation. "Justified freely by his grace" (Rom 3:24a) means

> not that the justification is without our will, but the weakness of our will is discovered by the law [*uoluntas nostra ostenditur infirma per legem*], so that grace may restore [*sanet*] the will and the restored will [*sana uoluntas*] may fulfil the law, established neither under the law nor in need of law [*non constituta sub lege nec indigens lege*]. (15)

The Latin shows that (a) the last words refer to the "restored will"—this owes nothing to the law and does not need the law (no *tertius usus legis* [third use of the law] here!)—and (b) Augustine is again using the imagery of healing, or making whole what is beset with weakness or infirmity, to describe justification. Most important, this will, "without which we cannot do the good" (20), is fundamental to the human self; this is what is to be healed by God's grace (cf. *The Spirit and the Letter* 6). How this in turn has affected Augustine's reading of some of the key terms that are of great interest to the modern exegete[24] is clear from his comment earlier in the section, on Rom 3:22:

> "The righteousness of God through the faith of Jesus Christ": that is, the faith whereby we believe in Christ. The "faith of Christ" here meant is not that by

24. For the modern discussion, which is voluminous, one may start with Manfred T. Brauch, "Perspectives on 'God's Righteousness' in Recent German Discussion," in E. P. Sanders, *Paul and Palestinian Judaism* (Philadelphia: Fortress, 1977), 523–42; Richard B. Hays, "ΠΙΣΤΙΣ and Pauline Christology: What Is at Stake?" in *Pauline Theology, Volume IV*, ed. E. Elizabeth Johnson and David M. Hay (Atlanta: Scholars Press, 1997), 35–60; James D. G. Dunn, "Once More, ΠΙΣΤΙΣ ΧΡΙΣΤΟΥ," in *Pauline Theology IV*, 61–81.

which Christ believes, any more than the righteousness of God is that by which God is righteous. *Both are our own;* called "of God" and "of Christ," because bestowed upon us by his bounty. (15; emphasis added)

Augustine's Interpretive Shift

At one point in his introduction to the text, Burnaby comments: "The effect of the Pelagian controversy was to sharpen the dilemma—either God's work or ours."[25] That may have been its ultimate effect, but it scarcely fits *The Spirit and the Letter.* There seems to be no question, for either Pelagius or Augustine, that the righteous life, when and where it is a reality, is "ours." Augustine's task was to transcend the dilemma and to show that justification is really "ours," that it makes a difference in the way human beings remain human, *and* that it is God's undeserved and gracious gift. But because being human is so closely identified with the freedom of the will (*liberum arbitrium,* freedom of choice),[26] the result is inevitable. Augustine rewrites Paul's text in Rom 3:21 in such a way that "the righteousness of God" is not "manifested" so much as it is "bestowed," being itself now the gift; "without law" (*sine lege,* for χωρὶς νόμου) has become an adjective modifying "righteousness" as much as an adverb qualifying "has been manifested." A shift has taken place, for the form of the "dilemma" in Paul, the true mystery, is not the conjoining of what is God's with what is "ours" but the holding together of freedom and fatefulness, responsibility and destiny, *both* in the behavior of humans, "saints" as well as sinners, and also in the sovereignty and faithfulness of God.[27]

After a somewhat labored excursus in section 16 to deal with "the lawful use of the law" in 1 Tim 1:8–9 (which of course was also attributed to the apostle), Augustine returns to Rom 3. What interests him now is v. 27, which exercises interpreters to this day, specifically the contrast here between "the law of works" (which does not exclude "glorying") and "the law of faith" (which does). This contrast sets in motion a new train of thought that dominates the remainder of the body of *The Spirit and the Letter,* forming what we may distinguish as its second major part (17–42).

What lies at the heart of this contrast? At first (18–20), Augustine turns to the beginning of Romans, where Paul sets over against the revelation of God's

---

25. Burnaby, *Augustine,* 192.

26. In his summary of the history of patristic exegesis of Romans, K. H. Schelkle has pointed out that *liberum arbitrium* (freedom of the will, of choice) is closely associated in patristic exegesis with τὸ αὐτεξούσιον (that which is in one's power or discretion), a major term in the vocabulary of Stoicism; it differs greatly from Paul's ἐλευθερία (freedom, the state of having been set free, liberation from oppressive and destructive powers, and therefore freedom *for* a new course of life) (*Paulus, Lehrer der Väter* [Düsseldorf: Patmos, 1956], 439–40).

27. Rom 1:21–23; 5:12; 6:17; 8:12–14; 9:33; cf. my "Romans: A Commentary," 163, 177–78, 182–84, 190–91, 199 in this volume.

righteousness (1:16–17) the revelation of God's wrath (1:18–2:11). Clearly recognizing the parallelism Paul establishes between a knowledge of God devoid of recognition and gratitude (the human creature of Rom 1) and a possession of the law lacking in true submission to God (the religious moralist and the Jew of Rom 2), Augustine drives home his point once more. As knowledge is not godliness, so ungodliness is not mere ignorance and cannot therefore be cured by instruction apart from the Spirit's help. "Without that aid, the teaching [*doctrina*] is a letter that killeth" (20; cf. 6).

But what are these *two* "laws" of 3:27? In an impressive display of exegetical sophistication, Augustine steadfastly refuses either to relegate "the law of works" to Jewish practices or cultic regulations left behind by Christianity, or to evaporate "the law of faith" into a spiritual principle unrelated to law. The law that produces covetousness (Rom 7:7), "the letter that killeth" (2 Cor 3:6), and the law by which no one is justified (Rom 3:20) are all the very same holy, just, and good commandment of Rom 7:12, 13b (24–25). Both "the law of works" and "the law of faith" say "Thou shalt not covet"; both refer to the Decalogue that the Christian is "bound to observe" (23).

> Where then lies the difference? To put it in a sentence: what is enjoined with threatenings under the law of works, is granted to belief under the law of faith. . . .
> So by the law of works God says, "Do what I command"; by the law of faith we say to God, "Give what thou commandest." (22)[28]

"The law commands, that we may be advised what faith must do" (22). Here is a nuance different from that of section 20; law is now much more closely related to faith. The law does not change; its content is the same in Judaism and Christianity, for both faith and unbelief. Faith knows that performance can come only by the power supplied by God's gift of the Spirit. Unbelief is exhibited by the Pharisee in Luke's parable (Luke 18:9–14), "who gave God thanks for what he had but asked for nothing to be given him—as though he stood in need of nothing for the increase and perfecting of his righteousness" (22). The wording fairly shouts out that "Pharisee" stands for the unnamed Pelagian.

The direction of the argument is now established on a new bearing. Subsequent sections draw on a range of passages, from Romans and beyond, to substantiate and to refine its two pillars: (a) "The law of works by which no flesh is justified" and "the law of faith by which the just lives" are one and the same Mosaic law; the law itself is not simply to be rejected as "letter" and divorced from spirit. (b) "Letter" and "spirit," no longer simply set against each other as polar opposites, the one as the "abounding of sin" and the other as "the abounding of grace," are two dimensions of the same law, two contexts in which the

---

28. Burnaby, *Augustine,* 212 n. 61: "The famous prayer of *Conf.,* X, 40, which gave offense to Pelagius" (Augustine, *Praed.,* 2:53).

one law functions. A long quotation from Rom 7:6–25 in section 25 serves to make clear:

> Not that the law itself is an evil thing, but that it holds the good commandment in the letter that demonstrates, not in the spirit that brings aid. And if the commandment be done through fear of penalty and not through love of righteousness, it is done in the temper of servitude not freedom—and therefore it is not done at all. (26; cf. 7)

The law remains one, the Decalogue. But clearly Paul's text provides the materials for constructing a comparison between "the law of works" and "the law of faith." Paul's (synonymous) use of the terms "law" and "commandment" (Rom 7:12) allows Augustine to distinguish (with an assist from 2 Cor 3:2–8 in section 24) one quality of law as "letter" from another in which law is associated with God's Spirit. Indeed, Augustine uses Paul's (for him, Latin) language and plays on it as his own:

> The man in whom is the faith that works through love [*per dilectionem* (Gal 5:6)] begins to delight [*condelectari*] in the law of God after the inward man; and that delight [*delectatio*] is a gift not of the letter but of the spirit. (26)[29]

Again, Augustine mines 2 Corinthians, first with a long quotation of 3:2–8 (24) and then with a series of citations in the order of the text from 3:3 to 5:21 (30–31). The law was always written by the finger of God (Exod 31:18), and that finger is God's Spirit (Luke 11:20). But in the one case it was given to a people "held back by a fearful dread" (Exod 19:21–23); in the other, the Spirit came upon an assembly waiting for his promised coming (Acts 2:1–4).

> There the finger of God worked upon tables of stone: here upon the hearts of men. So there the law was set outside men [*extrinsecus*] to be a terror to the unjust: here it was given within them [*intrinsecus*] to be their justification. (29)

"The law of God is charity [*caritas*]" (29, after quoting Rom 13:9), but in the one case it is "the law of works"; in the other, "the law of faith."

> [T]he one is written outside the man [*extra hominem*], to be a terror to him from without [*forinsecus*], while the other is written in the man himself [*in ipso homine*], to justify him from within [*intrinsecus*]. (30)

---

29. It is well known that Augustine changed his mind in the interpretation of Rom 7:7–25, believing at first that Paul's "I" describes "the man who is still under the law and not yet under grace," but coming later to believe that these verses "describe the spiritual man" (*Retract.* 2.1.1). The change is usually dated in 418–419 C.E. (e.g., Wilckens, *Römer*, 2:102). But since "delight" in Augustine's terms presupposes the healing of the will by the Holy Spirit, it seems that the change is already emerging here, in 412 C.E.

Further, from still another source: a full quotation of Jer 31:31–34, singled out by Augustine as the only passage from the Old Testament in which the new covenant is expressly mentioned (33), supplies another way of distinguishing one law from the other, as the laws of two covenants, the old and the new. We have noted above that an early answer to the question why, apart from God's Spirit, human beings do not delight in God's good, was to appeal to 2 Cor 3:6: "The letter killeth." But now we have another, more nuanced answer, triggered by Rom 8:3–4, showing again Augustine's fondness for healing as an image of salvation:

> The law was given that grace might be sought; grace was given that the law might be fulfilled. For the non-fulfilment of the law was not through its own fault, but the fault of the "mind of the flesh"—a fault which the law must exhibit, and grace must heal. (34)

Here "fault" (Paul's ἠσθένει [NRSV: "weakened"] in 8:3) was rendered *infirmabatur* ("was weakened, enfeebled") in Augustine's Latin text. But now in his interpretation it has become *uitium* ("a detect, blemish, imperfection"), to be made whole by grace. What in Paul is an incapacity in the *law* has become in Augustine a defect in the *self:*

> It is because of the sickness [*noxa* (a close synonym of *uitium,* specifically an injury or damage inflicted upon someone)] of the old man, which the commands and the threatenings of the letter did nothing to heal, that the former covenant is called old, and the latter new with the newness of the Spirit, which heals the new man from his old failing [*uitium*]. (35)

The difference between "the law of works" and "the law of faith," between the old covenant and the new, between Judaism and Christianity, does not lie in any change in the content of the law but in a change, a transformation, *within* the human self.

Sections 35–42 elaborate on that important passage from Jer 31:31–34 and the similarities and differences between the two covenants. But the entire argument is summed up and aimed back at the Pelagian in Augustine's Q.E.D.:

> Grasp this clear difference between the old covenant and the new: that there the law is written upon tables, here upon hearts, so that the fear imposed by the first from without [*forinsecus*] becomes the delight inspired by the second from within [*intrinsecus*], and he whom the letter that killeth there made a transgressor, is here made a lover [*dilector*] by the Spirit that giveth life. Then you can no longer say that God assists us in the working of righteousness and works in us both to will and to do according to his good pleasure, inasmuch as he makes us hear with the outward sense [*forinsecus insonat*] the commandments of righteousness. No, it is because he gives increase within us [*intrinsecus incrementum dat*], by

the shedding abroad of charity in our hearts through the Holy Spirit which is given us. (42)

This is the real conclusion to *The Spirit and the Letter.* What remains are two not insignificant appendixes. One (43–51) directly confronts the difficulty presented to Augustine's understanding of the differences between the two covenants by Rom 2:14–15a.[30] The second appendix (52–60) opens with a paraphrase of Paul's own rhetorical question in Rom 3:31: "Do we then 'make void' freedom of choice through grace? 'God forbid! yea, we establish' freedom of choice." The challenge is to support that claim, so close to Pelagius's own agenda, in a way that will preserve the difference from the Pelagian that the preceding body of the treatise has established. A conclusion (61–66) returns to Marcellinus's question but adds nothing significant to the preceding argument. Its most telling feature is that Augustine ends this "reading" of Paul by adopting as his own the words of praise with which Paul concludes his argument (Rom 11:33–36).

Conclusion

How close this argument stays to Paul—and yet how unlike Paul it resonates! One could try to enumerate similarities and differences, but such a list would miss the point, for it is often the case that Augustine displays his distance most clearly just when he is following Paul most closely. One interesting, and perhaps surprising, feature of *The Spirit and the Letter* in this respect is that Augustine chooses the question of the law, its nature and function, as the field on which to resist Pelagianism. Why? Of course, this is not Augustine's last word on Pelagianism, perhaps not his most definitive. Has the field of battle been determined here by Paul's letter? Augustine's treatise reflects clearly the variations and the tensions of the apostle's own arguments on this subject—another indication of the closeness of the "reading." But the conclusion of the argument is a measure also of the distance. Since the Christian life is understood in terms of the immanent qualities brought about by change within the believer, Paul's Christology and eschatology suffer heavy erosion. The cross and resurrection are moralized. Paul, in this reading, is left entirely vulnerable to the kind of development that took place in Corinth: the Christian life is a supernatural life.

30. This discussion of Rom 2:14–15a provides a fascinating look into the bishop's exegetical method at its best. He considers first one solution drawn from the context (44) but called into question both by an adjoining verse (45–46) and by a philological difficulty (47). A second solution is tried but proves less than convincing (48). Finally, Augustine advances beyond both by considering the rhetorical aim of the passage, with a surprisingly modern result (49). The upshot: in any case, whatever meaning is assigned the text, it provides no grist for Pelagius's mill (50–51).

Such a reading fails to grasp the full depth of Paul's understanding of sin as a power that corrupts even the most ardent love and desire of God as the highest good (Rom 7), and so could not alone check the drift toward Christian triumphalism and legalism. It is ironic that Augustine's assignment of *forensic* distance to God's command and *intrinsic* intimacy to God's grace had to be reversed in the Reformers' insistence on a *iustitia aliena* (alien righteousness) imputed in justification. There are signs that the reversal has raised questions of its own. Perhaps we will not find the balance the apostle had in mind until we put Christology again at the center of his teaching about justification.

Part III

Romans: A Commentary

INTRODUCTION

General Features

The position of Romans as the first letter in the New Testament is due to the simple fact that the earliest collections of Paul's letters were arranged in order of decreasing length and Romans is the longest.* Its resulting place has been oddly appropriate, however, since it is also the most deliberate and reflective of Paul's letters and its influence on Christian theology the greatest. The sixteenth-century reformer Philipp Melanchthon called it a "compendium of Christian doctrine," and it has in fact functioned as such for most of its long history. Its contents seem at first sight to conform to this assessment. In all other cases, Paul's letters clearly served as surrogates for his personal presence as an apostle and leader in situations of crisis that developed in churches he himself had founded. In those other letters, Paul writes because he has to—to protect, correct, or strengthen some aspect of the gospel in the life of a particular congregation at risk.

Romans appears to be an exception to this pattern. It is addressed to a church Paul did not establish. It does not seem to arise from an occasion that has been forced on him. There is no defense of himself, as in Galatians or 1 and 2 Corinthians, and no counterattack on those who have assaulted him or tried to seduce his converts. Instead, the argument of the letter proceeds by a serial treatment of interlocking and perennial themes, often in sections that stand out as independent literary "blocks." Indeed, one of the challenges in the reading of Romans is to see how these sections were intended to fit together as parts of a coherent whole.

These themes, furthermore, do not seem to be peculiar to Romans; there are very few of them that do not echo passages in the other letters. Some examples are the failure of the world to know God on his own terms (Rom 1:18–32; 1 Cor 1:18–25); justification by faith rather than by works of the law (Rom 3; Gal 3–4; Phil 3); Abraham (Rom 4; Gal 3); Adam and Christ (Rom 5:12–21; 1 Cor

*This commentary first appeared in *Harper's Bible Commentary*, ed. James L. Mays (San Francisco: Harper & Row, 1988), 1130–67. It was revised for the *HarperCollins Bible Commentary*, ed. James L. Mays (San Francisco: HarperSanFrancisco, 2000), 1038–73, and is reproduced here, with minor modifications, by permission. Unless otherwise indicated, all translations of texts drawn from Paul's letters are the author's.

15:21–22, 45–49); and the church as the body of Christ (Rom 12; 1 Cor 12). There are exceptions. Conspicuous by its absence from Romans is any discussion of the nature of Paul's apostleship, any defense of his credentials or cataloging of the trials he has endured to authenticate his ministry. That these are missing appears to be a function of the absence of polemic. Conversely, one major theme that is treated at length and with passion in Romans, but has no parallel in the other letters, is the discussion of the past and future destiny of Israel and its relation to the gospel (Rom 9–11).

If Romans is the first of Paul's letters in the order of the New Testament books, it is the last of his undoubted letters to have been written. The themes Romans shares with the other letters always come up elsewhere in situations of conflict or uncertainty that elicit Paul's discussion of them. But in Romans they are elaborated as part of a longer argument he has himself initiated, in deliberate and self-conscious progression. Many of its turning points are clearly marked by literary conventions (Rom 1:8; 12:1–2; 16:1), anticipated objections and queries (3:1; 4:1, 9; 6:1), short summations (6:11; 7:12; 15:5–6), rhetorical climaxes (8:37–39; 11:28–32), and the insertion of liturgical fragments (4:25; 9:5; 11:33–36). It seems that the historical concreteness of those earlier crises and conflicts has receded and been displaced by a more deliberate accounting of what Paul has come to regard as crucial and definitive in his total work as an apostle; he appears to transcend at least to some extent the particular situations he has lived through and make available for a new audience the fruits of his experience. As a result, there has always been a powerful temptation to read Romans with Melanchthon as a "compendium of Christian doctrine," or as a systematic statement of Paul's theology.

Yet there are three important reasons for not resting with such an appraisal. For one thing, it is clear from the other letters that Romans simply does not embrace everything that was important, even necessary, in Paul's own understanding of Christian faith and life (one may mention especially the Lord's Supper [1 Cor 11:23–26] and the resurrection [1 Cor 15:3–8, 12–19]). In the second place, no part of the New Testament was composed simply as a presentation of its author's ideas divorced from specific human occasions and needs. One should hesitate a long time before making Romans an exception to this rule and sundering it from early Christian history. Above all, Romans itself contains the most important evidence to help us understand its place in that history.

Occasion and Purpose

The most direct evidence for the occasion of Romans appears in the personal remarks Paul makes in the opening and closing sections of the letter. In 1:10–15 it is clear that he is preparing the way for carrying out a long-cherished plan to visit the church at Rome, a visit he hopes will be of mutual benefit. In 15:14–33 he is much more specific. He feels he has no more "space" to carry on his mission to the Gentiles in the eastern Mediterranean and wants to extend it to the west and to Spain, and to be "sped on his way" (15:24) there by the church at Rome, to be supported by them in this enterprise. Since Paul hopes for such help from a church he did not himself establish, one motive for writing is clearly implied: he wants to present this church with an authentic representation of his message to gain its trust and backing. Before he can come to Rome, however, Paul has to make one last trip to Jerusalem to deliver the collection of money he has raised for the Jewish Christians there.

This fixes the date and place for the writing of Romans fairly well, that is, during his last stay in Greece prior to his final trip to Jerusalem (at the point in the narrative of Acts represented by Acts 20:3), and probably from Corinth (Rom 16:23 mentions "Gaius, my host," and Gaius is one of the few persons Paul admits to having baptized in Corinth [1 Cor 1:14]). The time is probably the winter of 55 or 56 C.E. This generally undisputed dating of Romans has a significant bearing on the letter's content. Its composition comes after the writing of Galatians and all the letters to Corinth (whatever their number), after the resolution of the Corinthian crisis, and probably also after the writing of Philippians.

If this gives us time and place, it does not yet yield a very convincing account of Paul's purpose in writing. Why should a letter aimed at gaining trust and recognition deal with just the themes we have identified? Romans is much more than a neutral exposition of admirable ideas, however coherent. It is an argument with thrust and edge; it seeks to overcome resistance and counter objections. One may easily imagine that agitators and enemies from Paul's earlier conflicts over his mission to Gentiles have had some influence in Rome that he would have been anxious to neutralize before his visit, especially if the church in the capital city was linked to the synagogue community there. (Romans 3:7–8 shows in passing that Paul is aware of charges that have circulated against him.)

We have very little knowledge of the actual composition of the church in Rome. But the evidence from Paul's letter itself is perplexing. He seems to address the church clearly at certain points as Gentile (1:13; 11:13), at others as Jewish in background (2:17; 3:9). He seems to draw his justification for writing to the Romans and his right to be heard by them from his being an apostle to the Gentiles (1:13–14) and on their being a Gentile Christian community. Yet he does not incorporate into this letter some of the themes and preoccupations most characteristic of Gentile urban Christianity as these had emerged in Corinth. Instead, the argument itself is cast in profoundly Jewish terms: its controlling vocabulary, its appeals to authority and tradition, the values invoked, the techniques employed in interpreting scripture, and the things taken for granted in the minds of its readers.

The puzzle is compounded when one notes that Paul's missionary strategy included a "principle of noninterference," that is, a resolve not to pursue his missionary activity where others had begun theirs. This resolve is clearly stated in Rom 15:20–21; it appears earlier in 2 Cor 10:15–16. It is an understandable policy in the light of the division of labor agreed on at the Jerusalem conference (Gal 2:7–9) and is certainly congruent with the affectionate possessiveness Paul felt toward his own churches (e.g., Gal 4:19–20; 2 Cor 3:1–3; 11:1–3). How is it, then, that we find him writing to Rome at all? Is his departure from this principle adequately explained by his need of support from Rome for his mission to Spain? Answers to these questions have been sought by attempting to reconstruct in more detail the circumstances in which Romans was written.

These attempts have generally moved in one of two directions. The first may be called the "Roman exile hypothesis." On his first arrival in Corinth (about 50 C.E.), Paul made contact with a Jewish couple, Prisca and Aquila, who had recently come from Rome "because Claudius had ordered all the Jews to leave" that city (Acts 18:2–3). Apparently they were already Christian converts by that time. The Roman biographer Suetonius, in his *Life of Claudius* (25), gives the reason for the emperor's edict (49 C.E.) in words generally taken to refer to disturbances in the Roman Jewish community over the messiahship of Jesus. We may conclude that the church had been started in Rome by 49 C.E. and that it was sufficiently Jewish in composition to have come under Claudius's ban, though presumably an indeterminate Gentile Christian component would have been allowed to remain in the capital. When the ban was lifted after Claudius's death (54 C.E.), a good part, perhaps a majority, of the Christian community was allowed to return after its five-year exile. Enormous problems of reconciliation would have resulted. The situation faced earlier by Paul in Antioch (Gal 2:11–14) would have become an acute local Roman problem, but with a reverse twist: now it would not be the Jewish Christians who had to accept former Gentiles into the community, but the other way around. Gentile Christians would need to be reminded of their debt to their Jewish heritage (Paul seems in fact to do just this in Rom 11:18) and to be urged to be more tolerant of Jewish religious practices (cf. 14:3, 5–6, 14). For many scholars just such a situation is reflected in Paul's exhortations in the concluding chapters of Romans, thus confirming the exile hypothesis.

Yet this proposal does not answer all questions. The last chapters of Romans do more than simply reverse the arguments of Galatians. The contrast between the "weak" and the "strong" (Rom 15:1) appears to have developed not out of the Galatian debate but out of the distinction made in 1 Cor 8:7–13 between the "weak" and "those who have knowledge." Although this distinction is now subtly but firmly linked to the themes of Israel's history among the Gentiles and God's faithfulness (Rom 15:7–12), a thread that runs through the body of the letter, the connection appears contrived. Paul is very careful in Romans not to take sides; he no longer uses himself as a model (cf. Gal 6:14; 1 Cor 9:15–23; 10:32–33; 11:1), but points more directly to Christ (Rom 15:3, 7). In short, Paul's exhortations do not seem to address concrete problems so much as they present paradigms of Christian behavior generated out of his experiences in both Galatia and Corinth. But most important, all the previous bulk of Romans, the profoundly Jewish appeal of the argument, is not adequately accounted for by reconstructing a situation in which it is Gentile Christians who are being called upon to welcome back their exiled Jewish Christian associates.

Thus there has been another major attempt to reconstruct the occasion of Romans, which we may call the "Jerusalem crisis hypothesis." It is not time and place of writing that are in doubt, but Paul's motives, the circumstances that impelled him to write *this* letter. Proponents of this view point particularly to Rom 15:30–33, where Paul's anxiety over the outcome of his impending visit to Jerusalem is clearly expressed. That anxiety is in proportion to the importance attached by Paul to the money he has collected for the Jerusalem church and is about to deliver. The collection exemplified and actualized the unity of a church composed of both Jews and Gentiles, which had been the issue at the apostolic conference in Jerusalem (Gal 2:1–10) and constitutes one of the running themes of Romans (cf. Rom 1:16; 9:24; 15:7–12). With it, in Paul's view, the "truth of the gospel" stood or fell (Gal 2:5). Whether Paul's whole career had been worthwhile or futile depended in turn on Jerusalem's recognition of that truth (Gal 2:2). His anxiety therefore is not limited to what might occur in Jerusalem; it is at least in part an anxiety to be rightly understood in Rome not only so that he might have the Roman Christians as allies, but also that his entire mission should not be misunderstood as the irrelevant experiment of a freelancer.

The situation that occasioned Romans in this view is a crisis that lies before Paul in Jerusalem. The resources for facing it lie in his exposition of the gospel as its apostle. As a matter of fact, the themes of Romans fall rather precisely under two headings: first, the results of the controversies in Galatia, Corinth, and Philippi, now reflected upon in their interconnections and with more distance (Abraham and his promise, the Mosaic law, justification, spiritual gifts, unity and diversity in the church, eating and drinking in a religious context), and second, just those convictions Paul was going to have to defend in Jerusalem (the faithfulness and impartiality of God, the equal accountability of Jew and Gentile before God [chs. 1–2], the equal right of Gentile and Jew as offspring of the one Abraham "who is the father of us all" [chs. 3–4], the terms on which true obedience to God is possible [chs. 5–8], the meaning of Israel for the life of the church [chs. 9–11], the equal freedom and responsibility of Jewish and Gentile Christians in the everyday life of the community in the world [chs. 12–15]).

Such a reconstruction of the setting for Romans has the advantage of making historically intelligible the composition of this letter with its undeniable thematic and reflective character. Deeply rooted in the history of Paul's relations with his congregations, it is the rendering of an account of his gospel, its fundamental warrants, the major misunderstandings to which it is susceptible, its consequences, and above all the continuities and differences between it and the Judaism out of which Paul had come.

Significance

Although some find one more compelling than the other, the "Roman exile" and the "Jerusalem crisis" hypotheses are not, strictly speaking, mutually exclusive.

What they have most notably in common is the perception that the relation of the infant Christian movement to Judaism, a complex mix of both continuity and innovation as in the case of most significant new departures in religious tradition, is a fundamental motif of the letter. Being himself a participant in this transition, that is, being himself profoundly Jewish and Christian, Paul could not deal with the issues confronting him on either hypothesis—or on both—without involving his own religious identity. The "adversary," the debating partner, in Romans is not some enemy or some heresy; it is not Gentile Christianity, of which Paul is rather the advocate; nor is it Judaism, as though this were a rejected alternative left behind. It is, instead, in large measure the Hellenistic Jew that Paul himself was: a religious person in his highest aspirations, in his self-esteem but also his devotion to God, in his full knowledge of what God requires of human beings, in his loyalty to the Jewish Torah—yet one who despite all these virtues does not realize how religious life has been poisoned and perverted by the power of sin and needs to be shown how God has provided in his Son Jesus Christ a way of obtaining that integrity, that "righteousness," in one's relationship to God that has always eluded religious people.

The expository argument that results and that forms the substance of Romans has played an immeasurable role in the centuries since, most especially in two ways: first, in helping to shape the Christian community's understanding of its relationship to the Hebrew scriptures and to Judaism, both its debt and its distinctiveness; and second, in restoring and clarifying a sense of direction and identity in Christian reflection in times of great contention and change, such as the Pelagian controversy in the fifth century, the emergence of Protestantism in the sixteenth, and the breakdown of liberal optimism in the twentieth. These two ways in which Romans has functioned are intimately connected and are, one might say, but two sides of its significance.

The other letters of Paul have undergone various levels of editing in the process of circulation and canonization in order to make and keep available for subsequent generations what they initially intended and contributed in their original, contingently historical settings. Romans has been comparatively free of such modification. Its authenticity is not debated. Serious questions about its integrity, that is, whether it left the apostle's hand in the form in which we have it, are confined to chapter 16. The situation in which it was composed near the end of Paul's career called forth a type of argument that transcended that situation from the beginning by its comprehensiveness and because of the perennial nature of the issues of religious identity and integrity it addresses. Thus, even though it cannot be fully understood in isolation from the other letters that follow it in the canon, Romans has not unjustly been perceived as comprising the heart of the apostle's legacy to the Christian church.

COMMENTARY

1:1–17

Introduction

1:1–7, Salutation. Paul begins by using the conventional opening pattern of Hellenistic letters: "A (writer) to B (addressee): greeting" (cf. Jas 1:1; Acts 15:23). But this structural skeleton admits, and even invites, augmentation in a variety of ways. First, the greeting at the end (v. 7b) is modified under the influence of the Jewish "peace" greeting (also used in letters; cf. Dan 4:1; 2 Macc 1:1) and of Christian liturgical practice. Paul expects his letters to be read in public worship. Second, descriptive modifiers are attached to the designations of both sender and recipients, allowing Paul to present his credentials and at the same time to coordinate to his own calling "as an apostle" (v. 1) that of his readers "as saints" (v. 7). This last term is explained by the addition of "beloved by God" (v. 7) and "belonging to Jesus Christ" (v. 6) and is the closest equivalent in Paul's vocabulary to the later term "Christian." That is a reminder that all Paul's extant letters are written "within the family" to sustain, encourage, or correct people who are assumed to be baptized. God's calling initiative binds writer and recipients together, though it also distinguishes Paul by assigning him his own role as an apostle, an envoy commissioned for a particular purpose. That is Paul's principal credential: he "has" authority because he himself stands under it. The purpose of his calling is to serve "God's gospel," a message anticipated in the writings of the Jewish prophets, which formed part of the scriptures of the early Christian community from the beginning. As the subsequent argument will elaborate, this message has its roots in the continuity of God's past relationship to his people but has its goal in eliciting trust and obedience among non-Jewish peoples as well.

In the third place, Paul augments his salutation most strikingly in Romans by noting the content of God's gospel; it "concerns his Son . . . Jesus Christ our Lord." Two parallel relative clauses further identifying this Son in vv. 3b–4 show linguistic and formal signs of being a pre-Pauline creedal fragment and are of great interest for the light they shed on the early development of Christology (Christian understanding of Jesus' nature):

157

[his Son]
who was descended from the seed of David
    according to the flesh,
who was appointed Son of God with power
    according to the spirit of holiness by [or from] the resurrection of the dead.

This couplet is best explained as having originated from the combination of two strains of early Christian affirmation about Jesus. First, although it appears nowhere else in Paul, the origin of the Messiah from the royal line of David was one of the constants in Jewish messianic expectation based on 2 Sam 7:11b–16 and is found in the New Testament in the infancy narratives of Matthew and Luke (Matt 1:1; Luke 1:27; 2:4; cf. Mark 10:47 and parallels; Mark 12:35 and parallels; Matt 9:27; 12:23; 15:22; 21:9, 15; John 7:42; Rev 5:5; 22:16). Second, another tradition developed from the confession that with the resurrection Jesus was exalted to become the Son of God or the Messiah. This tradition made use of Pss 2:7 and 110:1 and appears in its simplest form in Acts 2:36; 5:30–31; 13:33. Such an understanding of "Son of God" as a titular office or role to which Jesus was "appointed" at a given moment in time is also without parallel in Paul. The two traditions, one oriented more around the earthly life of Jesus as a descendant of David, the other centered in the preaching of God's resurrection of the crucified Jesus, seem to have developed at first as alternative ways of affirming Jesus to be the bearer and fulfiller of Jewish messianic hopes.

In the couplet above quoted by Paul, the two traditions (which appear together again in looser order in 2 Tim 2:8) have been clamped together by means of the word pair "flesh" and "spirit." These terms appear in other early creedal or hymnic passages to distinguish the earthly sphere of reality (without morally pejorative connotations) and the transcendent realm of divine power (1 Tim 3:16; 1 Pet 3:18; 4:6; cf. John 3:6; 6:63). Combined in this way, the two sets of messianic ideas are no longer parallel but have become sequential, creating narrative movement in the creedal pattern. The earthly life of the descendant of David is a first stage, followed by the postresurrection reign of the Son of God installed in divine power. An important later development is then clearly observable in Ignatius's letters (Ign. *Eph.* 7:2; 18:2; 20:2; Ign. *Smyrn.* 1:1–2): the two sets of messianic categories are again brought into parallelism, but now, under the influence of the virgin birth tradition and to meet a new polemical situation, the link with the resurrection is broken and both are connected with the birth of Jesus to affirm a double origin of his person, one human and one divine. With that a major step is taken toward the patristic doctrine of the two natures of Christ. This is to go far beyond the meaning of the present passage in Rom 1:3b–4, but it indicates the historical significance of the creedal fragment Paul quotes.

In this context the quotation is an important part of Paul's initial move to establish the common ground of a shared faith with his unknown readers. Both the title "Son of God" and the mention of the resurrection, understood as God's vindication and authorization of Jesus "in power," show that what is decisive for Paul about Jesus of Nazareth is God's identification with him. The close operating association that results is central to Paul's Christology, appears in the liturgical blessing with which the salutation ends (v. 7b), and is seen in the way Paul embarks on his next paragraph, in which he prays to God "through Jesus Christ."

1:8–15, Thanksgiving. Another standard practice in Hellenistic letter writing was to begin with a prayer of thanksgiving for the favorable circumstances of recipient or writer or both. Paul often gives thanks for the faith of his readers, not only because he understands it to be symptomatic of God's working, but also because in his world confession is a public act with repercussions for the further spread of the gospel, not simply a private faith. In the present passage, the thanksgiving quickly merges after v. 8 into statements about Paul's desire to visit Rome (see the earlier section on the "Occasion and Purpose" of Romans). At the end (vv. 14–15) he explicitly traces this desire to the higher duty that governs his life and authorizes his mission; he is "one under obligation" to all alike. To register the universal range of that imperative he abandons for a moment (and only here in his letters) his customary division of humankind into Jew and non-Jew that always has a religious dimension and adopts the cultural and linguistic designations "Hellene" (among whom the Romans would have counted themselves) and "barbarian," "learned and simple" (NEB). Paul's thanksgivings often serve to signal certain concerns or themes of the subsequent letter bodies, and this deliberate point that his gospel pertains to all without regard to social standing and privilege confirms that pattern.

1:16–17, Statement of the Theme. In close logical continuity with the preceding, Paul asserts, "For I am not put to shame by the gospel." This somewhat surprising expression has little to do with moral disgrace or with personal pride. In the Septuagint (LXX), "to be put to shame" is to have a hope or expectation disappointed, a confidence proven to be misplaced (cf. Ps 119:6; Isa 54:4). Its opposite, as here, is to have the base on which one rests one's life turn out to warrant the trust placed in it. Paul can "have complete confidence in the gospel" (TEV) because it is God's powerfully effective way of working for human salvation. In itself that does not yet state an issue that is subject to debate. But with vv. 16–17, which bring the thanksgiving to its conclusion, Paul takes one additional step. Because the content of the gospel is God's Son (vv. 3–4), God's way of effecting salvation pertains from now on to all who believe, Jew and Greek alike, and it involves a revelation of "the righteousness of God" on these new terms. As a matter of fact, the ensuing argument of the letter elaborates this last step and in so doing rejects certain alternative understandings of salvation (see 3:21–26). Verses 16–17 thus function as a statement of the theme of the letter.

It is characteristic that Paul ends this introductory statement by appealing (for confirmation) to an Old Testament text (Hab 2:4) that brings together the three major terms "righteousness," "faith," and "life" (or salvation). But the sense in which Paul understands it is not immediately apparent. It differs in detail from both the Masoretic Text (MT) and the LXX. More important, the phrase "by faith" can be construed to modify either the subject, "the righteous person," or the verb, "shall live." A widely held view, choosing the first possibility, concludes that chapters 1–4 of the letter describe "the person who is righteous by faith," while chapters 5–8 show how such a person "shall live." That would suggest that Paul simply accepts the premise that righteousness is a condition of salvation and that the issue in Romans concerns only the terms on which that righteousness is to be attained. That is much too simple. In the actual course of the letter all three of the major terms of this text undergo basic redefinition and turn out to have more than one level of meaning. For example, although Paul is certainly concerned with human believing, his Greek term for "faith," as in the LXX version of Hab 2:4, is also used for the faithfulness of God on which human trusting rests. It appears wiser, therefore, not to press this key "title" verse too hard at this point, but to allow Paul's own line of thought to disclose his understanding of it.

1:18–11:36

The Central Argument

Romans 1:18–11:36 forms a first major whole in the composition of Romans; chapters 12–16 draw important consequences for the readers, but move at another level and incorporate materials of a quite different nature. One should avoid characterizing the first as "theological" or "dogmatic" and the second as "ethical" or "didactic," for in both parts Paul uses theological arguments of many kinds to inform, instruct, and guide his readers. Yet this first part of the body of the letter forms the base and must be taken on its own terms.

1:18–3:20

Preparatory Considerations

A clear indication of the deliberate nature of Romans in comparison with his other letters is that Paul does not move directly to the central content of his gospel. After the opening address, Jesus Christ is not mentioned until 3:21–26. Instead, Paul carefully prepares his readers and provides a context for his exposition in two ways. First, every interpretation of the meaning of Jesus Christ for human beings implies a certain understanding of the world, a diagnosis of the human condition to which that interpretation is addressed. Since 3:24–25 speaks of "redemption in Christ Jesus" and of God's provision of a "means for dealing with sin," this preceding analysis involves mounting a "charge that all human beings, both Jews and Greeks, are under sin" (3:9), demonstrating the world's need for God's saving action. Paul does not leave the diagnosis to be inferred; he develops it at some length. A careful reading of this preparatory argument is thus crucial to a correct perception of his intentions later. Second, and more important, if the exposition is to be persuasive and convincing, this diagnosis of the human predicament must also come to terms with the perceptions religious people have already formed about it. The tendency of religious moralists, in their scrutiny of the world about them, is to exempt themselves from their own negative judgments upon others. But since Paul wants to set forth the gospel as God's way of working for the salvation of all persons without distinction, he must also demonstrate that all stand on the same footing before God. This requires him to question certain typical and recurrent religious assumptions about God and about the terms on which salvation and life are bestowed on human beings. These two strategies of preparation are intimately intertwined in these first three chapters.

1:18–32, The Operation of God's Wrath in the World. Somewhat surprisingly, the point at which Paul begins is not human activity, but God's. The word "sin" does not appear until 3:9. In striking parallelism to his claim that in the gospel God's righteousness is revealed (1:17), he asserts that on the wider stage of the world apart from the gospel what is being disclosed is God's wrath in action upon and against human beings who suppress God's truth. Paul is quite specific about that suppression. Human beings have had every opportunity to know God; indeed, they have known God. Nevertheless, "in spite of knowing God, they did not honor him as God or give thanks to him" (v. 21). That is the central failure; everything else is a consequence of that. To be sure, it is a failure of human beings; they are responsible and indeed without excuse. But in presenting those consequences of their behavior, Paul insists three times (vv. 24, 26, 28) that it is God who has been at work.

Several features of this rehearsal call for attention. The first is the very notion of "the wrath of God." Although the wrath of the gods plays a role in many religions, in Israelite thought it had come to be understood as God's response to human provocation that violates the divine holiness and majesty (cf. 1 Sam 5:6; 6:9; 2 Sam 6:7). Following the trend of postbiblical Judaism, the New Testament writers tend to avoid terms for divine anger and rage that occur in Greek literature, to play down the elements of passion and arbitrariness, and to link the term "wrath" with God's impartial and just judgment, his zeal for righting the wrongs that have afflicted his creation (cf. such quite different texts as *1 En.* 91:7 and Wis 5:17–20). The interpretation of "the wrath of God" is subject to two tendencies. One is to construe it as an impersonal process of moral retribution built into the very structure of the world, a cosmic nemesis, to sunder it from belief in a living God. The other is to overpersonalize it and to dismiss it as reducing God to human terms.

But recognition of the background to Paul's use of this phrase in apocalyptic and wisdom traditions as represented by *1 Enoch* and the Wisdom of Solomon makes clear that his intent is not to trivialize the distance between God and humans, but to sharpen the sense for God's transcendent presence in the face of, and in spite of, human suppression of his truth. The revelation of God's wrath is here the reverse side of the manifestation of his righteousness; it is God's divinity asserting itself where it is not recognized by human beings. Paul does not suggest that the revelation of God's wrath is in any way the content of the gospel. Nor does he suggest that God's wrath is revealed to some (the ungodly) while his righteousness is revealed to others (the godly), as though God had different "faces" for different classes of people. The scope of Paul's canvas has no limits; in speaking of both sorts of revelation, he has all humankind in view. And there is no suggestion that the revelation of God's wrath belongs only to a bygone era, that it has been replaced by a revelation of God's righteousness, as though the two "faces" of God succeed each other. The revelation of God's righteousness in the gospel does not take place against the backdrop of the absence of God from a world that has repudiated him; its other side is God's reacting presence in a world over which he remains in charge even when it defies him.

The second feature of this depiction of God's wrath is the way in which it is executed. The passage has many similarities to the literature of Hellenistic Judaism, especially Wisdom of Solomon 11–15. In keeping with that tradition, there is a kind of ironic appropriateness to the reversals that follow upon human behavior "in order that they might learn that a person is punished by those very things by which one sins" (Wis 11:16): failure to perceive God's power and deity with the "mind" brings a darkening of the mind (Rom 1:20–21); those who claim to be wise turn out to be fools (v. 22); disregard for the Creator obliterates the distinction between Creator and creature and produces confusion about what befits nature and what violates it (vv. 25–26). The climax is reached in a traditional and artfully patterned "vice list" (vv. 29–31), the force of which derives from its cumulative impact in portraying an ordered world that has turned to moral chaos. Three times (vv. 23, 25, 26) human beings are said to have "exchanged" or "substituted" one reality for another, and three times (vv. 24, 26, 28) God is said to have given them up or "delivered them over" to the consequences of their own action. The language Paul uses, especially in depicting the power of human sensuality in vv. 26–27 (v. 27, "they were burned out by lust"), conveys the strong impression of a resulting impairment and perversion. This is not the outburst of an offended Victorian, though Paul does break off in v. 25 to utter a liturgical prayer at the thought of worshiping God's creature in place of the Creator. It is the response of a representative Hellenistic Jew to the spectacle of God's grand creation, which includes human sexuality, deformed. There is a moral dimension to this distortion, as the vice list shows, but the depiction itself is surprisingly free from moralizing. Idolatry and the abuse of sexual distinctions are not here the objects or cause of God's wrath but the symptoms of its operation, examples of the disorders that result from the root failure to honor God or give thanks to him. The worst distortions are those of human religious practice. "One does not thumb one's nose at God" (Gal 6:7b); suppressions of his truth produce corresponding negative realities to press with a new fatefulness upon the human race and shape its world. That is how a wrath traditionally associated with God's final judgment is already now being disclosed.

A third significant feature of this sober assessment of the world's condition is that the argument presupposes throughout that God is indeed known from his works, his deity manifest in his handiwork. Here too Paul shows his roots in a Hellenistic Judaism flavored with the language of Stoicism (cf. Wis 13:1–9). But he emphasizes the initiative of God in making himself known (Rom 1:19b) and universalizes access to this knowledge. The knowledge of God is not the special attainment of an intellectual elite, nor is godlessness the result of ignorance. This knowledge is not only open to all, it is given to all, "with the result that they are [all] without excuse" (v. 20b). Paul does not suggest that God is by nature or in principle unknowable, nor does he propose that what the world worships as an "unknown God" the Christian gospel now makes known (cf. the Lukan representation of Paul on the Areopagus [Acts 17:23]). He does not, like the author of the Fourth Gospel, claim that no one has ever seen or known God and that the point of Christ's coming was to make him known (John 1:18). The foundation lines of Paul's argument are laid down differently: God has been known, yet he has not been recognized or honored as God. Such an argument requires one to think of the knowledge of God on two levels: God is known, yet remains unknown; not necessarily unknown but actually unknown—and that paradox is the paradox of human sinfulness itself, which is not necessary but actually universal. That the manifest God should remain without the recognition and obedience due him is the fundamental perversion of the relationship between Creator and creature that draws every other kind of distortion in its wake.

We may for a moment anticipate Paul's later argument: the knowledge of God at this deeper level of recognition and honor, which otherwise is never actual because of the power of sin, is reached when the defeat of sin's power in Christ opens up a new life of obedience and righteousness. The whole argument of Romans may be summed up as an exposition of God's way of rectifying, setting right, that flawed relationship by his Son, Jesus (to whom Paul refers in his earliest letter as "the one who delivers us from the impending wrath" [1 Thess 1:10]). In the present section, some consequences of that failure of human beings to honor God are in abuse of their bodies (Rom 1:24), a distorted form of worship (v. 25), and a "reprobate mind," that is, one no longer capable of discerning good and evil (v. 28). After the conclusion of this whole argument, as Paul opens the other major division of his letter, he appeals to his readers to make their own that new life Christ has brought: "Present your bodies as a living sacrifice . . . which is your appropriate worship. . . . Be transformed by the renewal of your mind so that you may discern what the will of God is" (12:1–2).

2:1–16, Moral and Religious Persons before an Impartial God. So far Paul has not needed to name those he has been describing, for he has been referring to all inhabitants of God's creation. There has been one specification in 1:18: God's wrath is "against all ungodliness and wickedness on the part of those who by their wickedness suppress the truth." Now it is the inevitable reaction of all moral and religious people, all those who would agree with the preceding diagnosis of the world's condition, to suppose that these words exempt them from the wrath of God. The clear and simple purpose of this next section is to close off that imagined escape.

The first six verses make this apparent. It is a mistake to picture Paul as a prosecutor indicting first the Gentile (in ch. 1) and now the Jew (in ch. 2). Romans 3:9 may state his conclusion, but it does not describe his method. He does not now "prove" that religious moralists (there is no direct focus on the Jew until v. 17) in fact do the same things that they condemn in others. He simply assumes that they do (v. 1c). The moralist knows perfectly well the terms of God's judgment (v. 2, anticipated in 1:32). That is not the point. It is the presumption of those who put themselves on God's side in passing judgment, their illusory notion that they are exempt from judgment (v. 3), and the resulting "contempt" (v. 4) for a divine goodness and patience that ought to lead them to repentance, that is "storing up" God's wrath against them. For their denial of their own accountability to God is simply their form of a knowledge of God that fails to "honor God or give thanks to him" (1:21). In its place, in vv. 6–11, Paul rings the changes on God's impartial judgment: all persons without exemption, "the Jew first and also the Greek," stand on the same footing before God and must face the consequences of their actions, whether for good or ill. Just how axiomatic this impartiality of God is for Paul is shown by the form in which Ps 62:12 is echoed in v. 6, as an adjectival clause, almost an epithet for God. Paul's main point here stands firmly in the prophetic tradition; Amos (9:10), Micah (2:6–7), and Jeremiah (2:35; 14:13–16) all had to counter the tendency of religious people to turn trust in God into a self-immunization from his judgment, a shield behind which to evade accountability.

Just as Amos's oracles begin with the nations around Israel's periphery only to zero in on his own people (Amos 1:2–2:16), so Paul's argument quickly becomes more specific. Since he has referred now "to the Jew first and also the

Greek" (resuming Rom 1:16), the last verses of this section (2:12–16) press the point of their equal standing before God with regard to the one thing that most conspicuously divides them. Twice in one verse (v. 14) the Gentiles are defined as those who do not have the (Mosaic) law. The point of the verse is not to say that somehow Gentiles too have that law. What v. 12 states negatively, that the absence or presence of the law makes no difference in the consequences of human sinning, vv. 13–14 put positively: performance counts, and non-Jews who do "the things of the law" on their own, without being enjoined by the Mosaic law (this is the natural sense in Greek of the phrase "by nature"), do not need the Mosaic law when they come before God as their judge. Their conscience and the very existence of their moral disputations demonstrate their accountability for their own deeds. Paul carefully avoids saying that the law itself is "written on their hearts," which to a Jew could only mean the end-time realization of perfect obedience on the part of God's people (cf. Jer 31:33).

2:17–29, The Jew before an Impartial God. If the point that no one is exempt from accountability to God is to be carried through all the way, it must be made with explicit reference to the exemplary religious person. So Paul, in one of the most dramatically rhetorical passages in all his letters, addresses the Jew directly in the second-person singular—not because the Jew is the enemy or guilty of violation of God's law, but just because this person represents the very best in Paul's religious world, indeed the highest claims of his own religious tradition. Verses 17–21a are a single sentence, in which Paul itemizes a whole series of convictions that both reflected and shaped the Jewish sense of identity and of mission in the world during the intertestamental period. It is easy to translate with a sarcastic tone, but Paul has a sure eye for Jewish self-respect and pride, and the argument turns on that, not on Paul's demeaning his own tradition. The prerogatives of Judaism listed here (cf. Rom 9:4–5 for a less polemical enumeration) revolve around possession of the law as the hallmark of distinction from the non-Jewish world and are climaxed in v. 20b in the strikingly Hellenistic phrase "possessing in the law the very embodiment of knowledge and truth," that is, the answer to all human inquiry and searching. This possession notwithstanding, the rhetorical denouement at the end puts four ironic questions, two of which directly echo the Decalogue, challenging the Jew to answer to the same divine interrogation that every religious person is inclined to proclaim to the surrounding world. Using in v. 24 a text from Isa 52:5 that referred to the scorn of the Babylonians for the apparent weakness of the God of the Israelite exiles in their midst, Paul turns to charge that the goal of every serious religious person, to bring honor to God, is in fact subverted into its opposite by those who presume to judge the world but themselves evade accountability to God by taking their prerogatives as surrogates for obedience.

Returning in vv. 25–29 to his more sober argumentative style, Paul singles out circumcision, the most vivid symbol of individual participation in the covenant in the Hellenistic period, to make the point that all the formal tokens of religious identity depend for their meaning and validity on actual obedience, thus putting Jew and non-Jew once again on exactly the same footing before an impartial God. In the last two verses, far from obliterating the identity of the Jew, Paul proceeds to redefine and reclaim it by contrasting what is public and secret, flesh and heart, letter and spirit. (This last contrast, repeated in Rom 7:6 and 2 Cor 3:6, has become a major idiom of theological language.) Genuine religious identity (including that of the Jew in the first instance) is at once authentically human and immune to human manipulation, hidden except to God. Its ultimate approbation depends on the God who judges truly, not on human appraisal. This radical appeal from all outward criteria to an inner religious integrity known and determined by God alone is a positive ingredient in Paul's preparatory argument in Rom 1:18–3:20, apart from which his negative indictment (3:9) cannot be rightly understood. It taps the deep lode of the Old Testament prophets' critique of religion and is reminiscent of the sharp juxtaposition in the Sermon on the Mount between the visible marks of piety and what is recognized by "your Father who sees in secret" (Matt 6:4, 6, 18).

3:1–8, Two Objections Anticipated. A characteristic feature of Paul's didactic style is exemplified in this section. Not only does he directly address an imagined interlocutor in the second person, as in 2:17–24; he anticipates responses and answers them, thus ensuring that his own major conclusions are not misunderstood. Whereas in his other letters such dialogic interchange remains occasional, it is an index to the deliberate quality of the presentation in Romans that such rhetorical questions and replies mark stages in the argument and provide clues to the structuring of the letter (cf. 3:9; 6:1, 15; 7:7, 13; 9:14; 11:1, 11).

As is often the case, the first question (3:1) arises with unrelenting logic out of the preceding section. If that religious integrity that really counts before God has no connection with religious distinctions, what is the point of being a Jew? The question is only partially answered. The Jew has an "advantage," but it consists in the initiative and faithfulness of God, which does not depend on human fidelity. The answer is only partial because the question still lurks whether, in treating Jew and non-Jew on equal terms, God has not himself broken faith with the "direct utterances" he has entrusted to the Jews. That momentous issue, the connection between God's faithfulness and Israel's past election and future destiny, is suppressed here for full discussion in chapters 9–11. Deferring that side of God's faithfulness, Paul focuses for the moment on God's truth and righteousness instead. One who genuinely honors God will desire, in the words of the central penitential psalm of the Hebrew scriptures (Ps 51:4), that God be

"justified [i.e., shown to be right] whenever he speaks and be vindicated whenever he enters into court proceedings with his people." Justification, on its first
appearance in Romans, is not the justification of human beings but the vindication of God himself in the face of a world that fails to honor him as God and
in the face of evasive religious substitutcs for obedience.

This reply only hastens the second objection in vv. 5–8: if God is vindicated
no matter what the infidelities of human beings, what grounds are there for condemnation or wrath at all? Paul responds by turning the train of thought in the
opposite direction; the certainty that God is the judge of the world makes such
a protestation ridiculous. But the question only takes new forms. God's prerogative to judge may stand, but what about his integrity and the moral consequences? Wickedness and sin seem no longer to mean anything. Why not
conclude, "Let us do evil that good may come"? For a moment the curtain is
lifted on personal charges that have been leveled against Paul. But once again
no real answer is provided (until, in this case, 6:1–7:6), for a proper rejoinder
cannot come until Paul has begun his positive account of justification. Until
then, there is only a rough dismissal: people who talk like that deserve what
they get.

**3:9–20, The Solidarity of Jew and Gentile under the Power of Sin and
before the Law**. Having for the moment set these objections to one side, Paul
returns to his main line of thought to draw up his indictment. There is some sub-
tlety to the way he resumes the question of the Jew's "advantage" in v. 9. At
first he seems flatly to take back what he had granted in v. 2. But he has been
very careful so far—and remains so throughout Romans—not simply to obliterate the distinction between Jew and Gentile, even though he insists that they
stand as equals before God. It is the last point that now comes emphatically to
the fore. Whatever the "advantage," it makes no difference in this: all human
beings, both Jews and Greeks, are "under sin." This first mention of "sin" in
Romans personifies it as an oppressing power, setting a pattern that holds for
the rest of the letter. The "evidence" to verify the charge is not merely empirical; it is certified by scripture, here cited in a carefully constructed collage of
passages from the Psalms and Isaiah that first declares the nonexistence of a
single righteous person and then catalogs the symptoms of human debase-
ment in speech and action. At the end, Paul makes sure there is no room left for
religious self-exemption. The "law" (which here includes the passages just
cited from Psalms and Isaiah and thus stands for the whole of the Hebrew scriptures, as in 1 Cor 14:21) makes this declaration "to those who are covered by
the law," the Jews as well as Gentiles. It follows that the whole world is not
only answerable to God, but indictable. Something of Paul's distinctive view
of the Mosaic law emerges when he goes a step further to declare this silenc-
ing of every self-defense to be the very purpose of that law, a statement for

which no Jewish parallel is known. The psalmist, calling on God for deliverance, had cried (Ps 143:1c–2):

> [A]nswer me in your righteousness.
> Do not enter into judgment with your servant,
> for no one living is righteous before you.

By adding to that last line the expression "by works of the law," Paul had already in Gal 2:16 constructed a motto, which he now repeats (v. 20a). The true religious integrity that enables authentic obedience, but which all humankind lacks, cannot itself be produced by performing any deeds enjoined by the law. That would amount to self-salvation. It is precluded by the power of sin, which renders the law impotent to produce the obedience it calls for (cf. Rom 8:3–4; Gal 3:21b). Instead, "all that law does is to tell us what is sinful" (JB).

3:21–8:39

The Justification of the Unrighteous

The right knowledge of God, which truly honors God as God and gives thanks to him, the proper relationship of creature to Creator, and the genuine integrity that issues in true obedience are all wanting because of the power of sin. That void cannot be filled by human effort to live by the Mosaic law. Only a fresh initiative on God's part can recover for all human life a right relationship to him, the power of a new beginning, a restored integrity, and a hope for a future share in God's own glory. That this fresh initiative for the salvation of all has been effectively taken in Jesus Christ is the heart of Paul's gospel (1:16), and it is to the positive exposition of that claim that he turns at this point and for the remainder of his letter. Such a comprehensive claim requires an appropriately rich language. In Paul's usage, the controlling terms are "righteousness" and "justification"—first of God and then of human beings. This creates some problems of understanding for modern readers, but the first solution, as in every instance of listening to another person, is to follow his own explanatory line of thought, for these are not the only words or concepts Paul uses. Each subsequent unit of Romans adds another dimension to Paul's presentation of his gospel and so refines his use of these terms.

3:21–26, The Death of Jesus Christ as the Revelation of God's Righteousness. The most important step Paul takes in this introductory passage is to locate God's fresh saving initiative in the death of Jesus on the cross, the first mention of Christ in the argument of the letter. What is significant about Jesus here is not his teaching, preaching, expectation of the kingdom of God, or moral behavior, but his death. The righteousness of God now manifest apart from law is thus not first of all a divine attribute or a human moral quality bestowed by God and exemplified in Jesus' life, but God's delivering activity in the death of Jesus. Not until later does Paul elaborate his own understanding of the way this death alters the human situation. For the moment he simply accepts and uses in v. 25 what appears to be an early summary Jewish-Christian liturgical statement of the meaning of Jesus' death in terms drawn from the Old Testament institution of sacrifice. It refers to that death as an "expiation," a place or means of removing or covering sin. Since the Greek word behind this expression is used in the LXX (e.g., Exod 25:17) for the "mercy seat," the slab on top of the ark of the covenant that was sprinkled with the blood of the sin offering on the Day of Atonement, this liturgical language may have been composed originally to affirm that Jesus' death surpasses and replaces the atonement ritual of the Jewish temple (cf. Heb 9). But the reference to the temple may not be so direct; the same Greek term is used for the vicarious atoning effect of the deaths of the Jewish martyrs in the early Hasmonean revolt (4 Macc 17:22). In either case, Jesus' death is understood in terms of the atoning efficacy of the blood of a sacrificed life, that is, its power to remove not only the consciousness of sin on the part of those involved but also its objective consequences in the world, to break the guilt-punishment sequence that follows violations of God's will. Even elsewhere Paul does not develop such sacrificial ideas, though he frequently betrays their presence in his Christian traditions (cf. 1 Cor 15:3; Gal 1:4). Here he uses this traditional language to make a number of points that further his present argument.

The first is to emphasize God's own initiative in freely providing a solution to the problem described in the preceding chapters. The undeserved quality of this deliverance as a "free gift," prompted by God's own graciousness ("his grace" is not the gift itself but the generosity that produces it), will be developed further in Rom 5:1–11. Here Paul calls it "redemption," using a figure of speech for salvation that still has some of the financial overtones of its everyday sense (cf. 1 Cor 6:20; 7:23). But the emphasis is on its releasing effect. There is no suggestion whatsoever of compulsion on God to pay a price to anyone other than himself. What God has undertaken, in the formula Paul quotes, is "expiation," a means for dealing with human sin, and not "propitiation," a means for meeting God's wrath by offering something to appease it. In all Paul's references to atonement, Christ was crucified "for us," never for God; always as a gift, never as punishment.

That leads to the second point. Paul does not play God's graciousness off against his righteousness. Instead, God's gift in the death of Jesus is itself a manifestation of God's righteousness apart from the Mosaic law. In clear continuity with the Old Testament, especially the Psalms and Second Isaiah (Isa 40–55), the righteousness of God is in the first place his saving action in coming to the aid of his people, his "deliverance" (e.g., Isa 46:13; Pss 31:1; 143:1).

But vv. 25b–26, resuming a note struck in Rom 3:3–4, show that Paul under-stands righteousness to refer also to a quality of integrity and consistency on God's part. God cannot go back on himself; his faithfulness to his own covenant commitments means that the working of his wrath, which abandons human beings to the consequences of their actions (and which Paul never equates with his righteousness), cannot be the last word. Even patience and forbearance cannot, for by themselves they would mean God's capitulation in the end to the disorder and distortion in his creation. Justification cannot mean simply accep-tance and amnesty, though it includes these. God's claim over his own creation must finally be demonstrated by renewing its right relation to him and in this way restoring to it its own integrity and order. What justification, as this bestowal of a new righteousness and obedience, means for human beings will be discussed in 6:1–7:6. But in the meantime what is demonstrated in Christ's death is God's own integrity precisely in his acting to restore integrity to every person whose righteousness comes by faith in Jesus.

That faith is the third point. Four times in this paragraph Paul has inserted references to faith or believing (v. 22 [twice]; vv. 25, 26). Just what faith is like will become clear from the example of Abraham in chapter 4. But if a true rela-tionship to God cannot be brought about by human action, faith cannot mean some prerequisite condition to be fulfilled by human beings before God can act. It is not human performance at all (4:4–5). It describes, in deliberate contrast to the law, the terms God has set for his rectifying action. These terms are that Jew and non-Jew alike trust God, that is, rely completely for the renewal of life on God's act in Christ, just as Paul has staked his own life on the gospel (1:16). It is these terms that put all human beings on the same footing before God.

3:27–31, Jew and Gentile before an Impartially Justifying God. This sec-tion presses the previous point about faith in two ways. First, God's generous provision of a way out of the human predicament absolutely precludes the "boasting" that was detailed at some length in chapter 2, that vaunting of the advantage or position of one group over against another that evades account-ability to God, violates his impartiality, and denies the dependence of all on him for life. In explaining why this is so, Paul repeats in positive form (v. 28) the motto that was stated negatively in 3:20. The Mosaic law, by requiring certain behavior, appears to encourage boasting by suggesting that such behavior does not depend on a right relationship to God but can create it in the first place. Over against this Paul sets "the law of faith" (v. 27c), an expression without parallel in his letters, but similar to "the law of the spirit of life" in 8:2 and "the law of Christ" in Gal 6:2. Contrary to appearance, the Mosaic law presumes complete trust in God and reliance on his prior salvation, and so does preclude this boasting. In both Hebrew and Greek, one word for "faith" denotes both God's trustworthiness and reliability and the trust and reliance on him that is the appropriate human counterpart elicited by God's own faithfulness. This kind of trust is not a prerequisite for a healthy relationship to God; it *is* that right relationship. That is why faith is almost always mentioned when Paul writes about justification.

Second, v. 29 makes clear that behind these opposite and incompatible aspects or effects of law—one producing "boasting" and the other excluding it in favor of trust—is the fundamental issue of God himself. Every human claim to special position or advantage before God denies that all stand on an equal footing in relation to him. Making God the patron of this or that constituency carries with it the implicit denial that God is the God of all human beings. But that, Paul points out, contradicts the central watchword of Judaism that God is one (Deut 6:4). This creed requires one to embrace, instead, Paul's central claim that Jew and non-Jew alike are rightly related to God on the same terms. It is striking that in repeating that claim, while denying any difference in standing, Paul still carefully refuses to obliterate the distinction itself between Jew and Gentile. Nor, he adds, does his argument signal a dismissal of the Mosaic law. Instead, he claims, "We confirm the law." Only the later stages of Paul's argument can fill out what he means by that.

4:1–25, Abraham: The Paradigm of Justification and of Faith. At one level Paul understands his gospel to "confirm" the law (3:31) by the general congruity with the Old Testament that he now proceeds to demonstrate with the example of Abraham. But this is a very loose sort of confirmation, requiring Paul to return to the specific issue of law later. Actually the appeal he now makes to the Old Testament confirms his gospel, and therein lies its significance. The credibility of his own position is at stake. Since he had contended that this new demonstration of God's righteousness apart from the law was attested already in "the law and the prophets" (3:21), a whole range of claims made in 3:21–30 has to be supported with scriptural arguments. One of the most important premises shared by the early Christian communities with their Jewish antecedents was that scripture provides reliable access to God's truth. The appeal to scripture is thus a form of appeal to God himself to substantiate Paul's message, and this explains why Old Testament quotations form such a conspicuous part of Romans.

The methods by which Paul constructs these arguments are of course those of first-century Judaism; its study and use of scripture is, on the one hand, itself a tradition in which he stands and from which he draws. On the other hand, his recourse to scripture, exactly like every use of tradition throughout human history, is a selective process in which his own priorities and perspectives become evident. By appealing, one might say, over the head of Moses, the lawgiver, to Abraham, the recipient of the promise, Paul signals his new understanding of what is pivotal in his own Jewish tradition and reclaims it to undergird his gospel for his readers. Even this appeal to Abraham is selective. The traditions about the patriarch were extraordinarily varied in Paul's time. Abraham was a heroic figure whose story could be used to support a variety of ends. This can be seen within the New Testament itself. In Jas 2:21–24, the same verse Paul cites (Gen 15:6) is quoted, but because it is read in the light of Abraham's offering of his son Isaac (Gen 22:2, 9), the conclusion drawn from it is exactly contrary to Paul's. So Paul's appeal to scripture is circular in nature, drawing out of it only what his gospel has already determined he will find in it. Such a suspicion attaches to any use of the past. But in Paul's case, it is this ability selectively to find such corroboration in his scripture that alone enables him to maintain his religious identity as a Jew while proclaiming his gospel, indeed to find in his gospel the ultimate vindication of his Jewish tradition and faith (cf. 2:28–29). That ability has profoundly shaped Christian understanding of the gospel ever since.

In chapter 4, this invoking of Abraham proceeds in several clearly recognizable steps. In the first (vv. 2–8), Abraham, whose status in the collective memory as a paragon of rectitude is beyond question, illustrates what Paul has just written in 3:27–28: Boasting is precluded if a right relationship to God consists of faith. Verses 4–5 state the mutually exclusive alternatives that shape the argument. Justification is either earned or it is a matter of grace; it rests either on achievement that puts God in one's debt or on trust in a God who justifies the ungodly. The place of "grace" in the contrast of v. 4 is taken by "trust" in that of v. 5. And the text of Gen 15:6 clearly states that it was Abraham's believing God that God "regarded" as righteousness. Even Abraham was dependent on a God who "justifies the ungodly," who does not merely confirm the virtues of good people but takes the initiative in restoring a world that cannot save itself. Is that so clear if Abraham was such an exemplary figure? Was Abraham ungodly?

To close that loophole, Paul applies two well-established procedures of early rabbinic exegesis, adducing a second text that repeats some wording of the first, and supporting a text from the law (the Pentateuch) with another from the Prophets or the Psalms. Here it is the traditional penitential Ps 32:1–2a that fills the breach, for it shows that "reckoning righteousness" is the equivalent of "not reckoning sin," that is, forgiveness. Abraham, the model of religious probity, was as dependent on God's gracious initiative as David, the paradigmatic repentant sinner (assumed to be the author of that psalm). This yoking of Ps 32 with the Genesis text intercepts such a use of the latter as is made in Jas 2. So the precedent of Abraham confirms that God's justifying proceeds on the basis of trust in his undeserved graciousness and leaves no room for "boasting."

The second step (vv. 9–12) rests on chronological sequence: God's consideration of Abraham's faith as righteousness precedes his covenant with Abraham and Abraham's circumcision (Gen 17:1–27). The outward marks of

Abraham the prototypical Jew are therefore secondary to the faith that makes him a "true Jew" (cf. Rom 2:28–29). Another side of Abraham, his role as ancestor, like the blessing of the psalm just quoted, turns out to embrace all who believe without circumcision. Even in the relation of his physical descendants to him, the controlling factor in his patriarchal function is trust in God, theirs and his. So the precedent of Abraham also confirms that the terms of faith established by God for justification apart from the law mean that Jew and non-Jew stand on the same footing before an impartial God. In saying so, Paul again carefully avoids, this time only by tortured Greek syntax, a simple denial of the distinction between them (cf. 3:30).

In vv. 13–17 a third side of this powerfully symbolic figure Abraham emerges: he was the recipient of God's promise for the future. In Gen 15:4–5 this promise was for an heir and descendants (Rom 4:18); in Gen 17:6–7 it was for many nations among these descendants (Rom 4:17); by Paul's own time (Sir 44:21) the tradition had expanded it into an end-time promise of inheriting the whole world (Rom 4:13), a code word for all the benefits that the descendants of the patriarch might hope for. Paul's point now is that the transmission of this legacy is determined not by law but by "the righteousness of faith." This expression, used only here in Paul's letters, directly echoes v. 11 in Greek: it is "the righteousness that was attributed to the faith [Abraham had] in the uncircumcised state" he was in when he believed. One might expect Paul to use a chronological argument again (Abraham preceded Moses), but his own reason in v. 14 is more forceful: "If the heirs are those whom the law defines as heirs, then faith is empty and this promise has been voided." The issue is not what human beings do at all, whether they adhere to the law or whether they believe (as a substitute achievement). What is at stake is the competence to determine who the heirs are. Clearly that capability does not belong to the law, whose effect is rather to evoke wrath by marking human conduct as transgression and so to disqualify people from the inheritance (v. 15; cf. 3:20, 31; 5:13, 20). (These accumulating side remarks about the law will require special treatment; see the commentary on 7:7–12.) The terms that do define the transmission are "faith" (God's trustworthiness and human reliance upon God) and "promise," for that is the only way in which the legacy can remain a matter of God's undeserved graciousness and so be guaranteed to all the descendants of Abraham impartially in the inclusive patriarchal role that the promise itself assigned to him (v. 17a).

In these three ways, Abraham confirms the gospel's description of God's justification of the unrighteous. He not only provides the illustrative example; he furnishes the defining precedent for the way in which God deals with human beings. God has not changed between Abraham and Christ. In Christ he has done what Abraham trusted him to do. So Abraham's precedent helps interpret what God has done in Christ. Verse 17 restores this focus on Abraham's God, who not only justifies the ungodly but also gives life to the dead and calls into being the things that are not. That places justification as a life-giving act in an all-embracing context. God is the Creator of life at the world's beginning, the one who restores order and integrity to life in the world's crises, the one who bestows eternal life at the world's end.

But what about faith? Having so far provided the paradigm for God's action in justification, Abraham now provides also the model for human believing (vv. 18–22). Faith is not some internal condition in contrast to external acts, nor intellectual assent to propositional truths. It is not anything Abraham "does" (vv. 4–5). Instead, it is the unwavering reliance kindled by God's promise to him. It is to live by another, by what God has done and will do. Verses 19–21 play on the words: instead of being "disabled" at the contemplation of his own and Sarah's bankruptcy of life, Abraham was "empowered" by his confidence in God's "power" to carry out what he had promised, and he gave glory to God.

Verses 23–25 supply the bottom line. Abandoning his descriptive third-person language, Paul for the first time since his opening address shifts to a first-person plural style that signals the confessional stance of the Christian community. Abraham's God, who gives life to the dead, is the God who "raised Jesus our Lord from the dead"; Abraham's justification lies in store for those who trust in this God. The text of Gen 15:6, which has echoed throughout this chapter, was ultimately written for them. Paul ends by quoting another short two-part christological formula (v. 25; cf. 1:3–4): "[Jesus], who was delivered over [to death] because of our trespasses and raised for our justification." By employing parallel passive verbs, for both of which God is the implied active agent, the formula unites Jesus' death and resurrection as inseparable parts of a single action by God, one addressed to the expiation and forgiveness of sin, the other to the renewal of life. That "justification" is the term for the latter brings this whole first part of Paul's argument to a fitting conclusion and prepares the way for the next chapters.

5:1–11, Justification Interpreted as Reconciliation: The Death of Jesus Christ as the Basis of Confidence and Hope. From this section through chapter 8 an undeniable shift takes place, but it is important to note carefully what is altered and what is not. The change of style observed in 4:23–25 continues through chapter 8 except for a brief return to the more objective third person in the second section (5:12–21). Some dominant vocabulary changes. After the first two verses of chapter 5, "faith" and "to believe/trust" are scarcely used, whereas "death" and "life," "to die" and "to live" frequently appear. The "righteousness of God" is not mentioned again until 10:3. "Jew" and "Greek" disappear, along with mention of God's impartiality and faithfulness, until after chapter 8. Clearly there is a move away from the relationship of Christianity to Judaism and its traditions; only two brief quotations from the Old Testament occur (7:7 and 8:36) and exegetical arguments like those of chapters 3 and 4 drop out until chapter 9. Instead, there is a greater focus upon the Christian community and its experience, except again for that block in 5:12–21.

New theological terms appear, such as "enmity" and "reconciliation," "slavery" and "freedom," "adoption," and "peace." God's love and the (Holy) Spirit enter the discussion for the first time (and together, 5:5). Yet all this does not mean that the treatment of the justification of the unrighteous has been abandoned. Indeed, in some respects it has become more focused: the forensic language of indictment and acquittal becomes more specific than it has ever been before (5:13–14, 18–19; 7:1–3; 8:1, 3, 31–34); in just these passages Paul provides his own most telling reformulations of justification. Furthermore, if "righteousness" is now no longer "the righteousness of God," its new referent is the quality of rectitude and integrity in human life that belongs with obedience to God; it has a new synonym in "consecration" (or "sanctification"), a term that establishes a link in Greek with the word "saints" Paul had used in his address for "Christians" (1:7; 6:19, 22; cf. 1 Cor 1:30).

Law and sin continue to receive detailed attention, especially their relation to each other (5:20–21; 7:1–25). But above all, chapters 5–8 (5:12–21 is now not an exception) continue the connection made in 3:25 to the death of Jesus and elaborate, first from one side and then another, Paul's understanding of its meaning and consequences for all human beings as well as for baptized Christians. The clue provided in 4:25 turns out to be the right one to follow: the "justification of the unrighteous" means for Paul not only forgiveness and acquittal but God's gift in Jesus Christ of a reordered life and hope as well. It is the burden of chapters 5–8 to set forth this side of Paul's gospel, without any fundamental change of subject.

In 5:1–11 readers encounter a variety of new ideas for the first time in Romans; the task is to ascertain their relationship to each other and to what has preceded. Paul begins by saying that justification results in peace in one's relationship to God. Verses 8 and 10 show that peace here is the removal of enmity toward God by the reconciliation effected in Jesus' death. It is not God who is reconciled but human beings, because the enmity is not God's; it is human opposition and resistance to God (8:7–8). The removal of this barrier opens up access to "this grace" (v. 2), which is not a human condition but the undeserved graciousness on God's part that has been a key element in Paul's earlier argument (3:24; 4:4, 16). It may be "the sphere of God's grace, where we now stand" (NEB), for Paul later declares that his readers are "under grace" (6:14). In the present context, however, it seems to be that graciousness by which men and women are sustained through the trials of life, for to hold firm or fast under stress is the usual meaning of the everyday word "to stand" in Paul's letters.

But the most significant connection with the earlier chapters is concealed in many English translations, perhaps unavoidably. Both at the beginning of this section and at the end, Paul speaks of "rejoicing" (ASV, RSV, TEV), "glorying" (KJV), or "exulting" (NEB). The Greek root is the same one translated up to this point in the letter as "boasting" (2:17, 23; 3:27; 4:2), for Paul has been describing that self-protective, unrepentant, and presumptuous confidence in God that is a recurring trait of religious people but is irreconcilable with trust. Against that illegitimate confidence, Paul now sets a legitimate sort of joyful trust, a "boasting in God through our Lord Jesus Christ" (v. 11 NRSV). What makes possible the change from one to the other is God's undeserved justification of the unrighteous in Jesus' death, because it eliminates the need for that instinctive self-defensiveness before God that Paul calls "enmity."

Verses 3 and 4 contain a rhetorical sequence (cf. 8:29–30; 10:14) that draws attention to this life as one of suffering, testing, and patient perseverance. The point is that this legitimate confidence provides staying power through the afflictions of life, because it enables those who enjoy it to be "looking forward to God's glory" (JB). And this hope does not "put to shame," it does not in the end expose those who entertain it to the embarrassment of having followed a false hope (cf. Paul's own statement in 1:16). Why not? Because God has already demonstrated his love for human beings in Jesus' death (v. 8). In the meantime, Paul declares that God's love has been "poured out" in human hearts (v. 5), a striking statement found nowhere else in the Bible. Once (Sir 18:11) it is God's mercy that is poured out; frequently it is his wrath; but the conventional language is that God pours out his Spirit (cf. the narrative of Pentecost in Acts 2:17, citing Joel 2:28). Since v. 8 makes clear that "love of God" here means God's love for human beings, not their love for God, Paul is equating the sustaining assurance of God's demonstration of his love in the death of Jesus with the life-giving power of the Spirit, which is God's own presence with human beings in the world in spite of its afflictions and threats.

Just how the death of Jesus provides such supportive assurance for the future is spelled out in two steps in the second half of this section (vv. 6–10). First, Paul contrasts the death of Jesus with the rare but not impossible heroic death of an individual on behalf of another righteous person or in the name of "the good," some commanding cause like that perhaps of the Jewish martyrs in the Hasmonean revolt, an event that shaped the consciousness of many Jews under Roman rule in Paul's time. Jesus' death is totally different. Its force as a sustaining demonstration of God's love stems from its having occurred at just such a time as conventional religion would least expect it of God, on behalf of those who in no way deserve it—in short, from its being an act of Abraham's God who "justifies the ungodly" (4:5). Second, by using a standard rabbinic method of inferring a more comprehensive conclusion that is implied in what has already been stated, Paul argues that this given present reality of justification and reconciliation in the death of God's Son makes further salvation by his life "much more certain." So justification is the granting of life in an uncertain world by extending hope and certainty, the certain hope of sharing in the life of Christ for all those who have shared in his death by receiving its benefits of reconciliation.

By filling out in this way the import of Jesus' death for human life, Paul has anticipated dominant themes of chapter 8: present affliction and future hope, enmity and peace, the sustaining power of God's love and of the presence of the Spirit. These are all treated more fully in that climax to his presentation of the justification of the unrighteous. Thus the beginning of chapter 5 and the end of chapter 8 form a bracket marking these chapters as a major whole, distinct in content as well as style. The interpreter needs to ask how each intervening section advances Paul's thought.

5:12–21, Justification Interpreted as Acquittal and Life: The Universal Reign of Grace in Place of the Universal Reign of Sin. Paul himself provides the best summary of this section in an earlier letter: "For just as in Adam all die, so also in Christ all shall be made alive" (1 Cor 15:22). A parallelism is drawn between Adam, the biblical progenitor of the human race (Gen 1–3), and Christ. Each is the first of many. Each is also a single individual who represents all others and whose actions determine and affect all others. (Throughout these verses, "the many" and "all people" are simply interchangeable expressions, according to a well-established Semitic and biblical usage; cf., e.g., Isa 53:6, 12c.) Thus each is perceived as a universal and all-inclusive figure, not only a predecessor but a prototype of all humanity. Yet these two act and affect others in exactly opposite ways, so that they are symbolic of antithetical powers and realities of worldwide scope: disobedience and obedience, condemnation and acquittal, sin and righteousness, death and life. All of history is embraced in the cosmic conflict between these powers, a major sign of Paul's indebtedness to the apocalyptic tradition in Judaism.

The section falls naturally into three parts. The first is vv. 12–14. A full and balanced statement of the analogy between Adam and Christ is not reached until vv. 18–19, but Paul begins to set out the correlation on its negative side in v. 12. Without speculating on the origin of sin and evil, he simply takes for granted the biblical depiction of the original disobedience of Adam and Eve in Gen 3, with its correlate that death is the consequence of sin (Gen 2:17; 3:19), in order to affirm the universal penetration of sin and death through Adam to the whole human race. Because the Vulgate translation of v. 12c could be understood as "one man [Adam] . . . in whom all sinned," the verse has served for centuries as the main Pauline proof text for the notion of genetically transmitted sin, but a more natural translation is "because all sinned." This results in an apparent contradiction, but the verse summarizes a characteristic understanding in Judaism of sin as at once guilt and fate, both an individual responsibility and a destiny that overpowers each person (as in Paul's discussion of God's wrath in

Rom 1:18–32; cf. Wis 1:13; 2:23; Sir 25:24; *2 Apoc. Bar.* 54:15). It is to this second aspect that Paul turns first. In the period between Adam and Moses, "in the absence of law," sin was "not counted"; that is, each individual was not held responsible for sin. Nonetheless everyone died, showing clearly the fateful reign of death over all as a result of Adam's action, even over those who had not committed the same kind of explicit transgression of a command as Adam's. In thus determining the fate of others, Adam prefigured Christ. In so distinguishing the period prior to Moses, Paul already has in mind what he refers to later (v. 20) as the "intrusion" of the law.

Verses 15–17 form the second part of the section. Having just touched on the similarity that coordinates the two figures, Paul in these verses underlines the differences between the two sides of the typology. The correlation is decidedly unbalanced, both quantitatively and qualitatively. Death proceeded from a single act, but the gift of life began with a multitude of trespasses. There is a lavish profuseness, an "abounding" surplus on the side of God's gift that explicitly recalls the "much more" of 5:9–10. Paul's vocabulary clearly indicates that he now has in view the situation after Moses, created by the coming of the law. On the one side, trespass, judgment, condemnation, and death emphasize in juridical language the deserved guilt and responsibility of every sinner. On the other side, the language of free gift, grace, extravagant generosity, and life emphasizes the displacement of what is due to all sinners by a totally undeserved gift in God's act of justification (mentioned in v. 16).

Verses 18–21 form the final part of the section. With these verses a difficult train of thought emerges into the clear. Over against the trespass of the one is set "the righteous act" or, better, "the justifyinge" (Tyndale's translation, 1535) of the other (v. 18). Opposite Adam's disobedience, by which all "were constituted sinners," there is Jesus Christ's obedience, by which all "shall be constituted righteous." The restatement of 1 Cor 15:22 is complete; cast now in the language of justification, it shows that "justify" is for Paul a synonym for "make alive." Jesus' "obedience," mentioned for the first time in v. 19, is a new explanation for the way in which his whole life, but especially his death, saves others, namely, by reversing the effect of Adam's disobedience. This is an independent, alternative interpretation of Jesus' death, alongside "expiation" (3:25), "God's love for us while we were still sinners" (5:8), and "reconciliation" (5:10). (This use of obedience to explain Jesus' death, and the life that preceded it, appears elsewhere in Paul's letters only in Phil 2:8; cf. Heb 5:8. The idea, though not the word, is much more common in the gospels, e.g., Matt 3:15; Mark 14:36 and parallels; John 4:34; 6:38.)

In sum, apart from the law, sin and death (from Adam) and righteousness and life (from Christ) would be similar impersonal and inexorable destinies inflicted upon all people by virtue of the solidarity of all, first with Adam and then with Christ. But Paul recalls (v. 20) the "intrusion" of the Mosaic law between Adam and Christ (vv. 13–14). The law adds to trespass the "sting" of condemnation (1 Cor 15:56; Rom 4:15). Now that sin is "counted" (v. 13), magnified and deepened by the addition of guilt, death is more than a neutral destiny; it is deserved by all. But by the very same token, now that sin is counted against everyone, life has become something more than a neutral destiny; it is the free and undeserved gift of a gracious God. It has become the overflowing abundance of grace (v. 20). Verse 21 sums up what Paul has said about the law in a remarkable sentence: the purpose of God, served by its "intrusion" on the human scene, is that just as death has been the symptom of the reign of sin as a power over human lives, so righteousness (justification) might become the symptom of the new reign of grace. Just as the law turned the reign of death in Adam (v. 14) into the reign of sin, so that same law has turned the reign of life in Christ (v. 17) into the reign of grace.

It is not the purpose of this section to weigh determinism and free will, a problem that is simply not on Paul's horizon. Chapter 6 will show very clearly that he treats his Christian readers as responsible moral agents. The issue is the universal and pervasive tyranny of sin as a power, and Paul's gospel of an overwhelming liberating power of a grace that has replaced it (cf. 6:14). This section is still about the justification of the unrighteous. It does not just describe justification as the bestowal of life in place of death (5:1–11 does that in its own way). It does not merely portray the cosmic and universal scope of justification over against the universality of death (though it does also do that). It underlines the character of justification as an act of God's undeserved graciousness, elaborating the note struck first in 3:24 and then again in 4:4, 16; and 5:2—and does this in such a way as to make the Mosaic law contribute to its grace character.

6:1–7:6, Justification as the Gift of a Reordered Life. Paul has just made the astonishing claim that one of God's purposes with the Mosaic law was to use its "increase" of sin's power over men and women to augment and reinforce grace. If that is so, one must necessarily ask the question of 6:1: "Are we to continue in sin in order that grace might increase?" Paul's imagined interlocutor has already raised this question as part of an objection pertaining to God's own moral integrity in 3:5–8. It now serves as the transition to another facet of justification. But one should pause for a moment to reflect on its significance.

Romans 3:8 shows its personal importance for Paul, as a charge leveled against him by opponents who presumably thought his teaching undermined the Jewish law and invited irresponsible license in human behavior (cf. Acts 21:21). But the theological importance of the question "Why not sin?" lies in the fact that it is inevitably and regularly raised whenever the claim is made, as here, that human perversity cannot decisively frustrate God's benevolent purpose. Such a claim has always seemed to deny the reality and seriousness of sin, as Rom 3:5–7 exemplifies.

Throughout Christian history, the universal scope that Paul has clearly attributed to grace by pitting it against the worldwide grip of sin and death in 5:12–21 has seemed to undermine everything he set forth in the early chapters about human accountability to God for moral behavior. Every radical message of grace stirs the ghost of libertinism to life. For just that reason, in 6:1–7:6 Paul does not simply turn aside from his main argument temporarily to put down a local objection. Rather, his answer forms another carefully constructed stage in his presentation of the justification of the unrighteous. Chapter 5 showed that righteousness, the rectitude and integrity restored to human life in its relation to God through the death of Jesus, is "a matter of grace" (4:16). It shows God's love for human beings while they are still sinners (5:8); it is an undeserved gift, manifesting the lavish profuseness of God's generosity (5:17, 20). But in the present section Paul turns the argument in the opposite direction, answering the question of 6:1 by showing that God's grace involves for its recipients a new *righteousness,* a reordering and integrity that preclude an undisturbed continuation of life's previous patterns.

This sudden reversal has seemed to many interpreters to suggest a shift of audience, as though Paul were turning from the Jewish-Christian members of the Roman church to the Gentile Christians, correcting first the presumed legalistic tendencies of the former and now the libertarian proclivities of the latter. Such a reading gains a certain plausibility from the clear evidence that Paul had previously encountered both of these perennial religious tendencies in the churches he had founded, the one most conspicuously in Galatia and the other in Corinth. But one should avoid projecting stereotypes from his earlier correspondence onto the reading of Romans. There is little support from Paul's argument up to this point for such a hypothetical division.

On the contrary, the early emphasis on God's impartiality, the tight construction of his case, and its internal continuities suggest that in this letter, just because of diverse reactions to his preaching, Paul is fashioning a theological position that will effectively counter both tendencies at the same time. His instrument for doing this is a broad and flexible doctrine of justification that includes both God's free and undeserved initiative in the face of all kinds of conditions that legalism tries to set, and the restoration of integrity to human lives in the face of the moral chaos that libertinism breeds. The resulting exposition here in Romans has always resisted the artificial separation of justification and sanctification, of "forensic" and "sacramental" grace, of "imputed" and "infused" righteousness that the confessional debates of Christian history have produced and tended to impose on these chapters. It is just this separation that results in a corresponding literary isolation of chapters 6–8 from chapters 1–5, as though they were not written to the same audience. But this division should be resisted. If the formal instrument Paul uses is now the language of justification, the material heart of his theological position is his interpretation of the death and resurrection of Jesus. It was from this single vantage point that he had argued in both Galatia and Corinth. This remains the case here. As each stage in Romans, from 3:25 on, has involved recourse to the death and resurrection of Jesus as the decisive clue to God's nature and action, so this new section contains Paul's reflections on some hitherto unmentioned facets of the meaning of that event.

There are three stages to the argument of 6:1–7:6, so clearly distinguished as to amount to three separate answers to the question "Why not continue in sin?" The connection with 5:12–21 remains close, for the answers Paul now gives employ the polarities of sin and grace, death and life, disobedience and obedience that were set up by contrasting Adam and Christ.

6:1–14, Through Death to Life. The first answer to the question is that justification is a new life of righteousness because it is a death to sin. In 5:12–21, Christ was seen to be not an isolated individual but a figure who includes and represents others in such a way that he determines their circumstances and their lives; a solidarity or correspondence exists between them and him. Now Paul develops that idea. He takes it for granted that all his readers have been baptized, and that they understand this baptism to have been a baptism "into Christ's death." He does not here say that baptism created that solidarity (though it is possible to read Gal 3:27 and 1 Cor 12:13 as saying so), but as a "burial with Christ" (v. 4) it presupposes such solidarity and shows that it is now a solidarity in death. For his readers, too, a death has taken place that is irrevocable and involves the ending of each person's whole past way of life (v. 6). This is what precludes "continuing in sin."

This argument deserves a brief closer look. Paul's assumption that his readers will recognize the reference to baptism is an important indication that pre-Pauline development in Christian teaching about baptism revolved around the meaning of Jesus' death and included some kind of transfer of the benefits of that death to the baptized convert. Second, the argument rests on a very basic understanding Paul has of Jesus Christ as a representative figure, a rich idea capable of being nuanced in a variety of ways quite apart from baptism. In the discussion of Adam and Christ, it is apocalyptic and universal in its symbolic scope, embracing primeval beginnings and end time, the "first" and the "last Adam" (cf. 1 Cor 15:45). But there is also a cultic and sacrificial representation, in which Jesus died "for" others (Rom 3:24–25; 5:6, 8; and many other passages). And there is the more legal and political kind of representation, in which one person's actions commit and oblige others, as when someone has power of attorney for another. These are all intimately connected in Paul's Christology, as one can see in one of his clearest formulations of the idea of representation, 2 Cor 5:14–15 ("one has died on behalf of all; therefore all have died"). What happens to Christ happens to all those who are "in him." The phrase "in Christ Jesus," which runs through Paul's letters (occurring in our section at 6:11, 23, the two major dividing points), rests on this base perception, not on "mystical" ideas that have been anachronistically attributed to him.

Paul now refines this conception of Jesus Christ as a representative figure by drawing on the temporal sequence of Jesus' death and resurrection, as recounted in early liturgical summaries (in addition to Rom 4:25, cf. 1 Cor 15:3–4; 1 Thess 4:14; Phil 2:8–9; 2 Cor 5:15; Rom 8:34a). The adding of this new ingredient leads to various statements in Paul's theology about dying and rising, or suffering and living, "with Christ" (e.g., 1 Thess 4:14; Gal 2:19–20; Phil 3:10–11, 21; 2 Cor 4:10–11; 7:3; 13:4). In the present context this establishes a connection between the Christian's past and future: "For if we have been united with him in a death like his, we will certainly be united with him in a resurrection like his" (v. 5 NRSV). The solidarity that already exists between Christ and the individual in death must be followed by a solidarity in life as well. Since the latter still lies in the future, this solidarity has become a shared destiny. Verse 8 repeats this result as a flat indicative assertion about the future resurrection (like 1 Cor 15:22). But significantly, here in v. 4 this future indicative is deflected into a statement of God's purpose for men and women in the present: "The reason why we were buried with him through this 'baptism into death' is that, just as Christ was raised from the dead through the Father's glory, we also might [now] live a new life." What shall be, already ought to be; hope and ethical obligation are simply two sides of the same future given to each individual in Christ. Verse 11 draws the bottom line: "So you also should consider yourselves to be dead to sin and alive to God in Christ Jesus." That is why one should not "continue in sin."

Verses 12–14 press this conclusion home with general exhortations that return to the terms with which chapter 5 had ended: the reign of sin and the reign of grace as two contrary authority structures. One has displaced the other, and the Christian's allegiances are to be shaped accordingly. What is remarkable about these verses is the view of the human self implicit in the injunctions. "Mortal bodies" (v. 12), "members," and "selves" (v. 13) are interchangeable terms. Bodily existence, even though still subject to death, is an aspect of the self that one has at one's disposal, as an "implement" (v. 13) to be put in the service of a transcending allegiance (cf. 1 Cor 6:15). The self is not an end to itself; its end has been given to it in Christ.

6:15–23, Through Slavery to Freedom. The second answer to the question "Why not sin?" is that justification is a new life of righteousness because it is a being set free from the power of sin, but paradoxically it can have that quality only insofar as it is also a being brought into servitude to righteousness. Whereas the first answer was cast in terms of life and death, the categories now shift to freedom and bondage. But the most striking feature of this second answer is that it exists at all. Once one accepts Paul's premise, the destiny-creating role of Jesus as the Christ, the logic of his first reply would seem to be impregnable. Why then does he have to repeat the question once again in v. 15 and mount a second answer in these new terms? Verse 16 provides the clue by clarifying the issue of allegiance Paul raised in vv. 12–14. He does not think of human beings as autonomous creatures, or of freedom as a condition devoid of all commitment or obligation beyond oneself. No person can serve two masters, to be sure; but Paul presupposes that everyone has some "master," some controlling allegiance. The question is not whether life has such a point of orientation but which one it is, and what the outcome or goal is to which it ultimately leads. He sees the self either living in the service of sin as a power, the end result being death, or living in service of righteousness, the end result being life. By v. 22 it is clear that the latter is a life lived for God. But at the beginning, in v. 16, he seems to put it rather clumsily when he speaks of obedience "to obedience" as the opposite of obedience "to sin"; this awkwardness only shows that in the back of his mind is the contrast between obedience and the lack of commitment altogether, the total absence of a sense of obligation that lies behind the question "Why not sin?" Verse 16 shows why the language of slavery is appropriate, for here again (cf. 5:12) Paul balances the freedom of human life with its fatefulness. Choices have lasting consequences from which one cannot escape. And in moral decisions, the constraints within which one has to live have their roots in commitments one has already freely made. So slavery to sin was a kind of "freedom with respect to righteousness" (v. 20), and freedom from sin is to be found only in a "slavery" to righteousness and to God.

Paul seems to be fully aware of the scandalous incongruity of calling redemption and justification "slavery" (v. 19), but he retains the language nonetheless. Freedom, by itself, is not the answer to human existence; it is ambivalent, and its profounder dimensions open up only when one asks "Freedom from what, and for what?" and "Slavery to what?" Then the issue turns to what is being served, what allegiance is operative in every "slavery" or "freedom." As for his Christian readers, their conversion and baptism is clearly for Paul a point at which a transfer of allegiance and obligation has taken place, not because they were free to make it but because it has been made for them by God. They have "been committed" (passive) to a new pattern of living, yet they have concurred in it themselves "from the heart" (v. 17)—the same combination of fatefulness and freedom as before, but now in a liberating direction that restores human integrity ("righteousness"). That is the second reason one should not "continue in sin." (It is instructive to compare Paul's understanding of fate and freedom with that of contemporary Stoicism.)

Why was the first answer, which drew upon Christian baptism to characterize the Christian life as an irrevocable death to a past way of life, inadequate? It is hard not to conclude that the explanation lies in Paul's own experience in Corinth, where his invitation to "consider oneself dead to sin and alive to God in Christ Jesus" (Rom 6:11) had simply incited a libertinist absolutizing of freedom. A profounder exploration of human freedom and its ambivalences is required if those set free are to remain accountable to the God who set them free and are to "honor [God] as God and give thanks to him" (1:21). That is what made it necessary for Paul to add Rom 6:15–23.

7:1–6, Through Acquittal to Commitment. This third section in Paul's answer to the question "Why not sin?" consists essentially of a legal detail that provides, when applied to the Christian life, an example and conclusion for both of the first two sections. The chosen example transcends parochial usage and applies as easily to Greek and Roman society as to Jewish (and to the twenty-first century as easily as to the first). Considered by itself, the illustration (vv. 1–3) is one of the clearest definitions of justification in all of Paul's letters, for it exemplifies the way in which a person is put into a completely altered situation by the death of someone else. The extent of the change is apparent from the fact that for a married woman exactly the same action (living with another man) brings in its train the damning epithet of an adulteress before her husband's death, but has no such effect after he dies. In the latter case, the marriage legislation is still in force; it has not been abrogated. Paul is very careful not to suggest that it has, saying rather curiously that "she has been vacated from the law" (v. 2b) rather than that the law has been voided. But the law's power to condemn her has been broken. Her deliverance from this power, simply by virtue of a death having occurred, is the point.

All seems clear: the woman is the Christian set free by the death of Christ from the law's condemnation. But then the application in vv. 4–6 scrambles this neat analogy: the former husband is now the law, and it does not die; Christ, far from dying, has become the new husband to whom the Christian is now free to belong; and the effect of the death is not only to end a period of captivity but to legitimate a new relationship of commitment and productive loyalty. This reconstruction of the analogy is not the product of confusion but stems directly from the movement of Paul's thought from 6:1 on, which it in turn exposes to clear view. The Christian life is not merely a liberation, but is like ending one marriage and beginning a new one. Like the sequence of cross and resurrection adduced at the beginning (6:5, 6, 8, 10), solidarity with Christ (in his "body" [7:4a]) brings a past quality of life and service to an end and opens a new one for the future. Resuming the contrasting terms he had last used in 2:29 to distinguish the outward aspects of religion that are subject to manipulation and abuse from genuine religious integrity, Paul labels the old relationship "letter" and the new, "Spirit."

7:7–25, A Backward Look: The Power of Sin to Use the Law to Effect Death. In the course of Paul's presentation of justification, a great deal has been said about sin. Paul has always used the singular of the noun (except in 4:7, an

Old Testament quotation, and 7:5, where the plural functions as a modifier of "passions"). Almost personified, it has turned out to reign and have dominion (6:14). Death is the symptom of its rule (5:21), the daily ration it distributes to its subjects (6:23). Yet its power is curiously dependent on the Mosaic law, apart from which it lies dormant (7:8b, resuming 4:15b and 5:13b). Only the law confers upon the married woman's act of living with another man the result of condemnation (7:2–3). The law magnifies sin (5:20) and accords sin its power (cf. 1 Cor 15:56). Indeed, so closely have the roles of sin and the law meshed in Paul's reflections that death to the law (7:4) is required if one is to escape the power of sin. What in chapter 6 was a "dying to sin" (v. 10) has been replaced in the marriage illustration by "dying to the law" (7:4, 6). Correspondingly, what 6:18 referred to as "being set free from sin" has turned in 7:6 to "being exempted, vacated, from the law." It is hardly a surprise that the same logical necessity that produced the question of 6:1 now gives rise to 7:7: "What follows, then? That 'the Law is equivalent to sin'? Never!" (Moffatt's translation). When such questions have appeared earlier (in 3:1, 9, 27; 4:1, 9; and most notably in 6:1, 15), they have introduced clarifications and eliminated misunderstanding, but they have always advanced the discussion to new stages as well. That is the case here, but since the rest of chapter 7 clearly falls into two parts, each should be taken in turn.

Verses 7–12 form the first part. The inferential conjunction at the beginning of v. 12 shows that a first conclusion is being drawn to support the emphatic denial of v. 7. The Mosaic law is not the origin of sin; it is not to be confused with sin; it remains God's good and holy law. Yet law does in fact play a role in relation to sin: it identifies sin and makes it known. (Verse 7b explicitly resumes the point Paul had made in 3:20b, after affirming that the law impartially silences every attempt to evade indictment.) What law supplies, however, is no merely cerebral information about sin, nor does it bestow psychological enticement on evil by the mere act of forbidding it. As the experience of the Decalogue's prohibition of inordinate desire shows (in selecting just this one of the Ten Commandments, Paul may also have the story of the fall in mind; cf. Gen 3:6), it produces the very thing it is supposed to prevent. Just therein lies the exoneration of God's law; it has been captured and used by sin. The most striking feature of these verses is that, even though a question concerning law is being addressed here at the outset, the real subject whose activity is recounted through the rest of chapter 7 is sin. This is the power whose sinister rule has provided the foil for the reign of grace and the justification of the unrighteous in one form or another from 5:12 on. Just as in 5:12–21, its operation is chronicled in terms of the opposites, death and life. Continuing in the vivid first-person singular adopted in v. 7, Paul goes on: "in the absence of law" (v. 8b, a striking resumption of 5:13), sin was "dead," that is, dormant, and he was alive. But when the law "came on the scene" (v. 9, an echo of 5:20), sin "sprang to life" (NEB) and Paul died (v. 10). The climax is reached in vv. 10b–11: "The very commandment that was supposed to lead to life turned out for me to lead to death; for sin, by seizing an opportunity provided by that commandment, tricked me and by using it killed me."

The clear force of these words gives pause. The law held out the promise of life. Paul's phrasing here is carefully ambivalent. He does not say whether the arousing of such a hope was an intended function of the law in God's good purpose, frustrated by sin (as suggested by 2:13; 8:3a; and the quotations of Lev 18:5 in Rom 10:5; Gal 3:12), or whether it was a misunderstanding to expect life from it, a result of sin's deceitful use of the law (as seems required by Gal 3:21b; Rom 9:31–32; 10:2). The law, in scope and function, has many facets. In any case, the purpose of the law is not the first issue. It is enough that experience discovers that God's law in fact turns out to serve the strategies and ends of sin. Its result is not life but death, the symptom of sin's rule. There is not one syllable to suggest that this result is limited to those who have transgressed the law. Sin's deceit lies in its taking advantage of just those religious aspirations that make a person look to the law for life. By using the law precisely where it is honored and treasured and even obeyed, it destroys the integrity of a person's relation to God, corrodes trust, and replaces it with a defensive posture no longer gratefully dependent on God or unreservedly accountable to him.

Paul recounts this capture of the law and of the self by sin in the past tense and with the first-person singular "I." It is a mistake to read this as a personal autobiography and so to wring from it details of Paul's early life. Romans 3:7; 1 Cor 6:15; 10:29–30; 13:1–3, 11; 14:11, 14, 15; and especially Gal 2:18–21; 6:14 amply exhibit his penchant for casting his analyses of fundamental religious experience into the exemplary "I" of the born teacher. The past tenses depict the "history" of sin on the same epic scale as in Rom 5:12–14, 18–21. But the settings of Gal 2:18–21 and Phil 3:8–14 in the manifestly autobiographical contexts that precede these passages show that it would be equally mistaken to abstract Paul's description of sin from his personal discovery of its power to pervert devout allegiance to the Mosaic law. One can as little do that here as one can sanitize his perception of Jewish religious self-awareness in 2:17–29 from his own profound personal participation in it.

Verses 13–25 form the second part of the remainder of chapter 7. As 6:15 repeated the question of 6:1 in order to advance the train of thought to another level, so 7:13 renews the question of 7:7 and repeats the emphatic assertion that it was sin that was responsible for bringing about death. But there is a difference. "The law" has been replaced by "the good." Although this certainly has to do with God's law, the goodness of which Paul has just upheld, the reference now is to the good that the law holds out "to me" in its promise of life (as in 7:10), thus preparing for the following verses. In addition, two parallel purpose clauses now make clear that even in sin's use of it, the law remains God's instrument. The end result fits into God's purpose for the law, namely, to disclose the true nature of sin and show how "incomparably sinful" it really is. Continuing his intimately illustrative use of "I" but shifting to the present tense to emphasize its perennial quality, Paul turns to analyze more carefully the experience in which the religious self encounters this power of sin.

Paul shifts from the contrasting words "life" and "death" he used in vv. 7–12 to a closely related but quite different pair, "good" and "evil." (The same sort of shift occurs between the two stages of his argument in ch. 6.) This pair, in turn, is joined to contrasting verbs, and these contrasts carry the argument. This is clear in vv. 18–19: "For I know that the good does not dwell in me, that is, in my flesh. For to will the good is within my reach, but to produce it, to carry it out, is not. For what I do is not the good that I intend [desire, and prefer]; instead, what I actually accomplish is the very thing I do not intend [do not want, and wish to avoid]." Good and evil in this context are not abstract moral labels. They develop v. 13, where "that which is the good" is closely allied with the life promised "to me" by the law. The attraction of the law is that it seems to lead to the life that the religious person wants and desires above all else, the more so if it is God's holy, just, and good commandment. (In 12:2, Paul will equate "the good" with the will of God.) Paul is here touching on the deepest nerve of the Jew's allegiance to the Mosaic law. This is why the person who lives by the law, and not just under it, "delights" in God's law (v. 22, a clear echo of the psalmist's praise of the law; cf. Ps 1:2). Of course this is "moral" in a profound sense, for in religion at its best, represented for Paul by Judaism, the desire to attain life and the desire to do the good that God commands are fully joined. This willing and desiring are the more pressing the more one realizes that the good that amounts to life does not dwell within the native resources of the self taken on its own ("my flesh," v. 18).

But now, Paul goes on, this self that wants life and wills the good makes an astonishing discovery. What it does, creates, produces, and brings into being (the changes are rung on three overlapping Greek verbs) by its actions is not the intended good but exactly what it thought it could avoid by the law (exactly like the Decalogue's prohibition in vv. 7–8). The early chapters of Romans make clear enough what this means: the loss of inner integrity and of trusting reliance on God, the resulting claim to special standing that exempts one from accountability, and the denial that all stand on the same footing before the same God lead *every* religious person to abuse God's goodness and end up blaspheming his name. Verse 15 now gets its full force: "I don't understand the results of my own action!" One is compelled to paraphrase: "I know the law is good; the trouble cannot lie there. Indeed, it can't be I that am acting any longer; another power resides in me to which I am sold as a slave" (vv. 14, 17). To go a step further: "As a person wishing to do the good, I discover that God's own law, used by sin, has become a qualitatively different law, contrary to the one I adhere to in my sincere intentions. It has taken over my members, those aspects of myself by which my service and allegiance are implemented and which should be at the disposal of my own will [cf. Rom 6:12–13], and put them at the disposal of sin. The result is that I am a prisoner of war; when I want to do the good, evil is what comes out" (vv. 21–23). "Thank God that because of Jesus Christ our Lord this demonic power is not ultimate" (v. 25a).

This passage has been a battleground for debate almost since it was written. That is because it seems to lend itself to a wide variety of applications. What is needed is to take it on its own terms as far as possible, in its literary context in Romans, and in its religious and historical context in Paul's world. It is frequently understood as describing the common frustration produced by the discrepancy between ideal intentions and actual human performance, or between reason and desire (formulated, e.g., in Ovid, *Metam.* 7.18–21). This reading assigns the performance to the "flesh" as a lower self and the good intentions to an inner nature untouched by sin, and results in a dualistic conflict between passion and reason in the understanding of the self that is foreign to Paul. Such dualism is suggested by v. 25b, which is Paul's terse summary; but it is refuted by his analysis, in which the "inmost self" and "flesh" are not different selves at different levels but two aspects of the one person who is "sold under sin"— his sincere desire and his helpless vulnerability. What v. 15 describes is not the failure to produce results but the same bewilderment over the actual results of one's action that Paul spoke of in v. 10. Again, the experience that is detailed in this whole passage (7:7–25) is not the despair felt by a Martin Luther over his inability to live up to a demanding code; Phil 3:4–7 shows conclusively how different Paul's self-perception is. Nor is it the exposure felt by an Augustine at the discovery that he had oriented his life's striving around an attractive but inferior surrogate for God's highest good. It is the much more shocking encounter with sin's power to use genuine devotion to the true God, channeled through adherence to God's own law, to bring about exactly the opposite of what one has hoped for: a perverted relationship to God in place of an authentic one, evil in place of the good, death in place of life. That yields a far more sinister perception of evil operating at the very center of religious life to debase it and turn it into slavery. It is this slavery from which Paul gratefully acknowledges having been set free by Christ. Romans 7:7–25 is a backward look at "the old life of the letter" (7:6).

Finally, debate has raged over whether Paul is describing his experience as a Jew or as a Christian. That is the wrong question. There is for Paul one God of all human beings (3:29–30), and one authentic relationship to him for all, the trust exemplified by Abraham (ch. 4). All serious religious devotion is subject to being taken captive by sin and subverted into distrust and defiance of God. Of course one cannot abstract Paul's experience of that distortion from his experience with the Mosaic law. But he makes no suggestion that sin respects any boundary between Judaism and Christianity or any other religion, and his other letters show that he knew quite well that the best intentions of Christians are subject to the same falsification. Throughout all his letters, his gospel is that God has taken the initiative in his Son to break that power and set things right— for Jew and non-Jew alike. God's justification in Christ of the undeserving is what vindicates all devotion to God.

8:1–17, A Forward Look: The Power of the Spirit to Effect Life for Righteousness. To move to the other side of the contrast of 7:6, Paul first restates the change effected "in Christ Jesus" (for the meaning of this phrase, see the commentary above on 6:1–14). There is "no condemnation"; the power of the law to condemn has been decisively broken (the resumption of 5:16 and 7:3 is unmistakable). "The law of sin and death" (v. 2) is a shorthand summary of 7:7–25; it is the Mosaic law used by sin in such a way as to cause death. The parallel phrase "the law of the Spirit of life" is clearly intended as a rhetorical counterpart and suggests that life is the result when the same law is used by God's Spirit, his life-giving presence and power, instead of by sin. Like the expression "law of faith" in 3:27, it joins what Paul often sets in tension; only the context can supply its meaning. But that context is clear enough. The law itself is not demonic; to link law with Spirit instead of sin is the logical sequel to the argument of chapter 6 that freedom in Christ is aimed at the reshaping of human life, both individual and corporate, according to the good that God wills for it. Verses 3–4 supply the grounding for this new connection by declaring that this was the whole purpose behind God's "sending of his own Son." This reference to Jesus is cast in formal language closely paralleling Gal 4:4–5. It emphasizes first the complete entry of God's Son into the human condition. Paul is not worried about the "sinlessness" of Jesus (Heb 4:15), because he conceives of sin as a power, not as defilement or guilt. Without fully entering the domain of that power, "flesh," the Son could not have broken it. The fundamental contrast in the whole passage is between the inability and weakness, on the one hand, of the law to renew and reorder life so long as sin is in control, and the effectual life-giving power of God's own presence in the Spirit, on the other. The outcome is to open the way for the fulfillment of God's holy and just commandment. Only on these terms can Paul come back to the starting point of his letter, an impartial God whose righteousness is to be vindicated and acknowledged (3:4) if the relationship of creature to Creator is to have integrity and God is to be "honored as God and given thanks" (1:21–25).

Verses 5–8 elaborate briefly on the contrast between "flesh" and "Spirit" as these affect human beings. Each is a reality transcending the individual, but each is also a "mind-set" that involves a deliberate choice of values and human effort toward a goal. (How Paul conceives of such a mind-set is most clearly illumined by Phil 2:1–13 and the "Christ hymn," vv. 6–11, cited there as its source and norm.) Above all, each is most basically a relationship to God. The one, flesh, is a regression to the deadly "enmity" and defiance that preceded reconciliation (cf. Rom 5:10). The other, Spirit, is God's life-giving presence and power. It is renewing because it creates a new mind-set that is not inimical to God, that submits to God's law without the distrust that corrupts obedience into self-defensiveness, and that no longer allows God's law to be used as an instrument for holding one in its power.

If these definitions of flesh and Spirit suggest that human choices are the ultimate determinants of human destiny, vv. 9–11 quickly correct that impression by returning to God's primal life-bestowing act in the resurrection of Jesus (cf. 6:1–14). What is most striking about these verses is the free interchangeability of a whole series of phrases: "belonging to Christ" (v. 9b), "being in the Spirit" (v. 9a), "God's Spirit dwelling in you" (vv. 9a, 11b), "Christ's Spirit" (v. 9b), "Christ in you" (v. 10), and "the Spirit of the one who raised Jesus from the dead" (v. 11). Each interprets the others and is interpreted by them. God is the one who gives life to the dead (4:17); he has raised Jesus from the dead. The Spirit is not the possession of some elite group within the church. It is another word for God's life-giving power present through Jesus to all who belong to him, active already in their lives in spite of the mortality that still belongs to the body, working toward righteousness and undergirding the promise that the Son's identification with them will issue ultimately in their sharing in his resurrection (cf. 6:5, 8). The Spirit is neither only a mind-set nor merely the external power by which God raised Jesus from the dead. It is also the power of the risen Jesus to take men and women into his power and reshape life to make it well pleasing to God—thus doing what the law could not do and reversing the power of sin. That is why Paul could call the gospel "the power of God for salvation to all who rely on him, the Jew first and also the Greek" (1:16).

Verses 12–17 bring this unit to a close in two ways. First, Paul draws the consequences for his readers in a direct call for their response that reminds one of the challenge of the Deuteronomic covenant: "See, I have set before you today life and prosperity, death and adversity" (Deut 30:15 NRSV)—only here death and life are correlated to the conflicting claims of flesh and Spirit upon the self for its "deeds done in the body" (v. 13b; cf. 2 Cor 5:10). But second, Paul reminds his readers that, as in Deuteronomy, such a call only follows a change of allegiance and direction already made for them. Obedience is not finally the work of the self but the result of the Spirit's leading. The Spirit produces an authentic filial relationship to God in place of anxious slavery and verifies that gift by enabling people to address God with the intimate term "Father." The Aramaic word *Abba* suggests a liturgical acclamation of God in the mutually supportive worship of the gathered community and not simply the intimacy of private prayer. (This whole series of new terms occurs also in Gal 4:6–7 and seems to have formed a single cluster in Paul's preaching.) It is noteworthy that the full-fledged opposite of slavery, "freedom," is reserved by Paul for future salvation (v. 21). In the meantime (v. 17), the legal image of an "heir," one whose entitlement is firmly established even though actual possession remains outstanding, offers a way to affirm the certainty of the new life in the Spirit despite its provisional and unseen aspects, and to link it to the still unrealized future consummation of God's deliverance. Both certainty and hope are based once again on that central element in Paul's gospel, the inclusion of all in the one destiny of Jesus Christ: "if it is in fact true that we share his suffering in order to share also his glory" (v. 17).

8:18–30, Justification as the Gift of Hope in a Still Unredeemed World. Paul now returns to the afflicted and precarious quality of life mentioned in 5:3–4. The credibility of his many intervening affirmations is threatened by the falsifying power of the actual experience of transience and suffering, the footprints of death's continuing presence. Careful readers will have noted that Paul has never denied that presence, even in the last section (8:10a). Death is still "the last enemy" (1 Cor 15:26). This is exactly why the death of Jesus remains so central to Paul's gospel. The indisputable reality of death in human life is also the most public feature of Jesus' life. His destiny-creating role as the Christ rests on his prior identification with the human condition (Rom 5:5, 8; 8:3; cf. Gal 4:4–5). Only the irreversible sequence of Jesus' own crucifixion and resurrection clamps life to this death, discloses God to be "the one who gives life to the dead" (Rom 4:17, 24), and enables Paul to speak of life as a final destiny. For human beings, Paul is always careful to say, the culmination of that destiny remains future (cf. 5:10, 17; 6:5, 8; 8:11). "It is in this hope that we have been saved" (8:24, the only place in Paul's undisputed letters where he uses the verb "to save" in the past [i.e., aorist] tense). This insistence on the futurity of salvation is undoubtedly a residue of Paul's past experiences with the excessive enthusiasm of Christian perfectionism, against which he repeatedly drew the cruciform shape of his own life as an apostle and as a model for authentic life in others (cf. esp. 1 Cor 4:8–13; 2 Cor 4:7–12; Phil 3:12–16, 20–21). But here, as in so many other instances, a strategy in his churches became also an emphasis in his theology; the hard realism of this distinction between present and future reinforces the correspondence between Christ's life and those who are "in him," so that present affliction verifies the truth of the gospel instead of refuting it (e.g., 1 Cor 1:26–2:5; 2 Cor 4:7; 6:3–10; 11:23; 13:3–4; Gal 5:11; 6:17; Phil 1:14). In both Rom 8:17 and 8:29, Paul returns to this basic pattern of Christ's life; in between, as he moves to a first climax of his letter, this line of thought is elaborated in three progressive stages.

First, in vv. 19–22 the whole of creation is included in the same sequence. This is the only place in the New Testament where the natural world is singled out for attention, but the passage draws directly on the firm understanding of the affinity between human beings and God's total creation, of which they are a part, that runs through the Old Testament and apocalyptic literature. (Its opposite, an essential incongruity between human beings and their world, appears in many forms of dualism in the Hellenistic world.) Frequently in Jewish writings God's end-time redemption includes the renewal of creation (e.g., Isa 11:6–9; 65:17, 25; 66:22; *1 En.* 91:16; *Jub.* 1:29); an extension of this idea traces the ills and woes of the nonhuman world to the defilement and curse of human sin (e.g., Isa 24:1–6, 18–23; Jer 4:19–26; Ezek 32:6–8; with specific reference to Adam's transgression, 2 Esd 7:11). The pangs of childbirth (Rom 8:22) are conventional imagery for the cosmic woes accompanying God's judgment (Isa 13:8; cf. 1 Thess 5:3) and the coming of the new age (*1 En.* 62:4) or the Messiah (1QH 3:7–10); they are a fitting metaphor here for the universally shared pain that looks forward to new life (cf. John 16:21–22). Paul does not romanticize nature, nor does he treat it with contempt. The world's futility and "decay" (i.e., its vulnerability to the ravages of time), two of its most characteristic marks to Hellenistic thinking, are not the result of anything it has done; there is no "fall" of creation. Rather, they are part of the created order and fall under God's own "expectation that the creation itself will be set free" to share in the glorious liberty of God's children (Rom 8:20–21), so bearing their own testimony to God's transcending future.

Second, against any pious illusions about being "children of God," vv. 23–25 reassert that it is "not only creation but also the very ones who have the Spirit as a firstfruits" (a harvest metaphor for the advance portion that serves as surety for what is to follow) who participate in this urgent longing. The gift of the Spirit is not a partial resurrection or a certificate of exemption from the world's sufferings. As surety, it confirms the gap between present and future, but at the same time sustains the expectation and turns it into a certain hope. (As v. 24 demonstrates, "hope" in Paul's letters means both the act of expecting and the reality hoped for.) Hope is not a poor substitute for possession, but enhances it. As certainty about God's future, it makes meaningful connection between God's salvation and the miserable realities of the present world. What can be seen in this life remains changeable and transitory and bears the marks of death (2 Cor 4:16–18 is Paul's own best commentary). To identify God's end with that would be to defraud faith. Instead, hope is what gives faith patience and enables it to endure in its reliance on God (v. 25).

Third, "in the same way, the Spirit also stands by to assist us in our weakness" (v. 26). The imagery is that of a heavenly court (cf. vv. 33–34), in which the "inexpressible yearnings" of both creation and community are taken up and presented on their behalf to God. Paul is drawing on a tradition that perceives God's Spirit as an advocate or defender for God's people; it appears also in the Paraclete sayings of the Gospel of John and in sayings in the Synoptic Gospels that promise the Spirit's aid to the beleaguered community in times of persecution and trial (Mark 13:11; Matt 10:19–20; Luke 21:15). Human beings are not left to their own resources, even to the inadequacies of their praying, to bear the burdens of this time, for the Spirit's intercession is authorized by God himself, "the searcher of human hearts" (Ps 7:9; Jer 17:10; cf. Ps 139:1). Apart from this context, the assertion of Rom 8:28 must sound superficial; in this context, it summarizes what has gone before. The ultimate assurance that "all [these] things" eventually do lead to the good that God wills lies in his unfailing assistance to "those who love him," which Paul at once defines as those whom God has called into this new relationship (cf. 1 Cor 2:9; 8:3). A final rhetorical sequence of clauses stresses this divine purpose. Into it Paul inserts (v. 29b) another reminder of the Son: the branding mark of his life's pattern, in which glory and salvation come only by way of the cross, is what restores to human life the "image" the Creator had first willed to impress upon it (Gen 1:27; cf. Phil 3:21; 2 Cor 4:4).

8:31–39, Justification as Vindication by the Love of God in Christ. Finally Paul returns to the love of God, which 5:5–8 has identified as the ultimate basis for hope and for that kind of confidence in God that has integrity. But he does not name love until v. 35. What God's sacrifice of his own Son (the language echoes Abraham's "not sparing" Isaac [Gen 22:16]) proves first is that God is "for us" rather than "against us." That does not mean that he is "on our side" (JB) on every human issue, but it is the very heart of Paul's teaching on justification. The love of God does not mean a transmutation of earthly life into heavenly. It leaves history intact, with its choices, for which people and nations must still answer to God (cf. 2 Cor 5:10). Human beings still have blood on their hands, often in the name of religion. But the ultimate accuser in the heavenly court is now the one who has taken their side in Christ Jesus. Paul is back at his starting point in 3:23–24. The rest of this section unfolds that assurance with the help of two carefully constructed rhetorical lists: one (v. 35) a sevenfold recapitulation of Paul's own personal hardships as a paradigm of the Christian life, the other (vv. 38–39) a tenfold catalog of transpersonal powers that seem to threaten God's design. In between, v. 36 (unfortunately often passed over in the liturgical use of this passage) makes the first appeal for confirmation to the Old Testament since chapter 4. Psalm 44:22—originally a cry to God lamenting the assaults of Israel's enemies, now universalized as an apocalyptic truism that God's faithful are always exposed to violent death—becomes scripture's own reminder that tribulation is a sure mark of belonging to God. The love of the Christ (v. 35) is in the last analysis the love of the eternal and omnipotent God himself (v. 39); that is the meaning for this life of calling Jesus of Nazareth, crucified and raised, "Christ Jesus our Lord."

9:1–11:36

The Faithfulness of God

In 3:1–8, Paul had anticipated two serious objections to his argument. His exposition of the justification of the unrighteous in subsequent chapters has answered the second objection: that Paul is denying the realities of sin and human accountability, ignoring the moral consequences of God's graciousness, and casting doubt on God's own integrity. But the first objection remains unfinished business still clamoring for attention. Paul's early insistence on God's impartiality (2:6–29) had provoked the question, "Does the Jew have any 'advantage,' any privilege that others do not also have?" (3:1). In replying affirmatively, Paul pointed to the "direct utterances" entrusted by God to the Jews, referred cryptically to the faithfulness of God that does not depend on human fidelity, and then switched the emphasis to God's truth and righteousness. Even that answer he seemed to take back in 3:9, although from 1:16 on he has always been careful not to obliterate the distinction between Jew and non-Jew (1:16; 2:9–10; 3:1, 30; 4:11–12).

However, far from going away, the question has in the meantime only become more acute. On Paul's own terms, the gospel of God's gracious initiative for the deliverance of all in the death of Jesus has put Jew and non-Jew on the same footing before God (3:22b–23, 30) and even provided the non-Jew with equal access to what Paul located at the very core of Jewish identity, namely, God's promise to Abraham and Abraham's trust in that promise (ch. 4). Favoritism can never be claimed from God, as though God were the patron of one client people alone, for that would violate Judaism's central creed that God is one (3:29–30).

But what then becomes of God's faithfulness, that very reliability on which human trust, beginning with Abraham's, can alone depend? What about those "direct utterances" and God's calling of a people as his own, for which again Abraham is the prototype? Has God broken faith with his word, and with himself? What is at stake is not only the reality and future of Israel; it is above all a question about the God who has acted in Jesus Christ. That is why the argument of chapters 1–8 is unfinished. In this connection God's "faithfulness" has several levels of meaning. His trustworthiness is his power to do what he has promised (as in 4:20–21). But it involves also his constancy, the changelessness of his purpose. And another side of his reliability is the consistency with which he deals with different groups of people, that is, the very impartiality that raised the question in the first place. In the end, these are all aspects of God's righteousness.

These are the questions Paul addresses in the next three chapters. After a brief introduction, he proceeds in three major steps, though each section has some clear subdivisions.

9:1–5, Personal Introduction: The "Advantages" of Israel. In these intimate opening remarks, it is not at first apparent what Paul is talking about. He is affirming under oath his deeply pained concern for the Jewish people, in whom his own natural and historical roots are set. He makes no charges; there is not a syllable of reproach or blame. Yet in a manner reminiscent of Moses' impossible offer of his own life to atone for the worshipers of the golden calf (Exod 32:31–32), Paul entertains the fleeting thought of being accursed and cut off from Christ (something just declared impossible in Rom 8:35, 39) in their place, as if they are under a ban or spell. But he turns that thought aside (until 9:31–32) and instead enumerates all the "advantages" (3:1) of the "Israelites." This new name replaces "the Jew(s)" in these three chapters (except 9:24 and 10:12, where Paul needs to pair Jew with non-Jew) and is a calculated recall of Judaism's roots in the patriarchal history (Gen 32:28). The list itself rehearses the major tokens of the Jewish people's covenant relationship with God, the earthly branding marks of God's election—not the least of which is being the cradle of the Messiah. The thought moves Paul to a Jewish formula of thanksgiving and praise to "the God who is over all" (v. 5b) and who is the real subject of Rom 9–11. (Although some translations punctuate so as to make the formula refer to Christ, this fits neither the context nor Paul's Christology; cf. 1 Cor 15:28.)

9:6–29, Israel's Election as God's Free Initiative to Create a People. In this first major section, Paul reviews certain aspects of election in the patriarchal story in order to refute the suggestion that God's word has failed (v. 6). The first reason it has not is that God's past activity has been completely consistent with his justification of the unrighteous. Put another way, several of the points Paul has made in chapters 1–4 about the standing of human beings before God in his future judgment he now confirms by turning 180 degrees to look at Israel's past history. It is most important to note that throughout this first section it is God's nature and activity that are being described; there is absolutely no attack on the Judaism of Paul's own time or censure of Israel in the past. This review embraces three points.

First, in vv. 6–13, in a remarkable resumption of his earlier redefinition of the authentic Jew (2:28–29) and of the authentic Abraham (cf. the commentary above on 4:9–12), Paul now redefines Israel in such a way as to distinguish the "children of God" and "of the promise" (v. 8) from the simply physical posterity of Abraham. One should take some care in interpreting Paul. He is not trying to make room for believing Gentiles among Abraham's children (as he was in 4:9–12), much less suggesting a "spiritualized" definition of the Jewish people as a pretext for substituting the church for Israel (that would reduce vv. 1–3 to posturing). Nor is he dismissing the earthly history of the Jewish people as inauthentic; he is not abstracting an "essential" Israel from its history. Rather, in that history itself, as every Jew would agree, the descendants of Abraham through Ishmael (Gen 25:12–18; cf. *Jub.* 15:28–30; 20:11–13) and through Esau (Gen 36:1–8) were not included in "Israel." Historical Israel itself is determined by "promise" rather than by "flesh" (these terms are functioning here exactly as "spirit" and "letter" did in Rom 2:29). Of course Isaac and Ishmael, one born to Abraham's wife Sarah and the other to his maidservant Hagar, were not equals. So to make the point clear, Paul comes down one generation to the twin sons of Rebecca (Old Testament: Rebekah), "conceived from the same conjugal act with one man, Isaac" (v. 10). Here the determination of authentic Israel takes place "when they were not yet born and when they had not yet done anything good or bad, in order that God's elective intention might remain unchanged [i.e., consistent], dependent not on works but on the one who calls" (vv. 11–12a). The point is clinched, in rabbinic fashion, with one text from the Law and one from the Prophets (vv. 12b–13). Election, which means the calling into being of a people, exactly like the justification of the unrighteous, is God's free act, a gift, not something due (4:4); it results from the perduring intention of God, which operates "by election" (v. 11b). This is Abraham's God "who gives life to the dead and calls into being the things that are not" (4:17).

Second, vv. 14–24 reflect on the declaration "But Esau I hated." The last Old Testament text cited in v. 13 from Mal 1:2–3 creates a new problem. One may soften the language (since Hebrew has no comparative adverbs, there are Old Testament texts in which "to hate" simply means "to love less": Gen 29:30–31; Deut 21:15; cf. Luke 14:26), but there is no doubt about God's deliberate disfavor in that context in Malachi and throughout Israel's history. That raises the issue of injustice, the negative form of favoritism, on God's part. At first Paul seems merely to continue his preceding line when he adds the two counter-poised figures of Moses and Pharaoh. Verse 16 is a manifest reinforcement of v. 11: "So it all depends not on the person who wills, nor on the person who exerts himself, but on the God who shows mercy." But v. 17 shows that Paul's shift to (Moses and) Pharaoh introduces a new dimension: God is not guided by random or arbitrary whim but by a clear purpose to assert his power and presence in human affairs. In that connection Paul introduces the image of the potter and his clay.

Many readers, taking the side of the questioners in v. 19 and thinking only of the passive plasticity of the clay in the potter's hands, have taken offense at what they regard as this picture of an impersonal, unfeeling, and despotic God. It is imperative to consult the prophetic sources from which Paul is drawing this reply (Jer 18:6; Isa 29:16; but esp. Isa 45:9–13). The point is not the power of the potter but his "right" (v. 21 NRSV) to fashion each vessel for a function and to determine the use of each. A machine stamping out identical pots is impersonal. In Isa 45, the context concerns God's "raising up in righteousness" (v. 13) his "anointed," the Persian emperor Cyrus. The even more ludicrous parallel to the clay calling the potter to account is the helpless newborn infant holding its parents answerable for the procreative act that called it into being, as personal a caricature as one could wish. But the potter's example fits Paul's needs better than the infant's because, as vv. 21–23 make quite clear, his point is God's intention to fashion different instruments and use them in different ways—a latitude so far not yet achieved by human procreation. Neither rigid determinism nor arbitrary caprice, but creative and purposive divine freedom lies at the heart of Paul's understanding of election.

Corroboration for this comes in the difficult vv. 22–23. Paul's syntax is severely elliptical; v. 24 also is not a complete sentence, but it is clearly the goal toward which vv. 22–23 move. God is not simply like a potter. The purpose clauses with which both verses begin are parallel: God wishes to make himself known, first by showing his wrath and "what he can do" (a striking phrase; cf. its opposite in 8:3) by patiently enduring, that is, by not destroying, "vessels of wrath fashioned for destruction," and then by making known "the wealth of his glory" on "vessels of mercy" prepared for that use. "Vessel" in Greek normally also means an "instrument" or piece of gear in the hands of someone (Paul himself is a "chosen instrument," lit., a "vessel of election," for God in Acts 9:15). The harshness of this language results from combining terms from the imagery of the potter with God's wrath and mercy. Paul does *not* identify the "vessels of wrath designed for destruction" with Jews and the "vessels of mercy" with Gentiles, much less Christians. Such a correlation can be produced only by bringing elements of chapter 11, which is a different argument, up into chapter 9. These phrases refer to figures in Israel's own history, Pharaoh and Moses, respectively. Verses 22–23 thus reproduce in inverted order the juxtaposition of vv. 15–17 in order to reach toward the goal of v. 24, God's intent to create "us" as a people "not only from Jews but also from Gentiles," both of whom are included under "vessels of mercy."

This reappearance of the word pair "Jew and Gentile" and the confessional "us," both totally new elements in chapter 9, brings Paul back to the main track of his exposition of God's righteousness. Thus the juxtaposition in vv. 22–23 is not contradictory but progressive, remarkably like the parallel revelation of God's wrath and his righteousness with which Paul began the whole letter in 1:17–18. These are two "sides" or "faces" of God, but they are never in equilibrium and do not result in a schizophrenic duality of purpose in God himself. The hardening of Pharaoh served the deliverance of Israel under Moses, just as the revelation of wrath serves the manifestation of God's righteousness, or the "increase" of sin by the law serves the aggrandizement of grace (5:20). There is no inconsistency between God's behavior in Israel's creation and the justification of the undeserving that creates a new people from both Jew and non-Jew.

Third, vv. 25–29 buttress v. 24 with scriptural warrants in reverse order, first for the non-Jews (from Hosea), then for the Jews (from Isaiah), but in such a way that each passage also applies to both groups. The Hosea text (vv. 25–26) is a lucid and forceful equation of calling and election with God's undeserved love; its application to the inclusion of the non-Jews in what was originally Israel's election drives home God's consistency in his covenant love on which all alike depend. The text from "Isaiah," actually from a variety of prophetic passages, returns to God's reliability in the election of authentic Israel. "Remnant" in v. 27, like "seed" in v. 29, refers to that authentic line of descent from Abraham described positively in vv. 6–13 (it is not used reductively; there is no "only" in the Greek of v. 27; see the commentary on 11:1–10). The emphasis falls on the last line, which sums up Paul's answer to the question of v. 6 whether "the word of God has failed": No, "the elect strain that is called in Isaac" (v. 7) "shall be saved; the Lord will carry out his word on the earth conclusively and with dispatch" (vv. 27–28). A final quotation from Isaiah (v. 29) serves as a thanksgiving: apart from that constancy of God that has operated in Israel's election, we would all be like Sodom and Gomorrah, the Old Testament prototypes of annihilation.

9:30–10:21, God's Faithfulness in the Apparent Breakdown of Election. As often before (4:1; 6:1, 15; 7:7; 8:31; 9:14), a new stage in Paul's reflection is opened with the rhetorical question "What then shall we say?" This time, however, the words that follow are Paul's own answer and not an erroneous deduction he aims to refute. Verses 30b–33 leave behind the preceding account of God's role in the story of Israel's election and focus on the present status of that complex plot. Now for the first time Paul's readers get a clear glimpse of the reason for his pain in 9:2, for present circumstances are a baffling inversion of everything any participant in that story would have expected. In the language of the racecourse, Gentiles who were not even trying to reach God's righteousness have arrived at that goal on the proper terms of trust in God; Israel, on the other hand, pursuing a law that held out the promise of righteousness, has failed to reach even that law. By referring to the Mosaic law here not as a possession distinguishing Jew from Gentile (cf. 2:14, 20) but as Israel's unattained goal, Paul must have in mind something like that "law of faith" that precludes boasting in 3:27 (cf. the commentary on 3:27–31), the Mosaic law as presuming trust in God for its authentic obedience (2:25–29).

Of course Paul is contrasting the acceptance of "God's gospel" (1:1) among his Gentile converts and the resistance this gospel has encountered among his own people. But beneath those surface responses lies a deeper enigma. Something has gone seriously wrong (9:32), because Israel's pursuit of the goal was not carried out in trust but on the supposition that righteousness can come from performance of deeds enjoined by the law (i.e., in violation of the basic axiom under which Paul had begun his whole description of justification [3:20]). "The one who trusts in him [God] will not be put to shame." That assurance had been laid down by God as a foundation stone in Zion (Isa 28:16), but it has become a rock of stumbling, as the Lord of hosts said he would himself become to those who refuse his message (Isa 8:14), and Israel has stumbled on that rock (Rom 9:32). This is Paul's own people, and this is the reason for his anguish.

On the basis of Ps 118:22, Christianity after Paul developed a complex tapestry of Old Testament "stone" passages to apply to Christ (1 Pet 2:6–8; Matt 21:42; Mark 12:10; Luke 20:17; Acts 4:11; Eph 2:20; cf. Luke 2:34), so Paul's later readers have understandably assumed that the "stone" of v. 33 refers to Christ. But there is no use of Ps 118 here and no preparation for such a direct allusion. Instead, Paul seems to understand the second line of the quotation, to which he returns in 10:11, as the inscription on the stone or the "rock" itself (cf. the punctuation of Isa 28:16 NRSV). In any case, Rom 9:33 must count as one of the most remarkable of Paul's Old Testament quotations because of what it attributes to God: placing in the midst of God's people a base of security that is at the same time an obstacle over which they will stumble. Such an obstacle confronts those who encounter it with alternatives, yet their reactions only disclose things about themselves over which they have no control. This figure of speech thus combines the same fatefulness and freedom that have appeared in Paul's earlier analyses (Rom 1:21–23; 5:12; 6:17; 8:12–14). God's action is not unlike that law that was supposed to lead to life but in fact led to death, a result not outside God's purpose (7:10, 13b), or God's use of "an instrument of wrath" like Pharaoh on the way to disclosing his mercy in Moses. Such a perception of God recognizes in Israel's history what Paul has come in other ways to see about God from his disclosure of his power and wisdom in the offensive message of a crucified Messiah (cf. Paul's use of the figure of the stumbling block in 1 Cor 1:18, 21–24).

The rest of this section (ch. 10) explores these two sides of the strange reversal of 9:30–31. First, leaving the Gentiles aside, Paul first (10:1–17) concentrates on Israel's own responsibility for the current state of affairs. After a renewed personal testimony, he repeats (vv. 1–4) what has gone wrong, using the language of justification instead of his racecourse imagery; genuine zeal for God has been turned into disobedience and a pursuit of righteousness aborted into a search for "one's own" rather than God's (cf. Phil 2:9). This diagnosis of Israel parallels precisely what Paul wrote about religious moralists in Rom 2:1–5 and addressed to "the Jew" in 2:17–24. It should not have turned out so, for the real goal of the law as reached in Christ is to lead to righteousness for everyone who trusts in God (10:4; Paul's Greek word "end," like the English, can mean either "cessation," as in Luke 1:33, or "goal," as in Rom 6:21–22; both Paul's usage elsewhere and the racecourse motif here support the latter choice. But this is one of the most debated of Pauline texts).

Verses 5–13 supply the scriptural backing. Here Paul follows an established rabbinic procedure for dealing with apparently contradictory biblical texts, as in Gal 3:10–12. The law ("Moses," Rom 10:5) does indeed invite one to establish a "righteousness of one's own" that will divide Jew from non-Jew and make life dependent on performance. On that invitation Israel "stumbled." But the same law, when one reads Deut 30:12–14 prefixed by Deut 9:4, forbids presuming to do for oneself what God has already done (in Christ). The message about trusting in God, "which we preach," is already located "near at hand" by scripture, in the mouth by which human beings confess and in the heart by which they rely upon what God has done, and this is illustrated by two elementary Christian creeds (Rom 10:9). That is how righteousness is attained and salvation is found, not in one's own deeds. In the words of that foundation stone that God has himself placed in Zion (9:33), to which Paul now returns (10:11), "everyone who trusts in God will be vindicated." Paul adds the word "everyone" to that text of Isa 28:16. By what right? Because Joel 2:32 does just that (Rom 10:13). Just as there was no distinction between Jew and Greek in the matter of sin's power (3:22b), so there is no distinction between them before the riches of one and the same God, who is Lord of all (cf. 9:5b).

As in many of Paul's quotations from the Old Testament, "Lord" refers to God in 10:12 and should not be restricted to Christ. But this fusing of the text from Deut 30:12–14 with Paul's own "message about faith which we preach" (v. 8b), so clearly shown by his inserting explanatory comments into that text in vv. 6–8, is the result and confirmation of his perceiving complete continuity and consistency between the God of Israel and the Father of Jesus Christ. To exhibit that consistency, which is God's faithfulness, is Paul's aim in these chapters. If not all have obeyed the good news (v. 16), all the conditions for its reception have been provided by God; the bearers of his message were hailed already in Isaiah's time (vv. 14–15). Trust is created by that message, and that message comes (now) through the preaching of what God has done in Christ (v. 17).

Second, in vv. 18–21, the Gentiles come back into view as Paul returns from Israel's role to God's in that enigmatic reversal of 9:30–33. Can it be that Israel did not hear or understand? The next three Old Testament texts (in 10:18–20) indicate that it did indeed hear, as the earlier vv. 15–16 had confirmed, but that something else was going on. The second passage (v. 19, quoting Deut 32:21) comes from the context of Israel's defection to idolatry in the wilderness (1 Cor 10:7, 22 shows that Paul read Deut 32:21 in the light of Exod 32:6 and is probably thinking of the golden calf; cf. the commentary on 9:1–5). It was Israel's known provocation of God that elicited his return threat to provoke them with a "nonpeople" and a "foolish nation." Paul understands that as applying now to the unforeseen success of the Gentiles in reaching the goal that Israel has missed (9:30), as is clear from his third citation in 10:20. In deliberately showing himself to people who were not even trying to find him, and who had no comprehension of God's purposes ("a nation devoid of understanding" is an ironic echo of a Jewish label for Gentiles; cf. 2:20), God was not only pursuing his justification of the undeserving; he was goading his own people and showing his attachment to them (this striking motif will be resumed in 11:11, 14). Was that a breakdown in God's election? On the contrary, as Isaiah said, God has never ceased to reach out to Israel, even in the midst of its defiance (10:21).

11:1–36, The Impartiality of God's Faithfulness. In this final chapter, Paul closes in on his goal, pulling the pieces together now in a series of concluding steps, for which he provides the familiar rhetorical markers.

11:1–10, A remnant continues. The last part of chapter 10 still leaves a question. God's word to Israel has not failed. Israel, called into being by the God who shows mercy (9:6–13, 16), is an actual people, not a fantasy constructed out of future promises. If it has missed God's intent for it by a wide margin, and if God himself has had some hand in its doing so (9:31–33; 10:19), does it not follow that God has repudiated his own people? In reply, Paul uses the Old Testament concept of the "remnant." Like many other religious terms, this notion can be nuanced in different ways. Sometimes it refers to all the residue of God's people surviving a time of judgment and catastrophe; it then is used to emphasize its continuity and miraculous preservation. Paul understood the term in this inclusive sense when quoting Isa 10:22 in Rom 9:27, namely, as a synonym of "seed" in 9:29 (NRSV: "survivors"). But "remnant" may also be used exclusively to identify an "elite" minority within a larger whole, distinguished by special fidelity or piety; the Qumran community understood itself as such a faithful remnant. That Paul uses it in an exclusive sense here is clear from his differentiating "the elect" and "the rest" (clearly not those included in the "remnant") in v. 7, and from the analogy he draws with the seven thousand in the days of Elijah (1 Kgs 19:10, 14, 18). The difference in nuance is important. In Rom 9 Paul was distinguishing all of authentic Israel from that which was, even for Jewish perceptions, not Israel. Now he is drawing a distinction within Israel.

In this meaning of "remnant," the promissory assurance that the preservation of a part gives for the future of the whole is the key. The "oracle" (v. 4 NEB) to Elijah was God's own pledge then, as it is to Paul now, that God has not abandoned his people (v. 2). Paul, however, goes out of his way (vv. 5–6) to emphasize that this continuity-providing remnant is "a matter of the election of grace" (cf. 9:11–12), the product of that undeserved creative love of God that produced a Jacob alongside Esau, and not the result of one group's being any better or deserving than the rest of Israel.

Who is that remnant? There is nothing in the text to suggest that Paul is thinking of Christians. The empirical evidence he adduces is simply his own person, not by virtue of his Christian faith, which he does not mention (that would make it a "work" in the sense of v. 6), but in his unassailable flesh and blood identity as an Israelite (v. 1), a part of Israel's whole (vv. 1–5). Undoubtedly Paul does not feel himself alone; he does not liken himself to Elijah in that respect. But it remains a fact that he does not appeal directly to Christ here for assurance about Israel's future, but to the pledge of Israel's (and his) God. Although he uses the distinction between Jew and non-Jew, he simply does not draw any lines anywhere in chapters 9–11 between authentic Jews and authentic Christians (cf. 9:24), just as he perceives no split in himself—or in God.

A remnant of Israel, represented by Paul, did then arrive at that goal mentioned in 9:31, but (all) the rest did not. With two more texts (vv. 8–9), the first of them a complex mix of phrases from Deuteronomy and Isaiah, Paul not only documents the majority's lasting misunderstanding and blindness, but explains the painful reality of it as a deliberate work of God. Such use of these passages belongs to a broad early Christian tradition of appeal to Old Testament texts on God's causing blindness and misunderstanding in Israel, in order to explain the painful riddle of Jewish repudiation of the gospel (cf. the use of Isa 6:9–11 in Matt 13:14–15; Mark 4:12; Luke 8:10; John 12:40; Acts 28:26–27). Paul's point, however, is a continuation of Rom 9:33 and 10:18–21: to show God's continuing presence and purpose with Israel, and so to refute the suggestion that he has abandoned it. This becomes clear in the next step.

11:11–16, The part is surety for the whole. These verses should not be divided; they belong together in both thematic content and purpose. Verse 13a ("I am talking to you Gentiles") does not mark a change of audience; that largely Gentile Christian audience has been the same from 9:1 on. But Paul deliberately calls its attention to itself to accentuate these verses. If God is responsible for Israel's blindness, the question is still, has God become Israel's enemy and destroyer? "Have they faltered only finally to fall? Absolutely not! On the contrary, through their false step, salvation has been extended to the Gentiles in order to incite Israel to jealousy" (v. 11). Here is a double claim about God: first, that Israel's closure to God's righteousness (10:3) serves God's purpose to bestow his riches impartially upon all (10:12) and thus to extend his salvation to non-Jews; but second, that in that very action, by provoking them to anger over these outsiders (10:19), God's own "jealousy" or zeal for Israel, his undeterrable possessive claim on it and his faithfulness to it, is operating to awaken and recall it. Paul's own calling as an "apostle to the Gentiles" (cf. 1:5) is in service to this God, so that ultimately it coincides with his own deepest desire for his kinfolk, his "flesh" (v. 14), and one loyalty cannot be played off against the other. So the beneficiaries of God's hostile treatment of Israel are the non-Jews, and the beneficiary of God's reconciliation of the world is Israel.

Verses 12 and 15 are parallel and play on linguistic contrast: if Israel's "diminution" enriches the world, what will its "plenitude" produce (v. 12)? If its "being spurned" causes reconciliation, what will its "being embraced" bring about (v. 15)? The above two claims about God are so fused in Paul's mind that both these verses are ambivalent; one cannot really tell whether in describing

God's ultimate benefit, "life from the dead," he means its accrual to Jew or Gentile. The distinction has evaporated in the text. Both are equally indebted to the same life-giving God (cf. 4:12). And the part is surety for the whole: the remnant, for the indivisible whole of Israel; the Jew Paul, for his "flesh"; Israel, for God's whole creation. Significantly, Paul ends (v. 16) with two Old Testament symbols for the consecrating effect of the part upon the whole: the dedicatory cereal offering for the whole harvest (Num 15:17–21) and the root and the branch. One might suppose that he has only the remnant and the whole of Israel in mind with these allusions, but the next verses, into which the second figure leads, demonstrate conclusively the universal scope of their application.

11:17–24, The metaphor of the olive tree. Despite all the horticultural objections that have been raised about it, the theological point of Paul's metaphor of the olive tree is lucid and forceful (he concedes in v. 24 that it runs "contrary to nature"). Directed to the non-Jews (v. 13), it makes clear, first, that salvation is available for them only in continuity with Israel's history and in dependence on Israel's God. The root is now Israel of the patriarchs (cf. v. 28; 9:6–12; 15:8b), and the branches are the Jews and the rest of humankind. Everything Paul has said in Romans about God's justification of the unrighteous in Jesus Christ is empty unless this means a restored relationship to the God of Abraham, Isaac, and Jacob. It makes clear, second, that Jew and Gentile are alike utterly dependent on the creative freedom of this God to cut out and to graft in, to bestow life on his own terms where it is wholly undeserved, both "according to nature" and "contrary to nature" (v. 24). This leaves no room for either pride ("Do not become high-minded, but stand in awe," v. 20) or contempt ("God has the power to graft them back in," v. 23). God's freedom keeps the frontiers open for his mercy rather than closed; Paul is rejecting at every point that rigid determinism of conventional religion that divides humankind into the saved and the damned. And the illustration makes clear, third, that trust in this God is the issue for men and women, for Jew (v. 23) and for non-Jew (v. 20). The precipitous severity of God and his kindness are correlated to unbelief and faith. But it is God, in his goodness and righteousness, who determines these reversals; no one can manipulate him, and any attempt to do so is a dereliction of trust.

The chapter ends with three distinct conclusions.

11:25–27, Prophetic conclusion. The first conclusion answers the question about Israel's destiny. Using the term "mystery" in a meaning shaped by the apocalyptic tradition to refer to God's ultimate purposes for the world, hidden from human perception but disclosed on God's own terms (cf. Dan 2:27–28; *1 En.* 9:6; 63:3), Paul takes the stand of a prophet. Part of Israel has been "hardened" for the sake of all non-Jewish peoples, but "in this way" (v. 26) all Israel will be saved. The end-time miracle will consist in the justification of God's own people as ungodly (4:4), when God will "remove ungodliness from Jacob." Paul's supporting text in vv. 26–27 is a remarkable combination of Isa 27:9;

59:20; and Jer 31:33. In this deliverance, the two sides of God's righteousness (Rom 3:26) will again be evident: in not tolerating ungodliness, God is "himself righteous," but by bringing the Deliverer from Zion who will establish Israel's righteousness, God is also "the one who makes righteous those who are righteous by trust." Paul does not here call for Jewish conversion to Christianity or a separate Christian mission to the Jewish people. The mystery of Judaism's refusal of the gospel is an aspect of its misunderstanding of its own tradition and of the "near word" of Deuteronomy that called for faith (ch. 10), even its misunderstanding of God. But there is no break in the Jews' relationship to God, just as no Gentile is outside God's election love (9:25–26). From the very beginning of the letter, Paul has set forth the meaning of Christ not as an alternative or rival to God for the affections and trust of human beings, but as God's way of restoring integrity to the relationship of all, both Jew and Greek, to himself. The final salvation of all Israel is God's own "mystery," but the certainty of it, and the terms on which it must take place, like those of all God's world, are disclosed in God's revelation of his righteousness in Jesus Christ (see the commentary on 3:21–26).

11:28–32, Logical conclusion. To this certainty and these terms Paul returns in a second conclusion, crowning the whole of chapters 9–11, in which he speaks as a rhetorician and teacher. The tightly structured dialectic summarizes his argument:

> *A* In relation to the gospel, they are [God's] enemies on your account;
> *B* In relation to election, they are [his] beloved on account of the patriarchs.
> *C* For the gifts and calling of God cannot be rescinded.
> *A′* For just as you once disobeyed God but now have obtained mercy through their disobedience,
> *B′* So they too now have disobeyed the mercy extended to you, in order that they might themselves also now be recipients of mercy.
> *C′* For God has consigned all human beings to disobedience in order to bestow mercy on all.

Line C (v. 29) reaffirms God's election and his faithfulness to his promises, the point of chapter 9. Line C′ (v. 32) reaffirms God's impartiality, the point made by Paul in chapters 2–4 that raised the issue of Israel and required the writing of chapters 9–11. The two are not in conflict. God's justification of the undeserving embraces all human beings on equal terms, but this "universalism" is one that confronts them all with both judgment and mercy (cf. 5:12–21).

11:33–36, Liturgical conclusion. In this third conclusion, Paul takes the stance of the worshiper and uses an early Christian hymn. Its triadic structure is clear. Verse 33 is made up of three exclamatory lines: the first praises God's wealth, wisdom, and knowledge, three very Hellenistic religious categories; the other two repeat the exclamation in terms of the Hebraic notions of God's judgments and ways. Verse 34 consists of three rhetorical questions, all drawn from Old Testament poetic and wisdom passages, that resume in inverse order the three concepts of the first line. The implied answer to each "Who?" is "No one but God!" Verse 36 concludes with a couplet: the first line is a profoundly Hellenistic formula for God's omnipotence and transcendence (cf. 1 Cor 8:6; Col 1:16; Heb 2:10); the last is a conventional biblical doxology. Such praise of the God who transcends human understanding can easily slip into resignation and despair (cf. *2 Apoc. Bar.* 14:8–11). God remains beyond human manipulation. Still, authentic faith and obedience, and the undergirding hope of salvation, do not rest on God's withholding himself but on his making himself known, on his own terms, as a God who can be trusted. This is the God Paul praises at the conclusion of his argument.

12:1–15:13

The Community Exhortation

With 12:1 the nature and tone of the letter shift unmistakably to ethical and practical exhortation. Romans shares with other New Testament letters, not only those written by Paul, the tendency to gather such material at the end (cf. 1 Thess 4–5; Phil 4; Gal 5–6; Col 3–4; Eph 4–6; even such documents as Hebrews and 1 Peter, which incorporate hortatory passages throughout, follow this pattern in their conclusions: Heb 13; 1 Pet 5). This tendency of the letters reflects both the influence of Jewish and Hellenistic sermonic traditions on their composition and the personal experiences of their writers as leaders in their communities and participants in their worship assemblies, where such exhortation took place (and where Paul expects his letters to be read). Thus it is not surprising to find Paul incorporating into these final chapters of Romans material that bears many marks of traditional catechetical instruction and shows clear parallels with other letters, his own and others'. Yet Paul is never a slave to the conventions he follows, and it is important to reflect briefly on the inner connection between his use of this material and the argument of the first part of the letter.

Romans is peculiarly instructive because the concluding exhortations of this letter do not emerge from Paul's own personal familiarity with the church as its founder, nor are they a response to its appeals to him for guidance. The central argument itself has shown that no sharp separation is possible between Paul's "theology" and his "ethics." His exposition of the gospel as a revelation of God's righteousness, God's gracious initiative to restore integrity to the relationships of human beings to himself and to each other, has involved release from the patterns and condemnation of the past, the renewal of commitment, and the reordering of life in this world (cf. esp. the commentary on 6:1–7:6). That exposition can certainly gain now in both intelligibility and persuasiveness by the addition of concrete advice and counsel, but it is not the case that the truth of the argument depends on the exhortation or that the revelation of God's righteousness remains somehow defective or inconclusive until Paul's gospel is "applied" by its hearers to the practice of living. His position has clearly been that the human situation and the behavior it calls for have been defined by the death and resurrection of Christ, not the other way around. The "indicative" of his gospel entails and creates an "imperative" that the exhortations can now in one sense only elaborate and clarify.

But it also does not follow, on the other hand, that these concluding chapters remain essentially dispensable embellishments to his argument and, because they utilize tradition, contain no proper concerns and reflections of Paul's own. A closer look at these chapters will refute such a conclusion, but the earlier argument itself prepares the way, for in it, and especially in the diagnosis of human religious failure that accompanies Paul's exposition of God's righteousness all along, Paul nowhere represents his readers as morally disengaged or indifferent. The fundamental malaise is a distortion that the religious zeal of morally serious people has introduced into their relationship to God; the symptom of sin's power is not sloth but the breeding of just those results that an active religious commitment is seeking to prevent (cf. 2:1–24; 7:7–25; 10:1–4; 11:17–24). The human problem is not lack of religion but religion that lacks trust (faith) and for that reason does not honor God as God or give thanks to him (1:21; 3:27–30; 9:32), that misunderstands and resists God (8:5–8; 10:3).

This means that the point of chapters 12–15 is quite different from what modern readers, looking for religious encouragement in a "secular" world, may be inclined to hear. The function of these chapters is not to incite or inspire "religious" behavior or supply a moral dimension to life, as though these were missing; the world of Paul and his readers is full of both. Rather, what his readers now need are guidelines to help discern and promote integrity in a religious life that has been distorted, corrections to religious motivations that will bring these into line with the righteousness of faith, criteria for conduct suitable to the imperatives enunciated earlier (e.g., in 6:11, 12–14; 8:12). The revelation of God's righteousness does not remain defective, but the shaping of human lives to its patterns remains incomplete, an unfinished goal of the apostle's calling (1:5), and as indispensable a part of his gospel as the still unlived future conferred by the sharing of Christ's destiny (cf. the commentary on 6:1–14).

12:1–13:14

Basic Exhortations

The exhortations appear to fall into two groups: chapters 12–13 contain elemental appeals not related to a community problem under debate; chapters 14–15 present specific overtures occasioned by the major issue that called forth the writing of Romans, namely, the coexistence of Jews and non-Jews in one religious fellowship (Paul does not use the word "church" at all in Romans until ch. 16).

12:1–2, Transitional Introduction. Paul's opening words set the tone. "I appeal to you" (NRSV) means much more than a request; a summons and an encouragement are now being extended, in a deliberate reprise of Paul's diagnosis of human disorder at the beginning of the letter (see the concluding remark in the commentary on 1:18–32). Embracing all human life under the metaphor of an archetypal cultic act, Paul urges his readers, on the basis of God's "compassion," to offer their "bodies," that is, their selves, as these are at their discretion for allegiance and action (cf. 6:12–13, 19), to God as a "sacrifice" that will be at once animated by the life God has bestowed, dedicated to his purposes, and acceptable to him. Approbation by God is the ultimate sanction for every cultic action, but Paul adds another. Using a Stoic term for what is peculiarly human both in distinction from the animal or material world and in affiliation with the divine (and translated variously as "reasonable," KJV, or "spiritual," NRSV), Paul declares such dedication of themselves to be the authentic worship appropriate to a reordered human life. Such reordering is to consist now of their distancing themselves from the patterns and priorities of "this [present] age" (the expression appears here for the first time in Romans; cf. Gal 1:4; 1 Cor 2:6–8; 3:18; 2 Cor 4:4) for the sake of the renovation that the gospel provides (cf. Rom 6:4; 7:6; the transformation language used by Paul for this change recalls Rom 8:29; cf. 1 Cor 15:49; 2 Cor 3:18; Phil 3:21). Its signal manifestation will be a renewed "mind" possessing once more the lost capacity to "discern what the will of God is" (v. 2; cf. 1:21) and so to distinguish good and evil. The absence of casuistry or legalism from these verses only enhances the urgency of this call to individual accountability to God.

12:3–8, The Use of Diverse Gifts in One Community. A close comparison of this passage with 1 Cor 12:4–31, especially vv. 4–11, is instructive. Paul's Corinthian crisis had demonstrated the destructive effects wrought on the cohesion and harmony of a congregation when the religious standings of competitive individuals are linked to the inevitable variations in human talents and gifts. So Paul's first call is for a tempering of conceit in one's "mind-set" (cf. Rom 8:5–8) in favor of a more sober self-assessment "according to the measuring standard of faith God has provided to each" (v. 3). It is faith, to which all have equal access, that puts all on the same footing before God (cf. 3:22, 27, 30). All members are, like the apostle himself, beneficiaries of the one graciousness of God ("the grace given" [vv. 3, 6] appears to be a distinctively Pauline formula; cf. Rom 15:15; 1 Cor 3:10; Gal 2:9). But this one grace produces "different gifts" (v. 6) that so enable the exercise of diverse functions within the group that the gifts are identified only by listing the functions (vv. 6–8; unlike 1 Cor

12:28, this list contains no ordered ranking, for Paul is no longer disputing the Corinthians' priorities). The one grace is God's; the various gifts are human faculties (despite the formulaic expression, it is not until after Paul's time [in Eph 3:2, 7, 8] that these two are so identified that the grace becomes itself the possessed human gift). Unlike in 1 Corinthians, nothing in Paul's language here connects these gifts with the Spirit or traces the creation of this diversity to the Spirit (cf. 1 Cor 12:11); what is retained from the Corinthian experience is the solution to the threat posed by pluralism and diversity, but not the originating occasion for it in the Corinthians' glorification of ecstatic spiritual phenomena such as glossolalia (speaking in tongues).

Corresponding to this relationship of the many gifts to the one grace from which they derive is the parallel relation of the many members to the "one body in Christ" (v. 5), in the service of which the many gifts are to be employed. As in 1 Corinthians this social metaphor, widely used in the ancient world, of the body as a complex organism of many members, is used to reconcile diversity and unity in the community, though Paul does not here use the expression "the body of Christ" (in Rom 7:4 it denoted the solidarity of individuals with Christ in his destiny-creating role). Thus diversities are acknowledged but stripped of their divisive power by being subordinated to the interpretive norm of "faith." Each person is to exercise his or her own gift in recognition of its source and in a manner appropriate to its function for the whole; the gift itself has created the responsibility and supplies the norm for its right use.

12:9–21, Relations to Fellow Human Beings. Since in 1 Cor 12:31 Paul turns from the variety of gifts to focus on love, Rom 12:9a has seemed to form a topic sentence for the next section: "Let love be without dissimulation." One may recognize a certain controlling position for this first admonition, but the section itself scarcely offers a coherent exposition of love comparable to 1 Cor 13. The unit provides instead, in both syntax and content, a clear example of traditional catechetical admonition: short injunctions arranged in no obvious pattern, at best in small groupings linked by key terms or catchwords (cf. 1 Thess 5:12–22; Heb 13:1–17). Verses 9–13 appear to focus on relationships within the community and vv. 14–21 on external ones, but even this distinction is tenuous. More illuminating is the sudden increase of echoes and reminiscences of identifiable traditions: of the Jesus tradition in v. 14 (Matt 5:44) or vv. 17, 21 (Matt 5:39); of Deut 32:35 in v. 19b; of Jewish wisdom traditions in v. 15 (Sir 7:34), v. 16 (Prov 3:7), v. 17 (Prov 3:4 LXX), and v. 20 (Prov 25:21–22). This helps interpret the difficult v. 20b: in a certain Egyptian ritual, a basin of burning charcoal carried on the head was a token of penitence (cf. 2 Esd 16:53). Thus in vv. 17–21 a clear thematic unity emerges to be summed up in the last verse (which also resumes v. 9b): the tempering of violence and revenge in hostile human relationships is less an act of human love (v. 9a) than it is the fruit of a trust that has learned to rely on God's impartial love for all (cf. Matt 5:43–48). Human relations are nourished by security, not anxiety; the issue for Paul throughout Romans has been to identify authentic security and confidence in place of its illusory perversions (cf. Rom 5:1–11 and see the commentary above on that passage).

13:1–7, Relations to Those in Authority. Because of the many and controversial uses to which this section has been put since it was written, it is especially important to try to read it in its context in Romans and in Paul's world. A series of observations may be useful.

First, in this context the passage does not offer a comprehensive theoretical treatment of "the state" but simply guidance in relation to the specific and individual bearers of imperial authority, including the never popular collectors of taxes (v. 6); the last verse embraces a variety of civil obligations. That Christians would one day themselves exercise such authority is simply not envisaged. There is nothing specifically Christian about the appeal, and no distinction is drawn between Christian and non-Christian members of the social order; that simply underscores one intent of the passage: to urge on Paul's readers the fulfillment of their civil obligations, not just the pleasant ones, and to forestall any reading of his earlier plea "not to be conformed to this present age" (12:2) as an exemption from them. Paul's language accords with this; the words "servant" (v. 4, twice) and "officers" (v. 6 JB) are standard secular terms for public functionaries, and any religious connotation comes only from the attached possessive, "God's."

Second, the Greek verb used in the opening imperative belongs to the basic vocabulary of New Testament hortatory tradition; its root stem denotes "order" ("be subor*d*inate to"), and it is used in this tradition to invite and summon participation in an order presumed to be hierarchical in nature, whether political (1 Pet 2:13; Titus 3:1) or familial (of wives, Col 3:18; Eph 5:22, 24; 1 Pet 3:1, 5; Titus 2:5; of household slaves, 1 Pet 2:18; Titus 2:9). The verb is not a simple synonym for "obey"; it is never used in these New Testament codes of household obligations for the obedience of children to parents. Here in Rom 13:1–2, Paul's own use of three additional Greek cognates derived from the same stem (translated "instituted," "rebels," and "institution" by the NEB) shows he is deliberately appropriating this denotation of "order," which earlier in Romans embraces the natural creation (8:20; cf. 1 Cor 15:27–28). At the same time, Paul's use of this verb in 8:7 and 10:3 demonstrates that this subordination involves for him the recognition or acknowledgment that inspires voluntary submission. (Vivid corroboration is provided by 1 Cor 16:15b–16, where his appeal to "be subject" is grounded in recognition of the role played by leaders, probably including women, who have dedicated or "submitted" themselves to ministry; this "order" within the religious community [1 Cor 14:32, 40] is closely related to its health and "peace," for God is not a God of anarchy [1 Cor 14:33].)

Third, this (necessarily) hierarchical conception of order has two implications that connect the passage with well-established traditions and so shed further light on its meaning. One is that all authority is derivative and ultimately dependent on God's authorization and sufferance, a deep-seated Jewish conviction documented in the Old Testament prophets (Isa 41:1–4; 45:1–3; Dan 2:21), wisdom literature (Prov 8:15; Sir 10:4; 17:17; Wis 6:1–3), and apocalyptic (*1 En.* 46:5; *2 Apoc. Bar.* 82:9; cf. also *Let. Aris.* 196, 219, 224). This firm certainty, given its most vivid New Testament formulation in John 19:11, underlies both Rom 13:1–7 and Rev 13 (a passage that does not share Paul's present benign perspective on Roman imperial power and so is often too simply played off against Rom 13). Contrary to the use often made of Rom 13:1b to absolutize political authority, this perception subordinates all earthly power to God's ultimate sovereignty and thus limits and relativizes the former, just as the Old Testament claim that the earth is the Lord's desacralizes the earth's seasons and fertility and prohibits their religious veneration (cf. 1 Cor 10:26; Ps 50:7–15; Hos 2:8).

Closely allied with this view of authority as derivative is the Hellenistic Jewish premise, plainly underlying vv. 3–4, that the purpose of civil authority is to reward and encourage good conduct as well as to punish and inhibit evil (cf. 1 Pet 2:14; *Let. Aris.* 280, 291–92); the passage is thus informed less by a naive indulgence toward political power than by a traditional view of its noble ends that is neither contemptuous of authority as such nor extravagant in its esteem for it. This explains v. 5b, which introduces the sanction of conscience; these civil obligations are to be honored on the basis of one's prior cognizance of good and evil and one's own responsibility to the good. Beyond this, questions of illegitimate authority or the abuse of power are simply not raised; the passage shares with Mark 12:17; Matt 22:21; Luke 20:25 a basic assent to the legitimacy of Roman power.

Fourth, this passage is distinguished from its parallels in 1 Pet 2:13–14; 1 Tim 2:1–2; Titus 3:1, first, by Paul's warning against resistance or "defiance of order" (v. 2) and, second, by a striking emphasis on "fear" of authority (vv. 3a, 3b, 4). What is meant is a proper and deserved fear, since the authority itself is assumed to be legitimate, and the aim is to counsel a way to avoid such fear, not to aggravate it. Just these distinctive features of the passage have invited later political use of it to force submission to the holders of power, but they actually show that Paul is interested in stabilizing the attitudes of religious subjects toward existing bearers of authority. In Paul's world the tendency of religious movements was to clothe imperial power with the absolutes of either the divine or the demonic (cf. Rev 13), to heighten fear, and especially in some Jewish circles to spill over into active political resistance. Although Paul may have thought to quiet some particular political tendency in Rome such as the "tumults" that led Claudius to expel the Jews from Rome shortly before (see the introduction on the "Occasion and Purpose" of Romans), his overriding aim is to encourage the fulfillment of social obligations in a context of trust in God and recognition of his prevailing sovereignty and order. This is consistent with both Paul's preceding counsel against resorting to revenge (12:19–21) and his subsequent pointer to God's approaching salvation as reason for sobriety in daily conduct (13:12–13).

13:8–10, Love as the Fulfillment of the Mosaic Law. Verse 8a links this new paragraph both with the preceding, by repeating v. 7a in negative form, and with 12:9–13, by resuming its leading injunction to love. But the major contribution of this unit in the context of Romans as a whole lies in its interpretation of the law. The one continuing obligation of the Christian life that is never paid off is "the debt of mutual love" (v. 8a JB). The reason for this is not that the law remains unfulfilled or only partially fulfilled (in all of Paul's argument in Romans with respect to justification and the law, the issue has never revolved upon the degree to which the law is fulfilled or not). Instead, the reason is simply the law's abiding claim: one who loves "the other person" (v. 8b), the "next person" in one's daily contact (v. 10, almost universally translated "neighbor"), "has fulfilled the law" (v. 8b)—a gnomic statement of principle that defines what it is that the Mosaic law truly requires in human relations and what brings it to its "fulfillment" (v. 10b). Human relations are in view; the four commandments Paul cites (in the order of the LXX in Deut 5:17–18, as in Luke 18:20; Jas 2:11) are limited to the so-called second table of the Decalogue, those negative commands that shield human life from violation, but he makes clear that "any other [such] commandment" (v. 9) is included in the representation of these four. All are summed up in the command to love one's neighbor as oneself (Lev 19:18; cf. Gal 5:14).

While similar attempts to summarize the law are found in contemporary Judaism, Paul's straightforward use of Lev 19:18 as the summary seems to derive from the Jesus tradition (Matt 22:34–40; Mark 12:28–34; Luke 10:25–28; cf. Matt 7:12). On the other hand, there is no hint here of the "double commandment" of Jesus, which pairs love of neighbor to love of God. In Paul's letters "love of God" is always God's own love; human love for God is mentioned only in Rom 8:28; 1 Cor 2:9; and 8:3, in all three instances only to be overshadowed by human debt to God's generosity and initiative. For Paul the more appropriate human response to God's love and compassion (Rom 12:1) is honor and thanksgiving (1:21) and trust (4:20–21) in God, on the one hand, and, on the other, this love toward neighbor that is nothing else than the reordering of human life in accordance with God's will (12:2). For this is the substance of the law, the never-ending claim of God on human life embodied in God's "holy, just, and good commandment" (7:12), which Paul's gospel never undermines but only confirms (3:31b; cf. 8:4).

13:11–14, Living for God's Coming Day. A final section concludes these basic exhortations and forms a closing bracket to 12:1–2. Where Paul had begun by urging his readers to abandon the patterns of "this [present] age" (12:2), he now asks for conduct appropriate to God's certain and approaching salvation. This orientation to the future and a host of new images characteristic of New Testament catechetical and hortatory traditions give the section a unity and flavor of its own. The "day" of God's wrath and judgment (2:5, 16), often spoken of as "darkness" (beginning with the prophetic tradition; cf. Amos 5:18), is now the day of God's coming salvation and stands as the polar opposite to the darkness of this world. (It is usually referred to by Paul as "the day of the Lord" or "of Jesus Christ"; cf. 1 Cor 1:8; 5:5; 2 Cor 1:14; Phil 1:6, 10; 2:16; 1 Thess 5:2; also 2 Cor 6:2.) Such religious use of the opposites "light" and "darkness" is so widespread in the ancient world that it cannot be identified with any one tradition; Paul's clear dualistic use here is reminiscent of 1 Thess 5:4–8 (see also Eph 5:7–14; John 3:19–21; 12:35–36). When this antithesis is linked to the verbal imagery of "throwing off" and "putting on" attire (sometimes martial) and to the moral contrasts between indecency and propriety and the ethical metaphors of drunkenness and sobriety, the result is a telling hortatory fusion of images deeply rooted in the Greek religious and moral world with a Jewish apocalyptic sense of temporal urgency (cf. Col 3:8, 10, 12; Eph 4:22, 24; 6:11, 13–17). The final imperative to "put on the Lord Jesus Christ" (v. 14a) locates this homiletic-didactic language in the setting of early Christian baptism (cf. Gal 3:27): if baptism attests to the individual's identification with the life pattern of Jesus (Rom 6:1–11), and this "image" is the destiny set for each by the Creator (8:29), the companion ethical catechism will consist at its heart in the appeal to "assume" and embrace that image and live by it, for that is where each person's future lies, not with "the flesh" and the "desires" it serves (v. 14b).

14:1–15:13

Specific Exhortations

This second set of appeals forms the final block of material in the letter body of Romans. At this point and until he resumes some of the conventions of the letter conclusion in 15:14–16:27, Paul no longer makes use of the Christian catechetical or even quasi-liturgical traditions so apparent in 12:1–13:14. The lively dialogical style of his earlier chapters is recaptured. His characteristic mode of citing Old Testament scripture, with an introductory formula to ground an argument instead of relying on mere allusion, reappears (14:11; 15:3; cf. also 12:19); the catena of quotations in 15:9–12 exactly imitates the sequences of 9:25–29 and 10:18–21. Earlier in the letter, as the argument moved away from the relationship of Jew and Gentile and the deliberate appropriation of such Jewish traditions as those surrounding Abraham, the scriptural quotations themselves almost disappeared (the exceptions in 7:7 and 8:36 are all the more note-worthy); these citations return in thick abundance with the subject of Israel and the Gentiles in chapters 9–11. It is scarcely accidental that the earlier pattern of biblical documentation should reassert itself just as Paul's exhortations now converge on the specific issue of solidarity of Jew and Gentile within the Christian community. Finally, whereas the basic exhortations of 12:1–13:14 contain only two references to Christ (12:5; 13:14), this new division is replete with them. The second of those previous two, the concluding baptismal reminder of 13:14, supplies a leitmotif for these specific exhortations, and Paul's climactic appeal in 15:7 finds its leading warrant in a solemn christological dictum on the significance of Christ for both Jew and Gentile. In all these respects, the Paul of the main argument of Romans reemerges from his more comprehensive appeals to press his controlling preoccupation with the unity of Jew and Gentile—that is, all human beings—before the saving power of God. This section, once again, falls naturally into three parts.

14:1–12, Jewish and Non-Jewish Observance before an Impartial Lord. Paul's terminology bears careful observation. The person who is "weak in faith" (14:1) is one who does not "have the confidence to eat everything" (v. 2), but Paul does not put a premium on the degree of such confidence each one is able to demonstrate (he does not call anyone "strong" until 15:1; see the commentary on 15:1). Instead, it is apparent that differences of religious observance in matters of diet and holy days are under discussion because they occasion reciprocal disdain and contempt within the community (v. 3). The recurring tensions created between Jewish and Gentile converts to the Christian movement by such differences in daily religious routines constitute a running theme through the New Testament (e.g., Mark 2:13–17, 18–20, 23–28 and parallels; Acts 10:9–16; 11:11–18; 15:6–11; Gal 2:11–14), testimony to the long struggle to find effective bonds to transcend pluralistic practice. At first the issue in Rom 14 does not look like one created by this difference between Jew and non-Jew. Abstaining from meat and refraining from drinking alcohol (vv. 2, 21) are not themselves characteristic Jewish observances. They could become so because Jews (and Jewish Christians) would prefer abstinence to partaking of either in the urban settings of the empire in which both were regularly dedicated to pagan gods before being sold in the market. So one is tempted to read Rom 14 in the same terms as Paul's advice to the Corinthians (1 Cor 8:1–13; 10:12–33). But closer reading demonstrates that Paul is modulating his Corinthian experience to fit the argument of Romans (cf. the commentary on 12:3–8). At every point here the issue is the redefinition of values (cf. 12:2), and never, as in 1 Corinthians, the use or abuse of Christian freedom (the words "freedom," "conscience," and "knowledge," so central to 1 Cor 8 and 10, never occur in Rom 14:1–15:13; cf. 15:14).

Paul's fundamental appeal is to "accept" (JB, NEB), to take to oneself and into one's own community, the person of contrasting, even opposite, religious practice (14:1; 15:7); his desire is to break the cycle of mutual condemnation that regularly results from religious zeal when it is lacking in trust or faith (14:3–4). A person's "standing" (v. 4), that intangible worth so fatefully linked to public religious identity and usage, is determined by the Lord to whom each belongs— a direct practical application of what Paul wrote in 2:28–29. The confidence that counts is not the confidence to eat everything but the certainty that comes from integrity in each person's life-embracing relation to the Lord, whatever the practice that accompanies it, and it was to establish that integrity that Christ's death and resurrection took place (v. 9). Jew and Gentile stand on an equal footing before God, alike dependent upon his vindication of all human religious practice (v. 4b; cf. the concluding remark in the commentary on 7:13–25), alike beholden to his gift of life to all through their inclusion in Christ's own pattern of death and life (v. 9; cf. 4:25; 5:18; 6:10–11; 8:11; 2 Cor 5:15), and alike accountable to the God they must all eventually recognize (Rom 14:10b–12; cf. 2:6; 3:4, 19).

14:13–23, A Definition of "Right" and "Wrong." In this paragraph Paul clarifies the issues raised by eating and drinking in a religious context. Verse 13 plays on different nuances of the verb "to judge": one sense is to assess the worth of a fellow human being; another is to arrive at the settling of one's own values, the criteria by which those assessments of others are made. What is at stake is what one holds to be "the good" (v. 16; cf. 12:2b) or "right" and "wrong" (vv. 20b, 21a RSV). These, along with their equivalents in the ritual law of the Old Testament, "clean" and "unclean," are measured first by what violates the personal integrity and religious conviction of the fellow human being "for whom Christ died" (vv. 13–16). In v. 15 sparing such "injury" (NRSV) to the other is the specific form of "accepting" (14:1) the religiously different person; it is a concrete instance of "loving one's neighbor as oneself" (13:9).

Verses 17–19 generalize this process of definition by appealing to more conventional qualities associated with the kingdom of God, to what is "well-pleasing" to God or passes the test of human experience, and to what contributes to the common good. But vv. 20–23 return to the narrower subject at hand. Freedom is not the issue. Conceding to the one side that food does not defile (v. 20b; cf. v. 14; Mark 7:19), Paul nevertheless restates his earlier test, whether an action violates or reverses "the work of God" (v. 20a; cf. v. 15b). It is wrong for one to eat when one really believes one should not (vv. 20c, 23a), and right to abstain when not to do so would strike at the sensibilities of others (v. 21). The foundation of right action in every case is a right relationship to God, of trust (vv. 22a, 23). In the only use Paul makes in his letters of the common ancient beatitude form (Rom 4:7–8 is an Old Testament quotation), he pronounces that person blessed whose standing before God is not itself at stake in decisions about right and wrong (v. 22b), for whom that anxiety-producing link between diet and salvation has been subordinated to secure trust in God—a kind of ultimate practical application of the letter's argument concerning justification.

15:1–13, Christ the Paradigm for Jew and Gentile. Those who are "strong" and secure in the sense just referred to, Paul goes on, have an obligation not simply to put up with the failings of the less strong but to support them (cf. Gal 6:2). This is the only time Paul ever distinguishes some Christians from others as "strong" (a word not used in 1 Cor 8–10; cf. 2 Cor 13:9), and he includes himself among its referents. But he does so only to elucidate such "strength" with the model of Christ; Christ is the suffering righteous one of Ps 69:9, who remained obedient while enduring the ultimate derision that could be carried out in the name of religion. (For the role of Ps 69 in the passion narrative, see Mark 15:23, 36 and parallels; John 2:17; 15:25.) This is the Christ Paul's readers are to "put on" (13:14). Such commitment to "please" the other rather than oneself requires the endurance and encouraging support that come from God (v. 5a; cf. 5:3–5), that give life a dimension of hope, and that the scriptures just quoted are intended to provide (v. 4).

In vv. 7–13, a passage strikingly resumptive of chapters 9–11, the precipitating dietary occasion for friction between Jew and non-Jew vanishes completely before the vision of God's end-time purpose that they be joined in his praise. Once again, the vision is grounded in God's defining act in Christ (vv. 8–9), whose whole life was an act of "service": first to the Jews as a surety of God's truth and faithfulness (cf. 3:4), by confirming God's promises to the patriarchs; and then to the non-Jews, as a demonstration of God's mercy, by including them in the praise of Israel's God. That this "power of God that leads to salvation for everyone who relies on him, the Jew first and also the Greek" (1:16) should continue to fill and enrich the lives of his readers is the real substance of the petition with which Paul brings the body of his letter to its close (v. 13).

15:14–16:27

Conclusion

15:14–33, Paul's Ministry and His Plans. Resuming now the personal conversation with his readers that was broken off in 1:15, Paul speaks again of his desire to extend his work to Spain with the support and understanding of the Roman Christians. Since he was not the founder of the Roman community, both tact and the compulsions of his own self-understanding lead him to speak in vv. 14–21 of his own ministry to the Gentiles in order to explain his imposing himself on the Romans. Of special interest is the priestly metaphor in which he casts his role (v. 16); by his bringing them into the range of "God's agenda," the Gentiles are themselves Paul's "offering" to God, and so provide the grounds for his "self-esteem" (v. 17; cf. 11:13). Yet he will claim nothing apart from Christ's own action through him to bring about obedience among the Gentiles (vv. 18–19; cf. 1:5). Thus his work merges into Christ's own inclusion of the non-Jew in God's salvation (cf. 1:16). This explains why Paul lays such store by not interfering in the labors of other (Jewish-Christian?) missionaries, a policy that seems to go back to his agreement with Peter and the other apostles in Jerusalem (Gal 2:7–8) and that he justifies by applying to himself words from the Servant Songs of Second Isaiah (v. 21; cf. 2 Cor 10:15–16; Isa 52:15b; Rom 10:20). Paradoxically, just this practice explains his turning to a congregation someone else has founded for help in extending his own mission into untraveled territory beyond (vv. 22–24). In the meantime, however, Paul has to make a last trip to Jerusalem to deliver the monetary offering to which he committed himself at that Jerusalem conference and which symbolized for him the realization of one community from both Jews and Gentiles, a central theme of his letter (cf. 9:24; 15:8–12). Paul's plea to the Romans for their prayers in his support (vv. 30–33) betrays both the significance he attached to this trip and the anxiety he felt over its outcome.

16:1–27, Personal Greetings and Benediction. The concluding chapter comprises several items more or less typical of conventional letter closings. Some of them raise questions about the original termination of Romans. Verses 1–2 contain a recommendation of Phoebe, possibly as the bearer of Paul's letter to Rome. (For such recommendations, cf. Acts 18:27; 1 Cor 16:15–17.) She is an office holder, a minister or "deacon" (NRSV) of the church in Cenchreae, the port city for Corinth, the place from which Paul is writing.

Verses 3–16 add personal greetings to a large number of acquaintances, of whom twenty-six are identified by name. Since so many greetings in a letter to a church Paul has not founded or visited are surprising, and since there is evidence that Romans did at some time circulate without chapter 16 (see below), it has been suspected that this chapter was originally sent as a separate recommendation of Phoebe to a church much better known to Paul, such as Ephesus. However, chapter 16 in its present form could not have comprised an independent letter. The first two persons named, Prisca and Aquila, are known to have been in Rome earlier (Acts 18:2–3); they and others known to Paul may have returned to Rome after the lifting of Claudius's ban (see the introduction on the "Occasion and Purpose" of Romans). It would have served Paul's interests directly to name as many individual contacts in the Roman community as he possibly could, implicitly commending them to the rest as advocates for his cause.

Important for our knowledge of early Christianity is the number of women identified in these verses, nine in Rome in addition to Phoebe, all recognized for their leadership or service to the community. In v. 7, Andronicus and Junia are apparently a married couple like Prisca and Aquila. They are identified as fellow Jewish Christians ("kinfolk" is not "relatives" [NRSV] in a narrow sense) and as "outstanding apostles" (JB, NAB), converts before Paul, and thus part of the early circle of leadership beyond the Twelve (cf. Gal 1:17; 2 Cor 15:5, 7). Since the Middle Ages, but only since, Junia's name has often been accented as masculine, even though no other occurrence of the name as a man's has ever been found; most recent commentators agree that Paul is referring to a woman leader.

Verses 17–20a warn against false teachers. Their tone contrasts sharply with 15:14–32. The language is Pauline, but the content is reminiscent of Paul's earlier references to opponents (2 Cor 11:12–15; Phil 3:18–19; Gal 5:11; 6:17; Rom 3:8). Paul may be hoping to inoculate his readers in advance against possible similar opposition in the future. Ironically, these verses can be taken to refer to some more real and present danger in Rome that Paul knew about only if chapter 15 was composed largely with the impending situation in Jerusalem in mind rather than some crisis in Rome, that is, if Romans as a whole is best explained by the "Jerusalem crisis hypothesis" (see the introduction).

Verses 21–23 convey greetings from Paul's associates. Paul often adds general greetings from the place of writing (1 Cor 16:19–20; 2 Cor 13:13; Phil 4:21), sometimes from named persons (1 Cor 16:19; Phlm 23–24; cf. Col 4:10–14). The names given in v. 21 are especially intriguing. Timothy is Paul's oft-mentioned associate; Lucius (the Latin form of the Greek abbreviated name Luke) may be the Lucius of Cyrene of Acts 13:1; Jason may be the Thessalonian host of Acts 17:5–9; and Sosipater is very likely the Sopater of Beroea of Acts 20:4. Thus v. 21 may be a list of the delegates who are with Paul at the time of the writing of Romans, preparing for the trip to Jerusalem with the collection.

Verses 25–27 constitute a formal and liturgical doxology. Both content and style are more characteristic of letters written later by Paul's followers than of Paul in his undisputed letters (Eph 3:20–21; 1 Tim 1:17; cf. Jude 24–25). Since v. 26 does contain echoes of Rom 1:2, 5, this doxology may have been composed just for this letter, as a more stately conclusion for public reading. This is more likely to have occurred if Romans circulated in truncated versions without Paul's own conclusion. The evidence for this, in turn, is provided by the appearance of vv. 25–27 at different points in Greek manuscripts, even though chapters 15–16 or just 16 still always follow in extant copies: after 14:23 (the majority of late manuscripts); after 15:33 (one important papyrus manuscript of about 200 or 250 C.E.); here at the end of chapter 16 (the strongest early attestation); and sometimes in more than one, or none, of these places.

Verse 20b, which also appears in many manuscripts at different places, sometimes more than once, is Paul's own benediction, originally located as v. 24 after v. 23.

Bibliography

Achtemeier, P. J. *Romans*. IBC. Atlanta: John Knox, 1985.

Barrett, C. K. *A Commentary on the Epistle to the Romans*. New York: Harper & Brothers, 1957.

Barth, K. *The Epistle to the Romans*. London: Oxford University Press, 1933.

Cranfield, C. E. B. *Romans: A Shorter Commentary*. Grand Rapids: Eerdmans, 1985.

Dahl, N. A. *Studies in Paul*. Minneapolis: Augsburg, 1977.

Donfried, K. P., ed. *The Romans Debate*. Rev. and expanded ed. Peabody, Mass.: Hendrickson, 1991.

Dunn, J. D. G. *Romans*. 2 vols. WBC 38A–B. Dallas: Word, 1988.

Fitzmyer, J. A., S.J. *Romans: A New Translation with Introduction and Commentary*. AB 33. New York: Doubleday, 1993.

Godsey, J. D. "The Interpretation of Romans in the History of the Christian Faith." *Int* 34 (1980): 3–16.

Käsemann, E. *Commentary on Romans*. Grand Rapids: Eerdmans, 1980.

————. *Perspectives on Paul*. Philadelphia: Fortress, 1971.

Part IV

Exegetical and Theological Essays on the Gospel of John

CHAPTER 10

"THE FATHER": THE PRESENTATION OF GOD IN THE FOURTH GOSPEL*

"The Father and I are one." (John 10:30)

"Whoever has seen me has seen the Father. How can you say,
'Show us the Father'?" (John 14:9b)

In view of such passages as these, one might conclude that there is no such thing as a "presentation of God" in the Fourth Gospel. The unity of Father and Son, a prominent motif in the evangelist's Christology, seems to preclude any talk about God apart from the Son, or at least to render highly problematic any venture to devote a separate chapter on Johannine theology to "the Father." The Jesus of this gospel frequently claims to say and do and impart only what he has heard and seen and received from the Father (3:11; 5:19; 8:26, 28, 40; 20:21). Furthermore, the evangelist comments that the Father "has placed all things in [the Son's] hands" (3:35). The implications are restrictive: God is known and God's presence felt only because the Son alone "presents" God to the world, is wholly transparent to God, and is the only reliable vehicle for God's presence and action in the world. As Rudolf Bultmann observes, "apart from the revelation God is not here and is never here."[1] The only "presentation of God" in the Fourth Gospel is the self-presentation of Christ in its narratives and discourses.

I

The disconcerting fact that the gospel never spells out just what it is that the Son has seen and heard from the Father, except by what Jesus says and does, seems all the more to hide the Father behind the Son. Bultmann's reading of

---

*This essay reproduces, with minor revisions, Paul W. Meyer's contribution to a volume honoring D. Moody Smith: *Exploring the Gospel of John*, ed. R. A. Culpepper and C. C. Black (Louisville, Ky.: Westminster John Knox, 1996), 255–73. It is used here by permission.

1. Rudolf Bultmann, "The Eschatology of the Gospel of John," in *Faith and Understanding* (New York: Harper & Row, 1969), 173.

this is well known: "Jesus as the Revealer of God reveals nothing but that he is the Revealer. . . . John, that is, in his Gospel presents only the fact [*das Dass*] of the Revelation without describing its content [*ihr Was*]."[2] This seems to cut off even more conclusively any significant talk about God in distinction from the Christ and to signal a collapse of theology into Christology.

It will be well not to dismiss the point too quickly. Bultmann, as is well known, found in this feature of the evangelist's thought sure evidence of his dependence upon the gnostic redeemer myth.[3] But others have (more convincingly) seen in this exclusive orientation of Johannine faith around Jesus himself and the evangelist's refusal to spell out some body of esoteric teaching about God, delivered on earth by his emissary, precisely the one feature that most clearly differentiates the Fourth Gospel from the Christian gnostic literature that was to follow it. The content of the revelation here is not something different from the Christ himself, something (like Prometheus's fire) that he "brings" to earth.[4] "There are no heavenly mysteries revealed to Jesus by God except those disclosed in his own life and death."[5] And the process of the disclosure, the "presentation" of God, takes place for the reader in attending to the gospel narrative, which fuses historical recollection of the figure of Jesus with theological interpretation. This is far truer to the nature of the gospel's genre and more satisfying theologically than a notion of revelation that remains empty. But it still means that one may not abstract from the gospel some detached doctrine of God.

One might, on the other hand, come to just the opposite conclusion: that everything in the gospel's presentation of Christ is also a presentation of God. "When people confront Jesus, they are always dealing with the Father (8:16), and they see the Father (14:7); accordingly, Thomas can address the resurrected one quite directly as 'my Lord and my God' (20:28)."[6] But Thomas's confession is surely not to be interpreted to mean that the evangelist, after maintaining throughout the gospel a distinction between God and the one he has sent,

---

2. Rudolf Bultmann, *Theology of the New Testament*, 2 vols. (New York: Charles Scribner's Sons, 1951–55), 2:66. For a full discussion of this statement in the context of an examination of the gospel's concept of revelation, see especially John Ashton, *Understanding the Fourth Gospel* (Oxford: Clarendon, 1991), 515–53.

3. Rudolf Bultmann, "Die Bedeutung der neuerschlossenen mandäischen und manichäischen Quellen für das Verständnis des Johannesevangeliums," in *Exegetica: Aufsätze zur Erforschung des Neuen Testaments*, ed. E. Dinkler (Tübingen: Mohr [Siebeck], 1967), 57. Again, for fuller discussion and critique of Bultmann's position, see Ashton, *Understanding the Fourth Gospel*, 53–62.

4. Willi Marxsen, "Christology in the NT," *IDBSup*, 155; Hans Conzelmann, *An Outline of the Theology of the New Testament* (New York: Harper & Row, 1969), 340. For a clear summary of the crucial differences between John and Gnosticism, see Hartwig Thyen, "Johannesevangelium," *TRE* 17 (1976): 200–25, esp. 220.

5. Ashton, *Understanding the Fourth Gospel*, 551.

6. Marxsen, "Christology in the NT," 155–56.

between Father and Son, has finally abandoned it. The parallelism between the two nominative-vocatives means that in this climactic recognition-confession the fulfillment promised by the departing Christ to Philip in 14:9b has been realized. Does that come down to the same thing, a momentary evaporation of the distinction between the Son and the Father? Does that signal a collapse of Christology into theology? Ashton has remarked that Käsemann's famous characterization of the Johannine Christ as *der über die Erde schreitende Gott* (God striding across the earth) "conveys fairly accurately the impression that an unbiased reader would get from a first reading of the Gospel."[7] But a second reading will not rest with such an obviously docetic resolution. It will observe that the confession of Thomas results from recognizing the identity of this risen Lord with the one who was crucified. It will ask why the author has chosen a gospel form for his message, and why, if Father and Son are simply the same, so much is made throughout of their relationship to each other. Above all, it will continue to be brought up short by the text of the gospel, in which the term "Father," from whatever social location one might hear it, remains "God-language" that resists being swallowed up in Christology.[8] "There could hardly be a more Christocentric writer than John, yet his very Christocentricity is theocentric."[9]

After such introductory considerations, we may draw back from this fruitless alternative. The presentation of God in John's gospel will not suffer being treated as an independent locus in the evangelist's theology, but neither can it be simply suppressed and ignored. Perhaps we will make more progress in

7. Ashton, *Understanding the Fourth Gospel,* 72. See Ernst Käsemann, *The Testament of Jesus: A Study of the Gospel of John in the Light of Chapter 17* (Philadelphia: Fortress, 1968), 9 and passim; Käsemann credits earlier such characterizations to F. C. Baur, G. P. Wetter, and E. Hirsch.

8. On the problematic character of the image of "Father" for God in our time, when the brokenness of human relationships has served to make this traditional metaphor not only powerless for many but even destructive and offensive for some, one might well ponder some words of Donald Juel, written about the "Our Father" of the Lord's Prayer in Matthew and Luke but applicable as well to the Fourth Gospel: "Calling God 'our Father' has to do not primarily with traditional or 'natural' imagery. We do not pray to God as 'Male'; we do not speak of God as 'Father' because of some natural necessity—e.g., a 'natural law' according to which the cosmos is ordered according to gender distinctions. The God to whom we are invited to pray is known only in the particular—as the God whom Jesus addressed as 'Father' and who vindicated the crucified Jesus as Christ, Son of God, by raising him from the dead. We experience God as 'our Father' through Jesus. The words must be heard in their Gospel setting. The particularity of that setting . . . is the only promise of deliverance from ideologies of any sort that oppress and enslave and finally undermine the possibility of addressing God as one who cares and can be trusted to listen" ("The Lord's Prayer in the Gospels of Matthew and Luke," in *The Lord's Prayer* [*Princeton Seminary Bulletin,* Supplementary Issue, no. 2 (1992)], 63). "Father" never occurs in the Fourth Gospel with an "our" preceding it; it does not here belong in the community's prayer language. But that does not make it any less theological when used of God, or even confessional. The task at hand is to clarify "the particularity of that setting" in John's gospel.

9. C. K. Barrett, " 'The Father Is Greater than I' John 14.28: Subordinationist Christology in the New Testament," in *Essays on John* (Philadelphia: Westminster, 1982), 32.

understanding if we ask how the references to "the Father" in fact function in the "theocentric Christocentricity" of this complex book.

We may begin by noting the presence of a good bit of incidental "theology," in the conventional and straightforward sense of the term, in the traditions that have come to the evangelist. In this, of course, the Fourth Gospel does not stand alone. While the "doctrine of God is no longer the thematic center in the NT . . . this doctrine is always and everywhere the NT's most fundamental presupposition, for statements about God form the matrix of the Christian message, conditioning what is said about Jesus."[10] Not only individual verses in the Gospel of John but often logical and literary transitions as well are intelligible only if one is aware of some of these beliefs and teachings about God that are nowhere spelled out but are simply taken for granted by the writer. An example is the way in which the self-evident axiom of the constancy of the divine activity is presupposed in 5:17 and subsequent verses.[11] Nils Dahl, in discussing discourse about God as "the neglected factor in New Testament theology," has identified as one of the causes for neglect exactly this feature of the New Testament: its writers, dealing with other themes, presuppose or make only indirect use of some of these basic beliefs about God that are current in their environment, especially in contemporary Judaism. He enumerates several: "God is one"; "The Creator is the giver of life"; "God is the sovereign ruler"; "God is the righteous Judge"; and "God is merciful."[12] He goes on to indicate briefly how some of these traditional formulations acquire new nuances and distinctively Christian focus as they are applied in new settings; the result is "a new articulation of language used to speak about God," in which the traditional and the specifically Christian elements "are combined and interpenetrate one another."[13]

We may thus recognize, just beneath the surface of the text and at many points on it, the presence of a variety of traditional or conventional assertions about God. But because of the lively and creative process of reinterpretation to which Dahl refers, it would be unwise to try to codify these assumed elements into a "Johannine theology" and run the risk of forcing them into an artificial systematic pattern. This is not to say that it is unimportant to be aware of the rich funds of metaphorical language about God on which the Johannine community drew for the shaping of its symbolic world. The wide circulation and very diverse application of the idea of God as "Father" is a particularly strik-

10. Jouette M. Bassler, "God in the NT," *ABD* 2:1049.

11. Rudolf Bultmann, *The Gospel of John: A Commentary* (Philadelphia: Westminster, 1971), 246.

12. Nils Alstrup Dahl, "The Neglected Factor in New Testament Theology," in *Jesus the Christ: The Historical Origins of Christological Doctrine*, ed. Donald H. Juel (Minneapolis: Fortress, 1991), 158–60.

13. Ibid., 158. See also Bassler, "God in the NT," 1049.

ing instance in itself.[14] But this very wealth of material increases the temptation to draw lines of development or influence and to trace genetic relationships that can then take control of the interpretation of the gospel's text in questionable ways. Two examples of this have special bearing on the present essay.

In the earlier portion of his article on "Πατήρ" (Father) in the *Theological Dictionary of the New Testament,* Gottlob Schrenk devotes a section to "The Influence of the Roman *patria potestas* in the Hellenistic World," an indisputable and important aspect of the legal and social setting of the New Testament.[15] But then the specific appearance of some of these legal details in the parable of the Prodigal Son (Luke 15:11–32) leads to the generalization, "Whenever the NT uses the image of the 'father' it always builds on this concept of patriarchy."[16] The discussion of Πατήρ in John then takes its start by making the patriarchal notion of the head of the household (*Hausvater*) the controlling image, even to explain "the christological mystery" (997). The patriarchal traits of the language are exploited and emphasized in the subsequent discussion. The Son's love for the Father is interpreted primarily as unquestioning obedience, and the language of Luke 15 is specifically imported to illumine the Johannine text. This can hardly be the way to take the Fourth Gospel on its own terms.

A second example is provided by the almost obsessive desire, running through the literature, to trace the Johannine use of the term "Father" for God to the personal piety and religious intimacy of the historical Jesus. That Jesus referred to God as "[the] Father" is scarcely to be doubted; such usage was not uncommon.[17] What cannot be taken for granted is the extent to which this precedent accounts for the formulations found in John and their frequency. The

14. "The idea of God as Father and man as his child is found throughout the history of religion from the primitive stages onward" (Bultmann, *Gospel of John,* 58 [emphasis omitted]). For literature, see the footnotes there; cf. also Gottlob Schrenk and Gottfried Quell, "Πατήρ," *TDNT* 5:945–1014.

15. Schrenk and Quell, "Πατήρ," 950–51.

16. Ibid., 984.

17. The literature is extensive. To the article by Schrenk in the *TDNT,* referred to in n. 14 (esp. pp. 982–96: "Father according to the Jesus of the Synoptics"), one may usefully compare such widely different treatments as T. W. Manson, *The Teaching of Jesus: Studies of Its Form and Content* (Cambridge: Cambridge University Press, 1951), 89–115 ("God as Father"); Bultmann, *Theology of the New Testament,* 1:22–26 ("Jesus' Idea of God"); Conzelmann, *Outline of the Theology of the New Testament,* 99–106 ("The Idea of God"); and Robert G. Hamerton-Kelly, *God the Father: Theology and Patriarchy in the Teaching of Jesus* (Philadelphia: Fortress, 1979). More controversial is the significance of Jesus' use of "Abba"; cf. Joachim Jeremias, *New Testament Theology: The Proclamation of Jesus* (New York: Charles Scribner's Sons, 1971), 61–68; W. D. Davies and Dale C. Allison, *A Critical and Exegetical Commentary on the Gospel according to Saint Matthew,* ICC, 3 vols. (Edinburgh: T. & T. Clark, 1988–97), 1:601–2; and Ernst Haenchen, *Der Weg Jesu: Eine Erklärung des Markus-Evangeliums und der kanonischen Parallelen* (Berlin: Töpelmann, 1966), 492–94 n. 7a.

underlying issue, which can only be mentioned here because it would carry us too far afield, concerns "the specifically Christian usage" and where its roots lie.[18] References to God as the "Father" of Jesus Christ play an important role in the epistolary literature of the New Testament as part of the developing confessional, protoliturgical, and increasingly stereotypical formulations of the Christian community.[19] But the references are surprisingly scarce in the pre-Johannine gospel traditions.[20] "It is apparent that the earliest document, Mark, has the fewest references [to the divine Fatherhood], that the latest, John, has the most, and that documents which intervene in date occupy intermediate positions as regards their number of references."[21] This should suggest strongly that

18. The phrase is used, for example, by Bassler, "God in the NT," 1054.

19. For example, in Gal 1:1 God is the Father of Jesus Christ by virtue of having performed the essential act of a father, the giving of life. As a consequence, he is the Father also of Christians in vv. 3–4. (This was pointed out to me by J. Louis Martyn.)

20. The presentation of the statistics is often prejudiced by a theological argument. The data are as follows: In Mark, Jesus refers to God as "[the] Father" only three times (in direct address only once, in the Gethsemane prayer [Mark 14:36]; once in the apocalyptic discourse in conjunction with mention of "the Son" [13:32]; and once as the "Father" of the Son of Man [8:38]). Only once does he speak to the disciples of "your Father in heaven" (11:25). Jesus never refers to God as "my Father" in Mark. In the Q-material as it appears in Luke, Jesus speaks of God as "Father" of human beings four times: in two of these passages as "[the] Father" (once in the Lord's Prayer in Luke 11:2 and again in 11:13, where the text is uncertain [it may read "your heavenly Father"]) and in two as "your Father" (6:36 and 12:30). To this last-mentioned Q-saying in 12:30 Luke has attached another logion with "your Father" (12:32). The only other references to God as "Father" in the Lukan Q-material are in the much-discussed two verses, 10:21–22, the "bolt out of the Johannine blue," which are closely paralleled in Matt 11:25–27. Here "Father" is used absolutely of God four times (twice as a vocative and twice closely correlating "the Father" and "the Son") and once as "my Father." Five further examples occur in Luke, all in secondary traditions peculiar to this gospel: one or two instances of "Father" as a vocative, in Jesus' prayers from the cross (Luke 23:46 and the textually dubious 23:34), and three instances of "my Father" in 2:49; 22:29; and 24:49. It is Matthew who has augmented the synoptic tradition to the level of a representation of Jesus on intimate terms with God as "his" Father and the Father of his disciples. In the Matthean parallels to passages mentioned so far as occurring in Mark and Luke, Matthew adds the possessive "my" in 26:39 and "our" in 6:9 (the Lord's Prayer). To these parallels Matthew adds a single absolute reference to "the Father" in 28:19 (the trinitarian baptismal formula). But he adds another fourteen references in the mouth of Jesus to God as *his* "Father," always with the possessive "my" (7:21; 10:32, 33; 12:50; 15:13; 16:17; 18:10, 19, 35; 20:23; 25:34; 26:29, 42, 53); in six of these fourteen "in heaven" or "heavenly" is added (12:50; 15:13; 16:17; 18:10, 19, 35). Matthew also adds another nineteen references to God as the "Father" of the disciples (always "your" [sing. or pl.], except for "their" in 13:43: 5:16, 45; 6:1, 4, 6 (bis), 8, 9, 15, 18 (bis), 26, 32; 7:11; 10:20, 29; 13:43; 18:14; 23:9; in ten of these nineteen, "heavenly" or "in the heavens" is an added qualifier: 5:16, 45; 6:1, 18 (bis), 26, 32; 7:11; 18:14; 23:9. It is especially noteworthy that in all the synoptic tradition *only* Mark 13:32 (with its parallel in Matt 24:36) and the Q-logion in Luke 10:22/Matt 11:27 refer to God as "the Father" in correlation with reference to "the Son." This last point will be picked up below.

21. H. F. D. Sparks, "The Doctrine of the Divine Fatherhood in the Gospels," in *Studies in the Gospels: Essays in Memory of R. H. Lightfoot*, ed. D. E. Nineham (Oxford: Basil Blackwell, 1967), 259.

the comparatively high frequency of references to God as "Father" in the Fourth Gospel, indeed the very language itself, has its roots in post-Easter theological development and is part of the community's confessional language, *its* presentation of Jesus as the Christ in narrative genre. To appeal to Jesus' own religious usage at this point only stands in the way of examining carefully how this language functions in the evangelist's text.[22]

These two examples serve to demonstrate the importance of focusing on how the language about God as "Father" actually functions in this gospel before one draws conclusions about its genetic origins or antecedents. But they also serve to recall the point from which this essay began: the close connections between theology and Christology in this gospel. One can scarcely do justice to the gospel on its own terms if one does not at the same time account for some of the ways in which the presentation of God as "Father" is here related to the presentation of Jesus. On this last question there have been some important proposals in the literature on the Fourth Gospel that need to be considered before we can proceed.

In this connection it is useful to recall the striking thematic richness of the Christology of the gospel. Its opening chapter, with its prologue (vv. 1–18) and its testimonies (of John the Baptist and of the first disciples, vv. 19–51), confronts the reader with this diversity at the very start in the virtual catalog of titles it contains. These are here taken for granted and woven into the text, but they wait, so to speak, for elucidation as the gospel unfolds: Logos, Only (-Begotten), Messiah, Elijah, Prophet, Chosen One, Lamb of God, Son of God, King of Israel, and Son of Man.[23] The initial impression is one almost of confusion, or at least of such interchangeability among these terms that it would seem hopeless, perhaps even an act of violence upon the text, to try to break down the evangelist's Christology into some of its component strands and single out one that concentrates more than the others on Jesus' relationship to God as "Father." Yet on closer examination, that is exactly what the text does seem

22. After pointing out, in the words just cited, the low frequency of "Father" language in the early stages of the pre-Johannine tradition, Sparks disregards his own findings by reverting to an "explanation" offered by T. W. Manson years ago, before the impact of form criticism. The statistics do not matter; Jesus' "reticence" in speaking about God as "Father" is due to "the intense reality and deep sacredness of the experience [of the Fatherhood of God]. . . . [W]e cannot speak lightly of the things that most profoundly move us" (Manson, *Teaching of Jesus,* 108). Manson thought "that the only ultimately satisfactory explanation of the authority of Jesus is that which sets the foundation of it in his unique spiritual experience" (ibid., 106). But Manson's own immediate appeal to the analogy of the "inaugural vision" of the prophet in ancient Israel destroys at a stroke the category of "uniqueness." More important, what is missed is the fact that in the Gospel of John those references to God as "the Father who sent" Jesus function as the evangelist's way of "setting the foundation" of Jesus' authority outside and beyond the world of human religious experience, even and especially that of the prophets.

23. A review of these titles is found in Ashton, *Understanding the Fourth Gospel,* 253–62.

to allow. Within the overall coherence of the evangelist's Christology, certain constellations of motifs emerge. The titles are not confused with one another. In part at least, they even distribute themselves in different literary layers of the gospel. Each one that is resumed in the remainder of the gospel (not all are) is associated with certain recurring phrases, themes, and even topics of potential, and presumably actual, theological debate in the setting of the gospel during the stages of its composition. This is illustrated clearly by Wayne Meeks's study, "The Man from Heaven in Johannine Sectarianism."[24] Meeks has shown the close connections drawn in the gospel between the title "Son of Man" and the descent/ascent motif by which Jesus is repeatedly identified as one who has come into the world from heaven and is returning there.[25] This is not to say that the distinctions are watertight or that there is no overlap of one set of ideas or phrases with another. The spatial dualism of "heaven" and "earth" extends beyond the descent/ascent language, for example, but the close connection to which Meeks has drawn attention holds. Statements about the Son of Man and references to God as the "Father," especially as the one who "sent" Jesus, constitute quite distinct strands in the Johannine christological language.[26]

If "Father" language for God is not closely connected with the Son of Man, there can be little question that the title "Son of God" or simply "the Son" also occupies an important place in this Christology and does at once bring the reader to consider language about God as "Father."[27] It is, in fact, the presence of both terms in the theological vocabulary of the gospel that resists any easy collapse of the evangelist's theology into Christology or of his Christology into theology.

24. Wayne Meeks, "The Man from Heaven in Johannine Sectarianism," *JBL* 91 (1972): 44–72.

25. Ibid., 52: "There is a curiously close connection throughout the gospel between this title [viz., "Son of Man"] and the descent/ascent language." Similarly, Rudolf Schnackenburg has observed that the descent/ascent schema is constitutive for the title "Son of Man" ("'Der Vater, der mich gesandt hat': Zur johanneischen Christologie," in *Anfänge der Christologie: Festschrift für Ferdinand Hahn zum 65. Geburtstag,* ed. Cilliers Breytenbach and Henning Paulsen [Göttingen: Vandenhoeck & Ruprecht, 1991], 284).

26. The two strands come together most closely in 5:27 and 8:28. The distinction is preserved in the difference between 13:31 (God is glorified in the Son of Man) and 14:13 (the Father is glorified in the Son). Of course, both "the Son of Man" in 13:31 and "the Son" in 14:13 refer to Jesus, but there is no evidence in the Fourth Gospel for the simply synonymous use or interchangeability of "Son" with "Son of Man," or of "Father of the Son of Man" with the absolute "the Father," both of which Schrenk finds in the synoptic tradition ("Πατήρ," 989 n. 278).

27. The statistics of this "Father/Son" language alone compel this recognition. The following may be mentioned here: Whereas the title "Son of Man" occurs 13 times in the Fourth Gospel, Jesus is called "the Son" 20 times and "the Son of God" 9 times, for a total of 29. In 3 cases of these 29, "only" (μονογενής) is added. (The reading ὁ μονογενὴς υἱός ["the only Son"] is followed in 1:18, against UBSGNT, 3d ed., *Novum Testamentum Graece,* 27th ed., and NRSV; for decisive arguments supporting this choice, see Bart D. Ehrman, *The Orthodox Corruption of Scripture: The Effect of Early Christological Controversies on the Text of the New Testament* [New York: Oxford University Press, 1993], 78–82.) God is referred to as "the Father" (absolute) 74 times; with the

One might even venture to say that the reader is compelled by this language to redefine the term *Christology* itself and to recognize that in its profoundest dimension, not just in this gospel but in all its variations throughout the diverse traditions of the New Testament, it concerns not the person of Jesus or his identity ("who he is") and the consequences of his life so much as—first, foremost, and always—his open or hidden relationship to God, and of God to him.[28] Without that, there may be a religious hero in the gospels, but there is no Christology.

Both terms, "Father" and "Son," are of course figures originally drawn from the reciprocal relationships of human life. For that reason—perhaps also because of the long history of Trinitarian debate and the doctrinal and liturgical legacy left by it—the reader of the Fourth Gospel understandably tends to see and hear these words in similar reciprocity of meaning, as if one can never have one without the other. It is plain from the literature on John that the two terms are seen in close coordination with each other.[29] It is characteristic of those treatments of Johannine theology most explicitly attending to its presentation of God to do so under a heading such as "The Father and the Son."[30] Even more widespread is an emphasis on the unity of the Son with the Father in the thought of the evangelist.

---

possessive "my/your [sing.]" (always with Jesus as the antecedent), another 25 times; with the addition of "who sent me/him," another 7 times; in the anarthrous nominative/vocative of prayer, 9 more times; and as an (anarthrous) predicate, 3 times. This yields a total of 118 occurrences of "Father" for God (cf. the statistics for the Synoptic Gospels in n. 20). For purposes of comparison, one may note that God is referred to with θεός ("God") only 45 times; this count does not include the 31 instances of θεός as a genitive modifier (as in ὁ υἱὸς τοῦ θεοῦ, "the Son of God" [9 times], τέκνα τοῦ θεοῦ, "children of God" [2 times], ὁ ἀμνὸς τοῦ θεοῦ, "the Lamb of God" [2 times], etc.), nor the use of θεός as a predicate (1:1; 8:54) or predicate accusative (10:33), but it does include all uses of θεός with prepositions (22 times) and the one vocative (20:28). Finally, apart from the textually secondary 5:4, κύριος ("Lord") is used of God only in Old Testament citations (1:23; 12:13, 38). But since κύριος is used elsewhere always of Jesus—overwhelmingly in the vocative by those who address Jesus in the narrative, but also in the third person (whether the narrator is the evangelist or a character in the story) and even indirectly in gnomic statements in Jesus' own mouth (13:16; 15:15, 20)—one may ask whether the reader of the gospel is not intended to hear even these occurrences in Old Testament citations as referring to Jesus.

28. Though it no longer receives the attention it deserves, a major older presentation of Johannine Christology that presses this point and argues for its applicability to John is Ernst Gaugler, "Das Christuszeugnis des Johannesevangeliums," in *Jesus Christus im Zeugnis der heiligen Schrift und der Kirche,* BEvT 2 (2d ed.; Munich: Kaiser, 1936), 34–67, esp. 49–51.

29. Even the surveys of parallels that can be adduced from the history of religions seem either to presuppose this seemingly self-evident reciprocity or to find it confirmed (e.g., Bultmann, *Gospel of John,* 58–59; 165–66 n. 1).

30. So Conzelmann, *Outline of the Theology of the New Testament,* 339–41. Similarly, Rudolf Schnackenburg locates his principal discussion of the gospel's "Father" language for God in an excursus devoted to the Johannine "Son-Christology" (*The Gospel according to St. John,* vol. 2, *Commentary on Chapters 5–12* [New York: Crossroad, 1987], 172–86).

It cannot be disputed that there is strong support in the text of John for this emphasis on unity. Once again, however, it is the inordinate pressing of this otherwise valid point that threatens to collapse the distinction between Christology and theology. Interpreting the entire gospel from the motif of unity so prominent in chapter 17, Käsemann not only asserts that "the unity of the Son with the Father is the central theme of the Johannine proclamation," but goes on to say that it follows that "that unity is of necessity also the proper object of faith."[31] It is, indeed, not only 17:11 and 17:22 that assert that Jesus and the Father are "one"; 10:30 does the same. In 10:38; 14:10, 11, 20; as well as in 17:21, Jesus and the Father are said to be "in" each other. Those who respond negatively to Jesus' works "hate" both him and the Father (15:24). To know or not know one is to know or not know the other (14:7; 16:3; 17:3). Behind Jesus' life and activity lie the Father's will (6:40), the Father's life (6:57), the Father's acting (14:10), the Father's word (14:24), and the Father's love (15:10). "My Father" in the mouth of Jesus (ὁ πατήρ μου, 25 times) makes it clear that God is *his* Father as no one else's.[32] Throughout his life on earth, Jesus as the Son is portrayed as remaining in uninterrupted and direct association with the Father (8:16, 29; 16:32b).[33] "The Evangelist no longer perceives simply Jesus, the human being, in the earthly Jesus, but one who has come from God, one who has been identified as God's Son by the exaltation, one who does God's work on earth as if God himself were doing it."[34] The unity of Father and Son is continually set before the reader as a total coalescence of the two in the actual activity of giving life to the world.

Yet a crucial aspect of this unity in action for the evangelist is the "commandment" (ἐντολή, the order, warrant, or charge; cf. 11:57) that Jesus has received from the Father (10:18; 12:49–50), has himself "kept" or discharged (15:10), and passes on to his disciples (13:34; 14:15; 15:10). Because of this term, the correspondence of action between Son and Father has been misunderstood as obedience within a patriarchally structured relationship.[35] But this ἐντολή, in its first appearance in the gospel (10:18), is the Good Shepherd's act of laying down his life for the sheep—not the surrender of Jesus' own will to yield to God's, as in the synoptic Gethsemane scene (Mark 14:36; Matt 26:39;

---

31. Käsemann, *Testament of Jesus,* 24–25. Compare ibid., 25: "John's peculiarity [*Eigenart*] is that he knows only one single dogma, the christological dogma of the unity of Jesus with the Father." As is well known, Käsemann concluded that such a strong emphasis on the unity of Father and Son as he sees in the gospel leads to the danger of docetism (ibid., 26).

32. John 2:16; 5:17, 43; 6:32, 40; 8:19 (bis), 49, 54; 10:18, 25, 29, 37; 14:2, 7, 20, 21, 23; 15:1, 8, 10, 15, 23, 24; 20:17. Only in 20:17 is God referred to as the "Father" of anyone else (the disciples).

33. Gaugler, "Das Christuszeugnis des Johannesevangeliums," 49.

34. Ibid., 57.

35. So Schrenk and Quell, "Πατήρ," 984.

Luke 22:42), but the willing act of Jesus' own initiative and authority (ἐξουσία; cf. John 12:27), which is grounded in the relationship of mutual knowledge and love between Jesus and his Father (10:15, 17). "John himself uses neither the noun 'obedience' nor the verb 'to obey'. Instead he has the formula 'to do the will', which corresponds to the other formula, 'to hear the word'."[36] Jesus' constancy in doing the Father's will (4:34; 5:30; 6:38) or "doing the work[s] of God" (4:34; 9:4; 10:32, 37–38; 14:10; 17:4) does not *produce* unity with the Father—as would be the case if it were understood as obedience—but is grounded in, and springs from, the prior unity of Jesus with the Father.[37]

But how is this prior unity understood? How and in what sense are Jesus and the Father "one" (10:30)? The answer is clear: Jesus is the one who has been "sent" by God.[38] "The origin of his decisions and actions lies outside him; he has been 'sent' and acts on behalf of him who sent him."[39] Such language, while it maintains the evangelist's stress on unity in action, preserves also the distinction between Jesus and the Father—and is a principal reason why the evangelist's theology cannot be collapsed into his Christology.

Because this language about "sending" occupies such an important place in the gospel, it is not surprising that considerable attention has been paid to the motif of the divine envoy or emissary, or to what has been called, in German, the *Gesandtenchristologie* of the Fourth Gospel.[40] However, here once again, genetic considerations have controlled the discussion. For Bultmann, the combination of the commissioning of a divine emissary with the idea of his "coming into the world" from beyond cannot be traced to cultic or eschatological sources or to the precedent of Old Testament prophecy but has its analogues only in Gnostic notions of a Revealer figure.[41] A much larger number of interpreters have sought to illumine the evangelist's language by appealing to the presence in Jewish tradition of the idea of a divinely authorized agent or representative. This can vary all the way from the eschatological "prophet like

36. Käsemann, *Testament of Jesus,* 18. Käsemann goes on to make clear that if this doing of the Father's will is to be called "obedience" as a kind of "paraphrase," "this may not be understood moralistically," nor does it have anything to do with "what we usually mean by humility" (ibid.). See also Bultmann, *Gospel of John,* 249–50.

37. This point is emphatically argued by Thyen, "Johannesevangelium," 221.

38. Greek ἀποστέλλειν (leaving πέμπειν aside for the moment); sent by God (ὁ θεός): 3:17, 34; 6:29; 7:29; 8:42; sent by the Father (ὁ πατήρ): 5:36, 38; 6:57; 10:36; 11:42; 17:3, 8, 18, 21, 23, 25; 20:21.

39. Bultmann, *Gospel of John,* 249 (German: "handelt im Auftrag," i.e., "acts under commission"; *Das Evangelium des Johannes,* MeyerK [11th ed.; Göttingen: Vandenhoeck & Ruprecht, 1950], 186).

40. Bultmann, *Gospel of John,* 50 nn. 2 and 3. For a fuller discussion of parallels and background materials, see the excursus, "Jesus der Gottgesandte," in Walter Bauer, *Das Johannesevangelium,* HNT 6 (3d ed.; Tübingen: Mohr [Siebeck], 1933), 58–60.

41. Bultmann, *Gospel of John,* 50 nn. 2 and 3; 250–51.

Moses" (Deut 18:15–22) to what some have called the "institution" of the שׁלִיח ("emissary"), the basic principle of which is summarized in such rabbinic texts as Mishnah *Berakot* 5:5 ("The agent of a person is as the person himself") and which some have found perfectly restated in John 13:16b.[42]

What is involved in this rather extensive literature is a search for the juridical background that will make intelligible the notion of a divine envoy who does not merely bring information but mediates a fully authentic and genuine encounter with the God who "sent" him, and nothing less than that. At the same time, however, certain "subordinationist" connotations continue for some to cling to the very notion of an envoy or emissary that is "sent" and so seem to make it irreconcilable with the evangelist's claims for the unity of the Father and the Son. The result has been to stir up again, rather than to settle, a debate about Johannine Christology that pits one reading of the gospel, one that stresses the mission of Jesus as the divine emissary who has been "sent" into the world, against another that correlates the Father and the Son and emphasizes the unbroken unity between them and the mutual indwelling of each in the other. Genetic considerations continue to play a role, so that the debate turns in part on determining which christological strand is earlier and primary in determining the very structure of the gospel and which is derivative

42. Karl Heinrich Rengstorf, "ἀπόστολος," *TDNT* 1:414–24, esp. 415; Gaugler, "Das Christuszeugnis des Johannesevangeliums," 51–52; Théo Preiss, "Justification in Johannine Thought," in *Life in Christ,* trans. Harold Knight, SBT 13 (Naperville, Ill.: Alec R. Allenson, 1952), 9–31. Peder Borgen ("God's Agent in the Fourth Gospel," in *The Interpretation of John,* ed. John Ashton, IRT 9 [Philadelphia: Fortress; London: SPCK, 1986], 67–78) broadens the discussion of divine agency to include the early stages of Merkabah mysticism. Wayne Meeks *(The Prophet-King: Moses Traditions and the Johannine Christology,* NovTSup 14 [Leiden: E. J. Brill, 1967], 301–5) puts it in the context of the question about Mosaic traditions in John. John Ashton *(Understanding the Fourth Gospel,* 312–17) makes it part of a much broader discussion of the "mission" of the Son of God in the gospel. Jan-A. Bühner *(Der Gesandte und sein Weg im 4. Evangelium: Die kultur- und religionsgeschichtlichen Grundlagen der johanneischen Sendungschristologie sowie ihre traditionsgeschichtliche Entwicklung,* WUNT 2/2 [Tübingen: Mohr (Siebeck), 1977]) provides the most exhaustive investigation of the secular cultural and historical background for the evangelist's "mission-Christology," the key to which he finds in a synthesis of the legate or agent, the שׁלִיח, with the prophet. Of special value is his survey of previous discussion of the issue (7–115). A similar treatment, with a sharper focus on the eschatological prophet, is offered by Juan Peter Miranda, *Der Vater, der mich gesandt hat: Religionsgeschichtliche Untersuchungen zu den johanneischen Sendungsformeln: Zugleich ein Beitrag zur johanneischen Christologie und Ekklesiologie,* Europäische Hochschulschriften/European University Papers, Series 23: Theology 7 (Bern and Frankfurt a.M.: Herbert Lang/Peter Lang, 1972); and idem, *Die Sendung Jesu im vierten Evangelium: Religions- und theologiegeschichtliche Untersuchungen zu den Sendungsformeln,* SBS 87 (Stuttgart: Katholisches Bibelwerk, 1977). The sharpest cautions against an anachronistic use of the specific rabbinic terminology (esp. שׁלִיח) appear in discussions of the origin of the notion of apostleship in the New Testament, but they need to be heeded in Johannine studies as well (see John Howard Schütz, *Paul and the Anatomy of Apostolic Authority,* SNTSMS 26 [Cambridge: Cambridge University Press, 1975], 27–28, and the literature cited there).

and ancillary.[43] In an instructive and suggestive essay, Rudolf Schnackenburg has taken note of this discussion and its resulting dilemmas and proposed to show how, in the historical process of its formation, Johannine Christology could bring together such different traditions into a multifaceted whole. The end product of this development is for him perfectly symbolized in the pregnant, recurring phrase of the gospel, "the Father who sent me."[44]

II

If one pauses at this point to take stock, the results are far from satisfactory. The issue appears to have become, once again, a matter of refining our understanding of the evangelist's complex *Christology,* and we seem to be no closer to delineating his presentation of God. The way in which references to God as "Father" function in the gospel has hardly become clearer. There are several good reasons for pressing the question a step further.

One reason is a consideration of method. Hartwig Thyen has cautioned that genetic inquiries into the history-of-religions origins even of the motifs of Johannine Christology can never take the place of careful observation of the actual use and function of those motifs in their literary and historical contexts in the gospel itself.[45] That one should not allow the inquiry into the gospel's presentation of God to be swallowed up in the quest for the origins of its christological motifs is brought home also by James D. G. Dunn's reminder that the primary theological debate that the evangelist was engaged in with his Jewish contemporaries was a debate, sooner or later, about monotheism, that is, a *theological debate.[46]* Dunn has also forcefully argued that to focus on the pre- and posthistory of Johannine ideas is to invite anachronisms in interpretation.[47] One form of such anachronism is to project back onto the gospel a coherence and homogeneity among its diverse christological strands that were attained only in later interpretation and reflection. The fact, as we have already seen in part, is that the materials with which one has to work are not as homogeneous as they have often been taken to be. The gospel still confronts its reader as a layered

---

43. See especially Miranda, *Die Sendung Jesu im vierten Evangelium,* 90–92, and the sharp critique of Thyen, "Johannesevangelium," 221–22. For an admirably clear and balanced discussion of the tensions in Johannine Christology that feed this debate, see Ashton, *Understanding the Fourth Gospel,* 308–29. In the end, like the writers referred to earlier (n. 22), Ashton cannot resist suggesting, even if only by a rhetorical question, that the "original seed" of the "fine flowering" of Johannine Christology is to be found in "Jesus' own sense of the fatherhood of God" (326).

44. Schnackenburg, "'Der Vater, der mich gesandt hat,'" 275–91.

45. Thyen, "Johannesevangelium," 219.

46. James D. G. Dunn, "Let John Be John: A Gospel for Its Time," in *The Gospel and the Gospels,* ed. Peter Stuhlmacher (Grand Rapids: Eerdmans, 1991), 293–322, esp. 318.

47. Ibid., passim.

document in which the evidence of different traditions and stages in its history has not been completely suppressed in the process of assimilation.[48] John Ashton, who has contributed greatly to understanding the importance of mission and agency in the Christology of John, is clear that these motifs should not be indiscriminately combined:

> Essentially John saw Jesus' relationship with God in two clearly distinguishable ways, *sonship,* and *mission;* and the two names Jesus has for God ('Father' and 'the one who sent me') though often united in practice ('the Father who sent me') should not be assumed without further proof or argument to have been linked together in the traditions upon which John drew. In chapter 7 the term 'Father' is not used: nowhere in this chapter is there the slightest hint that Jesus regarded himself as the Son of God.[49]

In the second place, the language of "Father" and "Son" requires another look. We observed earlier a powerful tendency among the interpreters of the gospel always to coordinate closely the gospel's use of "Father" with that of "Son." Ashton shares this habit. I propose, however, to carry a step further his care in discriminating one tradition in the gospel from another and to try to show that the way in which references to God as "Father" function cannot be clearly seen until we break this habit. It is an understandable tendency. Whenever Jesus refers to God as "[my] Father," *we* unconsciously insert the evangelist's christological identification of him as "Son [of God]" but fail to notice that the resulting coordination is not matched by the evangelist's usage. The Q-logion in Luke 10:22/Matt 11:27 has long been dubbed a "bolt out of the Johannine blue," because it, along with only one other synoptic saying, makes this coordination direct and clear;[50] but actually the Johannine usage as a whole is much closer to the Pauline letters. In the undisputed letters, Paul refers to Jesus Christ as "Son of God" or "the Son" or "his [God's] Son" fourteen times but *never* in

---

48. For a finely nuanced discussion of the bearing of this fact upon method in interpretation, see M. C. de Boer, "Narrative Criticism, Historical Criticism, and the Gospel of John," *JSNT* 47 (1992): 35–48.

49. Ashton, *Understanding the Fourth Gospel,* 318. A similar example is provided by the two motifs of Jesus' "coming into the world" and his being "sent." Though Bultmann makes much of their combination (see n. 41), the evangelist does not combine them. Not one of the passages in which Jesus (whether himself or as "the light") is spoken of as "coming into the world" (1:9; 3:19; 6:14; 9:39; 11:27; 12:46; 16:28; 18:37) connects this coming with his being sent. The two motifs do lie side by side in 12:45–46, but this is a summary context that recapitulates a variety of themes from the "Book of Signs" (chs. 1–12), and there is no internal connection between them. On the other hand, the phrase "into the world" does follow the verb ἀποστέλλειν ("to send") in 3:17; 10:36; 17:18; in these cases the context offers clear reasons why the destination of the mission, the κόσμος ("world"), is named.

50. See the concluding remark in n. 20.

conjunction with any reference to God as "Father."[51] He refers to God as "the Father" (absolute) nine times (including "the Father of mercies," i.e., "the merciful Father," in 2 Cor 1:3), as the "Father" of human beings (always "our Father") eleven times, but as "the Father of [our] Lord Jesus [Christ]" only three times (Rom 15:6; 2 Cor 1:3; 11:31), and in none of these three contexts is Jesus Christ spoken of as "Son."[52] In the Fourth Gospel, as we have seen,[53] the occurrences of both "Father" for God and "Son" for Jesus are far more frequent. But the actual pairing of these terms as coordinates is surprisingly infrequent. "The Son of God" is linked with "Father" for God only twice (John 5:25; 10:36), while "the Son" (absolute) is coordinated with "the Father" for God fourteen times, with eight of these occurring in a single context.[54] These passages that bring the terms together form a distinct group, which when left to one side leaves the large number of remaining uses of "Father" for God far less susceptible to being subsumed under the Johannine "Christology."

A third reason for pursuing our inquiry is the most telling of all, a matter of basic Johannine usage that is the most surprising in the extent to which it has escaped notice in the literature. We come finally to the "sending" language of the gospel. The instances have already been enumerated in which God (ὁ θεός) or the Father (ὁ πατήρ) is said to have "sent" (ἀποστέλλειν) Jesus.[55] In these passages the verb is always in the finite active form, in the past tense (perfect

---

51. Rom 1:3, 9; 5:10; 8:3, 29, 32; 1 Cor 1:9; 15:28; 2 Cor 1:19; Gal 1:16; 2:20; 4:4, 6; 1 Thess 1:10. The coordination begins with the deutero-Pauline letters (Eph 4:13; Col 1:13).

52. Cf. Schrenk and Quell, "Πατήρ," 1009: "The rule is scrupulously observed that υἱός ['son'] should occur with θεός ['God'] rather than πατήρ ['father']." For the Synoptics, cf. the comment by Ferdinand Hahn: "Yet on the other hand it must be observed that in all the tradition about Jesus as the 'Son of God' the fatherhood of God and his union [*Bindung*] with the Father do not play any recognizable role; a distinction has therefore to be drawn between 'Son of God' and 'Son—Father'" (*The Titles of Jesus in Christology: Their History in Early Christianity* [London: Lutterworth, 1969], 313).

53. See n. 27.

54. John 1:18 (on the text, see n. 27); 3:35; 5:19 (bis), 20, 21, 22, 23 (bis), 26; 6:40; 14:13; 17:1 (bis). The concentration in chapter 5 is striking and has led Jürgen Becker to ask whether this entire group of passages may have its roots in an independent tradition that has left its mark also in Matthew and 1 Corinthians (*Das Evangelium nach Johannes,* Ökumenischer Taschenbuchkommentar zum Neuen Testament 4, 2 vols. [Gütersloh: Gütersloher Verlagshaus/Mohn, 1979–81], 1:239–40). On this tradition see also Eduard Schweizer, "Zum religionsgeschichtlichen Hintergrund der 'Sendungsformel' Gal 4,4f, Röm 8,3f, Joh 3,16f, 1 Joh 4,9," in *Beiträge zur Theologie des Neuen Testaments: Neutestamentliche Aufsätze (1955–1970)* (Zurich: Zwingli, 1970), 83–95; and idem, "What Do We Really Mean When We Say 'God sent his son . . .'?" in *Faith and History: Essays in Honor of Paul W. Meyer,* ed. John T. Carroll, Charles H. Cosgrove, and E. Elizabeth Johnson, Homage Series (Atlanta: Scholars Press, 1990), 298–312.

55. See n. 38. (In ch. 17, the second-person singular pronoun, σύ, is understood to have πατήρ ["father"; vv. 1, 5, 11, 21, 24, 25] as its antecedent.)

in 5:36 and 20:21; elsewhere, aorist).[56] The other verb in this language of sending is, of course, πέμπειν. Several writers have tried to identify a distinction in meaning between πέμπειν and ἀποστέλλειν, with varying conclusiveness.[57] What does appear to be consistent is the formulaic use of the definite singular active participle, always aorist, ὁ πέμψας με/αὐτόν ("the one who has sent me/him").[58] In this formula God is always the antecedent of the participle, the subject of the sending, and aside from the one use of the formula by John the Baptist in 1:33, Jesus is always the direct object of the participle. The formula can be combined with "Father" ("the Father who has sent me") but more often it stands alone as an epithet for God.[59] It never occurs absolutely (i.e., without a direct object, as though simply "the Sender"). In sum, the point in counting these verb forms is that nowhere in the Fourth Gospel is Jesus ever called the "Envoy" or "Emissary" or "one sent [ἀπεσταλμένος] by God"; only John the Baptist is. There is not so much a *Gesandtenchristologie* in the gospel as there is a *Sendertheologie.* "The Father who has sent me" or "he who has sent me" is *"God's name."*[60] The language of "sending" is *theo*logical language that undergirds Christology but refuses to be absorbed into it.

56. In addition, Jesus is the subject of the active verb, with the disciples as object, in 4:38 and 17:18. The verb is used twice of the Jews who sent a delegation to John (1:19; 5:33) and three more times in straightforward narrative contexts (7:32; 11:3; 18:24), still with at least mild "official" or legatine connotations. The perfect passive participle (ἀπεσταλμένος, "one sent," "emissary") is used twice of John the Baptist (1:6; 3:28), once of the Jewish delegates sent to question John (1:24), and once as a translation of "Siloam" (9:7), but *never of Jesus.*

57. Karl Heinrich Rengstorf, "ἀποστέλλω and πέμπω in the NT," *TDNT* 1:403–6; Miranda, *Die Sendung Jesu im vierten Evangelium,* 14–15. Schnackenburg sees no difference ("'Der Vater, der mich gesandt hat,'" 277). Bultmann (*Gospel of John,* 50 n. 2) seems to accept Rengstorf's distinction but to deny that the gospel observes it. (The translator's English sentence does not say this, and the original German [*Das Evangelium des Johannes: Ergänzungsheft,* 11] is ambiguous, but all the passages Bultmann here cites [1:19, 22; 5:36–37; 20:21] show the two verbs occurring side by side.)

58. The finite form of the verb is used once of God's sending the Spirit (future tense, 14:26), twice of Jesus' sending the Spirit/Paraclete (also future, 15:26; 16:7), and twice of Jesus' sending disciples (subjunctive, 13:20; present indicative, 20:21). The participial form is used once in the plural, of the authorities responsible for the delegation to John (1:22).

59. With "the Father": John 5:23, 37; 6:44; 8:16, 18; 12:49; 14:24. Without "the Father": 4:34; 5:24, 30; 6:38, 39; 7:16, 28, 33; 8:26, 29; 9:4; 12:44, 45; 13:20; 15:21; 16:5. There are two gnomic uses of the formula (7:18; 13:16); in both contexts the sender is still God.

60. Bultmann, *Theology of the New Testament,* 2:34 (emphasis added). Kendrick Grobel, the English translator, has inserted here into Bultmann's text the comment, "Both expressions, as *crystallized participial phrases,* might better be translated with nouns: 'my Commissioner, the Father,' and 'my Commissioner'" (emphasis added). For other stereotyped or formulaic participial phrases that serve as epithets or names for God in the rest of the New Testament, see the important study by Gerhard Delling, "Geprägte partizipiale Gottesaussagen in der urchristlichen Verkündigung," in *Studien zum Neuen Testament: Gesammelte Aufsätze 1950–1968,* ed. Ferdinand Hahn, Traugott Holtz, and Nikolaus Walter (Göttingen: Vandenhoeck & Ruprecht, 1970), 401–16.

We return, finally, to language about God as "Father" in the gospel. The statistics we have seen are high, and the present essay does not pretend to offer a full examination of all occurrences. But it is important to note their distribution. References to God as "Father" and as "the one who has sent [Jesus]" belong very conspicuously to the discourse material; in the few narrative contexts in which they appear, they stand out as editorial insertions of a late stage in the gospel's composition.[61] Since "the Father" in the absolute appears some seventy-four times and is frequently not coordinated with "the Son," we would expect it to function as a simple equivalent to "God" (ὁ θεός); indeed, the two words do alternate with each other in many contexts.[62] Yet there is a difference of flavor that goes beyond the statistical preponderance of "Father" over "God." For example, the evangelist speaks of "children of God" (1:12; 11:52) but never "children of the Father"; of the "wrath of God" (3:36) but never "wrath of the Father." Contrariwise, we hear of the "house of the Father" (2:16; 14:2) but never the "house of God"; the "will of the Father" (6:40) but never the "will of God"; the "hand of the Father" (10:29) but never the "hand of God." "Father" is the subject of eighteen verbs that never appear with "God" as subject, while "God" appears with only one verb that is not also used with "Father."[63] What is more significant for our purposes is that, while "the Father" and "God" easily and frequently alternate with each other, the formulaic epithet of sending, "the Father who has sent me" or simply "the one who has sent me," belongs strictly to the "Father" language of the gospel and with only two exceptions is

61. A word about the procedure on which such generalizations are based is in order, since the identification of "sources" or stages in the composition of the gospel is much debated. To stand for "narrative material," in an older edition of the *Novum Testamentum Graece* the text of Robert Fortna's reconstruction of the Signs Gospel (*The Gospel of Signs: A Reconstruction of the Narrative Source Underlying the Fourth Gospel,* SNTSMS 11 [Cambridge: Cambridge University Press, 1970], 235–45) has been highlighted in one color. Other colors have then been used to mark occurrences of πατήρ ("father") when used of God, υἱός [τοῦ θεοῦ] ("Son [of God]") when used of Jesus, θεός ("God"), and both verbs ἀποστέλλειν and πέμπειν (both meaning "to send"), all these instances checked against a concordance to the 26th edition of Nestle-Aland, *Novum Testamentum Graece* (Stuttgart: Deutsche Bibelstiftung, 1979). The patterns of attribution are thus both clear and striking. In only two passages (2:16; 18:11) does "Father" language for God appear in the Signs Gospel. References to Jesus' having been "sent" by God appear in such contexts only at 9:4, 7b; and 11:41–42, verses that Fortna regards as later insertions into the Signs Gospel.

62. John 1:(14?), 18; 3:35–36; 4:23–24; 5:18, 42–43, 44–45; 6:27 (here very emphatically joined as the twin subjects of one verb), 32–33; 6:45–46; 8:38–40, 41–42, 47–49, 54; 10:29–33; (11:40–41?); 13:1–3; 14:1–2; 16:2–3, 27–28 (v.l.), 28–30; 17:1–5; 20:17.

63. With πατήρ ("father") but never θεός ("God"): ἁγιάζειν ("to make holy"), γινώσκειν ("to know"), δεικνύειν ("to make known"), διδάσκειν ("to teach"), ἐγείρειν ("to raise"), ἑλκύειν ("to draw, pull"), ἐντέλλεσθαι ("to command"), ἐργάζεσθαι ("to work"), ἔχειν ("to have"), κρίνειν ("to judge"), λέγειν ("to say"), μαρτυρεῖν ("to bear witness"), μένειν ("to abide"), πέμπειν ("to send"), ποιεῖν ("to do"), σώζειν ("to save"), τηρεῖν ("to guard"), and φιλεῖν ("to love"). With θεός but never πατήρ: λαλεῖν ("to speak").

not even associated with "God" (ὁ θεός).[64] Thus "the Father" and "God" function in many ways synonymously, even though the former is more frequent; "God" and "Father" identify the source from which Jesus has "come" into the world and the goal to which he is "going" or "ascending"; they identify the origin of what Jesus says, of what he does, of the disciples he gathers. But it is the formulaic identification of the "Father" as "the one who has sent me" that gives this presentation of God its most characteristically Johannine nuance.

For our understanding of that nuance, we remain deeply indebted to much of the recent discussion of mission in the Fourth Gospel.[65] The problem is that the background materials have focused the discussion as a christological one, on the concept and figure of the one sent, the divine emissary, whereas the Fourth Gospel actually uses this language to point to God, the "Father," as the Sender of Jesus. "When we use the verb 'send' we make clear that God is not simply identical with the [saving] event but transcends it, although he encounters us in it and does so in his totality."[66] Not only does God transcend it; the sending language serves to legitimate and authorize the identity, the mission, and the claims of Jesus *as* the saving event. "His origin establishes his significance."[67]

Early in this essay I referred to Nils Dahl's article, "The Neglected Factor in New Testament Theology."[68] He writes about the New Testament: "The great majority of references to God occur in contexts that deal with some other theme. They serve as warrants and backing for promises, appeals, and threats, or for *statements about Jesus,* the Jews, the church, salvation, moral conduct, prayer, and so forth."[69] It is those "statements" that provide the content of New Testament theology, which today "does not speak about God but about the way in which the New Testament authors talk about God."[70] What we have in the Fourth Gospel, however, is something quite different. Here the evangelist's language about God as "Father" and specifically as "the one who has sent me" points to God as warrant and backing not for what the evangelist says to his readers but, in a second order of theological reflection, for Jesus himself—his words, his deeds, his life. The presentation of God as Father in this gospel is as the Vindicator and Authorizer of Jesus. By contrast, in the letters of Paul, God

64. The two exceptions are 7:16–18 and 9:4.

65. See n. 42.

66. Schweizer, "What Do We Really Mean," 310–11.

67. Bultmann, *Das Evangelium des Johannes,* 186, commenting on 5:19 (my translation; emphasis omitted); note especially his n. 3, attached to these words. (The translation in *Gospel of John,* 249, is simply wrong, reverses the point, and produces a caricature of Bultmann's theology: "his origin is grounded in what he means for us" [emphasis omitted].)

68. See n. 12.

69. Dahl, "Neglected Factor in New Testament Theology," 156; emphasis added.

70. Ibid., 153.

is the *eschatological* Vindicator, whose act "in power" (Rom 1:4) in the resurrection provides the ex post facto warrant, backing, and justification for Jesus.[71] "The conviction that the crucified 'King of the Jews' was right and had been vindicated by God, who raised him from the dead, forms the basis of the theology of the New Testament in all its varieties."[72] With regard to the historical basis, that remains true. But another stage has been reached in the Fourth Gospel. What is distinctively Johannine about this presentation of God as Father is that here eschatology has been replaced by *protology*. Jesus stands in no need of an eschatological vindication. He does not need to come again "in power." He is "right" because God is "the Father who has sent me."

---

71. For fuller discussion of Paul on this point, and as representative of a much wider literature, see Ulrich Wilckens, *Resurrection. Biblical Testimony to the Resurrection: An Historical Examination and Explanation* (Atlanta: John Knox, 1978), 1–27.

72. Dahl, "Neglected Factor in New Testament Theology," 157–58.

CHAPTER 11

SEEING, SIGNS, AND SOURCES IN THE FOURTH GOSPEL*

Part of the rich legacy bequeathed to the current study of the Fourth Gospel by Bultmann's massive commentary[1] is the question of the evangelist's sources and in particular that of his possible use of a *sēmeia*, or signs, source.[2] The case for such a signs source, from which the evangelist drew a large part of his narrative material, in contrast to the case for a discourse source, gains in plausibility in direct proportion to the force with which one is driven to conclude, on various grounds, (a) that this material is not freely composed but comes to the evangelist by a tradition of rather definite configuration, and (b) that the evangelist is not acquainted with the synoptic tradition accessible to us.

There is a curious complexity to the arguments involved here. Those parts of the Johannine narrative that most closely overlap with the Synoptics (the official's son, the feeding of the five thousand, the walking on the water, the anointing at Bethany) are the ones that most clearly preclude the alternatives that the evangelist either freely composed his narrative or had himself such direct access (say, as an eyewitness) to the events that he could operate in personal independence of the community tradition (thus supporting conclusion "a"). Yet just these portions of the narrative (and one should add here such sections as the calling of the disciples) keep raising the question of possible contacts on the part of the evangelist with the synoptic tradition (thus creating doubts about conclusion "b"). Conversely, those narrative portions that show minimal contact with the Synoptics (the marriage at Cana, the Nicodemus episode, the man

---

*This essay, published here for the first time, originated as a paper presented to the Society of Biblical Literature's Task Group on the Fourth Gospel, meeting in Dallas, Texas (October 18, 1968). Unless otherwise indicated, translations of New Testament texts are from the RSV.

1. R. Bultmann, *Das Evangelium des Johannes* (11th ed.; Göttingen: Vandenhoeck & Ruprecht, 1950); ET (from the 1964 printing): *The Gospel of John: A Commentary*, trans. G. R. Beasley-Murray et al. (Oxford: Basil Blackwell, 1971).

2. For a full discussion of Bultmann's source theories and the literature evoked by them, see D. M. Smith, *The Composition and Order of the Fourth Gospel* (New Haven, Conn.: Yale University Press, 1965). The fuller range of the Johannine source problem is reviewed by W. G. Kümmel, *Introduction to the New Testament* (Nashville: Abingdon, 1965), 142–54.

born blind, the raising of Lazarus) and thus seem flagrantly to demonstrate the evangelist's independence from the synoptic tradition (thus supporting conclusion "b"), manifest at the same time his editorial skill, his ability to knit narrative and theological dialogue into a single unit, and his freedom to use all his materials for his own ends—thereby challenging once more our confidence about having accurately discerned a distinct tradition behind him (casting doubt on conclusion "a").

It should be noted, in passing, that the complex question of John's relationship to the synoptic tradition both admits and requires discussion as a problem in its own right, apart from the identification of the evangelist's particular literary creditors. The matter is not disposed of by establishing the high probability that the evangelist had never seen our gospels Mark, Matthew, and Luke as they stand.[3] And, as an example, whenever we find the writer engaged in what appears to be internal polemic, as in his treatment of Peter, the question of a possible relation to the synoptic tradition is implicitly present, even if we were to say that the Johannine target is what the "mainstream" of the church has done with the Petrine traditions known from our Synoptics. Many details of Barrett's commentary, particularly the frequent suggestion that the intentions of the evangelist are here and there best understood in terms of residual problems latent in the earlier tradition, show quite clearly that the issue cannot be settled independently of exegesis, and thus offer at the very least grounds for taking care not to close prematurely this historical question, which has so many hermeneutical ramifications (i.e., to draw conclusion "b").[4]

On the other hand, there does seem to be something like a growing consensus on the first issue: dependence of the evangelist on a discernible tradition. Among a number of essays by Ernst Haenchen, one in particular, "Johanneische

---

3. P. Gardner-Smith is often and rightly cited as having most successfully established this probability (*Saint John and the Synoptic Gospels* [Cambridge: Cambridge University Press, 1938]); however, he makes no attempt to isolate the Fourth Gospel from the traditions that produced the Synoptics. The very plausibility of his contention that "John" did not know Mark requires as a premise the realization "that a wholly 'independent' account was hardly possible outside the irresponsible circles which produced the Apocryphal Gospel" (90). (We might today be far more ready to admit the existence of divergent, even irreconcilable "circles" in early Christianity, and far more reluctant to label them "irresponsible.") When, therefore, in conclusion, Gardner-Smith seems to yield to the longing for more historical information about Jesus and suggests the possibility that "in the Fourth Gospel we (may) have a survival of a type of first century Christianity which owed *nothing* to synoptic developments" (96, emphasis mine), he not only shows himself to have been ahead of his time in the general trend of Johannine studies; he also far outruns his own argument.

4. C. K. Barrett, *The Gospel according to St. John: An Introduction with Commentary and Notes on the Greek Text* (2d ed.; Philadelphia: Westminster, 1978). See esp. p. 53: "John probes into the meaning of the synoptic narratives and expresses it in other terms."

Probleme," may be mentioned as representative and influential.[5] By analyzing the stories of the nobleman's son, the feeding of the five thousand, the temple cleansing, and the crippled man at the pool, this essay seeks to show that a distinctive written tradition of a well-developed but still quite uneven sort lies behind John's narratives, and indeed imparts to them some of its own features. For example, the gospel's own stylistic fluctuation from the one extreme of high dramatic skill and power (ch. 9, the man born blind) to the other of colorless ineptitude (ch. 5, the crippled man at the pool) is better explained as having been imparted to it by this tradition on which it depends than as due to some later redactor. A reasonably persuasive demonstration of the presence of such narrative tradition is enough to preclude for Haenchen a number of options once treated as still viable: the notion that John "used" one or more of the Synoptics, that he was a literary artist of some stature who was free to borrow from his (synoptic) predecessors at will and able to incorporate his borrowings into his own composition; that he was an early evangelist, even a contemporary of Mark, and thereby deserving of great historical deference. It is clear that Haenchen hopes by his argument to dispense, once and for all, with these hardy apologetic perennials. Almost incidentally, he characterizes this tradition as nonsynoptic, even though it appears to have had some contacts with synoptic narrative units.[6]

All its fruitful detailed observations notwithstanding, this argument does not, as so far presented, suffice to establish the presence behind the gospel of Bultmann's *sēmeia* source. There is, of course, one detail that has widely been taken as offering the necessary literary clue to the evangelist's dependence on a source, thus tipping the scales in favor of the hypothesis: John 2:11 explicitly labels the changing of the water into wine as the "first of the signs" performed by Jesus in Galilee, and 4:54 similarly identifies the healing of the nobleman's son as the "second" after he had come from Judea to Galilee, despite the fact that in the meantime 2:23, 3:2, and possibly 4:45 refer to other signs (plural) done by Jesus in Jerusalem. At the very best, this clue would show that 2:11 and 4:54 have a common origin which already contained the sequential numeration; even that depends in part upon how stringently the evangelist intends his geographical references to Galilee to be noted by his reader and whether the choice of the word *archē* for the first is his own deliberate act, intended to mark this Cana episode as a "primary sign . . . representative of the creative and transforming work of

5. Ernst Haenchen, "Johanneische Probleme," in *Gott und Mensch: Gesammelte Aufsätze* (Tübingen: Mohr [Siebeck], 1965), 78–113 (originally published in *ZTK* 56 [1959]: 19–54). Cf. idem, "Der Vater, der mich gesandt hat," in *Gott und Mensch*, 68–77 (originally published in *NTS* 9 [1962–63]: 208–16); idem, "Faith and Miracle," in *Studia Evangelica*, ed. K. Aland et al., TU 73 (Berlin: Akademie-Verlag, 1959), 495–98.

6. Haenchen, "Johanneische Probleme," 110–13.

Jesus as a whole."[7] In any case, this clue hardly establishes the existence of a more extensive source. Something more is still needed, another element in the argument, before one can make a persuasive case not only for the extent and profile of such a source but even for its very existence. In the current discussion, this crucial additional ingredient consists of the claim that a discrepancy exists between the understanding of the signs imbedded in the tradition and the stories themselves, on the one hand, and what we find the evangelist doing with this material, on the other. This involves bringing into the discussion other passages as indicators of both points of view, as possible references drawn from such a signs source (such as 6:2; 7:3; 11:47; 12:37; and 20:30),[8] and as possible corrections and comments on the part of the evangelist. This step cannot be taken without opening up the exegetical discussion of these passages in particular and the place of the signs in Johannine theology in general.

Here, it seems to me, we come upon the heart of the issue, the question of the relationship of faith to sign in the gospel and, closely related but not identical to it, the relation between "seeing" and "believing" in the author's thought. It is to this set of issues that the following observations and reflections are addressed.

Let us return to examine in more detail the alleged discrepancy between the evangelist and the tradition on which he draws. It has become a commonplace to observe that the Johannine signs, in comparison to the synoptic miracle tradition, heighten the miraculous: the distance from which the nobleman's son is healed is greater than in the case of the centurion's son in Q; the blind man is *born* blind; Lazarus has been dead already four days when Jesus appears. It is also said that there is a corresponding tendency in the Fourth Gospel to suppress two kinds of factors observable in the synoptic stories: the accompaniment of dialogue containing specifically Christian teaching, and the influence of Old Testament motifs upon the narrative, the suppression of both of these resulting in an increased "secularization."[9] The evidence is not unambivalent. The synoptic tradition has nothing to compare with the way in which the healing narrative in chapter 5 (the crippled man at the pool) is subordinated, exploited, and even mutilated for the sake of dialogue. The best explanation for 6:21, which heightens by compounding a new miracle with the epiphany on the

---

7. Barrett, *Gospel according to St. John*, 193. Cf. my note on "John 2:10," *JBL* 86 (1967): 191–97 (pp. 264–70 in this volume), and, for the evangelist's interest in Galilee, my reference there to Wayne A. Meeks, "Galilee and Judea in the Fourth Gospel," *JBL* 85 (1966): 159–69. Bultmann treats the qualification "after coming from Judea to Galilee" (4:54) as a gloss by the evangelist. For a summary review of some of the literary pros and cons to the proposal of a Johannine *sēmeia* source, see esp. Smith, *Composition and Order*, 111 n. 183.

8. These passages are listed as having come from the "Book of Signs" by R. H. Fuller, *Interpreting the Miracles* (Philadelphia: Westminster, 1963), 88–109.

9. Ibid., 90–92.

sea, still remains the suggestion that an Old Testament motif is operating here.[10]
And in 9:1, the detail that the blind man was born that way is motivated for such
patently theological reasons, as the immediate question of the disciples and the
later progress of the drama show, that it is doubtful whether one ought to speak
at all of an interest in the miraculous for its own sake, much less for "secular"
reasons. It does not suffice to say that such details merely show that the miracle tradition exposed to view in our Synoptics continued to grow and develop
in the interim period before some of this material came to "John."

All the more welcome at first sight, therefore, is the suggestion that the more
important clue to the distinctive flavor of the Johannine miracles is to be found
in the theological perspective of the evangelist's source, a suggestion developed
in the articles by Ernst Haenchen mentioned earlier.[11] For Haenchen, the one
clear, characteristic feature of the tradition employed by John is that it regards
the miracles of Jesus as direct and compelling proofs of Jesus' divine status,
visible and "available" to all. Faith is elicited by them and rests upon them.
Nicodemus's response is the natural and inevitable one for the onlooker:
"Rabbi, we know that you are a teacher come from God; for no one can do these
signs that you do, unless God is with him" (3:2). Upon hearing that his son was
alive, the nobleman "believed, and all his household" (4:53). After the feeding
of the five thousand, those who saw the sign said, "This is indeed the prophet
who is to come into the world" (6:14). Again, 12:37 comes from the source; at
the end of the public ministry of Jesus, the ultimate reproach is that "[t]hough
he had done so many signs before them, yet they did not believe in him." And
at the conclusion of his gospel, the evangelist has taken for his own two verses
that originally brought the source to a close: "Now Jesus did many other signs
in the presence of the disciples, which are not written in this book; but these are
written that you may believe that Jesus is the Christ, the Son of God"
(20:30–31). The Christology of this source is accurately summed up by the
Peter of Acts, who declares Jesus of Nazareth to be "a man attested to you by
God with mighty works and wonders and signs" (2:22).

The evangelist, on the other hand, has quite another understanding of faith
as called forth by, and resting upon, Jesus' word and preaching, as a response
to direct personal address rather than amazement at something seen. The
Samaritan villagers of 4:39–42 do not even come to rest in the faith elicited
from them by the testimony of the woman who met Jesus by the well and had
all her past exposed to her; their knowledge of the Savior of the world comes
to realization when they hear him themselves and are no longer dependent upon
her. For the evangelist the miracles cannot provide the warrant for faith but are
instead signs pointing to Jesus. They do not *create* faith but *presuppose* it as the

10. Barrett, *Gospel according to St. John*, 281; W. Bauer, *Das Johannesevangelium* (Tübingen:
Mohr [Siebeck], 1933), 94.
11. See the articles cited in n. 5, and esp. Haenchen, "Der Vater," 68–69.

prerequisite for the proper understanding of their meaning. Thus Nicodemus is told that "unless one is born anew he cannot see God at work" (3:3).[12] So where the source had indicated that the five thousand "saw the sign which he had done" (6:14), the evangelist's own Jesus is heard to reprove them: "You seek me, not because you saw signs, but because you ate your fill of the loaves" (6:26). And at the end of the gospel, Thomas has to hear the reproof that his faith is less than perfect: "You have believed because you have seen me? Blessed are those who have not seen and yet believe" (20:29).

On such a view, John's *sēmeia* source appears to represent a christological development in which Jesus is being portrayed as a *theios anēr*, a Hellenistic miracle worker and healer. An important negative principle in the historical reconstruction of stages of development in a religious tradition is that any particular reconstruction gains in plausibility to the extent that it can be located in a given historical situation.[13] James M. Robinson finds important support for the hypothesis of a Johannine *sēmeia* source in this principle, and draws an analogy between Mark's way of curbing supernatural and crudely messianic tendencies in epiphany and miracle stories by linking them with his secrecy motif, on the one hand, and the Fourth Evangelist's critical annotation of his *sēmeia* source, his correction of the understanding of faith inherent in it, on the other hand. The historical implication is that the *sēmeia* source material belongs, despite the legendary inflation that the passage of time has inevitably produced in it, to the same logical stage as the pre-Markan miracle stories.[14] In both cases we see early Christianity striving to bring a crude and materialistic *Wunderglaube* under the control and discipline of a more authentically Christian dialectic in which not only the understanding of faith but also the church's retrospective view upon the earthly life of Jesus has been redefined. Such an appeal to analogous developments is, however, a negative argument, and must remain so. It cannot settle the question whether the alleged discrepancy is actually present in the texts; that must remain an exegetical enterprise in the narrower sense of the term.

The theory is attractive also because it allows the interpreter to assign the cruder and more "massive" miraculous element, as something upon which faith depends, to the source, rescuing the evangelist himself for a more sophisticated and dialectical understanding of faith.[15] Here the hermeneutical issue takes on

---

12. This is Haenchen's translation of *ou dynatai idein tēn basileian tou theou* (3:3): "kann Gottes Wirken nicht sehen" ("Der Vater," 69).

13. Johannes Schreiber, "Die Christologie des Johannesevangeliums," *ZTK* 58 (1961): 154–83.

14. J. M. Robinson, "The Problem of History in Mark, Reconsidered," *USQR* 20 (1964–65): 131–47, esp. 136–37.

15. Smith (*Composition and Order*, 62–63) has already pointed out that some such source theory which so disposes of the materials, putting a certain distance between the *prima facie* meaning of certain passages in the gospel (as their "original" meaning) and the evangelist's own intentions, is necessary for the survival of Bultmann's interpretation of the incarnation in the gospel as the *incognito* of the Revealer.

a sharper focus. For this latter kind of appeal, the very "sense" which the hypothesis makes at once raises the question whether this purported discrepancy of outlook is not the result of reading back into the gospel issues and connotations that originate in the modern discussions about miracle and faith, of reading back into the "signs source" a crasser supernaturalism and into the evangelist's mind a more idealized understanding, more congenial to the modern mind, than this late first-century document anywhere contains.

It is time to turn to one of the texts that occupies a central place in the discussion: the healing of the nobleman's son (4:46–54). It is a relatively small unit in the gospel, and one of the first issues in determining its context is the question whether it is intended to bring the preceding material to a close, or to pave the way for what follows. Much depends on how we interpret the officer's believing.

Barrett represents the first point of view; he argues that the story is used to show that the farther Jesus moves from Jerusalem, the more warmly he is received. This officer, "who in the end believes without signs and portents,"[16] is thus superior even to the Galileans who had seen signs in Jerusalem (v. 45). The momentum of the text thus begins with the temple cleansing: Jesus' home is Jerusalem, for salvation is from the Jews; yet he is the Savior of the world, and in him the Gentiles find their hope. In every scene he is the giver of life. In 2:13–22, he promises to raise up his body, the living temple; in 3:1–21 he offers new birth and eternal life; in 3:22–36, the same theme is renewed (v. 36); in 4:1–42, Jesus offers living water; and in 4:46–54 he gives life to the sick. The next chapter takes a fresh tack and opens a discussion of the person who claims to offer such exceptional gifts.

For Bultmann, however, the similarities and even the parallelism between 4:43–45 and 2:23–25 show that we have a new beginning. Both sections thus introduced consist in the main of two miracle stories and attached discourse material. To Nicodemus and the Samaritan woman correspond roughly the healing of the crippled man at the pool and the feeding of the five thousand (Bultmann inverts the order of the last two). Where in the first pair the conversations were with individuals, in the second they are with the leaders of the people in Jerusalem and with the people in Galilee. The climax to the whole comes in the division (*krisis*) that takes place in 6:60–71.[17] The place of 4:46–54 in this complex is not entirely clear and is in fact disturbing; it owes its present location to the fact that it stood between the Samaritan woman and the feeding in the signs source. Its climax (*Höhepunkt*) is in v. 48. By way of concession,

---

16. Barrett, *Gospel according to St. John*, 245, a statement I find simply incomprehensible.

17. The fact that Bultmann must rearrange the material to preserve this climax, in spite of his placing of the bulk of ch. 6 before ch. 5, is one reason for questioning his inversion of the order of these chapters.

the world is given the signs it seeks, but its general reaction is one of complete misunderstanding (ch. 6) or repudiation (ch. 5). Only in exceptional cases, of which the nobleman is a passing illustration, does the world come to faith. Thus the story's presence produces not only a literary fault (in the geological sense of that term) but disturbance in the theological continuity as well.[18]

Most of the commentators are prepared to acknowledge some kind of relationship with the Q narrative of the healing of the centurion's servant (or son) in Matt 8:5–13 and Luke 7:1–10.[19] But just what is this relationship? Here too, as in the determination of the role of the pericope in its context, everything seems to revolve around v. 48 and the widespread assumption that this is a rebuke, expressing, in Bultmann's words "Jesu Unwillen über das Verlangen des Wunders als Glaubensgarantie."[20] Never mind the plain fact that the text makes no mention of any demand from the nobleman for such a sign. Instead, on the assumption that this is what the verse means, all kinds of further conclusions are

18. Bultmann takes note of the fact that others (Heitmüller, Pribnow) find the point of the story in the thrice repeated verb "lives" (vv. 50, 51, 53) and its portrayal of Jesus as the giver of life. He offers no real counterargument to this very tangible clue; no one would pick v. 48 instead of v. 53b as the climax of the story without some such theological preconception as Bultmann's. Dodd also emphasizes the verb "lives" and shows its connection with 5:21: "the Son makes alive whom he wills" (*Interpretation of the Fourth Gospel* [Cambridge: Cambridge University Press, 1953], 319).

19. Even Haenchen writes: "Wir können ruhig zugeben, dass die Geschichte vom 'Königischen' und die vom Hauptmann von Kapernaum auf dasselbe Ereignis zurückgehen" ("Johanneische Probleme," 89), but because he claims to have distinguished, alongside the three written versions of the story that we have, the stages of "anonymous" tradition behind each of these (thus identifying no less than six separate versions), the conclusion he draws is that "wir sind nicht mehr zu der Annahme gezwungen, Johannes habe den synoptischen Stoff kühn umgedichtet." The very affinity of the story with the synoptic tradition thus leads to the result of asserting Johannine independence from our Synoptics. On its face, this looks like a tour de force; the reason for it lies in Haenchen's characteristic refusal to allow all analysis to revolve around the question of the individual writer and his written sources, instead giving a much larger role to the anonymous oral tradition and the changes effected in the material by it. This is a feature also of his commentary on Acts (ET: *The Acts of the Apostles: A Commentary*, trans. B. Noble et al. [Philadelphia: Westminster, 1971]).

Haenchen is not much impressed with the evangelist's gifts, at least as a narrator, and, as we have seen, believes that what he feels as the unevenness in dramatic and narrative skill in the gospel is best understood as having been imparted to the document from its source. Yet elsewhere ("Johanneische Probleme," 112 n. 2) he employs against Bultmann's discourse source the argument that if it is accepted, the role of the evangelist is reduced to that of a mere redactor who can only make incidental annotations to material that has come to him from others. These two lines of argument are not necessarily self-defeating, but they verge on being so; together, they highlight the importance of the task of determining just what the evangelist intended and actually did, and just wherein his true "skill," as a producer of a written document, lies, even if he did not share the literary ambitions of a Luke. The final reason why Haenchen cannot ascribe to him the passages that display dramatic gifts remains the theological one: the stories are said to imply a theology foreign to the evangelist (ibid., 14 n. 3).

20. Bultmann, *Das Evangelium des Johannes*, 151 (*Gospel of John*, 205–8).

drawn. First, concerning the identity of the central figure, the reader is not told whether he is a Jew or a Gentile. But Bultmann finds that the story takes it for granted that he is a Jew since, in the absence of contrary information, such a reproof is conceivable in the Fourth Gospel only as directed to a Jew.[21] Similarly Bauer: since the petitioner, far from putting Jesus to the test, expects something superhuman from him, Jesus' chiding reply is comprehensible only as aimed at "die wundersüchtigen Juden" whom he represents.[22] Haenchen is surely right in countering that whether the man be Jew or Gentile is inconsequential, but this is grist for his mill. He takes this very indifference to be symptomatic of the *sēmeia* source's tendency to put the miraculous power of Jesus at the center of attention, rendering more or less irrelevant the faith that is praised in the Matthean version. Bultmann (followed by Haenchen) draws a literary conclusion: just because no motivation for such rebuke appears in the story, v. 48 clearly betrays the intruding hand of the evangelist. The disturbance necessitates the addition of v. 49, which repeats in direct discourse the petition that is already present in indirect discourse in v. 47. This intrusion has had the additional effect of displacing the dialogue that is present in the Q story concerning authority and the centurion's "unworthiness" that Jesus should come under his roof. This displacement robs the story of its original point, in order to make it serve a new motif, that of "faith and sign."

The evangelist has therefore taken the motif of Jesus' refusal to provide authenticating signs, which in the synoptic tradition stands *alongside* the miracles, and woven it right into the healing narrative itself, making of it a general complaint about the human weakness that always requires such helps, uttered by Jesus before he gives the help sought. The story now has to take a fresh start: the repeated request now means something like "I am not asking for an authenticating sign, I only want help for my son before he dies." This recognition of need is a dimension of genuine faith, which Jesus then meets in v. 50. This is a faith without seeing, to which the healing is granted. In vv. 51–53, the healing is confirmed; that "he and his house" believed is a stereotyped ending, which nevertheless signifies for the evangelist the transition from a provisional to a genuine and full faith. The miracle, which the man has no right to demand, is given when faith is aware of its own need, in order to lead this faith to a higher stage beyond miracle faith. The subsequent chapters show, however, that this is the exception rather than the rule.

In support of this interpretation of v. 48 as a rebuff, it is frequently argued that this story closely parallels in structure 2:1–11, where Jesus first refuses to act with a rebuke to his mother, and then acts anyway to grant the request. Bultmann rightly cautions that this parallelism is more apparent than real. The moti-

---

21. Bultmann, *Das Evangelium des Johannes*, 152 n. 3 (*Gospel of John*, 206 n. 7).
22. Bauer, *Das Johannesevangelium*, 77–78.

vation for the rebuff—an explicit reason is given in 2:4: "my hour has not yet come"—and the reactions of the petitioners are quite different.[23] Yet Bultmann never doubts that 4:48 is a rebuke.

But v. 48 is neither rebuff, nor refusal, nor complaint.[24] Consider first the movement of the story. Where Bultmann finds genuine faith expressed in the father's second appeal (v. 49), the text makes its first mention of faith in v. 50, the nobleman's response to Jesus' word. And the construction is with the simple dative: *episteusen tō logō*. It is doubtful whether the meaning intended is more than a response of initial credence. The climax clearly comes with the absolute use of *episteusen* in v. 53. However much the stereotyped form of this conclusion reminds us of some of the conversion stories in Acts, it is impossible even for Bultmann to reduce its meaning to something like "he became a Christian"; his attainment to genuine faith is marked here as surely as that of the disciples in 2:11.

Consider also the synoptic parallel and what has been "suppressed" or displaced from the narrative, whether by tradition or by evangelist. Jesus is no longer in the vicinity of the man's house, or about to enter, so that the centurion's protestation of unworthiness no longer has a place. But with the increased distance imposed by the alterations in geography, how much *more* fitting than a request of Jesus to quickly traverse that distance would have been the synoptic centurion's appeal: "Only speak with a word, and my child will be healed!" (paraphrasing Luke 7:7). That would have been the implicit trust, the *Wortglaube*, without help of sign, which Bultmann and Haenchen value so highly. In the Synoptics this Gentile (just the point obscured in John), from whom such trust is not to be expected, comes to Jesus in the trust that where his military authority has reached its limits and is helpless, Jesus' word will suffice. But just this element is gone from the story. This kind of trust is not faith for the Fourth Evangelist, but at best a preliminary credence given to Jesus, and then only after he has spoken. Only after Jesus' act has been independently confirmed by the servants, and the cognizance of it made sure, does faith become genuine. Faith, even in its profoundest acknowledgment of need, does not call forth Jesus' act as its reward; Jesus' act calls forth faith, and faith rests upon this act, which is of course for the evangelist the act of one sent by the Father. That is exactly what v. 48 states: Faith cannot be self-generating but must have its ground in the recognition of something done by God. It is the radical elimination of, a slamming of the door upon, a fatal interpretation—namely, God's deliverance as a reward for the "right" kind of faith—to which the synoptic tradition, precisely

<hr/>

23. Bultmann, *Das Evangelium des Johannes*, 151 n. 6 (*Gospel of John*, 205 n. 5). Cf. the repudiation of the request of Jesus' brothers in 7:6, where the same reason is given.

24. For one of the exceptional discussions in the literature, where v. 48 is not taken as a rebuke, see Wayne A. Meeks, *The Prophet-King: Moses Traditions and the Johannine Christology* (Leiden: E. J. Brill, 1967), 40.

in its miracle stories with their refrain "as you have believed, so let it be done to you" was (whatever its own internal intent) dangerously exposed.[25]

Consider thirdly the form of v. 48. The aorist subjunctive with *ou mē* is the form of emphatic future negation, which Jeremias argues has something of the force of a negative oath.[26] This is not the form encountered in any of Jesus' refusals to grant a sign (though the Markan version of that refusal is cast in a strange Greek syntax explicable only in terms of another kind of Semitic oath form).[27] What is emphatically denied is not the granting of a sign but the possibility of faith apart from the prior meeting of a certain condition; signs must be seen before there can be any faith in the Johannine sense. Exactly the same form is used at one other point in the gospel where a certain harsh condition is laid down, having no immediate connection with the problem of signs but nevertheless very closely related to the Johannine sense of what is crucial in the delineation of faith; only there it is a condition put to Jesus by another. Yet, as in our passage, it is at once met by him. The passage is Thomas's statement in 20:25: "Unless I see in his hands the mark of the nails . . . , I will not believe." We shall have to return to this passage later.

This reading of 4:48 at its face value brings immediate relief to the interpreter at a number of points. The granting of the request, no longer coming on the heels of a disavowal, is no longer in itself a problem. Whether a prior link with the Cana episode existed or not, the story takes a more natural place in the present gospel as a sequel to the first manifestation of Jesus' glory to the disciples and their believing. On any count, v. 48 is the evangelist's comment; but if this is the meaning of it, then his own characterization of his book at the conclusion, in 20:30–31, is no longer an awkward relapse into a point of view foreign to his own theology. The whole purpose of his writing is to enable this fundamental condition for faith to be fulfilled for those who, coming after the departure of Jesus from the world, would otherwise be cut off by this condition. And we are, finally, in a position to make the most of just that basic difference from the Synoptics which makes the story serve, as Bultmann himself observes, the motif of "faith and sign," without at once suppressing this again to the status of a *Nebenmotiv*. The story, in relation now to the subsequent chapters, is no longer the exception that disturbs the theological continuity; it prepares the way for chapter 9, in which the sign given (the healing of the man born blind) sets in motion all the conflicting and polarizing reactions of both faith and unbelief.[28] There this

---

25. Characteristically, Johannine thought has *nothing* comparable to the saying about having faith (even as small) as a grain of mustard seed (Matt 17:20; Luke 17:6; cf. Mark 11:23).

26. J. Jeremias, *The Eucharistic Words of Jesus*, trans. N. Perrin (New York: Charles Scribner's Sons, 1966), 209–10; two of the more arresting instances of this construction appear in 1 Cor 8:13 (formally a vow of abstinence from meat) and Mark 14:25 (and parallels).

27. Matt 12:39; Luke 11:29; Mark 8:12. For the syntax in Mark, see BDF, par. 372 (4).

28. For the way in which the sign precedes and polarizes both faith and unbelief, see my essay "The Polarity of Faith," *USQR* 21, no. 1 (1965): 51–61 (pp. 254–63 in this volume).

motif is taken up in earnest, and indeed carried a step further. The giving of a sign is the prior condition not only of belief but also of unbelief, now in the radicalized sense of rejection and opposition. That development reaches its climax in the way in which the evangelist motivates the passion narrative from the opposition generated by the last of the great signs, the raising of Lazarus.

Käsemann was quite right, I think, in his discussion of the prologue, when he identified the key theme of 1:14 as the manifestation of Jesus' glory in the world (v. 14c), rather than its veiling in an incarnation understood as an *incognito*.[29] The incarnation of v. 14a is nothing else than the entry of the Logos into the world, as the necessary prerequisite for that manifestation and the subsequent reactions to it. John 4:48, read in the way suggested here, is but a further spelling out of that condition in terms required by faith. To be beheld, that glory must be made visible and available, and the signs of the Johannine narrative (in the very sense that compels Haenchen to assign them to a source) are the meeting of that condition.[30]

Of course, the meeting of that condition does not guarantee that faith will follow, and the documentation by the evangelist that it did not follow, in 12:37, is very nearly the ultimate reproach leveled against the world. There is no reason to tear this one verse out of its context and assign it to the *sēmeia* source. But it is a reproach at all only because it maintains that all the necessary conditions from God's side had been met: "Though he had done so many signs before them, yet they did not believe in him."

The evangelist is also quite aware that even a positive response to the signs is not necessarily faith. John 6:26 is a real rebuke, but it is not directed against *Wundersucht*; it lays bare the false motivation of the crowds that followed Jesus, in the immediate satisfaction of their appetites. Their misunderstanding is on the same level as that of the woman at the well, who wishes at first to be relieved of the necessity of drawing water. The rebuke does not accuse them of a false reliance on signs; it flatly denies that they are following because of having seen signs, and so comes close to suggesting that they have seen no sign at all. Indeed, only a few verses later (v. 30), they demand an authenticating sign of him.[31] For in one sense, to see a sign at all for the evangelist is to detect the

---

29. E. Käsemann, "Aufbau und Anliegen des johanneischen Prologs," in *Exegetische Versuche und Besinnungen*, 2 vols. (Göttingen: Vandenhoeck & Ruprecht, 1964), 2:155–80 (ET: "The Structure and Purpose of the Prologue to John's Gospel," in *New Testament Questions of Today*, trans. W. J. Montague [Philadelphia: Fortress, 1969], 138–67).

30. Cf. Käsemann's Shaffer Lectures, *Jesu letzter Wille nach Johannes 17* (Tübingen: Mohr [Siebeck], 1966), esp. 43–45 (ET: *The Testament of Jesus: A Study of the Gospel of John in the Light of Chapter 17*, trans. G. Krodel [Philadelphia: Fortress, 1968]).

31. Is the suggestion that they have seen no sign at all contradicted by 6:2? John 6:2 is part of the stage-setting for the feeding and clearly refers to earlier signs; 6:26 is part of the sequel to the feeding. In any case, there is no fundamental theological discrepancy that requires assigning different literary origins to these two verses.

presence of God in the one whom God has sent. But this does not mean that faith is a prerequisite to seeing signs; Haenchen's translation of 3:3, "unless one is born anew, he cannot see God at work," is an unwarranted bending of the text to his argument and contradicts the interpretation which the evangelist supplies in his own rewording two verses later. It is precisely the detection of the *praesentia dei* in the sign that produces opposite reactions, just as in 5:18 the detection by the Jews of the true claim implicit in Jesus' response to their raising of the Sabbath issue, namely, that he was "making himself equal to God," arouses their murderous reaction. When, therefore, Nicodemus comes to Jesus, having detected something comparable in Jesus' signs, there is no reason to call this *faith* and, with Haenchen, to put it on the same level as the nobleman's believing and so to be compelled to assign the passage to the signs source.

Finally, there is that Thomas pericope (20:24–29) to which appeal has so often been made on two counts: as support for the interpretation of 4:48 as a rebuke, and as disclosing the evangelist's own view of faith in its relation to seeing, in contrast to that of his alleged source. Both appeals presuppose that 20:29 also contains at least an implied rebuke to Thomas.

On one point there appears to be rather extensive agreement. The concluding beatitude, "Blessed are those who (have) come to believe [aorist participle] without having seen" (my translation), is aimed at the situation of John's readers, the second, third, and subsequent generations of Christians, the wider circle already envisaged in the third part of the "high-priestly prayer" (17:20–24). The intervening Farewell Discourses have as one of their controlling themes the situation and problematic of the disciples—who remain in the world after the return of Jesus to the Father, when there can be no further seeing of Jesus. One of the anxious queries put to Jesus in that context is: "Lord, show us the Father, and it will suffice for us" (my translation), to which the characteristically Johannine reply is: "He who has seen me has seen the Father" (14:8–9).

Indeed, the setting of the Thomas story emphasizes this orientation around the problems attendant upon the church after the crucifixion-glorification. What is narrated is not even described as an "appearance"; the synoptic word *ōphthē* is strikingly absent. Instead, Jesus "comes" to the disciples despite the obstacles of closed doors, in fulfillment of his own promise, and, also as he had promised, their anxiety is replaced with joy, they are given the Holy Spirit, and they are sent upon their mission.

But Thomas, the Twin, was not with them. Left out of this initial gathering, he already begins to encounter the difficulty of the second-generation disciple. This is especially clear in the way in which the members of the privileged circle press their advantage with him: "The other disciples kept saying [imperfect tense], 'We have seen the Lord!'" (my translation of John 20:25a). They use exactly the words, only in the plural, with which Paul, in another historical situation, asserts his apostolic credentials (1 Cor 9:1). It does not take much historical imagination to hear in their taunt the tendency in the "orthodox" mainstream of the church to exploit the more conventional resurrection appearance tradition in order to assert ecclesiastical prerogative. In the face of this claim, Thomas, who is explicitly said to be "one of the Twelve," states that other condition for believing which returns the church to the concrete reality of the crucifixion—in the Fourth Gospel the true *locus* of Jesus' glorification. The condition is met by a new "coming" of Jesus (the verb is now in the continuous tense; it is not explicitly narrated that Thomas touched the wounds). In his identification of the Lord with the crucified One, Thomas comes to the climactic confession of the gospel. The wording of it ("My Lord and my God") does not mean that Jesus is called God, but that in "seeing" Jesus Thomas has seen the Father; the definition of faith given in 14:9 is realized in this confession. But if there is a polemic here against a form of Christianity for which the only "seeing" important for faith is a resurrection appearance, Thomas remains in the gospel one of the disciples of Jesus' earthly life (11:16; 14:5). He is in a position to reassert, in the name of the genuine Johannine dialectic, and as a condition equally essential for faith, that other kind of seeing (namely, of the Crucified). Thomas *does* come to believe because he has "seen" Jesus. Whether we punctuate the sentence as a statement of fact or as a rhetorical question remains incidental. Jesus' reply is not a rebuke but an acknowledgment of even Thomas's prerogative. That kind of seeing is not to remain permanently available in the same direct way, either—which is why the beatitude is both necessary and reassuring.

John 19:35–37 may have been added by the redactor responsible for chapter 21, but it is not wholly discontinuous with the evangelist's work in the Thomas pericope. It contains the solemn insistence that faith requires testimony to Jesus' death and thus, by asserting the importance of "eyewitness" tradition, makes Thomas's kind of seeing available for subsequent generations in the same manner that the gospel as a whole, according to 20:30–31, makes available the seeing of the signs that "Jesus did in the presence of the disciples."

CHAPTER 12

THE POLARITY OF FAITH: A JOHANNINE PARADIGM FOR OUR TIME*

Contemporary reflection upon the identity and integrity of Christianity involves at almost every level some assumptions about the nature of faith. Whether the nature of faith determines the character of Christianity, or (the other way around) the distinctive peculiarities of Christian affirmation are determinative for the contours of (Christian) faith, these are but two of the available assumptions operative in this contemporary reflection. More pointedly, where such reflection is concerned with the analysis of the current theological situation and the role in it of the theological seminary—traditionally committed to the training of the pastor both as a person of faith and as one given to the nurture and increase of what Paul called "the obedience of faith among the Gentiles"—such assumptions readily take on a controlling influence. One would suppose that some unanimity, or at best clarity, with regard to these assumptions is of the greatest importance in our time; the fact is, however, that such clarity or unanimity is not within easy reach, and that the use of this central term in our religious vocabulary calls for some protracted reconsideration.

It is really not at all surprising that the use of this term should often become confused and confusing. For one thing, the history of Christian thought provides a wealth of reflection upon the meaning of faith; the many and various fruits of this thought, produced in diverse historical circumstances, cannot be reduced to a single coherent definition of what faith means. For another, this history displays a number of basic and recurring contrasts or ambivalences that inevitably accompany every discussion of faith. Perhaps the most notorious of these is the distinction between a *fides quae creditur,* a faith that is believed, faith as the content of affirmation, and a *fides qua creditur,* a faithfulness by which it is believed, faith as receiving and holding assent and answering posture. This contrast cannot be put at the center of theological reflection, for it is in some ways suspect of being an artificial distinction, since it can neither be drawn in the biblical elab-

*This essay re-presents in revised form an article first published in *USQR* 21, no. 1 (1965): 51–61, reproducing with minor modifications an address given by Paul W. Meyer at the opening of the academic year at Colgate Rochester Divinity School (September 15, 1964). It is used here by permission.

orations of faith nor maintained permanently in systematics. The nature of believing itself is so completely shaped by *what* it is that is believed that when, for example, one tries to speak of faith as a divine gift, one can no longer confine this to a single aspect, as though the content of faith were God's and its reception ours; one must rather speak in the end of both faith's content and its appropriation and results in human lives as the gift of God.

Yet the very artificiality of the distinction helps to shed some light upon the fateful oscillation between an emphasis first upon the one and then upon the other, or the flight from the one to the other, in which Christians have perennially been caught. We ourselves are caught by it today when the particular expositions and formulations of Christian tradition have become antiquated and hence irrelevant or discredited in our culture. The temptation is, on the one hand, to absolutize and insist upon these formulations of a faith once delivered and once believed, without regard to the present mode of their being believed (the tendency of orthodoxy), or, on the other hand, to think of faith as having no content and no ground but as consisting mainly in the posture and dynamics of believing, as though faith were what our believing makes it (the tendency of existentialism). It is strange that the modern temper and mood should so easily take to itself both forms, the orthodox and the existentialist; the reason is perhaps that in both, what has become important is *our* faith rather than the faithfulness of God. When that happens, the distinction between *what* we believe and *how* we believe it becomes irrelevant in the hegemony of the "we" that is established at the expense of God and of God's power to shape both what is believed and how it is believed.

The history of Christian thought displays other complexities in the definition of faith, of which we may very briefly remind ourselves. Great Christian minds have occupied themselves with understanding faith as *knowledge* and have so expounded it, in contrast both to the irrationalities of superstition and to the rationalities of logic or the demonstrabilities of scientific investigation. Others have interpreted faith as *trust* and consolation, and distinguished it either from the anxieties that beset the ancient and the modern person with regard to life, self, and world, or from the false securities to which we are prone, especially in times of abundance and prosperity. Yet others have been concerned to understand Christian faith as *motivating power,* and have drawn its profile against the background either of the perennial moral indifference that plagues every effective message of deliverance, or of the legalism that crouches in every system of ethical and religious merit.

These are some of the antinomies that necessarily accompany any full-fledged reflection upon our subject; they serve to warn us against any too facile declarations about faith. But it is not at all certain that they represent genuine polarities of faith from which we might start. Do they not all too obviously mirror the recurring one-sidednesses, the imbalances of Christian thought and practice? *For Christian faith is the human stance, condition, and behavior that is called forth by and appropriate to God's revealing and delivering action in Jesus Christ.* Its true understanding, whether as knowledge or as trust or as motivating power, depends upon our whole understanding of what God has done for us, and requires of us that we return to the gospel of Jesus Christ as the message that creates and nourishes Christian faith, not once only but whenever we wish to talk seriously and without partiality about faith.

The Johannine Paradigm

In choosing to discuss the "polarity of faith," however, I have had in mind not so much these antinomies as rather a paradigm provided for contemporary reflection by the Johannine narrative of the healing of the man born blind. Without denying the importance of these other questions, rather for their very sake and to shake them up into a new perspective, I should like to turn to this paradigm and to attempt a cursory exposition of it. Not all that can or must be said about faith is to be found here, not even all that the Bible says, not even all that the Gospel of John says. Yet what is told us here is worth our attending. And let us observe in passing that if we do attend to it, if we let our thinking be shaped by it, the gospel may in fact exercise among us some of that creative authority to which our age has become such a stranger. The authority of the gospel is not some inherent quality that we can deny or defend in the abstract; it is inseparable from its power to give new life to our theological reflection, and this power will be felt only when we resolve neither to ignore it nor, as the biblicist so often does, to allow it to say only what we have determined in advance.

Let us turn then to the ninth chapter of the Gospel according to John. The story is one of the most dramatic in the whole Bible—not only in the general sense of being a moving and vivid account but also in the very specific sense that it is composed of a series of scenes (eight of them, in fact), which follow each other in an artful and theologically purposeful sequence. In each scene there are essentially two characters or two parties, so that by naming these we can name each scene.

Scene 1: *Jesus and his disciples* (vv. 1–5)

As he passed by, he saw a man blind from his birth. And his disciples asked him, "Rabbi, who sinned, this man or his parents, that he was born blind?" Jesus answered, "It was not that this man sinned, or his parents, but that the works of God might be made manifest in him. We must work the works of him who sent me, while it is day; night comes, when no one can work. As long as I am in the world, I am *the light of the world*."[*]

---

[*]Translations from the Gospel of John throughout this essay are from the RSV. Emphasis has been added by the author.

This opening dialogue sets the stage. A man who is *born* blind defies the easy connection human piety tends to make between misfortune and the sin or wrongdoing of which it is the punishment, or between good fortune and the virtue of which it is the reward. If a man born blind is being punished at all, it must be for an act committed before birth, in some previous existence, or by his ancestors. Jesus' reply to the disciples makes it clear that the reader cannot begin with any such accusing ideas of punishment but only with the given fact of blindness. It soon becomes clear that this blindness has more than one meaning; perhaps it is the readers' own blindness. In contrast to this stands Jesus' "I am the light of the world." Finally, God himself, in his working and his willing to show his own reality to human beings, stands above and behind this man's blindness. Strangely enough, the whole story that follows is full of accusations brought against this man!

Scene 2: *Jesus and the man born blind* (vv. 6–7)

As he said this, he spat on the ground and made clay of the spittle and anointed the man's eyes with the clay, saying to him, "Go, wash in the pool of Siloam" (which means Sent). So he went and washed and came back seeing.

In two verses, the shortest scene of all, the act of healing is very briefly told. Two verses out of 41: this is fairly clear evidence that the writer of the gospel is not interested in the healing as a miraculous process, just as the man's being *born* blind is not a detail added for the sake of the miraculous alone.

Scene 3: *The man born blind and his neighbors* (vv. 8–12)

The neighbors and those who had seen him before as a beggar, said, "Is not this the man who used to sit and beg?" Some said, "It is he"; others said, "No, but he is *like* him." He said, "I am the man." They said to him, "Then how were your eyes opened?" He answered, "The man called Jesus made clay and anointed my eyes and said to me, 'Go to Siloam and wash'; so I went and washed and received my sight." They said to him, "Where is he?" He said, "I do not know."

This dialogue makes it clear that the apparently simple act of healing raises some important questions. Its reality is doubted by some—by denying the identity of the healed man with the one who formerly sat and begged. And the man healed is put into the position of having to identify himself ("I am the man"), thereby testifying indirectly to the reality of his transformation. Under further pressure, he refers to "the man called Jesus," obviously a way of identifying his healer without any statement of faith; no christological title is involved, but only Jesus' everyday proper name! The healed man knows his identity but not his whereabouts or presence.

Scene 4: *The man born blind and the Pharisees* (vv. 13–17)

> They brought to the Pharisees the man who had formerly been blind. Now it was a sabbath day when Jesus made the clay and opened his eyes. The Pharisees again asked him how he had received his sight. And he said to them, "He put clay on my eyes, and I washed, and I see." Some of the Pharisees said, "This man is not from God, for he does not keep the sabbath." But others said, "How can a man who is a sinner do such signs?" There was a division among them. So they again said to the blind man, "What do *you* say about him, since he has opened *your* eyes?" He said, "He is a prophet."

The tension mounts in this scene, which develops in the direction of a court-room drama—though it is not perfectly clear who is on trial. The motif of keeping and breaking the sabbath is introduced for the first time, so that Jesus is being tried in absentia for breaking the sabbath commandment; in another sense, it is the "beggar" who is on trial before the authorities of his religion and under pressure to take a stand. In the first-century background of the tension between Judaism and Christianity out of which this gospel comes, the beggar stands for the possible convert who is under pressure to leave the synagogue and come over into the Christian camp. But it is first of all Jesus' act of healing that puts people into a dilemma and raises the issue; the Pharisees say, "This man is not from God, for he does not keep the sabbath." The sabbath has been broken; how shall one react to this? For Judaism, the sabbath as a day of rest originated in the creation (Gen 1), in which God himself rested on the seventh day from all his work. Earlier in the Gospel of John (5:17), Jesus explains his having healed the crippled man at the pool of Bethesda on the sabbath by saying, "My father is working still and I am working." If the Jewish sabbath is explained by God's resting, Jesus' breaking of the sabbath is explained by God's working—which is to imply that in Jesus' healing, it is God who is at work, the Creator of heaven and earth and the sabbath!

The very next verse in chapter 5 tells the reader that "the Jews" sought to kill him because he made himself equal with God. So here in the story of the man born blind, the sabbath has been broken, but the question is, "What does that mean?" It must mean either that this man is not from God, or that he and the Father are one! To avoid these consequences (which represent unbelief or faith), his interrogators throw the question back upon the man himself: "You're the one whose eyes he opened; *you* tell us!" And the man answers: "He is a prophet"; this is a title one step closer to confession than the simpler identification of "the man called Jesus," but in itself it is still a perfectly conventional religious statement and not yet Christian confession.

Scene 5: *The Pharisees and the parents of the man born blind* (vv. 18–23)

The Jews did not believe that he had been blind and had received his sight, until they called the parents of the man who had received his sight, and asked them, "Is this your son, who you say was born blind? How then does he now see?" His parents answered, "We know that this is our son, and that he was born blind; but how he now sees we do not know, nor do we know who opened his eyes. Ask him; he is of age, he will speak for himself." His parents said this because they feared the Jews, for the Jews had already agreed that if any one should confess him to be Christ, he was to be put out of the synagogue. Therefore his parents said, "He is of age, ask him."

Nothing is to be gained by pushing the man himself—he is too obstinate and persistent—so the Pharisees turn to his parents in sheer refusal to accept the reality of Jesus' act. They are attempting to evade and deny what has been done by calling into question the identity of the man healed and the actuality of his former blindness. To both of these questions, the parents are able to testify: This *is* their son; he *was* born blind. But to testify to the healing is something beyond their competence, and they refer their questioners to their son himself. In addition, the element of fear is explicitly introduced into the narrative; for the parents to testify to anything more than they have done is to skirt that dangerous edge of confessing Jesus to be the Christ for which the penalty of excommunication had already been set. (Here we see most clearly how the struggle of church and synagogue at the end of the first century has sharpened the telling of the story.)

Scene 6: *The Pharisees and the man born blind* (for the second time) (vv. 24–34)

So for the second time they called the man who had been blind, and said to him, "Give *God* the praise; we know that *this* man is a sinner." He answered, "Whether he is a sinner, I do not know; one thing I know, that though I was blind, now I see." They said to him, "What did he do to you? *How* did he open your eyes?" He answered them, "I have told you already, and you would not listen. Why do you want to hear it again? Do you too want to become his disciples?" And they reviled him, saying, *"You* are *his* disciple, but *we* are disciples of Moses. We know that God has spoken to Moses, but as for this man, we do not know where he comes from." The man answered, "Why, this is a marvel! You do not know where he comes from, and yet he opened my eyes. We know that God does not listen to sinners, but if any one is a worshiper of God and does his will, God listens to him. Never since the world began has it been heard that any one opened the eyes of a man born blind. If this man were not from God, he could do nothing." They answered him, "You were born in utter sin, and would you teach *us?"* And they cast him out.

Now things are getting really warm. Having been unable to shake the man's testimony, or by way of his parents to discredit it by casting some doubt upon his identity or upon the reality of his former blindness, his questioners take another tack with him. "We *know* that this man [i.e., Jesus] is a sinner." Perhaps they can discredit Jesus by pinning a religious label on him, a not so unfamiliar technique. And to the once-blind man they say, "Give God the praise for your healing." Implicitly they accuse the one healed of impiousness and irreligion, of placing the credit in the wrong place and failing to give God his due! In the name of an appeal to religious piety, they try to get him to abandon his testimony. But he stands fast; the question whether or not Jesus is a "sinner" remains irrelevant. Over against what they claim to know, he holds fast to his simple "One thing I know": the reality of his healing. Weakly they persist in their questioning, raising another irrelevant question about the manner of the healing, thinking that perhaps some doubt can be cast upon it in this way. Then the man replies with absolutely beautiful irony: Does their persistent questioning mean that they are interested in signing up for catechetical instruction?

With perfect psychological insight, the narrative speaks then of the abuse to which this irony provokes them. They appeal to Moses, to whom God has spoken—of course because Moses is the giver of the sabbath law Jesus has broken. Then they add, "As for this man [Jesus], we do not know where he comes from." With these words they fall right into the condition that had been laid down earlier in the gospel when the crowds declared, "Can it be that the authorities really know this is the Christ? Yet we know where this man comes from; and when the Christ appears, no one will know where he comes from" (7:26–27). The man turns on his questioners with the eloquent judgment: "The really astonishing thing, the marvel, is that you do not know where he has come from, and here he has opened my eyes." He comes back to the simple reality of what has taken place, which his opponents will not face: that the eyes of a man born blind should be opened is something unheard of since the world began. The only possible conclusion is that this man Jesus must be from God—though this conclusion is still cast in negative form: "If this man were *not* from God, he could do nothing." This is a third stage on the way toward full Christian confession—but it is enough to bring the man's relationship to the religious community to the breaking point. He is condemned of total depravity and excommunicated. The irony is that his questioners now take his lifelong blindness to be the proof of this depravity, unaware of their inconsistency in thus admitting what they have up to this point been trying to deny!

Scene 7: *Jesus and the man born blind* (vv. 35–38)

Jesus heard that they had cast him out, and having found him he said, "Do you believe in the Son of man?" He answered, "And who is he, sir, that I may believe

in him?" Jesus said to him, "You have seen him, and it is he who speaks to you."
He said, "Lord, I believe"; and he worshiped him.

The man is alone now, separated from his community. But Jesus finds him and puts to him the ultimate religious question. It is not simply one of a theoretical knowledge about the eschatological bearer of salvation. One may be perfectly familiar with the doctrinal material concerning the Son of Man, and still ask, as he asks, about his identity: "Who is he, sir, that I may believe in him?" So far, the man has realized all the possibilities that are given within conventional human religion, stage by stage, but this question, put in direct personal encounter, is the decisive one. The formality of the dialogue confirms this presence of the climax in the words, "You have seen him, and it is he who speaks to you."

Jesus does not reply by granting the man a theophany, a vision of glory like Isaiah's in the temple or Paul's on the road to Damascus. If he were to have done that, the man's faith would rest upon that vision—and all the preceding experience, to which he has held so fast and for which he has had to pay such a heavy price, would become irrelevant. On the other hand, the tenacious assertion of his healing, even the willingness to make the right deduction from it—"If this man were not from God, he could do nothing"—is not Christian confession; this is reached only in the merging of the man's past experience with the fresh real presence, the self-authenticating encounter with his healer. And the result is that the man worships: he fulfills, as one commentator has observed, the true meaning of that "giving God the glory, the praise," which the authorities had demanded of him in scene 6.

Scene 8: *Jesus and the Pharisees* (vv. 39–41)

Jesus said, "For judgment I came into this world, that those who do not see may see, and that those who see may become blind." Some of the Pharisees near him heard this, and they said to him, "Are we also blind?" Jesus said to them, "If you were blind, you would have no guilt; but now that you say, 'We see,' your guilt remains."

This closing scene makes it clear that the "trial" goes in the end against those who so far have conducted it, who have condemned both Jesus and the man born blind. In their rejection of the light, they find themselves in darkness and condemned. "For judgment I came into this world." Just by *being* there, like a stone of stumbling set in their path, Jesus condemns them; or, more exactly, just by having healed the blind man. This is what they have not been able to accept, or avoid, or get around, or discredit, or deny; and this is their downfall. To receive Jesus and his divine work is to see; to reject him is to be blind.

Chapter 9 elaborates in detail both processes, simultaneously progressing toward their climax: the seeing in faith of the blind man, on the one side, and the blinding in unbelief of those who see, on the other. The paradigm describes vividly, if you will, the dynamics of unbelief and belief, reacting against each other, provoking each other, inciting each other in the heightening tension of dramatic encounter. At the same time, faith and unfaith here illumine and explain each other in their progressive and genuine polarization. Both begin from the one act of healing, which elicits opposite reactions as a catalyst elicits a chemical process of separation and division. "This is the judgment, that the light has come into the world."

For this polarization as a process there are many analogies. One that has struck me is to be found in the way in which complex and opposing reactions were set into motion in our public life by the single decisive event of the Supreme Court's declaration on segregation in public schools (1954). The dividing lines shift, the issues change from day to day, the frontiers are by no means closed, but all are ripples of reaction to the basic issue there posed of our nation's fidelity to its own constitution, and it is that issue to which we must give our answer in the interactions of frontlash and backlash that provoke each other to the point of threatening the very unity of our people. It does not matter that all people *claim* to uphold the constitution, any more than in the Johannine paradigm all claim to honor God.

The Memory of a Healing

Yet, illuminating as this polarity and this analogy may be, there is another kind of polarity in our paradigm, the noting of which brings us back finally to our own present situation and task. The blind man's memory of what has been done to him, and his persistence in holding to it at any price, is indeed like the memory of the Christian community that is embodied in the New Testament witness to the life and ministry of Jesus of Nazareth. It is not simply the memory of a memorable man; it is also the memory of a healing. Men and women know this man simply because they have known a delivering power at work through him and on them. Such a memory holds within itself the acknowledgment of former blindness and so differs from the contrasted memory of Moses. Theological training inevitably has also this aspect of imparting to each new generation this memory and tradition. But a collective religious memory is not yet Christian faith, and warming it over will never produce faith.

This memory is the necessary starting point, but the breakthrough to faith in a Christian sense is more than a deduction about Jesus drawn from this memory, and more than autobiographical honesty. Faith is not something to which the man healed penetrates on his own initiative; it is called forth from him in the self-disclosure of Jesus, as he finds the man who has held fast to his memory, and who for it has been excluded from the religious community. In exactly the same way, it must keep coming alive in our theological work; and the movement from a collective memory to the faith that worships God "in spirit and in truth" always takes place in that other polarization with unbelief—in the first instance our own unbelief and always also the unbelief of pious and religious people. The memory is there; the name of the "man called Jesus" is written once and for all in the annals of human history. But the question how we will react to it touches each person individually, so that faith must always be one's own, even when it rests most securely upon the communal tradition. Teachers can instruct and guide; they can deepen understanding; they can make more vivid a memory that has become, as it has so often for us, a dull thing—but they cannot produce faith.

Nor is faith given in a direct vision, a new and miraculous theophany. If one perversion of Christianity is to seek life in a lifeless tradition, the other is to look for it in a rootless and ecstatic religious fantasy, and it can scarcely be the business of a seminary to cultivate the latter. No mystical vision, no direct access to God is ever open to us that could render the earthly life and death of Jesus of Nazareth redundant. Faith never erases the church's memory; the Bible in its historical concreteness never becomes superfluous. Rather, to put it positively, faith springs from this memory when we hear the Son of Man addressing us directly in it. That is to say, as in the Johannine paradigm, faith does come with the presence of Jesus Christ himself as the Lord who declares, "You *have* seen him, and it is he who speaks to *you*."

CHAPTER 13

AN EXEGETICAL NOTE
ON JOHN 2:10[*]

This reconsideration of one verse in the narrative of the wedding feast at Cana
may begin with two observations about the passage in its entirety. First, the narrative appears to have clear connections with other parts of the gospel and occupies an important place in the general structure of this document. Karl Ludwig
Schmidt, in an essay in 1921,[1] emphasized already the need to distinguish
between tradition and composition in the analysis of this pericope, but he found
the integrating hand of the evangelist clearly discernible at at least three points:

(1) in vv. 3–4: the figure of the mother of Jesus and the word γύναι
    with which she is addressed, both of which reappear in 19:26; the
    reference to Jesus' ὥρα, which reappears in connection with the
    passion and glorification of Jesus in 7:30; 8:20; 12:23, 27; 13:1;
    17:1;
(2) in the parenthesis in v. 9 (καὶ οὐκ ᾔδει πόθεν ἐστίν . . . τὸ ὕδωρ);
    these words disturb the syntax of v. 9 and contain, in the question
    πόθεν ἐστίν, a Johannine christological formula that appears also
    in 7:27–28; 8:14; 9:29–30; 19:9; less directly also in 4:11; and
(3) in the appended notation of v. 11.[2]

---

[*]First published as the article "John 2:10" in *JBL* 86 (1967): 191–97, this exegetical study is
presented here with minor revisions, by permission.

1. K. L. Schmidt, "Der johanneische Charakter der Erzählung vom Hochzeitswunder in Kana,"
in *Harnack-Ehrung: Beiträge zur Kirchengeschichte ihrem Lehrer Adolf von Harnack zu seinem
70. Geburtstag* (Leipzig: Hinrichs, 1921), 32–43. Schmidt emphasizes (38ff.) the connections
between ch. 2 and the miracle stories of chs. 4, 5, 6, 9, and 11.

2. Ibid., 36–37, 41. Rudolf Bultmann (*The Gospel of John: A Commentary*, trans. G. R. Beasley-
Murray et al. [Philadelphia: Westminster, 1971; German orig. 1941], 118 n. 5) agrees in assigning
the parenthesis of v. 9 to the evangelist, but in general his estimate of the evangelist's intrusions
into the material is much more conservative than Schmidt's. In v. 11 the evangelist is responsible
only for the words καὶ ἐφανέρωσεν, etc., but even these may have stood in the source with a meaning different from the evangelist's reading of them (115; 119 n. 5). Verses 2 and 3 are assigned to
the source, for here Bultmann finds any possible symbolic reading of the figure of Mary incongru-
ous with 19:26, where she is taken to stand for Jewish Christianity (*Gospel of John*, 121 n. 2; for a
more convincing interpretation of this Johannine figure, see Eva Krafft, "Die Personen des

To be sure, the phrase ἀρχὴ τῶν σημείων in v. 11 appears to betray a sequential numbering from a written signs source which reappears again in 4:54. But other details strongly suggest that the verse as a whole is shaped at least as much by the evangelist's composition as it is by tradition: the emphasis on the location of Cana in Galilee;[3] the obvious connection this verse creates between the epiphany miracle just concluded and the revelation of δόξα in the evangelist's own comment on the Logos hymn in the prologue (1:14);[4] and the possibility that the phrase ἀρχὴ τῶν σημείων is deliberately turned to mean more than the πρῶτον σημεῖον ("first sign") of a source's sequence—"a primary sign . . . representative of the creative and transforming work of Jesus as a whole,"[5] in a sense commensurate with the place of the narrative at the head of the first major division of the gospel in chapters 2–12.[6]

Second, the interpreter needs to take seriously the symbolism of the story as a whole and of wine in particular. David Friedrich Strauss's devastating enumeration of the difficulties this pericope presents to the literalist reader—whether naturalistically literal or supernaturalistically so—is still worth reading.[7] Much wasted effort on the part of commentators to find a motivation for Jesus in performing such a "Luxus-wunder,"[8] and much of the pain the story

Johannesevangeliums," *EvT* 16 [1956]: 18–32). In addition, the reference to Jesus' ὥρα is assigned to the narrator of the source; the fact that it can be read in that context as simply exempting the miracle worker from human connections and motivations ("der Wundertäter untersteht einem eigenen Gesetz" [Bultmann, *Gospel of John*, 117; cf. n. 1]) is taken as sufficient grounds for separating this particular occurrence of ὥρα from the acknowledged Johannine thematic. In view of the striking reappearance of Jesus' mother at the very ὥρα of his death and *only* there, any suggestion that meets Bultmann's objection to connecting 2:3–4 and 19:26–27 would render this latter argument for attributing this instance of ὥρα in v. 4 to the source extremely unconvincing.

3. Cf. John 4:46; Bultmann, *Gospel of John*, 206 n. 3; Wayne A. Meeks, "Galilee and Judea in the Fourth Gospel," *JBL* 85 (1966): 159–69.

4. E. Käsemann, "Aufbau und Anliegen des johanneischen Prologs," in *Exegetische Versuche und Besinnungen*, 2 vols. (2d ed.; Göttingen: Vandenhoeck & Ruprecht, 1964), 2:155–80, esp. 170–71, 177–78 (ET: "The Structure and Purpose of the Prologue to John's Gospel," in *New Testament Questions of Today*, trans. W. J. Montague [Philadelphia: Fortress, 1969], 138–67, esp. 161–62).

5. C. K. Barrett, *The Gospel according to St. John* (Philadelphia: Westminster, 1978), 161.

6. Another reason for assigning v. 11 as it now stands to the evangelist may be the connection here made between the σημεῖον and the πιστεύειν of the disciples, but since the nature of such connection, or more precisely the existence of alleged discrepancies in the way in which such connections are drawn in different parts of the gospel, is a major argument not only in the delineation of a signs source but even for the very existence of such a source at all, it cannot be adduced as evidence here without much fuller discussion. Cf. E. Haenchen, "Johanneische Probleme," in *Gott und Mensch: Gesammelte Aufsätze* (Tübingen: Mohr [Siebeck], 1965), 80 n. 1, 88, 93.

7. D. F. Strauss, *Das Leben Jesu, kritisch Bearbeitet* (Tübingen: Osiander, 1835), 219–36 (par. 99) (ET: *The Life of Jesus Critically Examined*, ed. P. C. Hodgson [Philadelphia: Fortress, 1972], 519–27).

8. Ibid., 224 (ET: 521).

has produced for ascetic sensitivities, even in the textual transmission of the gospel,[9] would have been spared if the impressive evidence adduced by Bauer, Bultmann, and others for the place of οἶνος in the vocabulary of syncretistic religion had been known and taken seriously.[10] Whether or not Bultmann is correct in regarding the story as a pagan legend transferred to Jesus,[11] it is clear that it is not primarily about a humble Galilean village wedding but about the bringer of divine gifts to human beings.[12] Yet the precise nature and intent of this symbolism in the present Johannine context remains uncertain, and its interpretation depends still upon the handling of some of the details to which we have referred above.

One detail that has not received the attention it deserves is v. 10, the response of the chief steward upon tasting what the servants have drawn:

πᾶς ἄνθρωπος πρῶτον τὸν καλὸν οἶνον τίθησιν, καὶ ὅταν μεθυσθῶσιν τὸν ἐλάσσω· σὺ τετήρηκας τὸν καλὸν οἶνον ἕως ἄρτι.

By every standard of literary composition, the climax to the story should come with this saying, just as in the next episode, the cleansing of the temple, the climax is reached with the reaction of the Jews to Jesus' saying about the temple.[13] To be sure, as Bultmann asserts, vv. 9–10 serve to conclude the miracle story by supplying the confirmation of the deed done, which is a standard component of such narratives;[14] yet, to explain the concrete dialogue by means of which

9. Cf. H. J. Vogels, *Handbuch der Textkritik des Neuen Testaments* (2d ed.; Bonn: Peter Hanstein, 1955), 191–92.

10. W. Bauer, *Das Johannesevangelium*, HNT 6 (3d ed.; Tübingen: Mohr [Siebeck], 1933), excursus on pp. 46–47; Bultmann, *Gospel of John*, 119 n. 1; C. H. Dodd, *The Interpretation of the Fourth Gospel* (Cambridge: Cambridge University Press, 1953), 297–99.

11. Bultmann, *Gospel of John*, 118–19.

12. "Wir befinden uns hier im Bereich *religiöser Identifikation*—Christus ist das, was er spendet" (Schmidt, "Der johanneische Charakter," 41). "The primary meaning of the wine is clearly Jesus' gift of salvation, for which light, water, and food are other Johannine symbols" (Raymond E. Brown, *The Gospel according to John: Introduction, Translation, and Notes*, AB 29–29A, 2 vols. [Garden City, N.Y.: Doubleday, 1966–70], 1:110).

13. John 2:13–22 also ends with a comment by the evangelist referring to the (future) πιστεύειν of the disciples, and the reaction (v. 20) to which this comment is attached consists, just as does 2:10, of a contrast drawn between the novel performance that arouses it (emphatic σύ; here Jesus' word, there the bridegroom's "withholding") and something generally acknowledged to be true or expected in its place. We certainly cannot conclude, as does J. H. Bernard (*A Critical and Exegetical Commentary on the Gospel according to John*, ed. A. H. McNeile, ICC, 2 vols. [New York: Charles Scribner's Sons, 1929], 80), that since the story does not end with a saying of Jesus, it must go back to some historical reminiscence of an actual event in Jesus life!

14. Bultmann (*Gospel of John*, 118); his note 3 refers to his own discussion in *Die Geschichte der synoptischen Tradition* (2d ed.; Göttingen: Vandenhoeck & Ruprecht, 1931), 240–41 (ET: *History of the Synoptic Tradition*, trans. John Marsh [rev. ed.; New York: Harper & Row, 1976], 224–25).

the wonderful quality of the wine is here attested to the reader, Bultmann is forced to overinterpret the steward's response as upbraiding the bridegroom for withholding the good wine so long that the guests are no longer capable of appreciating it. It is doubtful that this is the natural meaning of v. 10. K. L. Schmidt noted in this connection the fact that the reader learns nothing (apart from the disciples' faith at the end of v. 11) about the effect of the miracle upon the persons present and involved. This ending does *not* fit the pattern of what Dibelius called the *Chorschluss* of the synoptic miracle stories, in which the deed arouses general astonishment and provokes praise.[15]

It is important to observe that v. 10 as it stands does more than declare the presence of wine where before there was, or was supposed to be, water. It does more than contrast old and new (as do such synoptic sayings as Mark 2:19–22 and parallels).[16] Instead, it sets up a contrast between πᾶς ἄνθρωπος and σύ (emphatic), between a generally valid expectation and what has just transpired. This contrast, furthermore, is a contrast in sequence, between the good first and then the poor in the one case, and the poor first and then the good in the other.

What is the generally valid expectation that provides the foil for this contrast? Hans Windisch understood it as *die johanneische Weinregel* and attempted to document this particular professional etiquette if not from the actual practice of ancient hosts and innkeepers, then at least from the scornful rumors which the more affluent connoisseurs of the grape would naturally circulate about low-class establishments.[17] The upshot is merely that some things have not changed since the first century: an innkeeper who slips bad wine to his guests after they are intoxicated is, and was then, a crook. Windisch is driven to explain the πᾶς ἄνθρωπος of v. 10 as either echoing the exaggerated defense made by any rogue caught in his swindle ("Everybody does it!"), or indicating that the evangelist came from just those lower classes, out in the eastern provinces of the empire to boot, where such behavior was presumably in fact the rule. Most commentators writing since seem to agree that Windisch failed to prove his point.[18]

Others have suggested that what gives the appearance of a general rule or axiom is instead an ad hoc formulation produced by the storyteller's art and colored by the dry wit of one who has had some experience with taverns.[19] For

15. Schmidt, "Der johanneische Charakter," 36; cf. H. Strathmann, *Das Evangelium nach Johannes*, NTD 4 (Göttingen: Vandenhoeck & Ruprecht, 1951), 58.

16. Such sayings may, of course, have contributed to the shaping of the Johannine narrative at a very early stage; see Bultmann, *Gospel of John*, 85; Bauer, *Das Johannesevangelium*, 47.

17. Hans Windisch, "Die johanneische Weinregel (Joh. 2,10)," *ZNW* 14 (1913): 248–57.

18. E.g., Bultmann, *Gospel of John*, 118 n. 4; Bauer, *Das Johannesevangelium*, 45; Brown, *Gospel according to John*, 1:100.

19. Bultmann, *Gospel of John*, 118; G. H. C. Macgregor, *The Gospel of John* (London: Hodder & Stoughton, 1928), 53: ". . . the words are intended as a pleasantry, and are not to be taken too rigorously. Lk. 5:39 is sufficient comment."

K. L. Schmidt, the problems of interpreting the Cana incident as a whole come to a head in the fact that the point of v. 10 is no real point at all but an utterly profane detail of popular narrative, the droll tone of which clashes with the exalted note struck by v. 11 and is therein representative of other details in the story that are wholly out of keeping with the tenor of the gospel.[20] C. H. Dodd calls the verse a "touch of homely humour" inserted to enhance the realism of the story; yet on the same page he emphatically urges the symbolic dimensions of a story that is "*not* to be taken at its face value."[21] Ordinarily, confronted by such double vision, a compassionate bartender would tell a man it was time for him to be on his way home.

Of course, Dodd himself is one of many commentators who have made it clear that if there is any writer of the New Testament who can make theological use of double vision or, more exactly, of double meanings, it is the Fourth Evangelist. The cases in point include not only such commonplace examples as ὁ ἄρτος ὁ καταβαίνων (καταβὰς) ἐκ τοῦ οὐρανοῦ (6:33, 41) but also such sentences in dialogue material as express transparently within the gospel narrative the issues and problems of the later Johannine church. The identical words, for example, with which both Martha and Mary greet Jesus in 11:21, 32 (κύριε, εἰ ἦς ὧδε οὐκ ἂν ἀπέθανεν ὁ ἀδελφός μου), taken together with that clause in Jesus' climactic reply of 11:25–26 which states that "he who believes in me shall live *even though he dies* [κἂν ἀποθάνῃ]," not only are a part of the Johannine reformulation of eschatological hopes but also, by expressing so poignantly the perfectly natural human response to the impact of death in the early Christian community (as we see it elsewhere in 1 Thess 4:13–18), are a part of the Johannine way of addressing the gospel to the human situation of his own time.

Is it possible to find a comparable further meaning in the wine steward's response of 2:10? So far as I know, the possibility has never been entertained save for the latter part of the verse, the second of the two sequences here contrasted, and then only in a most tentative sort of way, within the more general contrast between the water of the stone jars in v. 6 and the good wine of v. 10. So, for example, Raymond Brown writes: "Thus the headwaiter's statement at the end of the scene, 'You have kept the choice wine until now,' can be understood as the proclamation of the coming of the messianic days."[22] Similarly, Hoskyns: "It is not, however, the man whose marriage is being celebrated who has withheld the good wine, but God, who has now sent His Son, the bridegroom (Mark ii.19, 20), to give life to the world."[23]

20. Schmidt, "Der johanneische Charakter," 36, 38.
21. Dodd, *Interpretation of the Fourth Gospel*, 297; emphasis original.
22. Brown, *Gospel according to John*, 1:105.
23. E. C. Hoskyns, *The Fourth Gospel*, ed. F. N. Davey (2d ed.; London: Faber & Faber, 1947), 189.

Such an eschatological reading not only of the wine itself but of the bride-groom's remarkable withholding of it immediately reminds us that other writers of the New Testament are concerned with the question which, cast in the imagery of John 2, might be put as something of a taunt: If wine indeed stands for human salvation, why has God withheld it so long? Is he not as unlikely a God as the bridegroom is here observed to be an unlikely host? The author of Hebrews notes that Abraham and all the rest of the company of the old covenant did not receive what God had promised and did not themselves enter the heavenly city; the reason given is not merely earlier unbelief and disobedience (Heb 4:2, 6) but God's own intent to include a later generation in their perfection (11:39–40). Paul agonizes over the question why God has withheld final salvation from Israel, in seeming violation of his promise. He finds in God's having done so—having first consigned all people to disobedience in order *then* to have mercy on all—the reconciliation of the *whole* cosmos, proof that the God of Israel is the God of the Gentiles also and so truly God (Rom 11:11–15, 25–32). In 1 Cor 1:26–29, he points out that God's calling does not bring with it provision of wisdom, power, and nobility of birth; these are withheld *in order that* no flesh might boast in the presence of God.

Such an eschatological reading of the bridegroom's behavior must remain under the suspicion of being but an uncontrolled allegorization of John 2:10 until we return to our earlier observation that the verse itself sets up a contrast between two opposing sequences. What about the first half of the steward's response? What is the general expectation that provides the foil for the bridegroom's remarkable withholding?

This foil, I should like to suggest, is provided by a Hellenistic cosmogony that, in the terms of this narrative, would have to be called the story of the adulteration of God's good wine, the process of deterioration and defilement from what is originally divine, told in order to give an account of humanity's present condition. In such a scheme, the good wine always comes first, the heavenly man always comes before the earthly man, the spiritual before the natural. That Paul, in the interests of his eschatology, deliberately reverses the sequence of Hellenistic anthropology so clearly attested by Philo[24] (1 Cor 15:44b–47) is in fact a very clear and real parallel to the contrast in sequences that is the substance of the wine steward's reply. Salvation, in the Hellenistic worldview, is not ordinarily the changing of water into wine but the recovery of what has been cheapened and spoiled, a story about how the process by which the world came into being is reversed and undone. General Hellenistic expectation—I hesitate to say outright "gnostic expectation" only because of the terminological problems involved—has to do with a God who serves the good wine first; later, when the company is drunk, they have only the poor stuff left.

24. Cf. Philo, *Opif.* 134; *Leg.* 1:31, 53, 88–89.

C. H. Dodd provides indirect support for this suggestion and what it implies for the interpretation of the stone jars of v. 6 when he discusses the complexity of water as a symbol and remarks, only in passing, on its occasional highly negative meaning:

> In religious thought of the type of the *Hermetica* it [water] has cosmological significance as the prototype of the lower creation: it is the residue of the ὑγρὰ φύσις after fire and πνεῦμα have been refined out of it to make the heavenly sphere. There may be a reference to this side of water-symbolism where water, standing for the lower life, is contrasted with wine, standing for the higher (ii.1–12). . . . It is noteworthy that in the Gnostic Justin the water in which the ψυχικοί are cleansed is identified with the ὕδωρ τῆς πονηρᾶς κτίσεως, which is the 'waters beneath the firmament' of the Hebrew creation-story, and contrasted with the 'waters above the firmament', the ὕδωρ τοῦ ἀγαθοῦ ζῆν, in which the πνευματικοί are cleansed.[25]

The "hour" of Jesus for this evangelist is the hour of his death. The simple fact that there is such an "hour," which had once not yet come but which in his kerygmatic affirmation has come and now is, an hour in which one may behold the presence and glory of the Word made flesh and believe, is the real marvel, the miracle to which the Johannine story of the wedding feast at Cana points. The symbolism of the story is general and difficult to pin down, but it is characteristic of the evangelist to explicate his own earlier passages in the course of the book itself. Wine is a comprehensive symbol here, not anything as specific as the wine of the eucharist, to which not a few interpreters refer; yet, as such, it is suited for an opening story to introduce all the other signs that spell out the meaning of the Christ. The symbolism may be general, but the direction given to it by v. 10 is neither vague nor superfluous. For the salvation that appears in this gospel as miraculously new sets the Christian claim over against every dualistic cosmogony—indeed, against every *Heilsgeschichte* that starts with a heavenly, divine home for human beings. The heart of the evangelist's message does not have to do with the problem and existence of evil, or explaining humanity's present condition; it concerns the miracle of its transformation, the gift of salvation, of good wine, of truth, of faith, and of the authentic knowledge of God in the midst of falsity, darkness, unbelief, and anxiety. "No one," declares the evangelist, in a related comment in another setting, "has ascended into heaven except the one who descended from heaven, the Son of Man" (3:13 NRSV).

---

25. Dodd, *Interpretation of the Fourth Gospel*, 138; the reference for Justin is: Hippolytus, *Haer.* 5:22.13 (GCS, ed. Wendland: 5:27.3). All the texts ordinarily cited for the meaning of water in the Fourth Gospel (e.g., by Bultmann, *Gospel of John*, 180–87, esp. 182 nn. 3, 4; 183 n. 1) run in exactly the reverse direction, supporting the *positive* connection between water and "life." For the use of "water" with negative connotations, cf. Bultmann, *Gospel of John*, 184 n. 5.

CHAPTER 14

AN EXEGETICAL NOTE
ON JOHN 10:1–18[*]

The exegetical analyst has a right, and even a certain obligation, to adopt as a working hypothesis, until the text itself forces one to abandon it, the view that a passage under consideration possesses literary unity and integrity. Difficulties in the thought of a text that otherwise does not immediately present irregularities of style, vocabulary, and syntax ought not be taken at once as reason for abandoning this hypothesis, but should occasion first of all a reexamination of the author's argument and possible intentions.[1] It is the aim of this essay to attempt such a reexamination in the case of John 10:1–18.[2]

The difficulties connected with this passage have to do primarily with the substance and coherence of its thought; they are raised above all by what appears on first sight to be the incongruity existing between the concern with ἡ θύρα ("the door") in vv. 7–9, on the one hand, and the immediately subsequent and far clearer reference to ὁ ποιμὴν ὁ καλός ("the good shepherd") on the other. The incongruity is heightened if we take vv. 1–5 also to be primarily a description of the "good shepherd," as we seem almost by habit to do when we refer to the discourse of John 10.

The solutions vary—they involve necessarily some attention to the textual confusion of v. 7—but there seems to be a certain consensus that the interest of vv. 7–10 in the θύρα is secondary and represents a later interpretation of vv. 1–5

---

[*]This essay was previously published as "A Note on John 10:1–18," *JBL* 75 (1956): 232–35. It is reproduced here, with some revision, by permission.

1. Any other procedure, i.e., literary stratification on the basis of *Sachkritik* alone without verification from the side of *Literarkritik,* must always appear arbitrary and subjective. Conversely, even where literary considerations finally force the exegete to abandon this hypothesis, literary solutions must be intelligible from the point of view of *Sachkritik* and should include a plausible explanation of the present state and order of the text if this is not original.

2. Besides the commentaries, see J. Schneider, "Zur Komposition von Joh. 10," in *Coniectanea Neotestamentica XI, in honorem Antonii Fridrichsen* (Lund: Gleerup, 1947), 220–25; C. H. Dodd, *The Interpretation of the Fourth Gospel* (Cambridge: Cambridge University Press, 1953), 358–61; G. Bornkamm, "λύκος," *TDNT* 4:308–11; J. Jeremias, "θύρα," *TDNT* 3:173–80; E. Schweizer, *Ego Eimi: Die religionsgeschichtliche Herkunft und theologische Bedeutung der johanneischen Bildreden, zugleich ein Beitrag zur Quellenfrage des vierten Evangeliums,* FRLANT NS 38 (Göttingen: Vandenhoeck & Ruprecht, 1939), 141–51.

that missed the point of these verses and concentrated by mistake upon a secondary element within them, namely, ἡ θύρα, rather than upon the central idea of the ποιμήν (v. 2).[3] All such solutions, however, fail to be satisfactory for the one decisive reason that they ignore the actual importance of the word θύρα in vv. 1–5; ποιμήν is in fact only a predicate in these verses, and the crucial point is the criterion according to which this predicate is assigned to one εἰσερχό-μενος ("entrant") rather than to another. This criterion is provided by the contrast between διὰ τῆς θύρας ("through the door") and ἀλλαχόθεν ("from another point"). That vv. 7 and 9 concentrate on ἡ θύρα is very far from indicating a misunderstanding of vv. 1–5 on the part of some editor; in all the textual uncertainty of these verses there is evidence only that such an editor (if there is one here at all) "got" the real point of vv. 1–5, not that he missed it. The possibility therefore remains that vv. 7–10 are an integral part of the whole passage, vv. 1–18.

If we turn to the third and last part of the passage under review (10:11–18), the meaning is fairly clear. The good shepherd demonstrates his excellence as shepherd, the fact that he is ὁ ποιμήν rather than a μισθωτός ("hireling"), by his readiness not to flee but to meet the adversary and to lay down his life for the sheep.[4] Thus he demonstrates also his ownership of the sheep, in contrast to the hireling, οὗ οὐκ ἔστιν τὰ πρόβατα ἴδια ("to whom the sheep do not belong," v. 12; cf. the recurrent phrase of ch. 17: πᾶν ὃ δέδωκας αὐτῷ ["all that thou hast given him"]). This section "provides the evangelist with the clearest and most explicit statement he has yet permitted himself upon the Passion of Christ as a voluntary and vicarious self-sacrifice."[5] At this point the "logic" of the passage is fairly straightforward and the agreement of the commentators with each other fairly extensive. This is where the thought of the passage as a whole comes to a preliminary rest; what follows in vv. 19–21 concerns the response the discourse calls forth. If, bearing these points in mind, we go back to the first part and read 10:1–5 as a unit, remembering also that the main thrust of these verses stems from the contrast between διὰ τῆς θύρας and ἀλλαχόθεν as the criterion by

---

3. So Jeremias, "θύρα," 179–80; Schweizer, *Ego Eimi*, 143. Cf. Rudolf Bultmann, *The Gospel of John: A Commentary*, trans. G. R. Beasley-Murray et al. (Philadelphia: Westminster, 1971), 358–60; and W. Bauer, *Das Johannesevangelium*, HNT 6 (3d ed.; Tübingen: Mohr [Siebeck], 1933), 139: The explanation in v. 7 "knüpft an den relativ nebensächlichen Begriff 'Tür' an, während wir zu hören erwarten, wer der Hirt ist."

4. To insist that τιθέναι τὴν ψυχήν is here meant to indicate only a subjective willingness to "risk," "pledge," or "stake" one's life ("denn für einen Hirten ist es wohl charakteristisch, dass er sein Leben für die Schafe riskiert, nicht aber, dass er es für sie opfert" [Bultmann, *Gospel of John*, 370–71 n. 5]) is perhaps to press the evangelist's logic too relentlessly into the mold of a general and pragmatic definition of "shepherd," whereas actually the Christ event (with its culmination in death) governs the presentation and not infrequently threatens to break through the confines of the categories employed.

5. Dodd, *Interpretation of the Fourth Gospel*, 360.

which the "shepherd of the sheep" is distinguished from a "thief and robber," it is virtually impossible to avoid the conclusion that θύρα is here used to refer not to the *person* of Christ but to his *death* as the means of his passage εἰς τὴν αὐλὴν τῶν προβάτων ("into the enclosure, abode of the sheep"). The phrase ἀναβαίνειν ἀλλαχόθεν (lit., "to ascend from another point") makes the reference to Christ's death clearer still, inasmuch as ἀναβαίνειν ("to ascend") is several times the Johannine equivalent for ὑψωθῆναι ("to be lifted up"), being applied to Jesus' return to the Father and his entry into his glory.[6] The point of the contrast is therefore that a legitimate claim to be shepherd rather than thief must rest on legitimate entry—via death. Of course the reference to death is veiled at this stage of the gospel (10:6), but it is clearer than the earlier references in 3:13 and 6:62. It becomes clearer still in 10:11–18, as we have seen, and the climax is reached just before the passion narrative begins: "Truly, truly, I say to you, unless a grain of wheat falls into the earth and dies, it remains alone; but if it dies, it bears much fruit" (12:24 RSV).[7]

In other words, the whole passage 10:1–18 raises the question of true and false claims to messiahship. The claimants are contrasted first in terms of their means of entry ("entering through the door" versus "ascending from another point"), then in terms of their action in crisis ("laying down one's life" versus "leaving the sheep and fleeing"). This is the consistent and unifying thread that runs through the whole passage. The exegetical confusion arises from the fact that the claimants are not designated by nouns in the first part, whereas they are in the second; in vv. 1–5 the noun θύρα is the criterion, the means of entry, but in vv. 11–18 the criteria are expressed with verbs. In the transitional verses between these two parts (vv. 7–10), the exegetical confusion has to some extent become a textual one; the intent of the transitional section is that the messianic claimant who is known by the "door" he uses is himself the "door," first *to* the sheep (v. 7), then *of* the sheep (v. 9), in preparation for the changed perspective of vv. 11–18. What is at first the "door" by which the true ποιμήν enters becomes the "door" by which communion of the sheep with the shepherd is established (τῆς φωνῆς αὐτοῦ ἀκούειν, "hearing his voice"; τὴν φωνὴν αὐτοῦ εἰδέναι, "knowing his voice"; τὰ ἴδια πρόβατα φωνεῖν κατ' ὄνομα,

---

6. Cf. John 3:13; 6:62; 20:17 (bis). This is not to deny, of course, that within the figure the αὐλή is thought of as being surrounded by a wall the thief "climbs over" (Bultmann, *Gospel of John*, 372).

7. The pattern thus outlined is disturbed at only one point, namely, in the famous *crux* of 20:17, where οὔπω ἀναβέβηκα is spoken by the risen Jesus to Mary (cf. Dodd, *Interpretation of the Fourth Gospel*, 442–43). Nevertheless, the existence of the present, ἀναβαίνω, in the same verse and the absence of any resistance to Thomas's request in 20:26–29 seem to mean that οὔπω ἀναβέβηκα ought to be read with full emphasis on its *Aktionsart* (i.e., *not* as an aorist); in one sense, Jesus' ἀναβαίνειν is not complete until the "insufflation" (20:22), but it is already under way with the crucifixion.

"calling his own sheep by name" [10:3–4]); this in turn becomes the "door" for the sheep, by which they too find sustenance (νομὴν εὑρίσκειν, 10:9). At the same time, the discourse has shifted from the third to the first person, in line with the pattern that can be discerned also in chapters 4, 6, and 11. Christ is himself, by virtue of his death, the "door" as he is also the "way" (14:4–6); by precisely the same token he is the "good shepherd."

That this is the correct approach to the passage 10:1–18 as a whole is confirmed by the ease with which it now follows upon the reference to sight and blindness in 9:40–41, and by the natural way in which the "schism" of 10:19–21 and the demand of 10:24 for an open statement of messiahship follow in the subsequent context.[8]

John 10:1–18 thus finds Jesus' messianic claim confirmed and vindicated rather than contradicted by his death upon the cross. This it shares with other passages in the Fourth Gospel that also lead to the question of the meaning of Jesus' death for the evangelist—but the full development of this theme lies beyond the scope of this brief essay.

8. The backward reference to ch. 9 in 10:21 (τυφλῶν ὀφθαλμοὺς ἀνοῖξαι) does not disturb this sequence. In any case it is secondary; the σχίσμα is διὰ τοὺς λόγους τούτους.

Part V

Shorter Exegetical Studies
and Sermons on the Gospels

CHAPTER 15

AN EXEGETICAL REFLECTION ON MATTHEW 21:1–11[*]

The passion narrative in Matthew as in Mark clearly has two beginnings. In the narrower sense, the final events of Jesus' life are set in motion at Matt 26:1 (cf. Mark 14:1) with the decision of the authorities in Jerusalem to move against him. Here the headpiece, the ornamental and evocative figure that has been placed at the start (as a result of a process of development behind our written gospels), is the scene of the anointing at Bethany. The central clue to meaning provided to the reader in this intimate scene is the equation of two shockingly dissonant actions: the anointing of Jesus' head with oil (the Messiah being "the anointed one") *is* the anointing of his body for burial. That double action of the unnamed woman so marks the authentic center of the gospel that its telling shall always go where the true gospel is preached.

Yet in the broader reach of the gospel, there is another beginning when Jesus first enters Jerusalem. The shocking dissonance this time is between the way Jesus enters the "city of the great king" (Matt 5:35) and the way he leaves it. This dissonance is also a literary and compositional correlation of beginning and end, so that the story of the entry occupies a position in Matthew (as also in Mark) that can only be compared to the place of the foot-washing scene in John 13. A major new section in both the gospels of Mark and Matthew begins here. Both had concluded their major central sections with a dispute about greatness and Jesus' magisterial definition of ministry (Mark 10:45; Matt 20:28). The sole intervening material is the episode of the blind men (in Matthew; Bartimaeus in Mark) on the road from Jericho who hail Jesus as a deliverer with the epithet "Son of David" and whose one request is that their eyes be opened. At Jesus' touch they see and follow him into the city. The reader, drawn by the narrator into their movement, is invited also to share their gift of disclosing perception. The controlling imagery of this second beginning to the passion revolves around the royal figure of David.

David was a generator of symbolic meaning. In recalling a past, his name also shaped a people's hope for the future. He had been the founder of Israel as

[*]This essay reproduces, with minor revisions, a brief exegetical study first published as "Matthew 21:1–11," in *Int* 40 (1986): 180–85. It is used by permission.

a nation, with all the appurtenances of a capital, a court, a government—in short, a "kingdom." He had been the creator of Jerusalem as a symbol of beauty, of military strength, and of the dwelling presence of YHWH. His name preserved the memory, idealized but founded in fact, of a time when Israel was powerful and respected, when her enemies were held at bay, when the poor and oppressed were treated justly. So Judah's hopes were Davidic in shape: for a king who would not only rule Israel once again but would deliver his people from alien rule and so vindicate Israel's election, restore justice in the land, and above all increase the standing ("glory") of God himself among all the peoples of the earth. One text that speaks for many is *Psalms of Solomon* 17, which, by the way, shows that it is simply false to reduce Jewish messianic expectations in the first century to purely "political" terms or to a national warrior hero. In the New Testament, David is remembered not only as a prophet who, inspired by God's spirit, spoke about the Christ (Acts 2:25–30) but as a king himself; and as an ancestor of the messianic king, he was inevitably in his person also a representation of the Messiah. It is as this Son of David, as Israel's eschatological king coming into Jerusalem, that Jesus is hailed in the scene of our text.

Yet how is this Davidic material "applied" to Jesus by the evangelist? The interpreter is now faced with a crucial choice. It is not the only time this question arises; it is perhaps the fundamental issue everywhere in the interpretation of the gospels, but it is posed here with an uncommon directness and force.

One approach is to literalize the text, to read it as a descriptive report of Jesus' actual arrival in Jerusalem. The function of the text within the gospel was of course from the beginning to evoke, nurture, and refine the readers' understanding of Jesus of Nazareth as the messianic king. The temptation, almost irresistible in our culture and time, is to suppose that the way the text does that must lie in providing reliable historical detail about the episode. Yet it is extremely doubtful that this supposition furthers our ability to listen to the evangelist's text. It seems instead only to get in the way, to compound difficult questions for which the text itself provides no answers and shows no interest.

For example, if we historicize the text in that way, the dissonance undoubtedly intended by the evangelist between this entry and Jesus' exit from the city, alone, rejected, and mocked (Matt 27:32–44), is projected upon the pilgrim crowd of our passage and resolved by suggesting that the discrepancy is due to its "fickleness." The problem is that not one syllable from Matthew suggests such condescending contempt for the crowd or suspicion of the integrity of its acclaim. Again, if the historicity of the details is pressed, commentators are compelled to speculate about Jesus' motives in deliberately staging the scene as an "object lesson" in his own perception of himself as Messiah, this of course because the only words spoken by Jesus himself are those opening instructions to the disciples. To be sure, Jesus is at the center of the scene. Yet the heart of the passage lies in what is said by *others,* and the text makes no pretense of suggesting that it is Jesus who appeals to Zech 9:9 to define *his* conception of messiah. Again, a historically literal reading of this passage makes out of the hosanna of verse 9 "the expression of a momentary outburst of mistaken enthusiasm."[1] It is scarcely possible to imagine a more cheapening trivialization of what must be for the evangelist the very center of the pericope. A literalistic reading of the text, finally, creates artificial problems of chronology. Since the cry "Hosanna" and the carrying of branches (the last is found, strictly speaking, only in John 12:13) are activities more appropriate to the feast of Sukkoth (Tabernacles), the question is raised whether we should place the setting at another time of year. However, that would simply undo the evangelist's careful positioning of the narrative. The anachronisms are scarcely compelling; the narrator's emphasis upon festal acts of homage seems to have a symbolic momentum that has drawn upon a variety of festal practice in order to fill out the scene.

So one is bound to look for a different basic approach to the passage. As is well known, Matthew has inserted one of his characteristic "formula citations" (vv. 4–5) into Mark's account, and indeed has even altered the details of the scene to accord with that text from Zech 9:9, producing the notorious "doubling" of the animals used by Jesus in verses 2 and 7. Some commentators are appalled by the resulting clumsiness; how could the evangelist imagine Jesus riding on two animals at once (v. 7)? Others conclude that such a gross failure to appreciate the use of synonymous parallelism in the Hebrew poetry of the Zechariah oracle only proves that the evangelist could not have been a Jew. Actually, this detail provides an important clue to the passage: the whole narrative text derives its principal substance from two Old Testament passages on which the early church reflected deeply in its search for the meaning of what happened to Jesus in Jerusalem. This is apparent already from the way in which in Mark the animal is said never to have been ridden; prompted by the LXX text of Zechariah, even the animal's maiden use serves the eschatological dimension of the scene. It is the distillation of that exegetical reflection that the evangelist has set before us in this gateway scene to the whole passion narrative. These Old Testament texts were not invented; they were received and used by the early church as God's own clues to the meaning of Jesus' final days. So it is a slander to suggest that if we try to listen to the evangelist's reflections on these texts we are abandoning the only sound basis for true understanding or are making of this gospel the fictional product of the creative imagination of the early church.

Of course the fact of Jesus' entry into Jerusalem is beyond historical doubt. One can speculate about many of the precise circumstances that surrounded it, but that is rather unproductive. The one circumstance that is known most certainly and to every historian, that it takes no faith to know, and that may even

1. A. H. McNeile, *The Gospel according to St. Matthew* (London: Macmillan, 1949), 297.

perhaps be known more certainly to us than it was to Jesus, is that he entered the city on the way to his death—not only to his death, but to disgrace, to the discrediting of all that he had taught and done, and to the refutation of any hopes or expectations he might have had himself or might have aroused among his disciples or among the Passover pilgrims. So far as historical knowledge of Jesus is concerned, that is where we would have to leave the matter. If we want to know the historical reality behind this account, that is its brutal face.

The reasons why a literalistic historical reading of the text will not work are: (1) it evades and manipulates this historical reality, and (2) the evangelist views Jesus' entry into Jerusalem from another perspective. The claim from which distinctively *Christian* faith took its start, namely, that by raising Jesus from the dead God had identified himself with this one who had entered Jerusalem to die, meant that the outcome was no longer a disgrace and a discrediting but instead a new clue to an authentic and reliable understanding of God. That provided the warrant for looking again at what happened to Jesus in Jerusalem in the light of those Old Testament scriptures to find the proper categories in which to express and communicate this newly discovered eschatological perspective.

In this particular episode, the categories that came to hand were, as we have seen, those of the Davidic tradition. Nevertheless—and this is the most crucial point to observe—those categories were not employed to soften, to suppress, or to disguise the harsh public reality of the course of historical events, but to accept, reaffirm, and interpret it. The result is not only an imposition of Davidic roles and symbols upon Jesus (a "Davidizing" of Jesus) but a drastic reshaping of that David tradition under the impact of the brute historical reality of Jesus' death (a "Jesufication" of David, if one will—or better, simply a "Christianizing" of David's symbol-generating power). The result is not a "spiritualization" of militaristic or political hopes so much as it is a metamorphosis of eschatological symbols in the direction of real life and experience.

Every detail of Matthew's text seems to confirm and support this way of reading it. We may conclude by simply noting some of the most important.

Perhaps the most striking is the redefinition given to royalty itself. The actual word "king" (and its cognate "kingdom") has been completely removed in Matthew from the acclamation of the crowd and replaced with the single epithet "Son of David." To be sure, the Zechariah quotation makes it clear that the one riding into Jerusalem to die is to be proclaimed to Jerusalem as her king, but the quotation itself qualifies this king as "meek, gentle, humble." This predicate (picked up only in Matthew's use of this passage, not in John 12:15, the only other citation of it in the New Testament) is the same one that is used in Jesus' own pronouncement in the third beatitude (Matt 5:5) of blessing upon those who have no one to turn to for help and vindication but God. These are the suffering righteous of the Psalms. Jesus himself is one of these (cf. Matt 11:29; 27:43), destined for death and defeat and utterly dependent upon God for his own vindication. Matthew leaves out the line in Zechariah that says of this king, "triumphant and victorious is he." The oracle in Zechariah's own time may already have begun the process of redefinition, for it seems to have envisioned the restoration of God's order at the cost of such great suffering that the royal family itself would share the tribulations of the poor—a postexilic fusing of Davidic royal messianism with the tradition of the "poor" (the *anawim*). In any case, Matthew's intent seems clear: this Son of David is *this* kind of "king."

Again, in the opening verses of the pericope, Mark, by narrating how the disciples found things in the village just as Jesus had predicted, focuses attention on Jesus' clairvoyance (a hagiographical motif that is typical of Mark's way of conveying the eschatological dimension of the episode, or Jesus' "divinity"). Matthew drops such supernaturalism and highlights the congruity of the course of events with the prophet's eschatological message, which is inserted here between the instructions given by Jesus and their execution by the disciples. The disciples do not "find" things as Jesus has told them; they "do" as he "commanded." They do not create but they do act out the congruity between prophetic oracle and event that gives the episode its eschatological dimension. It is this congruity that *is* for Matthew Jesus' "divinity."

Finally, by altering the Zechariah quotation with words in the first line from Isa 62:11, Matthew turns a cry of jubilation ("Rejoice greatly, O daughter of Zion") into an imperative to deliver a message to Jerusalem ("Say to the daughter of Zion"). When the city is aroused (literally "shaken") by Jesus' entry to ask "Who is this?" the crowds accompanying Jesus carry out the command, but they do so with the formal pronouncement: "This is the prophet Jesus from Nazareth of Galilee." Such sudden relinquishing of all messianic titles and all supernatural or triumphalist claims, such shocking reference to Jesus' historical origin in apparent disavowal of any appeal to Bethlehem as his origin to verify his Davidic credentials, can hardly be accidental. It does not seem to be intended to suggest the crowd's stupidity. It rather finalizes in a breathtaking way the claim that the whole pericope has been driving home: Jerusalem's king, the authentic bearer of David's name, the fulfiller of all those dreams of restoration, the One coming in God's name to impart God's blessing, is this real historical figure, this Jesus who is entering the city to die.

CHAPTER 16

CONTEXT AS A BEARER
OF MEANING IN MATTHEW*

From form criticism, with its attention to the *Sitz im Leben* that shapes every tradition, through redaction criticism, right down to the latest suggestions on narrative plot, social setting and audience, one constant in the search for more adequate interpretation of New Testament texts has been the recognition of the role of context in determining meaning—including the meanings intended by those who shape the text and the meanings perceived by those who receive it and are shaped by it. Instead of trying, in these few pages, even to delineate the broad range of hermeneutical issues context generates, much less give an accounting of their present status, I propose simply to make a few observations about two texts in the Gospel of Matthew. These are, after all, the primary givens with which we have to work in any case; and this may be a way of keeping our feet on the ground. Yet I have chosen two texts rather than one in order to point beyond both to what I understand to be a characteristic dimension of this gospel.

Matthew 13:44–46

The first text is Matt 13:44–46, the twin parables of the Hidden Treasure and of the Pearl. Matthew begins his parable chapter with three sections closely parallel to Mark: the parable of the Sower (vv. 1–9), the reason for speaking in parables (vv. 10–17), and the interpretation of the parable of the Sower (vv. 18–23). The second of these sections is elaborated in a conspicuously Matthean way, and concludes with the Q saying that Luke uses at the end of the mission of the seventy (cf. Luke 10:23–24):

> But blessed are your eyes, for they see, and your ears, for they hear. Truly, I tell you, many prophets and righteous people longed to see what you see, but did not see it, and to hear what you hear, but did not hear it. (Matt 13:16–17 NRSV)

To this beginning, Matthew attaches six parables, in two groups of three. The first group opens with the parable of the Tares and adds the pair of the Mustard

---

*This essay first appeared in *USQR* 42 (1988): 69–72. It is reprinted here with minor revisions, and used by permission.

Seed and the Leaven. It is addressed publicly to the crowds, closing with a preliminary summary that takes Mark's final conclusion to all the parables and reinforces it with a formula quotation from Ps 78:2:

> I will open my mouth in parables;
> I will utter what has been hidden since the foundation of the world.
>
> (Matt 13:35 RSV)

But then the parable discourse resumes with a second group of three, this time spoken in the house to the inner circle of the disciples. The second section opens with the interpretation of the parable of the Tares, then introduces a new pair (the twin parables of our text, the Hidden Treasure and the Pearl), and finally concludes with the parable of the Dragnet. Thus the parables of the Tares and the Dragnet form a third pair, embracing the other two; they function as the inclusio or bracket for the Matthean arrangement, the center of which is occupied by the interpretation of the parable of the Tares. Matthew's emphasis lies here, where the point is not simply the fate suffered by the message of the Kingdom in the past time of Jesus but its fate in Matthew's time.

Surely the central point of the parables of the Hidden Treasure and the Pearl is connected in some way with the respective actions of the plowman in the field and the traveling merchant. When they are read by themselves, they seem to lead to an interpretation that lays all the stress on commitment, the willingness of each actor to venture all his resources, indeed to give up everything for the sake of the one ultimate value. Indeed, the common words shared by these two parables are "he goes [went] and sells [sold] all that he has [had] and buys [bought]." But what does that tell the reader about the *Kingdom?* The parable may describe a virtue that is perhaps an appropriate response to the Kingdom, but if one asks what it is about the Kingdom that calls for such a response one gets only the answer that by implication the kingdom of God is more to be desired than all else one has. That involves no disclosure about the Kingdom. The bankruptcy of this line of interpretation appears when one commentator gives these two parables the heading: "The Necessity of Economic Self-Deprivation to True Membership in the Kingdom" and sees no connection with the Matthean context; both were composed on this view by Matthew, and the common language about "selling all one has" "comes from the story of the rich young ruler."[1]

But what if these artfully positioned parables are *not* read by themselves? They are peculiar to Matthew (we set aside here the *Gospel of Thomas*). Between the interpretation of the Tares and the parable of the Dragnet, both of which promise that "at the close of the age" the angels will remove all causes

---

1. Robert H. Gundry, *Matthew: A Commentary on His Literary and Theological Art* (Grand Rapids: Eerdmans, 1982), 275–76.

of sin and all evildoers, these two parables set before the reader two people whose behavior is strangely ambivalent. From the world's point of view, they act in curious ways, even strangely. The merchant, whose whole existence is oriented toward acquiring, now suddenly sells all he has. The plowman behaves oddly because suddenly he knows something nobody else does. The commentators agonize over the question whether the plowman acts legally or not; if the pairing of the two parables means anything, it is that this question is irrelevant. Instead, the actions of both become intelligible and natural as soon as one recognizes that they have been seized by a perception that is hidden from the world around them. They are prototypes of persons to whom "it has been given to know the secrets of the kingdom of heaven" (v. 11), the mystery of the presence of the Kingdom in *this* unredeemed world. They have come upon "what has been hidden since the foundation of the world" (v. 35 RSV). They have seen and heard what "many prophets and righteous people have longed to see and hear" but have not seen and heard (v. 17).

Incidentally, that provides a link with the other pair of parables in the first group, taken from Q: the Mustard Seed and the Leaven. In Matthew's context, the point cannot be merely the contrast between small beginnings and giant consequences but rather the hidden, yet all-pervasive and all-embracing, operation of the kingdom of God. The woman hid the leaven in the meal; the tiny mustard seeds were scattered out of sight in the field. The operation of the kingdom of God is not conspicuous or apparent. It is hidden from the eyes of this generation. To some it is given to see it; to others not. The distinction between insiders and outsiders is not merely presupposed but caused and reconfirmed by the presence of a Kingdom that does not meet the world's standards or expectations.

Matthew 25:31–46

The second text is Matt 25:31–46, the Last Judgment. Conventional treatments of this passage have been less than satisfactory for three reasons:

1. They generally pay no attention to its context: its careful placement at the climax of Matthew's fifth and final large block of discourse material, that is, at the *end* of Jesus' teaching and just before the start of the passion narrative. To ignore this placement is a major breach of simple exegetical and literary observation.
2. They generally focus on the Son of Man's replies in vv. 40 and 45, that is, the equation of the hungry, the thirsty, the stranger, the naked, the sick, and the prisoner with the Son of Man, without asking either about the grounds for this equation or its connection with the "least" and the "little ones" elsewhere in Matthew. The result is a sentimentalizing or glorification of the poor that remains utterly arbitrary.

3. They generally pass over in silence the clear element of surprise expressed on both sides, the right and the left, at the Son of Man's verdict, and so do the ultimate violence to his reply of making it a self-evident truth.

Reconsideration of context can go a long way toward remedying all three counts. In the movement of this figurative narrative teaching (it is not a parable), the Son of Man disburses blessing and curse in God's place. The blessing is distributed not to the poor but to those *who have taken the side of* the hungry, the thirsty, the sick, the naked, and the imprisoned. When he says, "As often as you did it for one of my least brothers, you did it for me,"[2] the Son of Man is the one who identifies *himself* with these least. That is why to have done or not done in either case to these is to have done or not done to the Son of Man. Finally, *all* those before him are surprised at the verdict, at discovering what they have done or not done, because they are surprised at this alignment and identification. No one expected *that* of the Son of Man.

One must be discriminating in identifying the "least" or the "little ones" elsewhere in Matthew. It is not clear that all disciples are "little ones" or vice versa. But it is clear (e.g., 18:10–14) that the disciples are told to be advocates and defenders of these "little ones" just as Jesus himself has been identified as the one sent to heal the blind, free the captives, and deliver the "lost sheep of the house of Israel." That is why this passage occupies a position at the end of Jesus' teaching that is the chiastic opposite to the Beatitudes at the start of the first discourse: God himself has taken the side of the "poor in spirit," of those who mourn, and of those who hunger and thirst for righteousness.

And so the passion narrative takes over, in which this advocate of the naked and thirsty and in prison will himself be stripped, and flogged, and thirsty. The ultimate apportionment of blessing and curse will be determined by how individuals relate to this unexpected Son of Man, from whom all the disciples flee. For to this one, when God becomes *his* advocate in the resurrection, is given all authority in heaven and on earth (28:18).

---

2. This is the New American Bible's translation, which is close to that of the Rheims New Testament of 1582. There is no reason for introducing into the translation the familiar second partitive genitive ("the least of these my brothers," as in KJV, ASV, RSV, JB) that seems to have originated with Tyndale in 1525.

CHAPTER 17

THE PARABLE OF RESPONSIBILITY: A SERMON*

Text: Matthew 25:14–30

I am sure it has happened to most of you. Not long ago, my wife and I were driving up an access ramp onto an interstate. Ahead of us, instead of accelerating, an older driver—trying only to be safe and responsible—slowed to a near stop, making both his own entry into the river of traffic and ours more hazardous. Responsibility—but tinged with fear; it was making him a menace. This is a parable to prepare us for our text, to which Eduard Schweizer gives the apt title "The Parable of Responsibility."

Its exegesis is no great mystery. To describe this responsibility before God, the parable has instinctively and naturally drawn from the world of the ancient Near East the imagery of a powerful and rich master who entrusts his property to his slaves before departing on a journey. What he does is remarkable: not a contract drawn up with equals, but a free and sovereign act of conferring responsibility and opportunity to function in his stead. That he gives each "according to his ability" is no limitation on his generosity; it shows that he knows his servants and respects their differences. They are still his slaves; what they earn will still belong to him. Yet here is a master who generously involves them in his own affairs and invites their best performance. He does not spell out what they are to do, or do their work for them. In the best sense, he is one who intends to reap where he has not himself sown and to gather where he has not scattered. The parallelism in the narrative between the first and second servants shows that the degrees of ability and gift are immaterial. The faithfulness of both is rewarded alike: with greater responsibility, and most of all with an invitation to share in the master's joy.

But of course the movement of the parable shows that its focus is not on this master or on these two servants, but on the third. It is his example that is developed and dwelt upon. Our instinctive reaction, to identify ourselves with the first two servants, is pure evasion. Every detail of the text points us to this third.

*Paul W. Meyer preached this sermon on November 29, 1984, in Miller Chapel on the campus of Princeton Theological Seminary. It was first published in *PSB* 6, no. 2, NS (1985): 131–34, and is used here by permission.

In the first place, his digging in the ground and hiding his master's money is neither stupid nor irresponsible. In the world of the text, this was the correct action to take to keep silver secure from risk, the best insurance against theft. A telling stipulation in early rabbinic law provides that whoever buries at once and without delay property entrusted to him will not be liable if it should be stolen. Furthermore, this servant is acutely aware that his master will return and call for an accounting. He intends to give back, safe and undamaged, what has been entrusted to him. No, he is *very* responsible.

Yet he is called a "wicked" servant. Why? The text is very clear in identifying fear as the ingredient that subverts his sense of accountability. Suddenly what has been turned over to him is made to serve not his master's interests but his own skin. It is fear that perceives his master's generous offer of opportunity as harsh treatment, his reaping where he has not sown as a brutal demand on others to do the producing. He is condemned as *oknēros,* not for his "sloth" (RSV), but for his scrupling hesitation, his shrinking inactivity. In the end, he is "worthless"—a responsible guardian of his deposit, but as a servant of his master's interests, he is a basket case.

The exegesis is no great mystery. What about its application? One cannot be long at Princeton Seminary without being overwhelmed by the strong sense of responsibility that informs this campus—responsibility toward the tradition, obligation to make the most of resources given here that are the envy of other schools, commitment to the church and its mission. But anyone who reads the New Testament knows that spiritual danger lurks not in our weaknesses but in our strengths. And there are troubling signs that such an immense sense of responsibility breeds at times the very fear that is able to undo it.

As an institution the Seminary spends a lot of money—other people's money—on every student admitted. It rightly feels that in its admissions decisions it is responsible for serving the well-being of the church. Should it invest some of its treasure in an applicant who does not fit the Presbyterian mold? Most of us recognize that the ability of this school to serve the church depends upon preserving a significant measure of confessional diversity. But I have heard it asked seriously, "If we make one exception, where can we draw the line?" The question clearly advertises the fear that prompts it, fear of an accounting, a fear that strikes at the very root of the Seminary's historic ecumenical mission for which it is accountable. What would happen if the faculty were to shrink from teaching its best insights out of fear that they might raise objection among the presbyteries? Would we not all at a stroke become wicked and useless servants—most of all to the Presbyterian church?

And students? Many of you have brought God's gift of treasure here with you, charged to cultivate here what has been given in God's calling, to enlarge your skills and invigorate and stretch your faith. The Seminary exists to help you do that. But you cannot do that without risking change, without asking questions. The very sense of responsibility that brought you here threatens to flip over into a fear of being called to account, the fear that to change will be deemed itself an act of faithlessness to God's gift. It is a sad experience to see students choosing courses that will not threaten them in any way, or dropping others that they perceive will. That is to bury your gift in the ground.

Take that most precious gift, the Bible. The powerful sense that we are charged with the responsibility of interpreting it to a world in pain seems to breed among us a fear of using just those critical tools that might help us most in carrying out that mission. It is sad to read student papers that use only devotional commentaries and shy away from the tough questions. Fear turns the opportunity for critical study into a brutal assignment. But the fear is misplaced. Critical studies cannot change the Bible itself, or God's relation to it. They can change only our perceptions and our understanding. But these are just what we need to be able to risk if we are to use the gift to serve the master's intent and not our own skins. Where we cannot admit serious questions about our understanding of scripture, where there is no risk, there can be no delight in discovery, no sharing in the joy of the master. To use historical scholarship only to confirm what we already know and believe is like having sex without the commitment and vulnerability that alone make it genuinely human—and it is just as immoral. It is to keep the gift of the Bible intact, but to return it unused, as wicked and useless servants.

The parable ends on a harsh note, but that is because the Matthean Christ loves those whom he calls enough to warn them of the dangers of discipleship. Mere fidelity is really *infidelity*. A faith concerned only with avoiding mistakes out of fear of being held accountable fails the basic test of responsible discipleship. But those who will not shy away from losing their lives for his sake will be invited to share in the master's joy. Behind that promise—and the warning—stands the One who did not please himself but took upon himself the reproaches of all our faithless fears.

CHAPTER 18

THE DOOR THAT CLOSES:
A SERMON*

Text: Luke 13:22–30

Some years ago CBS devoted one of its special broadcasts to an "Essay on Doors." In what was at once a lighthearted whimsy and a kind of reflective visual and audio prose poem, the commentator, followed by the moving television camera, sauntered from one kind of door to another, opening, closing, demonstrating, and talking about: the warmly lit and inviting front door of a home; a much more heavily used kitchen screen door, with its long spring and the unforgettable sound of its slamming shut; a revolving door, simultaneously inhaling and exhaling customers of some busy emporium; a mysterious closet door; a conversational Dutch door; a tricky pair of louvered swinging doors—and many more.

One could conduct a comparable tour of biblical doors, and find a similar variety of denotation and connotation. A few, just within the New Testament, are: the temple doors, in one place shading a crippled beggar who arrested the passing apostles, and in another slammed shut to keep out Paul and the supposed defilement of his non-Jewish companions on the sacred precincts; the visionary door through which the seer of Revelation is admitted to the throne of heaven and its surrounding worship; the figurative door of missionary opportunity opened for Paul in Ephesus; the door of death and decay, shut and opened by the rolling of a great stone; the prison doors, from which here an earthquake and there an angel set apostles free; the gates of Hades, signaling the domain of an alien and hostile power; the door to the sheepfold, serving to test whether the one who enters is a real shepherd or an impostor; Jesus himself, *the* door to salvation; or the door of the hearer's indifferent heart, upon which the words of Jesus are a knock—a persevering, a persisting, a pressing knock.

One of these words of Jesus, which supplies our text, has itself to do with a door. Not two doors, mark you, one leading to life and the other to death, but one door, which is eventually a *closed* door. The only question about that kind

---

*On November 29, 1978, Paul W. Meyer preached this sermon in Miller Chapel on the campus of Princeton Theological Seminary. It was first published in *PSB* 2, no. 2, NS (1979): 121–23, and is used here by permission.

of door is which side of it a person is on, for a closed door has only two sides: an inside and an outside.

There is nothing particularly unclear about the parable. Jesus is asked to respond to a standard religious question of his day: whether in the end only a few will turn out to be saved (Luke 13:23). His reply is to speak of salvation as a door that God opens and human beings must enter, a door that opens only from the inside. And it is a *narrow* door: it takes some struggle and effort to get in; one cannot simply stroll leisurely through it! If some do not enter, that is not because God is unwilling to admit them, but because they fail to meet the terms the door itself imposes, and the running themes of Jesus' teaching in the synoptic tradition make clear what that involves. Salvation cannot be taken for granted; it is not enough to say "We have Abraham as our father." The very presence of God's open door poses the demand for a response, for obedience and the pursuit of his righteousness!

Even more important: this door is not rusted open permanently. A time comes when the door is shut, when it is too late for even the most strenuous effort to gain access. The last verses vividly contrast what goes on inside and outside this *closed* door. Inside is light and joy; here the patriarchs and prophets, and people from every quarter of the world sit down at the messianic banquet in the kingdom of God. Outside there is darkness and despair. "Weeping and gnashing of teeth" in this context is hardly an expression of remorse and fear—but the grinding fury of frustration on the part of those who thought they had some right to get in. This fury is their punishment, for the kingdom of God always turns things inside out. "I do not know where you come from" (vv. 25, 27). The reality of God and his repudiation is far more shattering than any silence of God ever could be; it always upsets the calculations of those who believe they have some prescriptive right to God's favor. "Indeed, some are last who will be first, and some are first who will be last" (v. 30).

Of course it has always been possible for some Christian folk to remain untouched by the sight of this closed door, to make out that *they* are the ones inside and that those who stand outside are someone else: the Jews of Jesus' own day, or the Roman Catholics of the time of the Reformation, or someone else today. Luke shows a profounder dimension to his gospel, to his Christian faith, when he does not merely repeat the parable and let it go at that. Instead, he introduces into the frantic conversation that goes on through the closed door precisely the uniquely Christian version of this false security, the last-ditch appeal on the part of those who are outside to the historical presence of Jesus! "Then you will begin to say, 'We ate and drank in your presence, and you taught in our streets'" (v. 26). "Come on, Lord! We still sit at our communion tables with you. We have more than heard, we have studied and learned the teachings you gave while you lived on this earth of ours. Doesn't that count for anything?!" "I do not know where you come from; go away from me, all you evildoers" (v. 27). By itself, an appeal to Jesus is in no respect different from an appeal to Abraham—and it does not matter under what theological banner the appeal is made.

This is a frightening door, this closed door, a profoundly unsettling door. One can leaf through the whole Gospel of Luke, through the whole New Testament, searching for some detour around it, some last hinged panel in this door to squeeze through, to relieve the finality of it. And there is none. Why is that? Because religious *insecurity* is as much a part of the authentic knowledge of God as religious certainty; "not having" is as crucial as "having"; the outside of the door is as important as the inside. If we dispense with the one, the other is gone as well, no matter how much we protest to the contrary. And why should that be so? Because in the New Testament all these things we prize: salvation, security, possession, joy, freedom, love, peace, realization—all are given in the form of *insecurity,* always proffered in a way that keeps them on God's terms and not on ours, always in a form that probes and challenges and unsettles. The love of God in Christ, from which, of course, neither death nor life, nor height nor depth can separate us, is either the burning love of Paul's righteous God who meets us on his own terms rather than on ours—on a cross—or else it is a pious illusion. "On God's own terms"—that is the meaning, in the New Testament, of God's transcendence, and it is utterly pointless to talk of Jesus of Nazareth without it. God's transcendence has very little to do with how much supernaturalism one may or may not be able to display in one's theology; no, it has to do rather with the difference between God's ways and ours. The gospel is always given in the form of our insecurity before God, always with a door slamming on our expectations and claims, for it is only God's terms that make it authentic and sure.

That is, finally, the real reason why authentic religious possession terminates in the prayer and worship for which we are assembled here. Not because in this chapel some inner life must be juxtaposed to the outer life of our studies (if your studies engage you only outwardly, how tiresome and dull they must be!). Why prayer? Because authentic religious security is found only in the God whom we cannot control, before whom we must remain ourselves insecure, ourselves always the petitioners. Real prayer is always prayer to the God of a door that *closes* and has an outside as well as an inside. And why worship? Because worship is fundamentally nothing else than this: once again to recognize and to acknowledge God's terms in place of our own. That is all—and yet that is everything! "Indeed, some are last who will be first, and some are first who will be last."

CHAPTER 19

MARK 14:1–11: A SERMON*

"I tell you this: wherever in all the world the Gospel is proclaimed, what she has done will be told as her memorial." (Mark 14:9 NEB)

Can we really take that verse seriously? In all the parade of biblical *dramatis personae*, among all those who became disciples in the New Testament, or all those who were healed, or all those who were forgiven, above all those who are remembered for praise or blame, all those whose names have become part of the church's recollection (like even Simon the leper, who is the host in this scene)—above all these, this nameless woman is singled out by a unique distinction: the story of her act is to go wherever the gospel goes!

To whom else does such a dignity belong? Certainly not to very many people! One may compare that famous person whose name has stuck in the Apostles' Creed, who has been singled out to serve as the historical mooring for Christian confession: ". . . suffered under Pontius Pilate." Yet his distinction pales before the honor accorded to this woman, whose act is linked not simply with the dating but with the preaching of the gospel. Or compare John the Baptist; the earliest preachers spoke of him as the starting point of the gospel, the one with whom the whole gospel began. Never has there appeared on earth a mother's son greater than he. Yet, since the least in the kingdom of heaven is greater than he, he must be kept in his proper place. His destiny is to decrease in order that one coming after him might increase. Or one may be reminded of another woman, as it happens far more celebrated in Christian history, who is distinguished in the gospels as having found favor with God when visited by the angel Gabriel. Yet her distinction lies only in her having received from God. There was some danger that that would be forgotten too. When, later in the Gospel of Luke, a woman in the crowd around Jesus raises her voice to cry out, "Blessed is the womb that bore you, and the breasts that nursed you," the hysteria of misplaced devotion is silenced with Jesus' reply: "Blessed rather are

---

*In a shorter form, Paul W. Meyer preached this sermon in Marquand Chapel at Yale Divinity School on March 12, 1963.

those who hear the word of God and obey it!" (11:27–28). It is almost as if Mary too must decrease, in order that the gospel might be kept in the center of the stage. But not so here: "I tell you this: wherever in all the world the Gospel is proclaimed, what she has done will be told as her memorial." A singular dignity, indeed!

How does she come by such an honor? Who bestows such dignity on this woman? On the face of the text, of course, it is Jesus who makes this promise. One doesn't ordinarily in a sermon make a point of this, but this is not an ordinary verse. There is scarcely a saying in all the gospels that is less likely to have been spoken by the historical Jesus than this one. It is one of the most obvious editorial disturbances in the Markan passion narrative that this anointing story has been given a place here at all. And the story of the anointing in itself reaches its climax and point quite well in Jesus' defense of the woman in the face of her critics without this tacked-on verse. It is not Jesus of Nazareth who speaks in this one verse, but the Markan missionary church, which lives and breathes in terms of proclaiming the gospel throughout the wide world.

What difference does that make? What does such an insight lend to our text? Part of the unique distinction accorded to this unnamed woman consists in just this: the honor itself comes out of the early church's mission. Readers of the gospel are transported out of the house of Simon the leper and across the centuries of Christian history—yet they are never to lose sight of this monument erected. They are never to be out of earshot of the telling of what this woman has done. It is not just that the woman found in Jesus her sufficient defender (of that there was no doubt!), but that Jesus' defense on her behalf has found echoing assent in the church, and her act has become part of the church's missionary gospel. In the end it scarcely matters whether the recognition given her is child or parent of the promise of our text. Has any comparable tribute ever been paid to Pontius Pilate, or to John the Baptist, or even to the venerated mother of Jesus?

But why such an honor and tribute? Is there any justification for this singular distinction? After all, we might well ask how Mark could justify giving her such preferential treatment. Wouldn't he have been better advised to nip it in the bud as drastically as Luke did in the case of the mother of Jesus? The later church in some respects has simply ignored Luke's warning about Mary and idolized her anyway. Should we repeat the error in the case of this woman? Why not simply ignore this text of Mark? What kind of a deed, by *any* human being other than Jesus himself, deserves or needs to be told like this: "Wherever in all the world the Gospel is proclaimed. . . ."

The woman's act was, of course, one of reckless generosity, and Jesus defends it against the objections of a recognizably conventional piety: "Why this waste? It could have been sold and given to the poor!" (Mark 14:4–5). Let us note, in passing, that this is an objection of perfectly righteous indignation;

in Mark there is no hint whatsoever of the editorial assignment of this protest to Judas, or of his motives, as in the Fourth Gospel (John 12:4–6). The terms of Jesus' defense are a little disturbing to us: "For you always have the poor with you, and you can show kindness to them whenever you wish . . ." (Mark 14:7). But since he goes on to say "you will not always have me" (v. 7), we are in the end willing to see it as an act of devotion to *him*, and so to side with the woman against those who thought such precious ointment wasted. It *was* a beautiful act. But why accord it such distinction? Has history not recorded many sacrifices to surpass this one?

Is it because she thought that she was anointing the Messiah? Under the circumstances, that was another kind of recklessness even worse than the waste of money. In a tense political situation, to enact an anointing that could recall Samuel's anointing of David, or Jehu's being anointed king of Israel in the middle of a meal, was a foolish way to tip the whole business of Jesus' presence in the vicinity of Jerusalem into the realm of political subversion and so to bring down upon him the police power of the state. With friends like that, who needs an enemy? Is that why those who tell the gospel remember this woman? They have remembered Judas for that!

Or should her act be rendered deathless because it is a touching deed of pity, not unlike Michelangelo's *Pietà?* The common pauper in Jerusalem could count on receiving burial in the name of philanthropy. But Jesus himself, poorer than these poor, was to receive no proper preparation for *his* grave. Should we be surprised if pious Christian imagination lovingly finds this lack made good in Jesus' defense of her act? She at least accomplished more to fill this lack than the good intentions of those other women who were interrupted as they bore their spices to the tomb on Easter morning (16:1–2). She *spent* her ointment. But should she be remembered for that? Were not those other women far more blessed in that their spices were suddenly superfluous?

"I tell you this: wherever in all the world the Gospel is proclaimed, what she has done will be told as her memorial." The pondering reader of the gospel will be satisfied with none of these explanations. Yet the woman does not need our defense; Jesus' alone suffices. But perhaps we should understand why the early church connected her act with the gospel if we could take Jesus' defense of her seriously. For her act documents for every age the fact that the anointing of the true Messiah is an anointing for *burial*. This distinguishes not her but him! It divides him from every false Messiah. And so, wherever the gospel is preached, throughout the world, the telling of her act marks the authentic gospel.

The various writers of the New Testament are astonishingly free with the gospel. They write for different audiences, in different crises, with different problems. The world was full of change already in the first century. So it really is something striking and unique when Mark goes out on a limb like this to say that wherever the gospel is preached, this story will be told. This king of Israel was anointed in a unique way—for *burial*. If that is forgotten, if that story is not remembered, the gospel will not remain the gospel for long, but will be forgotten or absorbed into something else.

Underneath the surface, of course, it is not the remembering of the story that makes the difference, but this fundamental point of which it is the expression. Jesus is not a conventional king. Of course he wasn't just a political Messiah. But the religious loyalty he calls forth from us is not just conventional religious piety either. Conventional religion always uses God to buttress and justify human values, the priorities of the status quo, what society already has or wants or needs. But a king whose anointing is an anointing for burial, whose coronation is an embalmment, is a king whose values conflicted with the status quo. Those who belong to his kingdom ought to be of an order different from the usual collection of hangers-on, the sycophants who surround any powerful political figure.

Just how they are different this particular text doesn't spell out. Working out the answer to that question is part of the search for a distinctively Christian life that engages all of us in a time of changing values. It has to have different answers where each one of us lives. And perhaps we ought not be as afraid, as we often seem to be, to consider that the answer for us here in an academic community, where our present responsibilities lie to the church and before God, may not be exactly the same as in a congregation. But this search had better sometimes make us raise questions about the world around us, wherever we are.

Let us, however, come back to our story and our text. Something about Jesus cannot be forgotten as long as the gospel is preached; something about the *kind* of "king" he is will always be remembered where his kingship is really celebrated. His anointing is an anointing for burial. That seemed like an awful waste then, and it seems like a waste today. Christianity would be a lot simpler if we could simply put charity to the poor in its place and live with that. But then life really would have become no different for us because of Jesus' coming. It is almost as if there is a gospel, good news about something new and different, only when and if we are prepared to accept how unconventional the New Testament is, only when we remember that the society of his time could not tolerate Jesus, only when and if his story makes us try new thoughts, new actions, new values—only when and if he really sets us free.

One final point: the line of reflection we have been following might suggest that any unconventional act, any defiance of the establishment (including the church), is by its very nature an act of Christian obedience, that it is by virtue of his own scorn for the status quo that Jesus of Nazareth is honored as our "king"—and that any story that results in new actions on our part and liberates us from the values of our society is indeed the gospel. This would be the final perversion of our story, the subtlest way of turning it on its head and violating the text.

The remarkable distinction accorded to this nameless woman is the *most* remarkable in that it does not confuse her seemingly wasteful act, her defiance of even righteous indignation, or her personal devotion with the gospel itself. The story is to accompany the gospel, not replace it. To put her, and by implication Jesus himself, upon a pedestal of nonconformity would be but a modern, more political version of the same romanticism that is awed by the beauty of her selfless act. As we have seen, that is not the point of Jesus' defense of her. She did not change the world; she only "did what she could." And in an important sense, his death shows that he did not change the world either. But the woman's act, anointing the true Messiah for burial, distinguishes not her but *him*, dividing him from every form of Promethean religion, no matter how attractive it might appear in a revolutionary world—for that kind of religion is itself not yet free. As Mark makes clear elsewhere, the ultimate test of discipleship is whether we can follow such a king, find his glory in his defeat, and so be really free to live as he did in this real world. In the end, this king does not lead us out of our world into another; instead, he has pursued us into the depths of this world. That is how he *remains* king. A Messiah who can be anointed only in being anointed for *burial* is alone your Messiah and mine.

CHAPTER 20

MATTHEW 27:38–44: A SERMON[*]

"He saved others; he cannot save himself." (Matt 27:42)

One can respond to this account of the mockery of Jesus in quite different ways. A late Victorian-era commentator remarks that a brutality that hurls such taunts at one suffering the agonies of crucifixion may seem incredible to us. Asking why, he answers that we think differently, "thanks to the civilizing influence of the Christian faith, which has made the whole details of the Passion history so revolting to the Christian heart."[1] But that was written before two world wars, Buchenwald, Hiroshima, and My Lai.

Or we can take a second look at the scoffers in our text and in the whole of Christian history. Why? Because they are the ones—not we—who have had the courage to give voice to the troubled doubts, the defiant objections, that move in every Christian breast, and because they could not scoff if they were not in the vicinity of the truth that lesser people avoid. Why is it, after all, that from beneath the cross no words are preserved from disciples, whether men or women, but only from scoffers? There may be something inevitable in the presence of these scoffers beneath the cross, something that may open our eyes if we heed their words aright.

"He saved others; he cannot save himself." The words "heal," "help," "make whole," and "save" are but one and the same word in the Hebrew and Greek of the Bible. The recognition that "he saved others" therefore clearly recalls to the reader of the gospel that long train of mighty and merciful acts throughout Jesus' ministry by which blind persons had come to see, crippled persons to walk, lepers to be restored to the ranks of the clean, deaf to hear, dead people to live, faithless ones to trust. Back then, these were the acts in which God's power had made itself felt with the advent of the kingdom of God. From our

---

[*]Paul W. Meyer preached this sermon on Good Friday (April 4, 1977) in Benton Chapel at the Vanderbilt University Divinity School.

1. Alexander B. Bruce, *The Synoptic Gospels*, vol. 1 of *The Expositor's Greek Testament*, ed. W. Robertson Nicoll (New York: Doran, 1897), 329–30.

perspective now, these acts trouble us theologically, not so much because we wonder whether they actually happened, but because even if they did, the Jesus who acts in them is *not human enough* for us, and because, in our very orthodox moments, we are inclined to feel that the reports about them are really, after all, a bit too docetic, or at least a bit too idealistic. At any rate, even if we have to call upon psychotherapeutic explanations of these acts of power in order to make this saving Jesus fully human again, the claim and the memory stand: "He saved others."

"He cannot save himself." This taunt forces upon the reader of the gospel the present reality of the cross, a sight in which all the power now is in the hands of others, and the power of God is conspicuous by its seeming absence. Back then, this was the act in which men of violence had taken the kingdom of God by violence. From our perspective now, this is an act that troubles us, theologically, not because we can't quite make out what legal precedents were broken or who was primarily responsible, but because this Jesus is *too human*, too barrenly exposed to the kind of cruelty and violence we like to tell ourselves we are free from, though it is an all too familiar part of our world—and because in our very orthodox moments we are inclined to feel that the reports are really, after all, a bit too Ebionite, or at least a bit lacking in a decent measure of idealism. But all the same, even if we have to appeal to Socrates or others who have died with visible nobility in order to soften the stark humanity of this death, the claim and the memory stand: "He cannot save himself."

"He saved others; he cannot save himself." As these scoffers look upon the cross and utter these words, the echo is an unbearably sharp formulation of a contradiction we can feel running right through the whole of the gospel material. As such, it is a compressed statement of the supreme irony of Christian faith. The words "he saved others" have to do finally not with some remote past in Jesus' ministry but with what is happening before their very eyes. Had he been able to save himself, he would have saved no one; to save others, he must be unable to save himself. The conclusion is not distant that he cannot be held there by their nails unless he is being held first by God's will to save them! The very mockers were those whom he was dying to save. Here the contradictory threads of power and powerlessness, of mighty deed and hunted weakness, that run through the gospels, are joined in an act that strains both to their very limit. Our orthodox objections that the portrait is too human or not human enough are simply of no avail; they cannot be applied, and we are faced with the possibility that this act itself provides the measure of what is both truly human and truly divine. "He saved others; he cannot save himself."

But let us not be too quick to take the taunt out of these words. Matthew's intent is clearly that we should not, for he has expanded and enlarged the incident of the mocking of Jesus with great care, making this (with the help of yet other verses in other places) the dominant theme in his narrative of the crucifixion. Is this to emphasize human cruelty? The details by which the evangelist has enlarged the scene show that this is not his aim, and that, instead, at least three other trains of thought meet in his mind.

One is the depth of the derision and the complicity of all in it. Before this Christ, all are involved: priests and criminals, Romans and Jews, leaders of the people and a people led. The incident, as a matter of fact, opens with the note that two robbers were crucified with him, one on the right and one on the left; it ends as these same robbers join in the invective. The disciples have long since fled. Those who most profoundly share his lot, or rather whose lot he has taken it upon himself to share, in the moment of their identity with him take rather the side of his opponents. There is a massive unanimity here in which *all* are involved.

Second, there are the lines that join this episode at the end of the gospel with the narrative of the temptation at the beginning. The devil's challenge, "If you are the Son of God, throw yourself down" (Matt 4:6), anticipates the taunt at the crucifixion, "If you are the Son of God, come down from the cross" (27:40; cf. v. 42). What the people demand here, Satan demanded there, and both times it was precisely the one thing that would have canceled Jesus' mission. The irony is that those for whose sake he had refused Satan's proposal that he cast himself down from the pinnacle of the temple now demand from him that very thing—a proof of his messianic credentials. His credentials, however, are of another sort. As the tempted was once victorious over the tempter, so the one mocked in his dying is to be the victor in his death on behalf of those who mock him. Yet how much is in the balance! As once the tempter, perceiving his true identity and mission, sought to distort it into the satanical and so to divert him, so here his own people, unknowingly perceiving his deepest truth, his obedience, his resolve *not* to tempt the Lord his God, seek to turn that against him.

In the third place, there are the lines that join this episode with the Hebrew scriptures. These scribes revile by using the sacred words of Holy Writ with which they have been entrusted. "Save yourself"—that is a derisive echo of the refrain that runs throughout the Psalter: "Deliver me, O my God!" By quoting Ps 22 against this Christ, they fulfill what Ps 22 had to say about the abuse suffered by God's righteous one, and thereby become witnesses to the very truth they are engaged in mocking. By thus confirming by what they do the truth that in their words they deny, they mock—but they mock themselves! And in the words they quote from this psalm—"He trusts in God; let God deliver him now, if he delights in him" (Matt 27:43, my translation; cf. Ps 22:5, 8)—their mockery achieves its height, for here they zero in precisely and unerringly on that which had been the very center of this servant's life and work: his trust and his obedience to God. So, as they mock, they disclose themselves as enemies of God and yet as witnesses to his truth, for the very psalm they quote to mock him provides his lips with their dying prayer: "My God, my God, why have you forsaken me?" (Matt 27:46, quoting Ps 22:1).[2]

In all these strains, the taunt and the derision are heightened; they are not to be removed from this episode! "He saved others; he cannot save himself."

"He *saved* others"? Should it not rather be "He *condemned*, or damned, others"? No, for they stand condemned by their words only because what they mock in him is for their salvation. But why must it be this way? Why is it that he saved others only by becoming unable to save himself? Why should this cross elicit such mockery?

Beneath all three of these lines of thought, behind the mockery itself, is a fundamental repudiation of the heart and center of Christian faith. And why not? What does the crucifixion mean but the basic refutation to every aspect of Christian recourse to Jesus of Nazareth? How can this one be the king of Israel? How can this one be the Son of God? How can this one save? "Let him come down now from the cross" (Matt 27:42) and *then* we will believe in this Christ! Then we will commit ourselves to live by his teaching and example. Then we will be able to answer the question of Feuerbach as to whether there is a reality behind our religious references, or whether they are but the projections of our own proclivities. Then we will be able to make Christ the norm by which to shape our common life, our ecclesial community. Then we will be able to take him as a model for the correct joining of our faith and our praxis. Then we will agree to derive the agenda of our mission from him rather than from the world.

These objections are no less and no more than the words, conscious or unwitting, of every Christian generation. But the evangelist presents them to us as ridicule, as a scoffing jeer, as a taunt, as mockery. Why? Why, indeed, do human beings mock? Because they sense the presence of a truth they have not created, a truth that threatens to unhinge them. Because all their securities are on the line, and they are engaged in a desperate attempt to recover their control and their presumed superiority. Who is the King? Who is the true emissary of God? Where is God's power to save? In this mockery, it is the securities of all human ways of talking about God and about salvation that are on the line.

Is Matthew recalling an actual mockery? There are no good grounds for denying that public derision was a regular part of crucifixion; indeed, we know that Rome adopted this oriental form of capital punishment not merely for its cruelty but also for the public exposure, the notoriety of outrage it poured upon those who had offended her order. Only, in the case of this man, Matthew indicates that it is offense against religious order that is the key. And by weaving

---

2. For these descriptions of the irony in Matthew's text, verging on sarcasm, I am indebted to the probing reflections of Ernst Lohmeyer in his *Das Evangelium des Matthäus: Nachgelassene Ausarbeitungen und Entwürfe zur Übersetzung und Erklärung*, ed. Werner Schmauch (Göttingen: Vandenhoeck & Ruprecht, 1956), 390–93.

into the mockery itself the themes we have identified—or rather, by carefully expanding upon them, for Matthew was not the first Christian to interpret in this way—he has made it clear that he views this whole intricate web of religious derision from the other side of Easter. What the resurrection means is that God has indeed identified himself with this servant who was delivered up to death, has taken pleasure and delight in his steadfast consistency to his own teaching about God's reign. It means that this crucified man belongs to God; the mockery is not hollow but, in all its human perversion, a witness to the truth. But it remains *God's* truth, a truth that exposes to outrageous affront not Jesus but the preconceptions, the conventions, the projections, the desperate moves for security, of *religious* human beings—a truth that affirms itself, when it does finally cross human lips, not in the piety of the faithful but in the derision of the scoffers. There is no more concentrated summary of what is going on in this text than the words of Paul: "For since, in the wisdom of God, the world did not know God through wisdom, God decided, through the foolishness of our proclamation, to save those who believe" (1 Cor 1:21).

My Christian friends, we arrive today at the climax of Lent, of our annual contemplation of the cross. If it is all simply wiped out by Easter, there is of course no point to such observance. Other religious communities celebrate their new years, commemorate the births of founders, clothe with religious solemnities the high and low points in the cycles of human life, both individual and corporate. And we do all these things too. But only Christians have a Good Friday—only they recall a public historical event that once made, and still makes, a mockery of their most central claim—and keep returning to it as their most central and certain truth. That cross, perceived never but dimly, and always against our natural inclinations, has been the mark of Christian identity from the beginning. Indeed, it *is* the beginning!

Make no mistake: the cross is not a symbol-set that we are free to leave or take from the much vaunted richness of our tradition as the mood may suit us. And God's authenticating signature is not to be found in every inversion of religious values, every violation of religious convention, every bold or even imaginative redefinition of God's salvation, every provocative and intriguing anacoluthon in the syntax of human piety, not even in every Christian use of the cross! The signature of God's truth does not emerge from a phenomenological analysis of human religious community or of the processes of moral decision making. It does not emerge from luxuriating in self-mockery and doubt and despair. It is not given by the zeal with which we seize the banners of liberation. It does not issue from our tracing of the vicissitudes of Christian history, or the profundities of the church's great theologians and philosophers. It does not emanate from our concentrated study of the words of scripture in their Hebrew and their Greek. If it came to us in any of these ways, it would not be God's but only our own.

No, God's signature is not an idea, or an insight, or a zeal, or a decision, or a process—of ours. It is the cross on Golgotha, outside the wall of Jerusalem, the public and ineradicable event we recall on Good Friday. Why? The apostle Paul perceived the reason perhaps most clearly, though he did not create it. He was only giving voice to the tradition that had laid hold of him when he spelled out that reason: true salvation, authentic faith, the right knowledge of God, sure participation in the common life of God's people, secure confidence to face the future—all of these can come only on God's terms, not on ours. That is what the transcendence of God means throughout the New Testament, and throughout the Old as well. For us its empowering signature is located in that public event we have not ourselves created, but which is given to us in our history, which created our history, and in which we are confronted—where no recourse of evasion is possible—by God's terms and not our own: in the cross.

BIBLIOGRAPHY

Achtemeier, Paul J. "Apropos the Faith of/in Christ: A Response to Hays and Dunn." Pages 82–92 in *Pauline Theology, Volume IV*. Edited by E. Elizabeth Johnson and David M. Hay. Atlanta: Scholars Press, 1997.

———. *Romans*. IBC. Atlanta: John Knox, 1985.

Anz, W. "Zur Exegese von Römer 7 bei Bultmann, Luther, Augustin." Pages 1–15 in *Theologia crucis–signum crucis: Festschrift für Erich Dinkler zum 70. Geburtstag*. Edited by Carl Andresen and Günter Klein. Tübingen: Mohr (Siebeck), 1979.

Ashton, John. *Understanding the Fourth Gospel*. Oxford: Clarendon, 1991.

———, ed. *The Interpretation of John*. IRT 9. Philadelphia: Fortress; London: SPCK, 1986.

Augustine. *Augustine: Earlier Writings*. Translated and edited by John H. S. Burleigh. LCC 6. Philadelphia: Westminster, 1953.

———. *Augustine: Later Works*. Translated and edited by John Burnaby. LCC 8. Philadelphia: Westminster, 1955.

Barrett, C. K. *A Commentary on the Epistle to the Romans*. New York: Harper & Row, 1957.

———. *Essays on John*. Philadelphia: Westminster, 1982.

———. *The Gospel according to St. John*. 2d ed. Philadelphia: Westminster, 1978.

Bassler, Jouette M. *Divine Impartiality: Paul and a Theological Axiom*. SBLDS 59. Chico, Calif.: Scholars Press, 1982.

———, ed. *Pauline Theology, Volume I: Thessalonians, Philippians, Galatians, Philemon*. Minneapolis: Fortress, 1991.

Bauer, Walter. *Das Johannesevangelium*. HNT 6. 3d ed. Tübingen: Mohr (Siebeck), 1933.

Beker, J. Christiaan. *Paul the Apostle: The Triumph of God in Life and Thought*. Philadelphia: Fortress, 1980.

Bernard, J. H. *A Critical and Exegetical Commentary on the Gospel according to John*. Edited by A. H. McNeile. 2 vols. ICC. New York: Charles Scribner's Sons, 1929.

Borgen, Peder. "God's Agent in the Fourth Gospel." Pages 67–78 in *The Inter-pretation of John*. Edited by John Ashton. IRT 9. Philadelphia: Fortress; London: SPCK, 1986.

Bornkamm, Günther. "Baptism and New Life in Paul." Pages 71–86 in *Early Christian Experience*. New York: Harper & Row, 1969.

———. *Early Christian Experience*. New York: Harper & Row, 1969.

———. *Paul*. New York: Harper & Row, 1971.

———. "Der Römerbrief als Testament des Paulus." Pages 120–39 in *Geschichte und Glaube*, vol. 2. Munich: Kaiser, 1971.

Braaten, Carl E., and Roy A. Harrisville, eds. *The Historical Jesus and the Kerygmatic Christ: Essays on the New Quest of the Historical Jesus*. New York: Abingdon, 1964.

Breytenbach, Cilliers, and Henning Paulsen, eds. *Anfänge der Christologie: Festschrift für Ferdinand Hahn zum 65. Geburtstag*. Göttingen: Vanden-hoeck & Ruprecht, 1991.

Brown, Peter. *Augustine of Hippo: A Biography*. Berkeley, Calif.: University of California Press, 1967.

Brown, Raymond E. *The Gospel according to John: Introduction, Translation, and Notes*. 2 vols. AB 29–29A. Garden City, N.Y.: Doubleday, 1966–70.

Bühner, Jan-A. *Der Gesandte und sein Weg im 4. Evangelium: Die kultur- und religionsgeschichtlichen Grundlagen der johanneischen Sendungschristolo-gie sowie ihre traditionsgeschichtliche Entwicklung*. WUNT 2/2. Tübingen: Mohr (Siebeck), 1977.

Bultmann, Rudolf. *Das Evangelium des Johannes*. 11th ed. MeyerK. Göttingen: Vandenhoeck & Ruprecht, 1950. ET: *The Gospel of John: A Commentary*. Translated by G. R. Beasley-Murray et al. Oxford: Basil Blackwell, 1971.

———. *Exegetica: Aufsätze zur Erforschung des Neuen Testaments*. Edited by Erich Dinkler. Tübingen: Mohr (Siebeck), 1967.

———. *Existence and Faith: Shorter Writings of Rudolf Bultmann*. Translated and edited by Schubert M. Ogden. New York: Meridian Books, 1960.

———. *Faith and Understanding*. Edited by Robert W. Funk and translated by Louise Pettibone Smith. New York: Harper & Row, 1969.

———. *Die Geschichte der synoptischen Tradition*. 2d ed. Göttingen: Van-denhoeck & Ruprecht, 1931. ET: *History of the Synoptic Tradition*. Trans-lated by John Marsh. New York: Harper & Row, 1963; rev. ed. 1976.

———. "Is Exegesis Without Presuppositions Possible?" Pages 289–96 in *Existence and Faith: Shorter Writings of Rudolf Bultmann*. Translated and edited by Schubert M. Ogden. New York: Meridian Books, 1960.

———. "The Primitive Christian Kerygma and the Historical Jesus." Pages 15–42 in *The Historical Jesus and the Kerygmatic Christ: Essays on the New Quest of the Historical Jesus*. Translated and edited by Carl E. Braaten and Roy A. Harrisville. New York: Abingdon, 1964.

————. "Romans 7 and the Anthropology of Paul." Pages 147–57 in *Existence and Faith: Shorter Writings of Rudolf Bultmann*. New York: Meridian Books, 1960. Translated from "Römer 7 und die Anthropologie des Paulus." In *Exegetica: Aufsätze zur Erforschung des Neuen Testaments*. Edited by Erich Dinkler. Tübingen: Mohr (Siebeck), 1967 (orig. 1932).

————. *Theology of the New Testament*. Translated by Kendrick Grobel. 2 vols. New York: Charles Scribner's Sons, 1951–55.

————. *Das Verhältnis der urchristlichen Christusbotschaft zum historischen Jesus*. SHAW 60/3. 2d ed. Heidelberg: Carl Winter Universitätsverlag, 1965. ET from the 3d German edition: "The Primitive Christian Kerygma and the Historical Jesus." Pages 15–42 in *The Historical Jesus and the Kerygmatic Christ: Essays on the New Quest of the Historical Jesus*. Translated and edited by Carl E. Braaten and Roy A. Harrisville. New York: Abingdon, 1964.

Byrne, Brendan. *Romans*. SP 6. Collegeville, Minn.: Liturgical Press, 1996.

Carroll, John T., Charles H. Cosgrove, and E. Elizabeth Johnson, eds. *Faith and History: Essays in Honor of Paul W. Meyer*. Homage Series. Atlanta: Scholars Press, 1990.

Chadwick, Henry, ed. and trans. *Lessing's Theological Writings*. Stanford, Calif.: Stanford University Press, 1957.

Conzelmann, Hans. *An Outline of the Theology of the New Testament*. Translated from the 2d German ed. by John W. Bowden. New York: Harper & Row, 1969.

————. "Zur Methode der Leben-Jesu-Forschung." *ZTK* 56 (1959), Supplemental Volume 1:2–13.

Cranfield, C. E. B. *A Critical and Exegetical Commentary on the Epistle to the Romans*. 2 vols. ICC. Edinburgh: T. & T. Clark, 1975–79.

————. "Some Notes on Romans 9:30–33." Pages 35–43 in *Jesus und Paulus: Festschrift für Werner Georg Kümmel zum 70. Geburtstag*. Edited by E. Earle Ellis and Erich Grässer. Göttingen: Vandenhoeck & Ruprecht, 1975.

Cullmann, Oscar. *The Christology of the New Testament*. Translated by Shirley C. Guthrie and Charles A. M. Hall. NTL. Philadelphia: Westminster, 1963.

Dahl, Nils Alstrup. *Jesus the Christ: The Historical Origins of Christological Doctrine*. Edited by Donald H. Juel. Minneapolis: Fortress, 1991.

————. "The Neglected Factor in New Testament Theology." Pages 153–63 in *Jesus the Christ: The Historical Origins of Christological Doctrine* by Nils Alstrup Dahl. Edited by Donald H. Juel. Minneapolis: Fortress, 1991.

————. *Studies in Paul*. Minneapolis: Augsburg, 1977.

Davies, W. D., and D. Daube, eds. *The Background of the New Testament and Its Eschatology* (in honor of C. H. Dodd). Cambridge: Cambridge University Press, 1956.

Davies, W. D., and Dale C. Allison, *A Critical and Exegetical Commentary on the Gospel according to Saint Matthew*. 3 vols. ICC. Edinburgh: T. & T. Clark, 1988–97.

de Boer, Martinus C. "Narrative Criticism, Historical Criticism, and the Gospel of John." *JSNT* 47 (1992): 35–48.

Dodd, C. H. *The Interpretation of the Fourth Gospel.* Cambridge: Cambridge University Press, 1953.

Donfried, K. P., ed. *The Romans Debate.* Minneapolis: Augsburg, 1977.

Dunn, James D. G. "Once More, ΠΙΣΤΙΣ ΧΡΙΣΤΟΥ." Pages 61–81 in *Pauline Theology, Volume IV.* Edited by E. Elizabeth Johnson and David M. Hay. Atlanta: Scholars Press, 1997.

————. *Romans.* 2 vols. WBC 38A–B. Dallas: Word, 1988.

Ehrman, Bart D. *The Orthodox Corruption of Scripture: The Effect of Early Christological Controversies on the Text of the New Testament.* New York: Oxford University Press, 1993.

Ellis, E. Earle, and Erich Grässer, ed. *Jesus und Paulus: Festschrift für Werner Georg Kümmel zum 70. Geburtstag.* Göttingen: Vandenhoeck & Ruprecht, 1975.

Farmer, William R., and Norman Perrin. "The Kerygmatic Theology and the Question of the Historical Jesus." *Religion in Life* 29 (1959–60): 86–97.

Farmer, William, et al., eds. *Christian History and Interpretation: Studies Presented to John Knox.* Cambridge: Cambridge University Press, 1967.

Fitzmyer, Joseph A. *Essays on the Semitic Background of the New Testament.* Missoula, Mont.: Scholars Press, 1974.

————. *Paul and His Theology: A Brief Sketch.* 2d ed. Englewood Cliffs, N.J.: Prentice-Hall, 1989.

————. *Romans: A New Translation with Introduction and Commentary.* AB 33. New York: Doubleday, 1993.

Flückiger, F. "Christus, des Gesetzes *telos.*" *TZ* 11 (1955): 153–57.

Fortna, Robert. *The Gospel of Signs: A Reconstruction of the Narrative Source Underlying the Fourth Gospel.* SNTSMS 11. Cambridge: Cambridge University Press, 1970.

Fortna, Robert T., and Beverly R. Gaventa, eds. *The Conversation Continues: Studies in Paul and John in Honor of J. Louis Martyn.* Nashville: Abingdon, 1990.

Friedrich, J., et al., eds. *Rechtfertigung: Festschrift für Ernst Käsemann zum 70. Geburtstag.* Tübingen: Mohr (Siebeck), 1976.

Fuchs, Ernst. "Die Frage nach dem historischen Jesus." *ZTK* 53 (1956): 210–29.

Furnish, Victor P. "The Jesus-Paul Debate: From Baur to Bultmann." *BJRL* 47 (1965): 342–81.

————. "On Putting Paul in His Place." *JBL* 113 (1994): 3–17.

————. "Paul the Theologian." Pages 19–34 in *The Conversation Continues: Studies in Paul and John in Honor of J. Louis Martyn.* Edited by Robert T. Fortna and Beverly R. Gaventa. Nashville: Abingdon, 1990.

Gaugler, Ernst. *Der Brief an die Römer.* 2 vols. Zurich: Zwingli-Verlag, 1945–52.

———. "Das Christuszeugnis des Johannesevangeliums." Pages 34–67 in *Jesus Christus im Zeugnis der heiligen Schrift und der Kirche.* 2d ed. BEvT 2. Munich: Kaiser, 1936.

Godsey, J. D. "The Interpretation of Romans in the History of the Christian Faith." *Int* 34 (1980): 3–16.

Haenchen, Ernst. "Faith and Miracle." Pages 495–98 in *Studia Evangelica.* Edited by Kurt Aland et al. TU 73. Berlin: Akademie-Verlag, 1959.

———. "Johanneische Probleme." Pages 78–113 in *Gott und Mensch: Gesammelte Aufsätze.* Tübingen: Mohr (Siebeck), 1965. Reprinted from *ZTK* 56 (1959): 19–54.

———. "Der Vater, der mich gesandt hat." Pages 68–77 in *Gott und Mensch: Gesammelte Aufsätze.* Tübingen: Mohr (Siebeck), 1965. Reprinted from *NTS* 9 (1962–63): 208–16.

———. *Der Weg Jesu: Eine Erklärung des Markus-Evangeliums und der kanonischen Parallelen.* Berlin: Töpelmann, 1966.

Hahn, Ferdinand. *The Titles of Jesus in Christology: Their History in Early Christianity.* London: Lutterworth, 1969.

Hamerton-Kelly, Robert G. *God the Father: Theology and Patriarchy in the Teaching of Jesus.* Philadelphia: Fortress, 1979.

Hammerstein, Franz von. *Das Messiasproblem bei Martin Buber.* Stuttgart: Kohlhammer, 1958.

Hay, David M., ed. *Pauline Theology, Volume II: 1 and 2 Corinthians.* Minneapolis: Fortress, 1993.

Hay, David M., and E. Elizabeth Johnson, eds. *Pauline Theology, Volume III: Romans.* Minneapolis: Fortress, 1995.

Hays, Richard B. "ΠΙΣΤΙΣ and Pauline Christology: What Is at Stake?" Pages 35–60 in *Pauline Theology, Volume IV.* Edited by E. Elizabeth Johnson and David M. Hay. Atlanta: Scholars Press, 1997.

Hengel, Martin. *Crucifixion.* Philadelphia: Fortress, 1977.

———. "Mors turpissima crucis: Die Kreuzigung in der antiken Welt und die 'Torheit' des 'Wortes vom Kreuz.'" Pages 125–84 in *Rechtfertigung: Festschrift für Ernst Käsemann zum 70. Geburtstag.* Edited by J. Friedrich et al. Tübingen: Mohr (Siebeck), 1976.

Hoskyns, Edwyn. *The Fourth Gospel.* Edited by F. N. Davey. 2d ed. London: Faber & Faber, 1947.

Hoskyns, Edwyn, and Noel Davey. *The Riddle of the New Testament.* 3d ed. London: Faber & Faber, 1947.

Jeremias, Joachim. *The Eucharistic Words of Jesus.* Translated by Norman Perrin. New York: Charles Scribner's Sons, 1966.

———. *New Testament Theology: The Proclamation of Jesus.* New York: Charles Scribner's Sons, 1971.

————. *The Parables of Jesus*. London: SCM Press, 1954.

————. "The Present Position in the Controversy Concerning the Problem of the Historical Jesus." *EvT* 69 (1957–58): 333–39.

Johnson, E. Elizabeth. "Romans 9–11: The Faithfulness and Impartiality of God." Pages 211–39 in *Pauline Theology, Volume III: Romans*. Edited by David M. Hay and E. Elizabeth Johnson. Minneapolis: Fortress, 1995.

Johnson, E. Elizabeth, and David M. Hay, eds. *Pauline Theology, Volume IV*. Atlanta: Scholars Press, 1997.

Käsemann, Ernst. "Aufbau und Anliegen des johanneischen Prologs." Pages 155–80 in *Exegetische Versuche und Besinnungen*. Vol. 2. Göttingen: Vandenhoeck & Ruprecht, 1964. ET: "The Structure and Purpose of the Prologue to John's Gospel." Pages 138–67 in *New Testament Questions of Today*. Translated by W. J. Montague. Philadelphia: Fortress, 1969.

————. *Commentary on Romans*. Grand Rapids: Eerdmans, 1980. German original: *An die Römer*. HNT 8A. Tübingen: Mohr (Siebeck), 1973.

————. *Jesu letzter Wille nach Johannes 17*. Tübingen: Mohr (Siebeck), 1966. ET: *The Testament of Jesus: A Study of the Gospel of John in the Light of Chapter 17*. Translated by G. Krodel. Philadelphia: Fortress, 1968.

————. *Perspectives on Paul*. Philadelphia: Fortress, 1971.

————. "Das Problem des historischen Jesus." *ZTK* 51 (1954): 125–53. ET: "The Problem of the Historical Jesus." Pages 15–47 in *Essays on New Testament Themes*. Translated by W. J. Montague. London: SCM Press, 1964.

Keck, Leander E. "Paul as Thinker." *Int* 47 (1993): 27–38.

Knox, John. "The Epistle to the Romans: Introduction and Exegesis." In *IB*. Vol. 9. New York: Abingdon, 1954.

Kümmel, Werner Georg. *Introduction to the New Testament*. Translated by A. J. Mattill. Nashville: Abingdon, 1966.

————. *Das Neue Testament: Geschichte der Erforschung seiner Probleme*. Munich: Karl Alber, 1958. ET: *The New Testament: A History of the Investigation of Its Problems*. Trans. S. McLean Gilmour. Nashville: Abingdon, 1972.

————. *Römer 7 und die Bekehrung des Paulus*. Leipzig: Hinrichs, 1929. Reprinted in *Römer 7 und das Bild des Menschen im Neuen Testament*. Munich: Kaiser, 1974.

Küng, Hans. *On Being a Christian*. Garden City, N.Y.: Doubleday, 1976.

Kuss, Otto. *Der Römerbrief*. Vol. 3. Regensburg: Verlag Friedrich Pustet, 1978.

Landes, Paula Fredriksen. *Augustine on Romans: Propositions from the Epistle to the Romans; Unfinished Commentary on the Epistle to the Romans*. Early Christian Literature Series 6. Chico, Calif.: Scholars Press, 1982.

Leenhardt, Franz-J. *L'Epitre de Saint Paul aux Romains*. Neuchâtel: Delachaux & Niestlé, 1957.

Lietzmann, H. *An die Römer*. Tübingen: Mohr (Siebeck), 1971.

Lohmeyer, Ernst. *Das Evangelium des Matthäus: Nachgelassene Ausarbeitungen und Entwürfe zur Übersetzung und Erklärung.* Edited by Werner Schmauch. Göttingen: Vandenhoeck & Ruprecht, 1956.

Luther, Martin. *Lectures on Romans.* Translated by Wilhelm Pauck. LCC 15. Philadelphia: Westminster, 1961.

Manson, T. W. *Ethics and the Gospel.* New York: Charles Scribner's Sons, 1960.

———. "The Life of Jesus: Some Tendencies in Present-Day Research." Pages 211–21 in *The Background of the New Testament and Its Eschatology* (in honor of C. H. Dodd). Edited by W. D. Davies and D. Daube. Cambridge: Cambridge University Press, 1956.

———. *The Teaching of Jesus: Studies of Its Form and Content.* Cambridge: Cambridge University Press, 1951.

Martyn, J. Louis. "Apocalyptic Antinomies in Paul's Letter to the Galatians." *NTS* 31 (1985): 410–24.

———. "Paul and His Jewish-Christian Interpreters." *USQR* 42 (1988): 1–15.

Meeks, Wayne A. "Galilee and Judea in the Fourth Gospel." *JBL* 85 (1966): 159–69.

———. "The Man from Heaven in Johannine Sectarianism." *JBL* 91 (1972): 44–72.

———. *The Prophet-King: Moses Traditions and the Johannine Christology.* NovTSup 14. Leiden: E. J. Brill, 1967.

Meyer, Paul W. "Augustine's *The Spirit and the Letter* as a Reading of Paul's Romans." Pages 366–81 in *The Social World of the First Christians: Essays in Honor of Wayne A. Meeks.* Edited by L. Michael White and O. Larry Yarbrough. Minneapolis: Fortress, 1995. (With revision: pages 133–48 in this volume)

———. "Context as a Bearer of Meaning in Matthew." *USQR* 42 (1988): 69–72. (With revision: pages 282–85 in this volume)

———. "Faith and History Revisited." *PSB* 10, no. 2, NS (1989): 75–83. (With revision: pages 19–26 in this volume)

———. "'The Father': The Presentation of God in the Fourth Gospel." Pages 255–73 in *Exploring the Gospel of John.* Edited by R. Alan Culpepper and C. Clifton Black. Louisville, Ky.: Westminster John Knox, 1996. (With revision: pages 221–39 in this volume)

———. "The Holy Spirit in the Pauline Letters: A Contextual Exploration." *Int* 33 (1979): 3–18. (With revision: pages 117–32 in this volume)

———. "John 2:10." *JBL* 86 (1967): 191–97. (With revision: pages 264–70 in this volume)

———. "Matthew 21:1–11." *Int* 40 (1986): 180–85. (With revision: pages 277–81 in this volume)

———. "A Note on John 10:1–18." *JBL* 75 (1956): 232–35. (With revision: pages 271–74 in this volume)

————. "Pauline Theology: A Proposal for a Pause in Its Pursuit." Pages 140–60 in *Pauline Theology, Volume IV*. Edited by E. Elizabeth Johnson and David M. Hay. Atlanta: Scholars Press, 1997. (With revision: pages 95–116 in this volume)

————. "The Polarity of Faith: A Johannine Paradigm for Our Time." *USQR* 21, no. 1 (1965): 51–61. (With revision: pages 254–63 in this volume)

————. "The Problem of the Messianic Self-Consciousness of Jesus." *NovT* 4 (1960): 122–38. (With revision: pages 27–40 in this volume)

————. "Romans." Pages 1038–73 in *HarperCollins Bible Commentary*. Edited by James L. Mays. 2d ed. San Francisco: HarperSanFrancisco, 2000. (With revision: pages 149–218 in this volume)

————. "Romans 10:4 and the 'End' of the Law." Pages 59–78 in *The Divine Helmsman: Studies on God's Control of Human Events, Presented to Lou H. Silberman*. Edited by James L. Crenshaw and Samuel Sandmel. New York: KTAV, 1980. (With revision: pages 78–94 in this volume)

————. "The This-Worldliness of the New Testament." *PSB* 2, no. 3, NS (1979): 219–31. (With revision: pages 5–18 in this volume)

————. "The Worm at the Core of the Apple: Exegetical Reflections on Romans 7." Pages 62–84 in *The Conversation Continues: Studies in Paul and John in Honor of J. Louis Martyn*. Edited by Robert T. Fortna and Beverly Roberts Gaventa. Nashville: Abingdon, 1990. (With revision: pages 57–77 in this volume)

Michel, Otto. *Der Brief an die Römer*. 5th ed. MeyerK. Göttingen: Vandenhoeck & Ruprecht, 1978.

Miranda, Juan Peter. *Die Sendung Jesu im vierten Evangelium: Religions- und theologiegeschichtliche Untersuchungen zu den Sendungsformeln*. SBS 87. Stuttgart: Katholisches Bibelwerk, 1977.

————. *Der Vater, der mich gesandt hat: Religionsgeschichtliche Untersuchungen zu den johanneischen Sendungsformeln: Zugleich ein Beitrag zur johanneischen Christologie und Ekklesiologie*. Europaische Hochschulschriften/European University Papers, Series 23: Theology 7. Bern and Frankfurt a.M.: Herbert Lang/Peter Lang, 1972.

Morgan, Robert. *The Nature of New Testament Theology: The Contribution of William Wrede and Adolf Schlatter*. SBT 2/25. Naperville, Ill.: Alec R. Allenson, 1973.

Niebuhr, H. Richard. *The Responsible Self*. New York: Harper & Row, 1963.

Nygren, Anders. *Commentary on Romans*. Philadelphia: Muhlenberg, 1949.

Patte, Daniel. *Paul's Faith and the Power of the Gospel: A Structural Introduction to the Pauline Letters*. Philadelphia: Fortress, 1983.

Perkins, Pheme. *Resurrection: New Testament Witness and Contemporary Reflection*. Garden City, N.Y.: Doubleday, 1984.

Preiss, Théo. "Justification in Johannine Thought." Pages 9–31 in *Life in Christ*. Translated by Harold Knight. SBT 13. Naperville, Ill.: Alec R. Allenson, 1952.

Robinson, James M. *A New Quest of the Historical Jesus*. SBT 25. Naperville, Ill.: Alec R. Allenson, 1959.

———. "The Problem of History in Mark, Reconsidered." *USQR* 20 (1964–65): 131–47.

Sanday, William, and Arthur C. Headlam. *A Critical and Exegetical Commentary on the Epistle to the Romans*. ICC 36. 11th ed. New York: Charles Scribner's Sons, 1906.

Sanders, E. P. *Paul and Palestinian Judaism*. Philadelphia: Fortress, 1977.

Schelkle, K. H. *Paulus: Lehrer der Väter*. Düsseldorf: Patmos, 1956.

Schmidt, K. L. "Der johanneische Charakter der Erzählung vom Hochzeitswunder in Kana." Pages 32–43 in *Harnack-Ehrung: Beiträge zur Kirchengeschichte ihrem Lehrer Adolf von Harnack zu seinem 70. Geburtstag*. Leipzig: Hinrichs, 1921.

Schnackenburg, Rudolf. *The Gospel according to St. John*. 3 vols. New York: Crossroad, 1982–87.

———. "'Der Vater, der mich gesandt hat': Zur johanneischen Christologie." Pages 275–91 in *Anfänge der Christologie: Festschrift für Ferdinand Hahn zum 65. Geburtstag*. Edited by Cilliers Breytenbach and Henning Paulsen. Göttingen: Vandenhoeck & Ruprecht, 1991.

Schoeps, H. J. *Paul: The Theology of the Apostle in the Light of Jewish Religious History*. London: Lutterworth, 1961.

Schreiber, Johannes. "Die Christologie des Johannesevangeliums." *ZTK* 58 (1961): 154–83.

Schüssler Fiorenza, Elisabeth. "The Ethics of Biblical Interpretation: Decentering Biblical Scholarship." *JBL* 107 (1988): 3–17.

Schütz, John Howard. *Paul and the Anatomy of Apostolic Authority*. SNTSMS 26. Cambridge: Cambridge University Press, 1975.

Schweitzer, Albert. *Das Messianitäts- und Leidensgeheimnis: Eine Skizze des Lebens Jesu*. Tübingen: Mohr (Siebeck), 1956 (orig. 1910). ET: *The Mystery of the Kingdom of God: The Secret of Jesus' Messiahship and Passion*. Translated by Walter Lowrie. London: A. & C. Black, 1925.

———. *The Quest of the Historical Jesus*. New York: Macmillan, 1968 (ET orig., 1910; German orig., 1906).

Schweizer, Eduard. *Ego Eimi: Die religionsgeschichtliche Herkunft und theologische Bedeutung der johanneischen Bildreden, zugleich ein Beitrag zur Quellenfrage des vierten Evangeliums*. FRLANT NS 38. Göttingen: Vandenhoeck & Ruprecht, 1939.

———. "Der Menschensohn." *ZNW* 50 (1959): 185–209.

————. "The Son of Man." *JBL* 79 (1960): 119–29.

————. "What Do We Really Mean When We Say 'God sent his son . . .'?" Pages 298–312 in *Faith and History: Essays in Honor of Paul W. Meyer*. Edited by John T. Carroll, Charles H. Cosgrove, and E. Elizabeth Johnson. Homage Series. Atlanta: Scholars Press, 1990.

————. "Zum religionsgeschichtlichen Hintergrund der 'Sendungsformel' Gal 4,4f, Röm 8,3f, Joh 3,16f, 1 Joh 4,9." Pages 83–95 in *Beiträge zur Theologie des Neuen Testaments: Neutestamentliche Aufsätze (1955–1970)*. Zurich: Zwingli, 1970.

Smith, D. M. *The Composition and Order of the Fourth Gospel*. New Haven, Conn.: Yale University Press, 1965.

Stowers, Stanley. *The Diatribe and Paul's Letter to the Romans*. SBLDS 57. Chico, Calif.: Scholars Press, 1981.

Strathmann, H. *Das Evangelium nach Johannes*. NTD 4. Göttingen: Vandenhoeck & Ruprecht, 1951.

Strauss, D. F. *Das Leben Jesu, kritisch Bearbeitet*. Tübingen: Osiander, 1835. ET: *The Life of Jesus Critically Examined*. Edited by P. C. Hodgson. Philadelphia: Fortress, 1972.

Suggs, M. J. "'The Word Is Near You'; Romans 10:6–10 within the Purpose of the Letter." Pages 289–312 in *Christian History and Interpretation: Studies Presented to John Knox*. Edited by W. R. Farmer et al. Cambridge: Cambridge University Press, 1967.

Taylor, Vincent. *The Gospel according to St. Mark*. London: Macmillan, 1952.

————. *The Life and Ministry of Jesus*. London: Macmillan, 1954.

————. *The Person of Christ in New Testament Teaching*. New York: St. Martin's, 1958.

Theissen, Gerd. *Psychological Aspects of Pauline Theology*. Philadelphia: Fortress, 1987.

Thyen, Hartwig. "Johannesevangelium." *TRE* 17 (1976): 200–25.

Tödt, Heinz Eduard. *Der Menschensohn in der synoptischen Überlieferung*. Gütersloh: G. Mohn, 1959. ET: *The Son of Man in the Synoptic Tradition*. Translated by Dorothea M. Barton. NTL. Philadelphia: Westminster, 1965.

Toews, John E. *The Law in Paul's Letter to the Romans: A Study of Romans 9:30–10:13*. Ph.D. diss., Northwestern University, 1977.

Walter, Nikolaus. "Zur Interpretation von Römer 9–11." *ZTK* 81 (1984): 172–95.

White, L. Michael, and O. Larry Yarbrough, eds. *The Social World of the First Christians: Essays in Honor of Wayne A. Meeks*. Minneapolis: Fortress, 1995.

Wilckens, Ulrich. *Der Brief an die Römer*. 3 vols. EKKNT. Neukirchen-Vluyn: Neukirchener Verlag, 1978–82.

————. *Resurrection. Biblical Testimony to the Resurrection: An Historical Examination and Explanation.* Atlanta: John Knox, 1978.

Windisch, Hans. "Die johanneische Weinregel (Joh. 2,10)." *ZNW* 14 (1913): 248–57.

Wrcdc, William. *Das Messiasgeheimnis in den Evangelien: Zugleich ein Beitrag zum Verständnis des Markusevangeliums.* Göttingen: Vandenhoeck & Ruprecht, 1901. ET: *The Messianic Secret.* Translated by J. C. G. Greig. Cambridge: James Clarke & Co., 1971.

INDEX OF ANCIENT SOURCES

INDEX OF MODERN AUTHORS

INDEX OF SUBJECTS